TAKING SIDES

Clashing Views in

Early Childhood Education

SECOND EDITION

Selected, Edited, and with Introductions by

Karen Menke Paciorek
Eastern Michigan University

**McGraw-Hill
Higher Education**

Boston   Burr Ridge, IL   Dubuque, IA   New York   San Francisco   St. Louis
Bangkok   Bogotá   Caracas   Kuala Lumpur   Lisbon   London   Madrid   Mexico City
Milan   Montreal   New Delhi   Santiago   Seoul   Singapore   Sydney   Taipei   Toronto

**McGraw-Hill
Higher Education**

TAKING SIDES: CLASHING VIEWS IN EARLY CHILDHOOD EDUCATION,
SECOND EDITION

Published by McGraw-Hill, a business unit of The McGraw-Hill Companies, Inc., 1221 Avenue
of the Americas, New York, NY 10020. Copyright © 2008 by The McGraw-Hill Companies, Inc. All
rights reserved. Previous edition(s) 2002. No part of this publication may be reproduced or
distributed in any form or by any means, or stored in a database or retrieval system, without the
prior written consent of The McGraw-Hill Companies, Inc., including, but not limited to, in any
network or other electronic storage or transmission, or broadcast for distance learning.

Some ancillaries, including electronic and print components, may not be available to customers
outside the United States.

Taking Sides® is a registered trademark of the McGraw-Hill Companies, Inc.
Taking Sides is published by the **Contemporary Learning Series** group within the McGraw-Hill
Higher Education division.

 This book is printed on recycled, acid-free paper containing
10% postconsumer waste.

1 2 3 4 5 6 7 8 9 0 DOC/DOC 0 9 8 7

MHID: 0-07-351530-2
ISBN: 978-0-07-351530-4
ISSN: 1537-0712

Managing Editor: *Larry Loeppke*
Production Manager: *Faye Schilling*
Senior Developmental Editor: *Jill Peter*
Editorial Assistant: *Nancy Meissner*
Production Service Assistant: *Rita Hingtgen*
Permissions Coordinator: *Lori Church*
Senior Marketing Manager: *Julie Keck*
Marketing Communications Specialist: *Mary Klein*
Marketing Coordinator: *Alice Link*
Project Manager: *Jane Mohr*
Design Specialist: *Tara McDermott*
Senior Administrative Assistant: *DeAnna Dausener*
Senior Operations Manager: *Pat Koch Krieger*
Cover Graphics: *Maggie Lytle*

Compositor: ICC Macmillan Inc.
Cover Image: © BananaStock/PunchStock

Library of Congress Cataloging-in-Publication Data

Main entry under title:
    Taking sides: clashing views in early childhood education/selected, edited, and with
    introductions by Karen Menke Paciorek.—2nd ed.

    Includes bibliographical references.
    1. Early childhood education. 2. Education, preschool. 3. Education, primary.
    I. Paciorek, Karen Menke, *ed.* II. Series.
                                                            372.21

www.mhhe.com

Preface

The study of young children, their families, and those who care for and educate them is an ever-changing field. What complicates the study of issues affecting young children is many of the topics studied cannot be carried out as true experimental studies. Subjects cannot be randomly assigned to an unhealthy versus healthy cafeteria food cohort or a high-quality versus poor-quality early childhood setting. So many independent variables come into play when examining the effects of life on young children and their families. Parental education, parental occupation and income, marital status and life-styles, public education available in the area, and geographical location can affect the ways in which children are raised and educated. Caring for and educating young children is often viewed as something that comes naturally to people. Little, if any, preparation or prior knowledge has traditionally been viewed as required. When examining the many issues involving the raising and educating of children, one can see how knowledge of the issues that affect young children can be valuable when making important decisions.

Plan of the book. The eighteen issues in this book are ones that the reader might see discussed on any of the morning talk shows or read about in weekly news magazines. They have been selected to appeal to students in early childhood education (ECE) issues courses or seminar discussion classes, parents, or school administrators and boards of education examining the issues. Eight of the issues were presented in the first edition of this book. The ten new issues represent current topics of concern to policymakers, parents, and educators across the country. The topics are divided into three parts: Children in Families and Society, Children in Educational Programs, and Educational Policies. There is not a suggested order for reading and discussing the selections. The group could decide as a whole in which order they would like to investigate the separate issues. As the editor, I carefully chose the eighteen issues to represent current controversial topics in the field. Each issue is posed in the form of a question. I then conducted a thorough search of the literature and read many hundreds of articles. From those readings I chose two articles that represent a yes and no, pro and con, or point and counterpoint side to the issue for a total of thirty-six different readings. These are presented as YES or NO in response to the topic question. The articles were chosen from a variety of sources, some weekly magazines, some professional early childhood journals, as well as other professional education journals and Web sites. I first provide and issue summary and background information, explaining why it is controversial, and how it may have been viewed historically or how it varies from state to state. This overview is followed by a summary of the controversy in a point-counterpoint format. I then pose some challenge questions for reader reflection and end with a list of additional readings for further study. Of course, the reader may view the issue from other angles than are presented in this book. Controversial issues generally do not have a right or wrong side, just different ways of viewing an issue. People usually form an opinion after becoming educated about an issue by having read and discussed the many points surrounding the topic. The aim of the *Taking Sides* series is to provide the reader with a vehicle for becoming more knowledgeable about clashing views on controversial issues and then being able to carry on a thoughtful, informed discussion with others.

A discussion on the issues could center on decisions made in educational settings based not on evidence or research but instead on past practice or a gut feeling. As a publicly elected school board member, this editor would never be party to approving an educational policy that was made based on unsupported evidence. Examples of this practice that are most relevant for the issues in this book are those issues on school retention, transition grades, and the elimination of recess, among others. When decisions are made based on past practice or commonly held beliefs, we are setting ourselves up for problems down the road.

A word to the instructor. You are strongly encouraged to have your students read the Introduction to this book, which is an overview of early childhood education including a historical perspective. Students will have a clearer understanding of the profession by reading the Introduction before they read the issues. An Instructor's Manual is available through the publisher for the instructor using this volume of *Taking Sides*, including suggestions for discussing the issues in class. A general guidebook, *Using Taking Sides in the Classroom*, which presents methods and techniques for integrating the pro-con approach into any classroom setting, is also available. An online version of using *Taking Sides in the Classroom* and a correspondence service for *Taking Sides* adopters can be found at http://www.mhcls.com/usingts. For students, there is a field guide available for analyzing argumentative essays, *Analyzing Controversy: An Introductory Guide*, with exercises and techniques to help them to decipher genuine controversies. *Taking Sides: Clashing Views in Early Childhood Education* is only one title in the *Taking Sides* series. If you are interested in seeing the table of ontents for any of the other titles, visit the *Taking Sides* Web site at http://www.mcgraw-hill.com/takingsides/

For exploration of other issues in early childhood education, I suggest the instructor review *Annual Editions: Early Childhood Education* and *Sources: Notable Selections in Early Childhood Education* (2nd ed.), both published by McGraw-Hill.

Acknowledgments. My husband Michael and sons Clark and Clay deserve my heartfelt appreciation and love for their support during the writing of this book. Their suggestions and ideas were always welcome. I am fortunate to have two wonderful parents, Audrey and Kenneth Menke, who raised my sister and me to be accepting of all, and to broaden our horizons through travel, reading, and thoughtful discussions. For that I am thankful. In addition, I want to thank the administration at Eastern Michigan University for supporting me with a faculty research award so I was able to complete this project and my colleagues Margo Dichtelmiller, Brigid Beaubien, Sue Grossman, and Martha Baiyee for their extra effort while I was gone. I am very grateful for the assistance provided by Tony Derezinski and Justin King of the Michigan Association of School Boards for assistance in surveying school board members. Jill Peter and Larry Loeppke at McGraw-Hill have been extremely supportive and accessible throughout this project.

As always, I welcome your feedback on any book I edit for McGraw-Hill. The books are revised and improved based on the suggestions of attentive readers and instructors. For that I am grateful and encourage your comments. Feel free to contact me at: kpaciorek@emich.edu. I look forward to hearing from you.

Karen Menke Paciorek
Eastern Michigan University

Contents In Brief

UNIT 1   Children in Families and Society   1

Issue 1.   Should Brain Science Guide Educational Practice?   2
Issue 2.   Should Young Children Use Computers?   26
Issue 3.   Is Time-Out an Effective Guidance Technique?   39
Issue 4.   Does Nightly Homework Improve Academic Performance?   51

UNIT 2   Children in Educational Programs   65

Issue 5.   Should Superhero or Violent Play Be Discouraged?   66
Issue 6.   Should Transition Grades Be Abolished?   82
Issue 7.   Is Being Older Better When Entering Kindergarten?   96
Issue 8.   Is Grade Retention Harmful to Children?   115
Issue 9.   Should Educators Address Students' Unhealthy Lifestyle
               Choices?   126
Issue 10. Are English Language Learners Best Served in an Immersion
               Language Model?   144
Issue 11. Does Learning to Read Involve More Than Phonics?   161
Issue 12. Should Recess Be Included in a School Day?   177
Issue 13. Are Looping Classrooms Effective Learning Settings?   192

UNIT 3   Educational Policies   207

Issue 14. Should Public Money Be Spent on Universal Preschool?   208
Issue 15. Is Regular Testing the Best Way to Improve Academic
               Performance?   223
Issue 16. Will School Improvement Efforts Alone Narrow the
               Racial/Ethnic Achievement Gap?   237
Issue 17. Should Corporal Punishment in Schools Be Outlawed?   257
Issue 18. Are Boys in Crisis in Our Schools?   265

Contents

Preface   iii

Introduction   xiii

UNIT 1   CHILDREN IN FAMILIES AND SOCIETY   1

Issue 1.   Should Brain Science Guide Educational Practice?   2

YES: **Stephen Rushton and Elizabeth Larkin,** from "Shaping the Learning Environment: Connecting Developmentally Appropriate Practices to Brain Research," *Early Childhood Education Journal* (September 2001)   *4*

NO: **Olaf Jorgenson,** from "Brain Scam? Why Educators Should Be Careful about Embracing 'Brain Research'," *The Educational Forum* (Summer 2003)   *18*

Stephen Rushton and Elizabeth Larkin from the University of South Florida at Sarasota support early childhood educators fostering developmentally appropriate learning experiences based on what is known about early brain research. Olaf Jorgenson is headmaster of the Hawaii Preparatory Academy in Walmea, Hawaii. He states that brain science should not be used to affect educational practice or policy.

Issue 2.   Should Young Children Use Computers?   26

YES: **Regina G. Chatel,** from "Computer Use in Preschool: Trixie Gets a Screen Name," *The New England Reading Association Journal* (vol. 41, 2005)   *28*

NO: **Edward Miller,** from "Less Screen Time, More Play Time," *Principal* (September/October 2005)   *33*

Regina G. Chatel is a professor of education at St. Joseph College in West Hartford, Connecticut. Dr. Chatel states we are past the debate of should young children use computers to the discussion of how computers should be used. She raises many of the key issues related to the use of computers with young children. When appropriately done with young children related to age of introduction, support provided and teacher training, she advocates for the use of computers by three- and four-year-old children. The Alliance for Childhood, based in College Park, Maryland, released a report in 2004 critically examining the use of computers with young children in the twenty-first century. Presented here is a summary of the findings by Edward Miller, a founding partner and senior research at the Alliance for Childhood.

Issue 3.   Is Time-Out an Effective Guidance Technique?   39

YES: **Lawrence Kutner,** from "The Truth About Time-Out," *Parents* (April 1996)   *41*

NO: **Kathy Preuesse,** from "Guidance and Discipline Strategies for Young Children: Time Out Is Out," *Early Childhood News* (March/April 2002)   *44*

Lawrence Kutner is a contributing editor of *Parents* and a psychologist at Harvard University Medical School. Dr. Kutner supports time-out when effectively managed by parents or teachers. Kathy Preuesse teaches at the Child and Family Study Center at the University of Wisconsin–Stout in Menomonie, Wisconsin. She finds time-out to be an antiquated practice that is not effective for helping guide the behavior of young children.

Issue 4.   Does Nightly Homework Improve Academic Performance?   51

YES: Mary H. Sullivan and Paul V. Sequeira, from "The Impact of Purposeful Homework on Learning," *The Clearing House* (July/August 1996)   *53*

NO: Alfie Kohn, from "The Goldilocks Paradox," *American School Board Journal* (February 2007)   *59*

Mary H. Sullivan from Western Connecticut State University and Paul V. Sequeira, superintendent of schools, New Britain, Connecticut, report there is sound research to support teachers assigning homework to students for the purpose of improving academic performance. Alfie Kohn, long known as a powerful advocate for education, questions the entire practice of teachers assigning homework and does not find support in the literature for the nightly ritual of children sitting at the kitchen table doing homework.

UNIT 2   CHILDREN IN EDUCATIONAL PROGRAMS   65

Issue 5.   Should Superhero or Violent Play Be Discouraged?   66

YES: Diane E. Levin, from "Beyond Banning War and Superhero Play: Meeting Children's Needs in Violent Times" *Young Children* (May 2003)   *68*

NO: Brenda J. Boyd, from "Teacher Response to Superhero Play: To Ban or Not to Ban?" *Childhood Education* (Fall 1997)   *73*

Diane E. Levin is an author of eight books on the effects of violence and the media on the behavior of young children and a professor in the Department of Early Childhood at Wheelock College in Boston, Massachusetts. She describes why children find superhero and violent play attractive and how teachers can best meet children's needs for self-expression. Brenda Boyd, from Washington State University, does not view superhero play to be aggressive and believes banning this type of play will not teach children how to develop the social skills necessary for healthy living.

Issue 6.   Should Transition Grades Be Abolished?   82

YES: Vera Estok, from "One District's Study on the Propriety of Transition-Grade Classrooms," *Young Children* (March 2005)   *84*

NO: Barbara S. Harris, from "I Need Time to Grow: The Transitional Years," *Phi Delta Kappan* (April 2003)   *89*

Vera Estok was a pre-first-grade teacher in Springfield, Ohio. Her district formed a committee to research their 23-year practice of offering transitional grade classrooms. After studying the literature and their program, the committee determined transitional programs were not in the best interest of the children they served. They abandoned the program and moved to full-day kindergarten classrooms. Barbara S. Harris, associate headmaster at Presbyterian Day School in Memphis, Tennessee, participates in presentations to parents and others on the benefits of giving the gift of time to young children by placing children in transition classes.

Issue 7.   Is Being Older Better When Entering Kindergarten?   96

YES: **Nancie L. Katz,** from "Too Young for Kindergarten," *The Christian Science Monitor* (July 21, 1997)   *98*

NO: **Hermine H. Marshall,** from "Opportunity Deffered or Opportunity Taken? An Updated Look at Delaying Kindergarten Entry," *Young Children* (September 2003)   *100*

Nancie Katz, a writer for *The Christian Science Monitor,* examines families who chose to keep their children out of kindergarten for a year and are pleased with the decision. She cites research that found children with later birthdays were retained at a higher rate. Hermine Marshall, a professor emerita at San Francisco State University in California, presents arguments to dispel any myths about older students performing better and suggests children should attend kindergarten when they are age eligible.

Issue 8.   Is Grade Retention Harmful to Children?   115

YES: **Susan Black,** from "Second Time Around," *American School Board Journal* (November 2004)   *117*

NO: **Joellen Perry,** from "What, Ms. Crabapple Again?" *U.S. News & World Report* (May 24, 1999)   *122*

Susan Black, a contributing editor for the *American School Board Journal,* reports that grade retention has never been a positive experience for children when it happens, later in their schooling or well into their adult life. She finds little, if any, benefits for the well-entrenched practice. To many parents and children, the only solution for getting back on the right track in school is to start again. For these children, repeating a grade offers the student a chance at a positive experience. Ms. Perry, a writer for *U.S. News & World Report,* shares stories from families for whom retention was successful.

Issue 9.   Should Educators Address Students' Unhealthy Lifestyle Choices?   126

YES: **Sheree Crute,** from "Growing Pains," *NEA Today* (March 2005)   *128*

NO: **Michael I. Loewy,** from "Suggestions for Working with Fat Children in the Schools," *Professional School Counseling* (April 1998)   *133*

Sheree Crute, a freelance health and medical writer and editor, reports on what many call an epidemic in overweight children and the urgent need to have children make immediate changes in their eating habits and activity choices. Michael I. Loewy is a professor in the Department of Counseling and School Psychology at San Diego State University, San Diego, California. He contends we need to stop being obsessed with weight and instead focus on having children feel positive about their body.

Issue 10.   Are English Language Learners Best Served in an Immersion Language Model?   144

YES: **Christine Rossell,** from "Teaching English Through English," *Educational Leadership* (December 2004/January 2005)   *146*

NO: **Jill Wu,** from "A View from the Classroom," *Educational Leadership* (December 2004/January 2005)   *153*

Christine Rossell, a professor of political science at Boston University in Massachusetts, found English language immersion programs best for students learning English. Jill Wu, a graduate student at the University of Colorado, supports programs that first teach students basic skills in their native language prior to teaching them English.

Issue 11.   Does Learning to Read Involve More Than Phonics?   161

YES: **Judy Willis,** from "The Gully in the 'Brain Glitch' Theory," *Educational Leadership* (February 2007)   *163*

NO: **National Reading Panel,** from "Teaching Children to Read: An Evidence-Based Assessment of the Scientific Research Literature on Reading and Its Implications for Reading Instruction," htpp://www.nichd.nih.gov/publications/nrp/smallbook.htm (April 2000)   *170*

Judy Willis is a board-certified neurologist who specialized in clinical research prior to becoming a classroom teacher. Dr. Willis found that enjoyment and understanding of the reading process is more important than phonics when learning to read. Members of the National Reading Panel concluded that students need a strong foundation in systematic phonics instruction in kindergarten through sixth grade to be successful readers.

Issue 12.   Should Recess Be Included in a School Day?   177

YES: **Tom Jambor,** from "Recess and Social Development," *Earlychildhood News,* http://www.earlychildhoodnews.com/ earlychildhood/contact.aspx   *179*

NO: **Kelly King Alexander,** from "Playtime Is Cancelled," *Parents* (November 1999)   *186*

Tom Jambor, an associate professor of early childhood development at the University of Alabama at Birmingham, strongly supports daily recess for young children. He cites many benefits and ways to advocate for recess. Kelly King Alexander writes about the required additions to state-mandated curricula. Many school administrators have no choice but to eliminate nonacademic time from the schedule. With life and times changing rapidly she raises questions about having free time scheduled into the school day.

Issue 13.   Are Looping Classrooms Effective Learning Settings?   192

YES: **Mary M. Hitz, Mary Catherine Somers,** and **Christee L. Jenlink,** from "The Looping Classroom: Benefits for Children, Families, and Teachers," *Young Children* (March 2007)   *194*

NO: Allan S. Vann, from "Looping: Looking Beyond the Hype," *Principal* (May 1997) *202*

Mary M. Hitz, Mary Catherine Somers, and Christee L. Jenlink, all educators in the state of Oklahoma, encourage teachers to loop with their students to the next grade and see many positive benefits to the practice. Allan Vann, a principal at the James H. Boyd Intermediate School in Huntington, New York, cautions teachers to think carefully about looping. He states it is not for everyone and there may be disadvantages of having a child stay with the same teacher or peers for two years.

UNIT 3 EDUCATIONAL POLICIES 207

Issue 14. Should Public Money Be Spent on Universal Preschool? 208

YES: Julie Poppe and Steffanie Clothier, from "The Preschool Promise," *State Legislatures* (June 2005) *210*

NO: Darcy Ann Olsen, from "Universal Preschool Is No Golden Ticket: Why Government Should Not Enter the Preschool Business," *Policy Analysis* (February 1999) *215*

Both Julie Poppe and Steffanie Clothier are policy researchers in areas related to child care and early childhood education for the National Conference of State Legislatures in Washington, D.C. They see preschool education as extremely important for all young children and urge state legislatures to become involved in supporting preschool education. Darcy Ann Olsen, an entitlements policy analyst at the Cato institute, argues that government should not pay for education of preschool children. She finds that public schools cannot provide education for the children for whom they are responsible now; to add younger children would be a poor decision.

Issue 15. Is Regular Testing the Best Way to Improve Academic Performance? 223

YES: Matthew Gandal and Laura McGiffert, from "The Power of Testing," *Educational Leadership* (February 2003) *225*

NO: Kenneth A. Wesson, from "The 'Volvo Effect': Questioning Standardized Tests," *Young Children* (March 2001) *230*

Matthew Gandal and Laura McGiffert are on staff at Achieve, Inc., an organization whose goal is to raise academic standards and improve schools. They make the analogy that teachers testing students is similar to the medical tests doctors run on patients to determine what needs to be done to improve the patient. Kenneth A. Wesson, from San Jose/ Evergreen Community College District in San Jose, California, also works as a consultant with educators in preschool through university level. He fears that tests do not adequately demonstrate what children have learned and may lead to teaching a narrow set of tested skills.

Issue 16. Will School Improvement Efforts Alone Narrow the Racial/Ethnic Achievement Gap? 237

YES: Kati Haycock, from "Closing the Achievement Gap," *Educational Leadership* (March 2001) *239*

NO: **Richard Rothstein,** from "Class and the Classroom: Even the Best Schools Can't Close the Race Achievement Gap," *American School Board Journal* (October 2004) *247*

Kati Haycock is the executive director of Education Trust and follows the belief that adequate funding and high standards will improve academic achievement. Richard Rothstein is a research associate of the Economic Policy Institute and a visiting professor at Teachers College, Columbia University in New York City. Rothstein believes the achievement gap will be narrowed when collaboration occurs from a number of outside groups, not just those functioning within the schools.

Issue 17. Should Corporal Punishment in Schools Be Outlawed? 257

YES: **Paul Ferraro and Joan Rudel Weinreich,** from "Unprotected in the Classroom," *American School Board Journal* (November 2006) *259*

NO: **Greg Gelpi,** from "Some Small Area School Systems Use the Paddle," *Augusta Chronicle* (October 2006) *262*

Paul Ferraro is an elementary teacher in Connecticut and Joan Rudel Weinreich is an associate professor at Manhattanvillle College in New York. They provide information on the 21 states that allow the striking of students in schools, why it's wrong and should be abolished. Greg Gelpi, a writer for the *Augusta, Georgia Chronicle*, writes about the popular practice of administering corporal punishment to students in the state of Georgia.

Issue 18. Are Boys in Crisis in Our Schools? 265

YES: **Peg Tyre,** from "The Trouble with Boys," *Newsweek* (January 30, 2006) *267*

NO: **Sara Mead,** from "The Truth About Boys and Girls," *An Education Sector Report* (June 2006) *274*

Peg Tyre, a Pulitzer Prize–winning editor at *Newsweek* covers a number of issues related to the care and education of children. Her focus in this issue is on what many see as a learning gap between boys and girls. Sara Mead, a senior policy analyst at Education Sector, says there is ample evidence that boys are not doing worse, and that girls have narrowed the achievement gaps that have existed for years.

Contributors 286

Introduction

Early Childhood Education

Karen Menke Paciorek

Issues affecting young children and their care and education have always been controversial. People make decisions based on their own childhood, their involvement with children on a daily basis, their educational level, and their perception of what is best for their children or the children in their educational setting. For those of us who make early childhood education (ECE) our profession, we strive to provide optimal care and educational experiences for children from birth through age eight. We diligently work to educate their families, advocate for resources and support, and develop appropriate learning experiences that will meet the needs of all young children. We are rewarded daily with smiles, stories of achievements, and opportunities to participate in the education and development of young children who will grow to be contributing members of society. Our job as citizens concerned for the care and education of young children is not new; neither are many of the issues we face. Some of the issues chosen for this second edition have been discussed by educators and families for over a hundred years. For other issues involving modern technology, the debate is in its infant stages. The early one-room schoolhouses that dotted the rural territories of the United States and Canada were the initial discussion settings for many issues. As populations grew, so did the controversies and the importance of making the right or best decision. When making decisions affecting children, passion runs deep. We may view an educational experience for children today based on our memory or experience of when we were younger. As adults we tend to think that if a certain practice was good enough for us, and seemed to work, then it will also be good for the current generation of children.

Historical Perspective of Care and Education of Young Children

For many thousands of years little was known about the development of children. Parents were ill-informed about rudimentary skills like crawling, walking, or eating. Much of family life depended on basic survival and healthy children were prized for their ability to help in the fields or in the home. The period of time we know today as childhood did not exist for most children. For wealthy families, care was provided by nursemaids and education was conducted by private tutors. Children would rarely see their parents and would be trained to take over the family business. For the majority of children who lived in poverty, life was extremely difficult and often involved hard physical labor beginning at an early age. Care was provided by the parents as they went about their daily work, and education was minimal, if at all. The skills necessary for survival were taught. Families were not concerned with educational skills as much as with obtaining food and shelter. As countries throughout the world explored and traded, more knowledge was gained and more resources became available as additional economic opportunities were developed. Religious influence into the care and education of young children brought a more humane focus and there were efforts to provide quality educational experiences for young children. The care and education of young children were dominated by European men in the 1600s and 1700s. Men like Martin Luther, John Amos Comenius, John Locke, Jean-Jacques Rousseau, Johann Pestalozzi, and Friedrich Froebel laid the foundation for a child-centered, exploratory-based learning environment. Books, materials, and music were developed specifically for children and school settings were established for their education. As exploration moved west, influences from Europe, Asia, and Africa were spread to North America. In the late 1870s the American kindergarten movement gained momentum. The 1876 Centennial Exposition in Philadelphia had an exhibit of a kindergarten classroom complete with a teacher and young children who went about their day of playing and exploring while millions of visitors watched. Women became interested in the care and education of young children as families struggled to work during the period of time known as the Industrial Revolution in the late 1800s and early 1900s. Elizabeth Peabody, Susan Blow, Patty Smith Hill, Margaret and Rachel McMillan, and Maria Montessori worked diligently to educate others about current trends and practices.

The public wasn't yet ready to accept public education for children under the age of six, but many private kindergartens flourished. Unfortunately, there were many children who were left to fend for themselves or were cared for by siblings or relatives while parents worked hard to establish financial resources for the family. Child care outside of the home was almost nonexistent. Educational settings grew as did the population in cities and rural areas. The first generation of children who had more education than their parents was being raised. Education began to be viewed as a viable option for a better life. Parents wanted their children to learn to speak English, no matter what their native language may have been. They also wanted them to learn to read and to attend school for a period of time. Kindergartens, modeled after the work of German educator Friedrich Froebel, were spread throughout the country. Formal schools were built and a calendar developed based on the weather and the planting and harvesting of crops. In cities, children had the hot summer months off from being in a classroom all day. In rural areas, children had the months of June through September off to help with chores on the family farm. That academic calendar still operates today for most school children, even though air-conditioning is available and the majority of families no longer live on a farm.

Programs for Young Children in the Past 100 Years

The late 1890s brought prosperity for many families. The United States had rebuilt cities after the Civil War and industry grew as products were exported all over the world. Education of young children became a concern for many. People were especially interested in the lives of young children who were living in unstable families or in poverty. Day nurseries were opened to care for children as young as two. Children were given daily health assessments, provided with warm nutritious meals, and information on childrearing was shared with the mothers. Nursery schools were started for middle-class children to provide them with social experiences as well as opportunities for large muscle development through free play. Colleges and universities began to offer classes in child development and opened child-care centers on the campus for university students to observe young children in groups. Professional organizations were formed and information and research about appropriate practices for young children began to be disseminated through conferences and seminars. In 1909, President Theodore Roosevelt convened the first White House Conference on Children. These conferences, held every ten years, highlighted children's health and well-being. Most of the recommendations that came forth from the White House Conferences over the years were not legislated, but some progress was made. A Children's Bureau in the Department of Labor was organized as a result of the 1909 conference. The stock market crash of 1929 and the Great Depression that followed brought a new dimension to programs for young children—government funding. Up until that time day nurseries and nursery schools were supported by private charities, colleges and universities, or parent tuition. The Depression put many people out of work, including elementary teachers. In rural areas schools closed due to lack of funds and in the cities children stayed out of school to get jobs. The United States government developed a massive federal relief program in 1933 called the Works Projects Administration (WPA) with the aim of providing jobs for unemployed Americans. Many of our public parks, zoos, and town halls were built by WPA workers. Nursery schools were started so the unemployed teachers could be paid. These schools and parent education programs were coordinated through a national advisory agency. Although the 1,700 WPA nursery schools were created to augment temporary relief programs and existed for only ten years, their effect is still evident today in early childhood education. These programs did not just provide basic services like food, but were comprehensive programs of preschool education. The young children received health services, as well as nutrition and physical, social, and intellectual development in a safe and nurturing environment. This massive federal program employed 3,775 teachers over the course of its existence of which only 158 had previous nursery school experiences. There was a commitment to high standards and teacher training in new methods to provide a quality early childhood experience for the children from struggling families.

The new focus of psychologist John Watson in the 1920s and 1930s on helping children to become detached from their mothers had a profound impact on preschool education and pedagogy. Watson strongly urged parents to never hug and kiss their children or let them sit in their laps. This advice caused many to wonder exactly what the role of parents and teachers was in the early care and education of young children. As a result of this confusion by many on the abilities and needs of young children, child development professors and teachers at laboratory nursery schools observed, recorded, and wrote on children's behavior regularly. Advice was given to parents and knowledge about child development was disseminated to families and the community. Parent education was seen as a way to make an impact on the lives of young children. The study of young children received attention from noted psychologists and educators like G. Stanley Hall, Jean Piaget, Lev S. Vygotsky, John Dewey, Arnold Gesell, and Erik Erikson.

As problems throughout the world escalated in the 1930s and 1940s, and a Second World War loomed, the need for the federal government to once again become involved in the care and education of young children was the result. The Lanham Act was passed by Congress and was in effect from 1940–1946. Lanham early childhood centers were developed to provide child care for children whose mothers were employed in industries supporting government efforts during World War II. With most of the males in the military contributing to the war effort, young women, many of whom were mothers, were needed to work in the factories. Maternal employment wasn't a controversial issue then. The war effort required mothers to work, so they answered the call without repercussions from those in society who did not approve of mothers working. The out of family care options available for the children of working mothers ranged from no care available for mothers working at the B-24 bomber plant in Willow Run, Michigan, to new child-care centers built for the children whose mothers were employed at the Kaiser Ship Yards in Portland, Oregon. In 1943, Edgar Kaiser was concerned that the Lanham child-care centers located in Portland neighborhoods were not convenient for his workers. He sought to build his own child-care centers and staff them with employees from the shipyard. Mr. Kaiser quickly found out that one does not staff programs for young children with welders or carpenters. The general community at large, and the early childhood community specifically, quickly educated Kaiser about the importance of quality early childhood programs. He responded by supporting what many called the best child care there ever was. In addition, he recognized the importance of high-quality staff and recruited some of the best in the field to establish the centers and started teachers at a salary of $3,000 per year. In 1943 that was considered a very high salary. The two Kaiser Centers served 1,125 children each from eighteen months to six years and were opened 24 hours a day, seven days a week, and 364 days a year. Services unheard of at the time were available for the families. Mothers could pick up cooked meals at the end of the day, have their children's hair cut, pictures taken for fathers off at war, drop off clothes to be mended, or have school-age children cared for during school breaks. Most people hearing about the Kaiser Child Service Centers for the first time wonder what happened to these marvelous programs after the war. If the best child care that America ever had was available seventy years ago, then we haven't made much progress in the past half of a century. As James L. Hymes, who served as manager of the Child Service Centers, stated in 1970 at a conference on industry and day care, "We did it all at a tremendous expense." He went on to say, "I have to end by saying this was wartime. This was a cost-plus contract. . . . I am taken with how costly good services to children and families have to be. I am taken with how costly bad services always are."

The war ended; the fathers returned to seek employment or attend college, and the mothers stayed home to care for children. The federal government's involvement in care and young children ended for the second time. The 1950s were a decade of expansion and prosperity for most Americans. The country rebounded after sacrifices made for the war effort, and suburbs blossomed overnight outside of major cities. Full-day child care was extremely limited but half-day preschool programs began to open serving middle-class children. These children were living in families with many options available. However, children living in poverty were less fortunate. They had limited options for formal education before first grade.

When the Murfreesboro, Tennessee, Public Schools recognized the difficulty children living in poverty were having when they entered first grade, they looked to George Peabody College for Teachers in Nashville for help in the late 1950s. Kindergarten was not universally available then, so first grade was often the initial school experience for many poor rural children. Drs. Susan Gray and Rupert Klaus from the psychology department enlisted the help of doctoral students to develop a six-week summer program in 1962 called the Early Training Project. Up until this time it was believed that an early intervention program for children living in poverty could not help. The curriculum was aimed at teaching disadvantaged children language and other skills necessary for success in elementary school. Gray and Klaus gathered data and found their program better prepared children living in poverty for first grade. In fact, the earlier the intervention, the greater the gain. Their final report for the funding they had received from the federal government for the program was sent to the Department of Health, Education, and Welfare. The results meshed with the goals of the Economic Opportunity Act of 1964, which resulted in the establishment of the Head Start Program on February 12, 1965. This became the third time the federal government provided services for young children to fulfill economic goals. Head Start serves at-risk three- and four-year-olds in many types of programs in a variety of settings. All Head Start child development centers were initially based on five major components: health, nutrition, education, parental involvement, and social and psychological services. Many question why Head Start has had to constantly struggle for its basic existence. With the vast amount of evidence supporting early intervention programs, why are there not more funds available to meet the needs of all children?

As one can see, there are recurring themes in the past century related to programs for young children.

1. Federal involvement in early childhood education has primarily been in response to economic or social crises of the country, not as a result of the needs of young children.
2. Much of the focus and money has been spent on children from disadvantaged or at-risk families as opposed to all children.
3. Early childhood education was viewed as a panacea, the solution to all social ills in society.

This was, and is, huge pressure to put on an overworked and underpaid profession, especially when long-standing federal commitment to programs for young children has not been forthcoming.

Current Trends and Issues

The last quarter of the twentieth century was marked by an increase in single-parent families and the participation of mothers with young children in the workforce. There was also high mobility of families resulting in a lack of extended family upon which to rely for child care and other child-rearing assistance. The availability of child care, coupled with the problem of ensuring that the care is high quality and that the staff is compensated at an appropriate level, has become a major dilemma.

What was once a private family matter, child care has entered corporate board rooms and community discussion groups as families struggle to provide for their families and care for their young children simultaneously. Much attention has been paid to the lack of quality early childhood programs being available for all children and the high turnover of teaching staff. Teachers who can make more money at fast-food restaurants leave the profession at a national rate of approximately 40 percent each year. The long-term effects for young children who spend the majority of their formative years in poor quality child care are still being investigated. Teachers in elementary schools are encountering children who show effects of having participated in a wide range of child-care situations during their early years. The effects of children living in poverty are being met with success through quality early childhood programs, but there are not enough programs available, or teachers prepared to work with young children from a variety of backgrounds. The United States has yet to address the problem with sufficient resources and attention to sufficiently meet the challenge of early care and education. The offering of universal preschool education for all children has been met with criticism from some and strong praise from others.

We have children coming to our schools from diverse families. Parents may not speak English, children may have disabilities, and education beliefs may differ greatly from what is practiced in the school. It is the job of educators to meet each child at his or her level and move them forward. The need to accommodate programs instead of making young children change to fit into programs has never been truer than it is today. The focus in many schools has changed from one of assessing which children are ready to enter school to one of preparing the schools for the many different students who are eligible to attend. Teachers of young children need to be constantly aware of the needs and abilities of each child in their classroom. Teachers are under great pressure to improve academic standards, elevate failing schools to acceptable levels, and produce children who score passing marks on state-mandated tests. It is incumbent for ECE teachers to use their knowledge of child development and current research on best practices to advocate for what is most appropriate for young children. Federal and state policies related to No Child Left Behind (NCLB) are causing school personnel to constantly monitor the many regulations affecting education and work to improve academic performance for all students. Early childhood education plays a key role in any reform as the initial learning setting for all children. The importance of the strong foundation that can be forged during the years from birth through age eight must be shared with others. We must also address the need for the appropriate resources to do the job necessary to prepare every child for a lifetime of learning.

Public policy efforts are more crucial today than ever because future generations of children are dependent on sound educational and social practices receiving support today. Teachers have more responsibilities than just teaching children. They must inform parents of the kind of learning experiences children are receiving in their classroom, and stay professionally involved to keep up with current trends.

The good news for the ECE profession is that there has been tremendous growth in professional organizations, journals, and conferences. There are many articles in weekly news magazines on children's issues and the availability of products for young children has flooded the market. With this new information must come some caution though about the developmental abilities and needs of young children. Parents still want information on parenting and the proliferation of information about the abilities of young children has only served to confuse many parents on what are the best ways to raise children in today's world. Many of the issues contained in this volume are controversial because they may directly conflict with what has been standing practice for many generations, or are new issues Americans have not had time to think about.

A Call to Action

One indicator of a profession is that a body of research guides its practice. I am continually amazed that often in education, unlike other fields, we do not heed the research. Our grandmothers and great grandmothers would tell us years ago that for a simple kitchen burn, the best remedy was to slather the burn area with butter. There have been numerous studies conducted finding running a burn under cold water is best way to treat a burn. Medical personnel today use that research when educating others about burns. They do not continue to recommend the use of butter even though it has been proven to make the burn worse. For many of the issues in this second edition of *Taking Sides: Clashing Views in Early Childhood Education*, it was difficult to find a yes or no side to the issue. But that doesn't mean the practice is not occurring: far from it. In many cases we continue to carry out unsound educational practices, even though there is no sound research to back up the practice. For some of the issues chosen for this edition, that is the case. It is my hope that the reader will use sound research to guide decisions that are made regarding the care and education of young children. Alfie Kohn, in a 2007 interview said, "I'm always intrigued when the data point in one direction but practice goes in another."

When editing the two editions of *Sources: Notable Selections in Early Childhood Education* (McGraw-Hill), I realized just how little the field of early childhood education has changed over the years. Many of the sound educational principles upon which quality early childhood programs are based are deeply rooted in practices from 200, 100, or 50 years ago. Educational philosophies have a cyclical pattern where they are all the rage for a period of time, then fall out of favor with the general public for years, before being revived again. Change is evident. What must be kept in mind is that we learn from change and make improvements to practice based on what we learned. This is true of some of the issues chosen for this edition of *Taking Sides: Clashing Views in Early Childhood Education.*

Whether you are a student preparing to enter the field of education, a parent of young children, or a seasoned teacher or administrator, the issues in this edition will be of interest. Throughout the country, school board members are wrestling with many of these issues and might find reading the clashing views in this edition helpful when discussing critical topics. Decisions affect budgets, educational performance, and the views parents in the community have of the school system. Informed decisions can be made based on a thorough study of the issues. Understanding the issues can also lead to additional research. For many of the topics presented here, there has been limited research on the issue and how it affects young children. This can serve as a reminder to public policy specialists and researchers who investigate issues affecting children and their families. We need more data on many topics to make informed decisions. I invite you to read and reread the following articles. Have discussions with colleagues, neighbors, and friends. Develop an informed opinion that is not carved in stone, but one that could be altered based on new information, data, or experiences with the issue.

Internet References . . .

Administration for Children and Families

This site provides information on federally funded programs which promote the economic and social well-being of families, children and communities.

http://www.dhhs.gov

American Academy of Pediatrics

Pediatricians provide trusted advice for parents and teachers. The AAP official site includes position statements on a variety of issues related to the health and safety of young children.

http://www.aap.org

Children's Defense Fund (CDF)

At this site of the CDF, an organization which seeks to ensure that every child is treated fairly, there are reports and resources regarding current issues facing today's youth, along with national statistics on various subjects.

http://www.childrensdefense.org

Children, Youth and Families Education and Research Network

This excellent site contains useful links to research from key universities and institutions. The categories include early childhood, school age, teens, parents and family and community.

http://www.cyfernet.org

Connect for Kids

This nonprofit site provides news and information on issues affecting children and families, with over 1,500 helpful links to national and local resources.

http://www.connectforkids.org

Zero to Three

Here one will find developmental information on the first three years of life—an excellent site for both parents and professionals.

http://www.zerotothree.org

Children in Families and Society

*E*very family is different and operates with its own traditions, practices, and beliefs from all other families. Parents make parenting decisions based on their own experiences and the values they hold dear for their children. How parents support, guide, and educate their children changes as their children grow and they gain experience as parents. In addition, the society in which the family lives, which can mean the extended family, the community, state, and country, all make decisions that affect the family. The issues in this section relate to young children growing up in families, which are a part of the society at large.

- Should Brain Science Guide Educational Practice?

- Should Young Children Use Computers?

- Is Time-Out an Effective Guidance Technique?

- Does Nightly Homework Improve Academic Performance?

ISSUE 1

Should Brain Science Guide Educational Practice?

YES: **Stephen Rushton and Elizabeth Larkin,** from "Shaping the Learning Environment: Connecting Developmentally Appropriate Practices to Brain Research," *Early Childhood Education Journal* (September 2001)

NO: **Olaf Jorgenson,** from "Brain Scam? Why Educators Should Be Careful About Embracing 'Brain Research,'" *The Educational Forum* (Summer 2003)

ISSUE SUMMARY

YES: Stephen Rushton and Elizabeth Larkin from the University of South Florida at Sarasota support early childhood educators fostering developmentally appropriate learning experiences based on what is known about early brain research.

NO: Olaf Jorgenson is headmaster of the Hawaii Preparatory Academy in Walmea, Hawaii. He states that brain science should not be used to affect educational practice or policy.

T he research on early brain development had been called by many the shot in the arm the early childhood profession needed to validate the work they do. Parents, policymakers, and government leaders may now begin to see the importance of the first three years of life and how truly crucial they are for a child's future learning and development. Researchers now know 50 percent of brain development occurs during the first year of life. The National Education Goals Panel found that over 50 percent of infants and toddlers in America are not spending their days and nights in environments that will provide them the stimulation and assistance so important for future success in school. Many children under the age of three face one or more of the following risk factors: poor prenatal care, inferior child care, poverty, lack of sufficient attention, and isolated parents. Children being raised in these environments are facing great odds as they begin a life of learning.

Connections, or synapses, formed during the early years will help the child think and learn as he or she grows. Children who lack early brain stimulation have brains that are not as active and able to engage in complex thought processes or form lasting secure relationships. Early experiences strengthen the synapses so the brain will be better able to absorb and acquire new information as they grow and learn.

Over fifty years ago initial learning opportunities were provided for children when they entered kindergarten at age five. Efforts to provide additional stimulating materials or environments to children younger than five were not thought necessary. With the creation of the federal program, Head Start, in 1965, attention turned to preparing four-year-olds to enter school ready to learn. As time went on, it was found that four was not quite early enough to prevent the myriad of problems and deficiencies of many young children. Nor was it early enough to build a neurological foundation for math and logic. Brain research, made possible by new technology, has led researchers to focus intervention efforts even earlier than once thought necessary. Just as an electrician will tell you it is easier to wire a house during the construction phase than after the house is built, early intervention for strong brain development is easier during the child's first three years of life than into middle childhood and adulthood.

Stephen Rushton and Elizabeth Larkin report on the need for quality early experiences that are developmentally appropriate for stimulation of neuron development to form synapses or connections in the brain. They share some strategies that can be implemented in an early childhood classroom to enrich brain development.

Olaf Jorgenson cautions us against jumping to conclusions about the brain science findings saying that for centuries children have been raised in homes by parents who may not have paid 100 percent attention to the growth and development of their children or attended schools with little teacher expertise on early brain development and they turned out just fine. Jorgenson urges more research on early brain development before educators rush to make changes to our present educational system.

POINT

- The early years are critical for future learning.

- Parents and educators must capitalize on the early years by providing stimulation for young children.

- Research on how the brain develops should inform practice.

- Teachers should align developmentally appropriate practices and brain-based principles for effective learning to occur.

COUNTERPOINT

- The rapid growth of synapses in the early years does not mean children have the ability to learn more than adults.

- Extra stimulation is not necessarily better.

- The research can provide information on brain development but should not affect social policy.

- Educators must be cautious about jumping on the brain research bandwagon.

YES

**Stephen Rushton and
Elizabeth Larkin**

Shaping the Learning Environment: Connecting Developmentally Appropriate Practices to Brain Research

Introduction

The past several years have seen an explosion of published articles, books, and documentaries as well as a proliferation of conferences and workshop seminars focused on connecting recent neuroscientific research findings relating the child's developing brain to educational strategies. President of the James S. McDonnell Foundation, Bruer (1998), questions the validity of this marriage, stating clearly that "brain science has little to offer education practice or policy" (p. 14). He is supported by others who warn the educational community that knowledge gleaned from today's brain science may well be out-dated in several years due to its rudimentary nature. Indeed, many educators are quick to exert pressure on the educational pendulum in order to substantiate their philosophical position. However, although brain science is relatively new, Wolfe (1998), an educational consultant and expert on brain research, postulates that the bridge between neuroscience research and education is not the job of neuroscientists, but instead, that of educators.

Studies about how the human brain learns need to be interpreted in light of the classroom environment, because children spend a great deal of their time in these settings at a critical period in their development, and expectations for our professional success carry high stakes. The good news is that new research appears to be affirming what many early childhood educators have always known about effective learning environments. The bad news is that we have yet to fully explore the implications of this rapidly expanding area of knowledge in terms of generating widely recognized practices in the field of early childhood education. This paper is a beginning attempt to draw some parallels between brain research and the early childhood classroom, and so it should be acknowledged at the outset that the connections we propose here are tentative.

The National Association for the Education of Young Children's position statement on developmentally appropriate practices (DAP) for children birth through age 8 (Bredekamp & Copple, 1997) originally stated two main objectives, namely, (a) to provide "guidance to program personnel seeking accreditation by NAEYC's National Academy of Early Childhood Programs; and (b) to counter persistent beliefs in the prevailing traditional approach to early childhood education. The educational emphasis was on a didactic, teacher-centered approach to learning that encompassed primarily whole group instructional techniques (Bredekamp & Copple, 1997, p. v). Subsequently, DAP was revised to describe a philosophical orientation that now implies a constructivist approach to teaching young children. It is built on the premise that children are social learners who actively construct meaning and knowledge as they interact with their environment.

Research on what constitutes appropriate early learning experiences has focused during the past decade on both the social-emotional (Burts, Hart, Charlesworth, & Kirk, 1990; Hyson, Hirsh-Pasek, & Rescorla, 1990) and the cognitive (Dunn, Beach, & Kontos, 1994; Sherman & Mueller, 1996) development of young children. Studies indicate that children actively engaged in learner-centered environments score higher on measures of creativity (Hyson *et al.*, 1990), have better receptive verbal skills (Dunn *et al.*, 1994), and are more confident in their cognitive abilities (Mantzicopoulos; Neuharth-Pritchett, & Morelock, 1994; Stopek, 1993). Additionally, Frede and Barnett (1992) reported that children who attended developmentally appropriate programs in preschool performed better in first grade on standardized assessments of achievement. A study by Burts *et al.* (1993) indicated that children from low socioeconomic home environments who were enrolled in DAP kindergarten classrooms showed higher reading scores in first grade than their counterparts who attended more traditional classrooms.

Unfortunately, even with these studies, there exists a wide discrepancy between what research recommends and how children are currently being taught. Dunn and Kontos (1997) postulated that DAP programs are not the norm in early childhood programs as teachers have difficulty knowing how to implement such practices. They also reported that many parents are unaware of the significant benefits of a DAP program and therefore choose a more traditional learning environment for their children.

During the past decade a parallel body of literature has emerged, one that has potentially important implications for teachers and young children alike. Research in the fields of neuroscience (Diamond & Hopson, 1998; Fitzpatrick, 1995; Sylwester, 1997), cognitive psychology (Gardner, 1993; Goldman, 1995; LaDoux, 1996), and education (Caine & Caine 1991, 1997; Jensen, 1998; Kovalik, 1994; Wolfe, 1998), has provided some new information for teachers to better understand the learning process with implications for how to create more effective classroom environments. Combining knowledge across these disciplines could benefit teachers seeking ideas about best practices in designing environments that are consistent with what we now know about how the human brain learns. Specifically, brain research will help provide educators with strategies that can stimulate specific areas of the brain (thalamus, amygdala, hippocampus, and the frontal cortex) in order to gain the learner's attention, foster meaningful connections with prior understanding, and maximize both short- and long-term memory.

Brain research also supports the importance of developing and implementing a curriculum that is appropriate for the learner's particular developmental age. Early childhood teachers have been acutely aware for some time now that certain periods in a young child's life are more receptive for some kinds of learning. It is exciting to observe how the literature also indicates that particular "windows of opportunities" for learning do exist when the brain's plasticity, or adaptability, allows for greater amounts of information to be processed and absorbed (Wolfe, 1998).

Many teachers who embrace the early childhood philosophy are already practicing brain research-based strategies. Rushton (in press) describes a typical early childhood setting, for example, encouraging verbal interaction, integrating curriculum content areas, and providing meaningful problem-solving opportunities. Brain research, in and of itself, does not introduce new strategies for teachers; however, it does provide very concrete and important reasons why specific approaches to teaching and certain classroom strategies are more effective than others. As we will show, brain research seems to affirm many DAP principles and the underlying early childhood educational philosophy. With each DAP principle and brain research corollary, examples are provided on how to create, organize, and/or implement a learner-centered classroom that is compatible with both bodies of research. Not all principles are addressed since clear connections are not always evident. Table 1 outlines the parallels between the DAP standard and what we termed Brain Research principle. Additionally, the chart provides a few classroom strategies [that] connect the two similar bodies of research.

DAP Principle 1

Domains of children's development—physical, social, emotional, and cognitive—are closely related. Development in one domain influences and is influenced by development in other domains.

Educators have known for some time that development in one area is either influenced by, or is influencing another area of development. For instance, Graves (1983), Adams (1990), Weaver (1990), and others have articulated how reading and writing are connected; as a child begins to explore letters, sounds, and writing the desire and capacity to interpret, recognize, and understand these symbols increases simultaneously. And of course, this is conditional on the child's ability to see and hear—two very separate, yet interconnecting physiological functions. With even younger children, becoming mobile increases their ability to explore and understand their immediate environment. This increased activity also helps to stimulate cognitive development as they begin to interact and make sense of their surroundings (Kostelnik, Soderman, & Whiren, 1993; Sroufe, Cooper, & DeHart, 1992).

Each region of the brain consists of a highly sophisticated neurological network of cells, dendrites, and nerves that interconnect one portion of the brain with another. New stimuli entering the body via the five senses are directed immediately to the thalamus. The thalamus acts as a sorting station and reroutes the sensory input to various parts of the brain that deal specifically with each sense. These portions of the brain, called lobes, consist of millions of cells related to the specific sense that is being stimulated. For instance, the occipital lobe

Table 1

Different Strategies and Principles

DAP position[a]	BR principle[b]	Classroom environment[c]
1. Domains of children's development—physical, social, emotional, and cognitive—are closely related. Development in one domain influences and is influenced by development in other domains.	Each region of the brain consists of a highly sophisticated neurological network of cells, dendrites, and nerves that interconnect one portion of the brain to another. The brain's emotional center is tied to the ability to learn. Emotions, learning, and memory are closely linked as different parts of the brain are activated in the learning process.	Good curriculum naturally engages many of the five senses and activates more than one of Gardner's eight intelligences at the same time. Learning is a social activity, so children need opportunities to engage in dialogue. Multiage grouping is a strategy that can support and challenge a range of learning styles and capabilities. Good learning environments build trust, empower learners, and encourage students to explore their feelings and ideas.
2. Development occurs in a relatively orderly sequence, with later abilities, skills, and knowledge building on those already acquired.	The brain changes physiologically as a result of experience. New dendrites are formed everyday, "hooking" new information to prior experiences. An enriched environment increases cell weight and branching of dendrites.	Hands-on activities stimulate the various regions of the brain, and active participation helps young children to form stronger associations with existing understanding. Different stages of play (solitary, parallel, associative, collaborative), for example, can be identified and appropriate activities designed to build increasingly complex ideas through play.
3. Development proceeds at varying rates from child to child as well as unevenly within different areas of a child's functioning.	Each brain is unique. Lock-step, assembly-line learning violates a critical discovery about the human brain: each brain is not only unique, but also is growing on its own timetable.	Environments should allow choices to accommodate a range of developmental styles and capabilities. Large blocks of time, and systems for planning and tracking work, can be organized for children to share responsibility for their activity choices. Teachers need to adjust expectations and performance standards to age-specific characteristics and unique capabilities of learners.
4. Early experiences have both cumulative and delayed effects on individual children's development. Optimal periods exist for certain types of development and learning.	Brain research indicates that certain "windows of opportunity" for learning do exist. The brain's "plasticity" allows for greater amounts of information to be processed and absorbed at certain critical periods (Wolfe, 1998).	Children need opportunities to use sensory inputs, language, and motor skills. Young children also require frequent opportunities to interact verbally with peers.

(continued)

Table 1 (Continued)

Different Strategies and Principles

DAP position[a]	BR principle[b]	Classroom environment[c]
	The critical period for learning a spoken language is lost by about age 10 (Sorgen, 1999).	Repeated opportunities to interact with materials, peers, and ideas are critical for long-term memory.
		Second language programs will be most successful before 5th grade and should start as early as possible.
5. Development proceeds in predictable directions toward greater complexity, organization, and internalization.	The brain is designed to perceive and generate patterns.	Finding patterns can be built into math, language arts, science, and other subject area curriculum. Learning environments need to be organized for both low and high order thinking skills.
	The brain is designed to process many inputs at once and prefers multi-processing. Hence, a slower linear pace reduces understanding. (Caine & Caine,1997)	The use of metaphor, and repeated opportunities to compare and contrast through multiple modalities, allow children to differentiate increasingly complex schemas.
7. Children are active learners, drawing on direct physical and social experience as well as culturally transmitted knowledge to construct their own understanding of the world around them.	When a child is engaged in a learning experience, a number of areas of the brain are simultaneously activated.	Learning should be presented in a real life context so that new information builds upon prior understanding, and then generalizes to broader concepts.
	Children raised in nonaca-demically oriented environments have little experience in using decontextualized language. They are more inclined to reason with visual, hands-on strategies (Healy,1990).	Field trips, guest speakers, interactive technology, and multicultural units of study will help children better understand themselves and succeed in today's world.
		In environments where children can interact with diverse populations (various cultures and generations—including grandparents), and use language as well as visual-spatial strategies, their learning will be enhanced.
8. Development and learning result from interaction of biological maturation and the environment, which includes both the physical and social worlds that children live in.	Each of the senses can be independently or collectively affected by environmental factors that in turn will affect the brain's ability to learn. Enriched environments increase dendritic branching and synaptic responses (Diamond, 1998).	Environments should be carefully monitored for appropriate lighting, aromas, ionization (fresh air), and noise. Water and appropriate foods should be made available to children, remembering that each person's internal clock differs.

Table 1 (Continued)

Different Strategies and Principles

DAP position[a]	BR principle[b]	Classroom environment[c]
	The simple act of reading a book may be one of the most challenging tasks the brain must perform. Speech comes naturally, but reading does not (Sorgen, 1999).	Environments should offer a wealth of materials and activity choices to explore. Children need to understand the relevance of learning to read. Learning to read should be connected to the child's speaking and writing. Reading aloud and reading for meaning are two different processes, and children need opportunities to do both.
9. Children demonstrate different modes of knowing and learning and different ways of representing what they know.	"The mental mechanisms that process music (and rhyme and rhythm) are deeply entwined with the brain's other basic functions, including emotion, perception, memory, and even language" (Sorgen, 1999, p. 56). The most powerful influences on a learner's behavior are concrete, vivid images. The brain has a primitive response to pictures, symbols, and strong, simple images (Jensen, 1995).	A classroom should provide opportunities for individual children to learn via modalities other than just verbal/linguistic or logico-mathematical tasks. Rhyme and rhythm are memory aids. Children should be able to express knowledge in a variety of forms. Dramatization, music, and the visual arts should be made readily available as modes of both learning and expression. Symbolic representation can easily be built into the arts.
10. Children develop and learn best in the context of a community where they are safe and valued, their physical needs are met, and they feel psychologically secure.	Brain research has clearly demonstrated that high levels of stress, or a perceived threat, will inhibit learning. (Caine & Caine, 1997) The brain is primarily designed to survive. No intelligence or ability will unfold until or unless given the appropriate model environment" (Jensen, 1996).	The classroom environment should connect learning experiences to positive emotions. Students need to make decisions and choices about learning that is meaningful to them. The classroom culture should support risk-taking, and view failures as a natural part of the learning process.

[a]NAEYC's positions on Developmentally Appropriate Practices (DAP)
[b]What brain research (BR) suggests about how the brain learns.
[c]Strategies that incorporate both BR and DAP.

relates to the receiving and processing of visual information, and is located near the rear of the brain. The temporal lobe relates to language development, writing, hearing, sensory associations, and, to some extent, memory. It is located in the mid-left portion of the brain. The parietal lobe relates to higher sensory, language, and short-term memory. Finally, the frontal lobe helps us in our ability to judge, be creative, make decisions and plan. Learning does not take place as separate and isolated events in the brain—all these parts work together.

When a child is engaged in a learning experience a number of areas of the brain are simultaneously activated. Each lobe interacts cohesively, not as separate or isolated organs, but as interdependent collective units (Sylwester, 1997), and all of them are needed in order to read and write. For instance, reading a book requires that the child picks up a book (activating the motor cortex: movement); she looks at the words (activating the occipital lobe: vision); she attempts to decipher words (activating the temporal lobe: language); and finally, she begins to think about what the words mean (activating the frontal lobe: reasoning) (Sorgen, 1999).

We know that learning and memory are strongly connected to emotions, and thus, the learning environment needs to be both stimulating and safe. Classroom experiences can be designed to allow children to investigate, reflect, and express ideas in a variety of ways that are increasingly complex and interconnected. Gardner (1993) proposed that each individual draws on multiple intelligences and generally relies on some more than others. Thus, learners need ample opportunities to use and expand their preferred intelligences, as well as adapt to and develop the other intelligences, which are all interdependent within the one brain. Then, they need opportunities to express what they know and understand in a variety of formats.

Early childhood teachers need to recognize developmental characteristics among children in a group, as well as each learner's unique capabilities. Multiage grouping is one strategy that helps to facilitate learning for a range of abilities (Kasten & Clarke, 1993). Because all the children in the class are not the same age, children can recognize more readily how individual approaches to learning tasks are both distinctive and viable. Here, what a child knows and how he knows it is not so much a factor of age as of prior experience and learned meanings. In this, or any environment, teachers of all ages will want to foster a learning context that builds trust, promotes self-direction, and encourages students to freely exchange their feelings and ideas so that the social/emotional realm is connected positively to cognitive and physical experiences.

DAP Principle 2

Development occurs in a relatively orderly sequence, with later abilities, skills and knowledge building on those already acquired.

DAP Principle 3

Development proceeds at varying rates from child to child as well as unevenly within different areas of a child's functioning.

We learn to sit before we crawl, and crawl before we walk. In this way, human development is ordered and sequential. Developmental psychologists have described how stages of physical, cognitive, and social development are stable and predictable over time especially in children during the first 9 years of life. Notable pioneers such as Piaget (1952) and Erikson (1963), for example, proposed different stages of play and socialization that, providing normal development, are observable, predictable, and measurable. In these hierarchies, no stage can be skipped over as the developmental process unfolds.

Wolfe and Brandt (1998) stated that the brain changes physiologically as a result of experience. As the child experiences an event for the first time, either new dendrites are formed, or the experience is associated with a similar past event hooking new information to old understanding. Much of our behavior and development is "hardwired" through a long history of human evolution (i.e., breathing, circulation, and reflexes). However, individual brains are also "softwired" in order to adapt and create new neurological networks in response to the unique environmental stimuli encountered in our individual lives. It is in the interplay between environment and genetics, hardwired automatic behaviors and softwired developing neuronetworks, that we need to be sensitive to differences among children.

Each child's uniqueness is expressed in a number of ways: personality, temperament, learning style, maturation, speed of mastering a skill, level of enjoyment of a particular subject, attention, and memory. These attributes help to identify how a particular child will learn and what style of teaching is best suited for him or her. Further, each brain's growth is largely dictated by genetic timing, and therefore is as individualized as DNA (Sylwester, 1995). In truth, there are no homogeneous groups of children; as no two children are the same, no two brains are the same. Wolfe (1998) put it succinctly when she stated: "The environment affects how genes work, and genes determine how the environment is interpreted" (p. 10).

Implications for Practice

Early childhood teachers have learned that children progress through various stages of development, knowing that each child's rate of development (and each brain) is unique and different. Providing hands-on activities that both cater to the differences among children and stimulate various regions of the brain reinforces stronger associations of meaning and makes learning inherently more interesting. Teachers who are trained to observe each child's development can establish a responsive environment for different documented stages of play (solitary, parallel, associative), and carefully design appropriate activities for the child's level. Teachers of older students can pay attention to higher order thinking skills in a similar manner, challenging students with engaging problem-solving opportunities. Teaching complex skills too soon may impede learning, and conversely, not teaching children when they are ready may result in boredom and a lack of interest.

Activities that have different levels of complexity allow every child access both to the content ideas and to conversation with peers. Creating centers around the classroom with a range of problems to solve and materials to use can accommodate the differences among learners. A general overall theme may permeate the activities in each center so that the children see connections across subject areas. A center (Rushton, in press) approach can easily be adapted from preschool to third grade, using planning sheets and individualized contracts to help children discover for themselves what their particular strengths and challenges are.

Because each learner is so different, children should be able to choose activities that fit their level of development, experience, and interest. Thus, teachers will want to use a variety of teaching methods and materials to ensure that every child becomes interested in exploring ideas, so that their auditory, visual, tactile, or emotional preferences are accounted for. More important, teachers need to remember that each child's educational experiences inside the classroom plays a part in shaping a lifetime of learning habits. Different children feel challenged by different problems, and threatened by different social circumstances, and these matter in what and how they learn.

DAP Principle 4

Early experiences have both cumulative and delayed effects on individual children's development. Optimal periods exist for certain types of development and learning.

Principle 4 suggests that each learning experience lays groundwork for future learning, either positively or negatively. The child's ability to learn and interpret new information is directly related to the frequency of prior experience with related ideas. Brain research also indicates that certain windows of opportunities for learning do exist (Sorgen, 1999). In some instances, it is vital to development that a particular sense be stimulated. For instance, it has been demonstrated that some animals have had their vision obscured at key times in their development and were unable to ever see again. The blueprint, so to speak, relating to vision simply cannot be reestablished if not stimulated to grow in the first several years (Wolfe, 1998). The same can be said for developing oral language. In extreme cases in which a child has been abused, neglected, and cut off from society, speech pathologists have been unable to help those individuals speak normally.

Language and motor development both require children to actively engage with others. Conversation and physical activity are extremely important for the development of the brain. To facilitate optimal development, young children require opportunities to interact with each other regularly, to encounter new vocabulary, construct arguments, express emotions, and stretch their muscles. Thus, learning environments should encourage verbal interactions, moving around the room as children work on projects or pursue a line of inquiry, and plentiful occasions to use manipulative materials including gross motor equipment.

Second language acquisition is most successful prior to fifth or sixth grade when the necessary structures in the brain for language learning are still in place. Young children seem to be particularly adept at mimicry, especially when language is rhythmic and rhyming. Also, the brain looks for patterns and connections, and repetition is critical for long-term memory. Introducing young children to more than one language is extremely beneficial, even if they do not yet understand how language is structured grammatically or written down. This early learning creates a foundation for later, more formal, study of another language.

DAP Principle 5

Development proceeds in predictable directions toward greater complexity, organization, and internalization.

The brain is designed to perceive and generate patterns and is constantly seeking to place new information into existing neurological networks. If no prior network exists, then new dendrites will be formed. Each layer of learning builds upon former networks. It has been suggested that the myelin sheath that surrounds the axons (the long tentacles of a dendrite) thicken with repeated exposure to a thought, idea, or experience. The greater the complexity of an experience, the thicker the myelin becomes. The belief is that thicker myelin results in faster recall of an event and greater memory (Diamond & Hopson, 1998). If this is true, then repetition of activities helps to thicken the myelin and thus, reinforce students' understanding.

Since no two children learn at the same rate, it is crucial that children be given repeated opportunities and ample time to explore, play, and socialize while they work in various curriculum areas (paint, blocks, dramatic play, listening center, water table, science). A typical K–3 classroom covers content in reading, writing, and mathematics, and time permitting, social studies, science, and the arts. Curriculum is often presented as separate subjects in distinct units with little overlap. Information would be better presented in a context of real life experiences where new information can build upon prior knowledge, so that learners understand how it is meaningful to them. Field trips are an excellent strategy to connect new learning to real world applications. When studying pollution, for example, students might visit the landfill, clean water treatment center, the recycling plant, or local municipal garbage collection center rather than just viewing pictures and reading texts about the subject. The learner should be able to connect new information to well-established conceptual frameworks in an experiential manner, not as isolated bits of information that have no meaningful connection.

DAP Principle 7

Children are active learners, drawing on direct physical and social experience as well as culturally transmitted knowledge to construct their own understanding of the world around them.

DAP Principle 8

Development and learning result from interaction of biological maturation and the environment, which includes both the physical and social worlds that children live in.

The environment in which a child learns, both the explicit physical surroundings (people, manipulative materials, books) and the implicit cultural norms, (alphabet, numerical symbols, values) shapes that child's understanding of the meaning of his or her experiences. Bredekamp and Copple (1997) stated that "young children actively learn from observing and participating with other children and adults" and that they need to "form their own hypotheses and keep trying them out through social interaction, physical manipulation, and their own thought processes" (p. 13).

The human brain is constantly seeking information from a variety of stimuli. These data are interpreted through all the senses and are then organized by the brain. Since each of the senses can be independently or collectively affected by environmental factors, they will affect the brain's overall ability to learn. Therefore, it stands to reason that the learning environment should make children physically comfortable—they need good lighting, fresh air, and a reasonable level of noise. In addition, children cannot learn when they are hungry or tired because their minds will be focused on the body's signals to eat or sleep. They need to move around to oxygenate their blood and exercise their muscles.

The social environment in a classroom relies heavily on language, and the simple act of reading is one of the most challenging tasks the brain performs. But the brain perceives patterns, and so we can help children develop language skills by looking for letter patterns in words, word patterns in sentences such as rhyming or alliteration, patterns in story sequence, and the like. Most importantly, we need to help children see the relevance of learning language and becoming competent readers, so that their motivation to learn and attention to the challenge are both high. The learning environment can reflect children's interests by including them in conversations about which books will be read.

Children who have been raised in nonacademically oriented environments have less experience using decontextualized language than their peers. In other words, they are less apt to rely on words to describe events to others outside the context where they occurred, and oral language skill development will affect later reading ability (Snow, Tabors, & Nicholson, 1995). These children may communicate more readily through using visual images, physical activity, and symbolic representation.

The curriculum can include practice in storytelling as a way to develop oral language skills and to make connections with children's real world experiences at the same time. The more children are exposed to and talk about experiences that are new to them, the more connections they can make to what they already know. Children also need opportunities to express ideas and understanding in physically active ways, such as through visual and dramatic arts. Repeated practice helps children to recall information and master physical tasks. As new information builds on prior understanding, children are able to generalize their own experiences to broader concepts.

DAP Principle 11

Children demonstrate different modes of knowing and learning and different ways of representing what they know.

Gardner's (1993) work in multiple intelligences and assessment has pointed to the need for classrooms to provide more occasions for children to use music, bodily-kinesthetic, visual-spatial, and interpersonal domains to learn and express understanding. Brain research has indicated that the "mental mechanisms that process music (and rhyme and rhythm) are deeply entwined with the brain's other basic functions, including emotion, perception, memory, and even language" (Sorgen, 1999, p. 56). If music and movement can be used to build children's social/emotional experiences in the classroom, and to reinforce memory, language development, or even mathematical skills, we are likely to reach more kinds of learners than we would if we relied solely on narrowly defined subject areas.

Jensen (1998) has said that the most powerful influences on a learner's behavior are concrete, vivid images. The brain, he added, has a primitive response to pictures, symbols, and strong, simple images. It follows, then, that our systems of symbolic representation (the alphabet and numbers) are learned better if they can be connected to concrete, vivid images such as pictures and expressive motions. Children's memories are helped by physically representing what they know in addition to using language, so the arts should hold an important place in the curriculum. Children can draw, paint, construct, and dramatize what they know and understand.

DAP Principle 12

Children develop and learn best in the context of a community where they are safe and valued, their physical needs are met, and they feel psychologically secure.

Research on the brain and learning has clearly demonstrated that high levels of stress, or a perceived threat by the child, inhibits learning (Caine & Caine, 1997). It is the brain's principal job to ensure survival. The brain's emotional center is tied to its ability to learn. The amygdala checks all incoming sensory information first to see if it fits a known impression of danger. If a threat is perceived, the ability to learn is greatly impeded as the entire body automatically gears up to defend itself.

Teachers have a central responsibility to create a learning environment that feels relaxed enough to allow children's attention to focus on the curriculum, and challenging enough to excite interest. Evaluation is one component of the educational milieu, and thus, all assessment situations need to avoid generating a perceived threat. Clearly, using a variety of methods for collecting data enhances the likelihood of matching an individual learner's ways of knowing, and provides a more complete picture of what is known and understood.

Emotions, learning, and memory are closely linked as different parts of the brain are activated in the learning process. It is crucial, especially during the first several years of the child's life, to provide a rich and safe environment that lays groundwork for this neurological network to develop. Early childhood programs ought to invite children to make choices about what and how they learn so that they are more willing to take risks and view their experiences as both relevant and positive. Children need to explore, play, and discover, in a safe and healthy environment, using all of their senses in making connections from one part of the curriculum to another.

Conclusion

Technological advancements during the past decade have seen the development of some sophisticated equipment that has helped to better understand the functions of the human brain. This technology and subsequent understanding of the brain, albeit overwhelming for most educators, supports many of the philosophical tenets of constructivism, rooted in the philosophy of Dewey (1964). He believed that children learn best when interacting in a rich environment. He also believed that children constructed meaning from real life applications, and further, he knew that when various senses were used simultaneously, the probability of learning would be greater. Our modern educational terminology—such as integrated curriculum, whole language, hands-on learning, authentic assessment, and developmentally appropriate practices—not only echoes brain research, but also, we believe, contains many of the underpinning beliefs, thoughts, and tenets of Dewey.

Brain research helps to explain further why constructivist educators such as Dewey (1964), Piaget and Inhelder (1969), and Vygotsky (1967) still prevail. It is hoped that with new understanding about how the brain works, combined with the tenets of Developmentally Appropriate Practice, our ability to educate future generations will be greatly enhanced. The neuroscientist's job is to better understand the workings of the mind and brain; it is our job, as educators, to carefully sift through their findings and connect them to what we know empirically about how children learn best.

References

Adams, M. J. (1990). *Beginning to read: Thinking and learning about print*. Urbana-Champaign, IL: The Reading Research and Education Center.

Bredekamp, S., & Copple, C. (1997). *Developmentally appropriate practice in early childhood programs* (Rev. ed). Washington, DC: National Association for the Education of Young Children.

Burts, D., Hart, C., Charlesworth, R., & Kirk, L. (1990). A comparison of frequencies of stress behaviors observed in kindergarten children in classrooms with developmentally appropriate versus developmentally inappropriate instructional practices. *Early Childhood Research Quarterly, 5*, 407–423.

Burts, D., Hart, C., Charlesworth, R., DeWolf, D., Ray, J., Manuel K., & Fleege, P. (1993). Developmental appropriateness of kindergarten programs and academic outcomes in first grade. *Journal of Research in Childhood Education, 8*(1), 23–31.

Caine, R. N., & Caine, G. (1997). *Education on the edge of possibility*. Alexandria, VA: ASCD.

Dewey, J. (1964). The relation of theory to practice in education. In R. Archamault (Ed.), *John Dewey on education: Selected writings* (pp. 313–338). New York: Random House.

Diamond, M., & Hopson, J. (1998). *Magic trees of the mind: How to nurture your child's intelligence, creativity, and healthy emotions from birth through adolescence*. New York: Penguin Putnam.

Dunn, L., Beach, S., & Kontos, S. (1994). Quality of the literacy environment in day care and children's development. *Journal of Research in Childhood Education, 9*(1), 24–34.

Elkind, D. (1981). *The hurried child*. Reading, MA: Addison-Wesley.

Erikson, E. H. (1963). *Childhood and society*. New York: Norton.

Fitzpatrick, S. (1995). Smart brains: Neuroscientists explain the mystery of what makes us human. *American School Board Journal*.

Frede, E., & Barnett, W. S. (1992). Developmentally appropriate public school preschool: A study of implementation of the High/Scope curriculum and its effects on disadvantaged children's skills at first grade. *Early Childhood Research Quarterly*, *7*, 483–499.

Gardner, H. (1993). *Multiple intelligences: The theory in practice*. New York: Basic Books.

Graves, D. (1983). *Writing: Teachers and children at work*. Portsmouth, NH: Heinemann.

Hirsh-Pasek, K., Hyson, M., & Rescorla, L. (1990). Academic environments in preschool: Do they pressure or challenge young children? *Early Education and Development*, *1*, 401–423.

Hyson, M., Hirsh-Pasek, K., & Rescorla, L. (1990). The classroom practices inventory: An observation instrument based on NAEYC's guidelines for developmentally appropriate practices for 4- and 5-year-old children. *Early Childhood Research Quarterly*, *5*, 475–494.

Jensen, E. (1998). *Teaching with the brain in mind*. Alexandria, VA: Association for Supervision and Curriculum Development.

Kasten, W., & Clark, B. (1993). *The multi-age classroom: A family of learners*. New York: Richard C. Owen Publishers.

Kostelnik, M., Soderman, A., & Whiren, A. (1993). *Healthy young children: A manual for programs*. New York: Macmillan.

LaDoux, J. (1996). *The emotional brain: The mysterious underpinnings of emotional life*. New York: Simon & Schuster.

Piaget, J. (1952). *The origins of intelligence in children*. Toronto: George J. McLeod.

Piaget, J., & Inhelder, B. (1969). *The psychology of the child*. New York: Basic Books.

Rushton, S. (in press). A developmentally appropriate and brain-based compatible learning environment. *Young Children*.

Sherman, C., & Mueller, D. (1996, June). *Developmentally appropriate practice and student achievement in inner-city elementary schools*. Paper presented at Head Start's Third National Research Conference, Washington, DC. (ED 401 354)

Sorgen, M. (1999, June). *Applying brain research to classroom practice*. Materials presented at the University of South Florida Brain/Mind Connections Conference, Sarasota, FL.

Spodek, B. (Ed.). (1993). *The handbook of research on the education of young children*. New York: Teachers College Press.

Snow, C. E., Tabors, P. O., & Nicholson, P. A. (1995, Fall/Winter). SHELL: Oral language and early literacy skills in kindergarten and first grade children. *Journal of Research in Childhood Education*, *10*, 37–48.

Sroufe, L. A., Cooper, R. G., & DeHart, G. G. (1992). *Child development: Its nature and course* (2nd ed.). New York: Knopf.

Sylwester, R. (1997). The neurobiology of self-esteem and aggression. *Educational Leadership*, *54*(5), 75–79.

Vygotsky, L. (1967). Play and its role in the mental development of the child. *Soviet Psychology*, *12*, 62–76.

Weaver, C. (1990). *Understanding whole language: From principles to practice*. Portsmouth, NH: Heinemann.

Wolfe, J., & Brandt, R. (1998). What we know from brain research. *Educational Leadership*, *56*(3), 8–14.

Olaf Jorgenson  **NO**

Brain Scam? Why Educators Should Be Careful About Embracing "Brain Research"

Glance through the program of virtually any recent professional-development conference for educators, and you will find at least one presentation linked to "brain research." Indeed, for the past several years, our profession has been inundated with articles and in-service sessions connecting brain research and topics as varied as understanding teen behavior (Brownlee 1999), developing the meaning and relevance of curricula (Westwater and Wolfe 2000), or recognizing how movement can enhance learning (Jensen 1998). The vast majority of brain-research information has been packaged and presented by energetic, visionary educational consultants, almost none of whom carry credentials in neuroscience or the study of brain chemistry or anatomy. Their work is lucrative, as educators across the country have ferociously devoured teaching aids and strategies allegedly rooted in brain research—so much so that it is now possible to order "brain-based" educational materials from catalogs devoted to such wares. . . .

At a rapid pace, "brain learning" has inundated educational theory and practice in the United States; in some circles, it would be blasphemous to voice criticisms of its principles or its proponents. The possibilities of the brain-research phenomenon—like its implications for the future of teaching and learning—are dizzying. Yet educators must recognize the limitations of the fledgling cognitive-neuroscience movement as it currently can contribute to our profession. Limited findings in several instances have led to an avalanche of speculative "brain research" assertions from educational consultants and professional developers—nonscientists—initiating and propagating numerous misunderstandings and myths in the guise of science. This speculation in turn has led to widespread commercial exploitation of teachers and school systems eager to implement promising (if pseudoscientific) educational programs and products. So is any of the new "brain science" really new, or really science?

Where's the Science Here?

These developments have led some seasoned educators to be wary of embracing yet another professional trend that will likely fade away in a few years. As Bruer (in Lawton 1999, 6) noted, "There's a whole industry of brain-based education

From *The Educational Forum*, vol. 67, Summer 2003, pp. 364–369. Copyright © 2003 by Kappa Delta Pi. Reprinted by permission.

based on no research at all." The brain-based learning advocates to which he referred have repackaged progressive educational principles favoring active learning and constructivist methods, but "none of the evidence comes from brain research" (Bruer 1999, 649).

Because much of the data is relatively new, confusion arises when scientific findings are unclear or contradictory. Brain laterality, for example, is the widely accepted proposition that "right brain/left brain" distinctions may explain differences in aptitudes depending on which hemisphere in the brain is "dominant" in a person. Some neuroscientists, including Bruer, have dismissed such claims, asserting that ample research conducted over the past two decades supports the position that complex mental processes involve subsystems from both hemispheres of the brain. Yet educators eager to learn more about brain research can snatch up copies of David Sousa's (1995) widely read *How the Brain Learns: A Classroom Teacher's Guide.* This text includes a chapter exploring brain bilaterality, citing "split-brain" studies that appear to support this model of brain function. In the absence of a definitive posture in the scientific community, brain bilaterality has been presented as a model for understanding thinking and learning—right or wrong.

Critics of the brain-research bandwagon point to careless misrepresentations of neurobiological research perpetuated by consultants and educators peddling brain commercialism. For instance, the notion of a so-called "critical period" or "window of opportunity" within which children learn faster and easier in conjunction with increased brain development has been promoted by leading brain-research consultants including Sousa, Pat Wolfe and Ron Brandt (1998), and Eric Jensen (1998); in some cases, it has been embellished far beyond its original research findings. The "critical period" assertions are actually rooted in a limited truth with regard to language acquisition. As Kluger and Park (2001, 54) have explained, "At birth, babies have the potential to learn any language with equal ease, but by six months, they have begun to focus on the one tongue they hear spoken most frequently." This period does indeed appear to be a "window" for language acquisition; but, "when it comes to other skills, such as math or music, there is virtually no evidence for learning windows at all" (Kluger and Park 2001, 54).

Our sweeping acceptance of such learning windows can be traced back to a single scientific study (Chugani, Phelps, and Mazziota 1987) conducted with 29 epileptic children ranging in age from between five days to 15 years. The popular notion of critical learning periods for children (often cited as those aged four to ten years old) "is an instance where neuroscientists have speculated about the implications of their work for education and where educators have uncritically embraced that speculation" (Bruer 1999, 653). A number of studies make the leap from the limited finding on windows of opportunity with language acquisition to broad assumptions about optimal time frames for cognitive development in general (Miller 1998; Southwest Educational Development Laboratory 1998). Similar interpretive leaps are evident in the literature; for example, if in principle researchers find that "the brain is designed to perceive and generate patterns," are educators justified in concluding that "thematic teaching, integration of the curriculum, and life-relevant approaches to learning" (whatever those terms mean specifically) are now scientifically credible or justified because they somehow involve pattern recognition (Metropolitan Omaha Educational Consortium [MOEC] 1999, 3)? Such carelessness exposes much of the brain-research movement's "scientific" foundation as "a popular mix of fact, misinterpretation, and speculation" that may be "intriguing, but not always informative" (Bruer 1999, 657).

Perhaps the best-known misconception associated with brain research is the "Mozart effect." The brain product catalogs, and even many department store children's sections, currently feature classical music collections for stimulating young, growing minds. Compact discs and tapes may be purchased that allegedly "enhance spatial reasoning and perhaps musical and artistic abilities too" (Kluger and Park 2001, 52). Even babies in utero can benefit, as suggested by products like "pregaphones"—tummy headphones that pipe music into the mother's womb (Kluger and Park 2001, 54). Harvard University's Project Zero (Hetland 2000) analyzed research concerning the effects of background music on its listeners, demonstrating that college students under study did in fact benefit from listening to music when they were assessed through paper-and-pencil tests of spatial reasoning—but these were adults, and the effects lasted only 15 minutes before fading away (Kluger and Park 2001, 54). There is no evidence that listening to Mozart or any other background music improves a child's "brain power," and certainly none that shows any benefit for babies (Seiden 1998, 1). Nonetheless, the governor of Georgia in 2001 proposed that the state purchase a classical music disc or cassette for each Georgia newborn—at a cost of more than $100,000 annually to taxpayers—"to spur brain development" (Kluger and Park 2001, 1).

As the Jensen Learning Center (1998, 4) noted, "The Mozart studies were not proven wrong; they were clarified." Marketers seeking profit, and a general public (including at least one governor) unaware of accurate science, allowed fact to become fad. As the results of brain research are increasingly institutionalized in educational theory and practice nationwide, however, the proportions of other brain myths we may unwittingly buy into—literally—are significant.

Counterpoint: If It Works, Use It

As the influence of the brain-research movement spreads, educators and governing boards are implementing "brain compatible" (Westwater and Wolfe 2000) programs and techniques intended to improve student achievement, increase engagement in lessons, and move teachers away from passive models of direct instruction that have proven ineffective in many modern educational contexts. Institutionalization of these techniques, questionably founded as some may be on science, has led to reports of successes. Lawton (1999) cited an example of a Wisconsin superintendent who outfitted her elementary schools with expensive keyboards after she learned of a single study appearing to connect music lessons with enhanced spatial and abstract reasoning in preschoolers. Subsequently, student achievement improved among the district's kindergartners, apparently as a result of the experiment, and at least one brain-research believer was vindicated. Other favorable outcomes are emerging in districts and schools nationwide, though it is hard to isolate the different factors leading to the success in such system-wide reform efforts. It is difficult to know whether the improvement is due to "brain-based" theory, increased attention paid to hands-on activities and engaging teaching strategies, improved teacher awareness and attention to student needs, the pressure of a unified district mandate with support throughout the chain of command, or one of many other variables contributing to increased student achievement. Yet, as Jensen (1998) has argued, teachers and administrators can't always wait for definitive evidence and redundant studies before implementing new research findings in the classroom. As Lawton (1999, 7) noted, "If we waited until we knew absolutely for sure, it would be 30 years [and] that is unfair to millions of kids."

On some levels, the criticism of brain research as it has been applied to K–12 educational practice smacks of academic elitism, the pervasive quest for quantitative data and disdain for unscientific application of theory. When Westwater and Wolfe (2000, 52) described enticing lesson ideas linked to claims about how the brain prioritizes information, and then referred to "the many brain compatible activities available to teachers," should it matter whether these assertions and activities are grounded in "hard" neuroscience rather than "soft" behavioral psychology? As Bruer (1999, 649–50) argued, "Teachers should know about short- and long-term memory; about primacy/recency effects; about how procedural, declarative, and episodic memory differ; and about how prior knowledge affects our current ability to learn." In the attempt to nudge schools away from the so-called "factory model" of education, rife with the long-suffering reliance on lecture and memorization of rote information, these brain-based approaches are inherently appealing to many progressive education reformers whether they are scientific or not.

To be fair, other reformist agendas are similarly unfounded in "hard" research. The inquiry-science approach, for example, encourages students to *do* science—preparing hypotheses, designing experiments, evaluating conclusions—as opposed to learning *about* science by passively reading textbooks and watching teachers conduct experiments. Comparatively little research supports inquiry methodology as an improvement over traditional science instruction, yet districts across the nation are implementing inquiry-based programs and lauding the merits of the approach anecdotally. We may not be certain that inquiry works; but decades of international science education comparisons have confirmed that our traditional methods of teaching science do not work. Given this sort of analogy, educators confront the mandate of reform and must put all promising tools to the test in the hope of advancing our success with children in schools.

A New Cognitive Epoch

The debate over the merits of brain research is just beginning, like the field of cognitive neuroscience itself; but the awareness that education is poised before a revolution is inescapable regardless of which side of the argument you support. As Scheibel (1997, 23) noted, "We are all travelers in a new cognitive epoch, plumbing unfamiliar extensions of the human experience. We must use the new knowledge about our remarkable thinking organ to understand the way we learn and to change the ways we teach. The coming generations have a right to expect no less of us."

The potential of the brain-research movement, viewed in this light, extends to the very nature of what it means to be a "professional" educator. Research about brain anatomy, chemistry, and processes applied to how humans learn is still in its infancy and surely might revolutionize our field. Just as attorneys earn their credibility by acquiring mastery of the law, engineers by commanding the principles of math and physics, and physicians by gaining expertise in the biological sciences, so too could education one day be founded on cognitive science, the "core knowledge" that will establish teachers once and for all as true professionals and experts in the disciplines of teaching and learning. Luckily for those of us headed to emergency rooms and operating tables, however, "we can only be thankful that members of the medical profession are more careful in applying biological research to their professional practice than some educators are in applying brain research to theirs" (Bruer 1999, 657). Following this analogy, our carelessness in misinterpreting and decontextualizing the findings of brain research amounts to a sort of educational malpractice. Perhaps teachers and administrators are as much to blame for the rampant brain-based misinformation permeating our profession as those consultants and marketers getting rich by selling dubious "brain products" to us. As the Jensen Learning Center (1998, 1) argued, "Educators who are going to use or quote research ought to know what makes a good study, who is funding it, the reputation of the researcher, the design of the study, what are the implications and constraints on the findings." At issue is not whether brain research and cognitive psychology offer potential to change or support educational practice; rather, it is a question of making sure our applied practices are sifted from speculation, interpretation, and assumptions based loosely on scientific research.

Our rush to embrace brain research is evident. As MOEC (1999, 1) noted, "Researchers caution [educators] about making sweeping changes without thoughtful consideration, but the information and its implications are too important to ignore." As the Southwest Educational Development Laboratory (2001, 1) declared, "Brain research provides rich possibilities for education. . . . Enterprising organizations are translating these findings into professional development workshops and instructional programs to help teachers apply lessons from the research to classroom settings." Scientific researchers have cautioned educators about the limitations of their findings, yet educators plow ahead, attending expensive workshops and designing "brain-based" lessons—while "enterprising organizations" get rich selling products to unwitting—if well-intentioned—teachers and parents.

Brain research represents an enigma to educators today: we want desperately for "brain science" to validate teaching methods with which we have realized some success; yet, to protect the integrity and longevity of its eventual promise, and to keep it from peaking on its current trajectory as a pseudoscientific fad, we must in the meantime be wary of less careful claims. Our professionalism, and millions of children, depend upon it.

References

Brownlee, S. 1999. Inside the teen brain. *U.S. News and World Report* (9 August), 44–54.

Bruer, J. T. 1999. In search of . . . brain-based education. *Phi Delta Kappan* 80(9): 648–54.

Chugani, H. T., M. E. Phelps, and J. C. Mazziota. 1987. Positron emission tomography study of human brain function development. *Annals of Neurology* 22: 487–97.

Hetland, L. 2000. Listening to music enhances spacial-temporal reasoning: Evidence for the 'Mozart effect.' *Journal of Aesthetic Education* 34(3–4): 105–48.

Jensen, E. 1998. *Teaching with the brain in mind.* Alexandria, Va.: Association for Supervision and Curriculum Development.

Jensen Learning Center. 1998. Brain-based learning: Truth or deception? San Diego: JLC. . . .

Kluger, J., and A. Park. 2001. The quest for a superkid. Time (30 April), 50–55.

Lawton, M. 1999. The brain-based ballyhoo. *Harvard Education Letter* (July/August), 5–7.

Metropolitan Omaha Educational Consortium. 1999. Principles of brain-based learning. Omaha: University of Nebraska. Available at: http://www.unocoe.unomaha.edu/brainbased.htm.

Miller, J. 1998. Brain research and education: Neuroscience research has impact for education policy. Denver: Education Commission of the States. . . .

Scheibel, A. 1997. Thinking about thinking. *American School Board Journal* 184(2): 20–23.

Selden, A. 1998. The 'Mozart effect': Can we get implications for pedagogy from neuroscience? Cookeville: Tennessee Tech University. . . .

Sousa, D. A. 1995. *How the brain learns: A classroom teacher's guide.* Reston, Va.: National Association of Secondary School Principals.

Southwest Educational Development Laboratory. 1998. How can research on the brain inform education? *Classroom Compass.* Austin, Tex.: SEDL. . . .

Westwater, A., and P. Wolfe. 2000. The brain-compatible curriculum. *Educational Leadership* 58(3): 49–52.

Wolfe, P., and R. Brandt. 1998. What do we know from brain research? *Educational Leadership* 56(3): 8–13.

POSTSCRIPT

Should Brain Science Guide Educational Practice?

Challenge Questions

1. What have we learned from the research on early brain development?

2. Should major educational reform take place as a result of the brain science?

3. How should teachers best apply this research?

4. Does the early brain research have implications for the many parents who adopt children from orphanages in developing countries?

5. If early brain development is so critical, what help is available for those children who, because of medical or other reasons, did not receive sufficient early stimulation?

6. What determines if a neuron is thick instead of thin thereby increasing its capacity to store information?

7. Are the findings conclusive enough to warrant what may be, in some cases, dramatic changes in our educational programming?

Suggested Reading

Berger, E. H. (1999). Supporting parents with two essential understandings: Attachment and brain development. *Early Childhood Education Journal*, 26(4), 267–270.

Bruer, J. T. (1998). Brain science, brain fiction. *Educational Leadership*, 56(3), 14–18.

Jensen, E. (2000). Brain-based learning: A reality check. *Educational Leadership*, 57(7), 76–79.

Kulman, L. (1997, March 10). The prescription for smart kids. *US News & World Report*, 122(9), 10.

Lindsey, G. (1998/1999). Brain research and implications for early childhood education. *Childhood Education*, 75(2), 97–100.

Mead, S. (2007). *Million dollar babies: Why infants can't be hardwired for success.* Washington, D.C. Education Sector.

Newberger, J. J. (1997). New brain development research—A wonderful window of opportunity to build public support for early childhood education! *Young Children*, 52(4), 4–9.

Puckett, M., Marshall, C. S., & Davis, R. (1999). Examining the emergence of brain development research: The promises and the perils. *Childhood Education, 76*(1), 8–12.

Wolf, P. (1998). Revisiting effective teaching. *Educational Leadership, 56*(3), 61–64.

ISSUE 2

Should Young Children Use Computers?

YES: Regina G. Chatel, from "Computers Use in Preschool: Trixie Gets a Screen Name," *The New England Reading Association Journal* (vol. 41, 2005)

NO: Edward Miller, from "Less Screen Time, More Play Time," *Principal* (September/October 2005)

ISSUE SUMMARY

YES: Regina G. Chatel is a professor of education at St. Joseph College in West Hartford, Connecticut. Dr. Chatel states we are past the debate of should young children use computers to the discussion of how computers should be used. She raises many of the key issues related to the use of computers with young children. When appropriately done with young children related to age of introduction, support provided, and teacher training, she advocates for the use of computers by three- and four-year-old children.

NO: The Alliance for Childhood, based in College Park, Maryland, released a report in 2004 critically examining the use of computers with young children in the twenty-first century. Presented here is a summary of the findings by Edward Miller, a founding partner and senior research at the Alliance for Childhood.

College professors are dealing with the first generation of students raised with regular access to computers and the Internet from preschool on. Preschool and primary teachers have encountered those children for years. The age at which American children begin to interact with computers and the Internet starts young and is prevalent even at the earliest years. A 2005 survey found 67 percent of preschoolers and 80 percent of kindergartners use computers. Use of the Internet among those same age groups is 23 percent and 32 percent, respectively. The fastest growing market for educational software is what developers are calling lapware, software specifically developed for infants and toddlers from six months to two years of age to use while seated on a parent's lap. Miller reports the phrase "the earlier the better" to be a common marketing tool used by technology companies.

Doctors are concerned about muscle strain, obesity, and poor posture related to computer use. Preschoolers generally sit in a chair adjusted for an adult body and may develop poor posture as a result of tilting their head back to see the screen or reaching their fingers to the mouse and keyboard located on an adult-sized desk. Hours spent in uncomfortable positions can result in sore wrists, neck strain, back pain, and headaches. In addition, eye strain and fatigue is a common problem in young children who may sit too close to a computer screen. More serious concerns are the physical activity in which young children are not engaging while they are passively sitting and staring at a computer screen and the access child predators have to innocent children in online chat sites. The early years are years for active learning where children acquire knowledge through the use of their body as well as their mind. When they sit for long periods of time without being active, obesity and a sedentary lifestyle may be the end result. The media have aggressively publicized the explosion of online child predators trolling my. space and other Web sites for innocent children.

In a national study conducted by the Milken Exchange on Education Technology it was reported that 87 percent of parents gave computers high marks for their importance to learning. These findings were found to be consistent across all educational levels, occupations, and incomes. This seems to be a case where even though access to computers was not something parents had when they were in school, they certainly want to make sure they are available for their children. Parents are willing to support school fundraising efforts if the money earned will be used to purchase additional computers or software.

Regina G. Chatel in "Computers Use in Preschool: Trixie Gets a Screen Name" presents the appropriate ways in which computers can be introduced to young children. She argues that with parental support, knowledgeable teachers, and ready access to computers, young children can begin using a tool that will be a major part of their lifelong learning.

Edward Miller would like to see children spending more time doing those things most associated with childhood such as free exploration, imaginative play, and opportunities for social development over time spent on a computer.

POINT

- Technology can be found everywhere today and children need to get used to using computers.
- Children can develop problem solving and other useful technology skills through computer use.
- Children will use computers their whole life so starting to use them early will be beneficial.

COUNTERPOINT

- There is no rush to develop technology skills during the preschool years.
- It is more important to develop creativity and social skills at a young age.
- Spending long hours in front of a computer screen can cause eye strain and muscle fatigue.

YES

Regina G. Chatel

Computers Use in Preschool: Trixie Gets a Screen Name

The role of technology in early childhood education is complex and controversial. Parents and educators are concerned with possible harm as well as potential benefits of technology to young children. The debate is often characterized by questions such as, "Doesn't the computer foster passive learners?" "Shouldn't children use concrete objects and play for learning?" "Young children just aren't ready to manipulate the computer effectively!" and "Is it really developmentally appropriate to use computers with young children?" (Lynch & Warner, 2004) However, societal realities suggest that the question is no longer one of *should* we use computers in early childhood education but one of *how* should we use technology in order to significantly impact the way children learn, what they learn, how they interact with their peers and adults (Clements, 1999; Haugland, 2000; Scoter, Ellis & Railsback, 2001). For example, computers and the Internet have arrived in one of my favorite comic strips, *Hi & Lois*. As a parent I can certainly empathize with Lois' absolute amazement when Trixie's older brother, Skip, not only sets up his baby sister with her own screen name but she gets her first instant message before she can even speak!

Just like *Hi & Lois'* family; the National Center for Educational Statistics (2005) in analyzing data from 2003 found that computer use and the Internet start very early in real American homes as well. According to the NCES survey (2005), "use of these technologies begins at young ages; 67 percent of children in nursery school were computer users, as were 80 percent of those in kindergarten. About one-quarter (23 percent) of children in nursery school used the Internet, and about one-third (32 percent) of kindergartners did so" (p. 1). Therefore, the discussion must now focus on *how* to use technology with children to help them learn and develop socially, emotionally and intellectually rather than on *should* we use technology with young children since computers are already in most homes and they are being used by young children (Bers, New & Boudreau, 2004; Lynch & Warner, 2004; Scoter, Ellis & Railsback, 2001).

From *New England Reading Association Journal*, vol. 41, no. 2, 2005, pp. 49 50, 52. Copyright © 2005 by New England Reading Association Journal. Reprinted by permission.

Child Development: What Research Says About Technology and Child Development

Studies have found that computers help develop fine motor skills, alphabet recognition, pre-mathematical skills, concept learning, cognitive development, self-esteem, collaborative social skills, decision making skills, and school readiness skills (as cited in Li & Atkins, 2004). A study published in the June 2004 issue of the journal *Pediatrics* concludes that preschool children who use a computer appear to develop better learning skills than their peers who don't use computers. It found that those children who had access to a computer performed better on measures of school readiness and cognitive development. The researchers hypothesize that early computer exposure, before or during the preschool years, is associated with the development of preschool concepts and cognition. However, the study found no such association with how frequently young children used computers nor with using child electronic or video games. The children's computer use included typing, playing games, using learning software, manipulating the mouse or joystick, watching images, or observing and imitating parents or siblings when they used the computer (Li & Atkins, 2004).

Children 3 and 4 years old are developmentally ready to explore computers (Bers, New & Boudreau, 2004; Haugland, 2000a; NAEYC, 1996). However, children need ample time to experiment, explore, and play with the computer. Young children are comfortable manipulating a mouse and clicking various options to see what is going to happen. Although teachers may want to intervene when children appear frustrated or when nothing seems to be happening, it is better not to do. As my 5 year-old nephew, Adrian, told me once when I was frustrated with the computer, "Patience! Auntie Regina. Patience!" Children are less anxious and concerned about the computer than adults. They learn through play, in small steps and at their own pace while enjoying the opportunity to explore the computer. By providing minimal assistance, teachers show children that they believe not only in their ability to learn to operate the computer successfully but, also, to work independently and make good decisions. In addition, by observing rather than intervening, the teacher is better prepared to ask guiding questions and pose problems in order to enhance and expand children's computer experiences. (Bers, New & Boudreau, 2004; Murphy, DePasquale & McNamara, 2003).

When Considering Software for the Classroom

Research (Clemens, 1999; Clemens & Samara, J. 2003; Li & Atkins, 2004; Scoter, Ellis & Railsback, 2001; Wardle, 2002) has identified qualities of effective computer software targeted for the pre-school child. For young children, the value of the computer is in its open-ended use as a tool for experimentation, creativity and exploration not for creation of a product. The child needs to be in control of the pace and direction of the experience. Additionally, effective software builds on the child's prior knowledge. The teacher's role is to structure an environment in which children explore and experiment with in a safe setting, and then act to support their exploration and inquiry in different ways. Therefore, effective software must be appropriate to the child's developmental needs; foster exploration, imagination, and problem solving; contain sound, music and voice; allow exploration without fear of making mistakes; encourage further investigation; elicit excitement and so encourage language; and provide immediate feedback to children. In contrast, drill-and-practice or computer-assisted instruction (CAI) software, similar to electronic worksheets or flashcards should be used for limited amounts of time, and should not be the major focus of computer use (Haugland, 2000b; Brown & Dougerty, 1994; Clements, 1999; Scoter, Ellis & Railsback, 2001).

Enchanted Learning . . . produces children's educational web sites and games which are designed to be creative, educational, and fun. It reflects the belief that children learn when they are actively involved in activities that are clear, logical, stimulating, and fun. The software is easy for children to use by providing a clear, simplest computer interface, and intuitive navigation and control. It truly is an invitation to learning.

Although it is tempting to recommend some software, the reader is better served by becoming familiar with a web site such as *Children's Technology Review* . . . which reviews software. According to the web site, "Children's software" has evolved to "children's technology"—a broader category of products that a child and parent today have to choose from. Want to find out about The Polar Express, My Little Pony, VSmile and much more, visit the site for free reviews. However, you will have to subscribe for more information by searching the database, or read the last eight issues of the print version of CTR in PDF format. . . .

Suggestions for Effective Use of Computers in the Early Childhood Classroom

The following list of suggestions is based on theory and research in the use of computers with young children (Davis & Shade, 1994; Haugland, 2000c; Lynch & Warner, 2004; NAEYC, 1996; Scoter, Ellis & Railsback, 2001; Wardle, 2002),

- Place the technology in its proper perspective! Although computers can facilitate learning, they should not be used to divert children's time and attention from childhood activities such as art, music, play, social interaction, exploration of books, and playing on the playground. Computers cannot take the place of concrete experiences, hands on learning, interactions with adults and peers, and discovery of the real physical and natural world. Balance computer time with real life play and experiences.
- Provide a computer center as one of many learning centers in the classroom. Allow use, access, and choices as you would any other center but not as a reward for other activities, behaviors, and tasks. The teacher must provide equal access to the computer for all children, not only the 'well behaving' ones.
- Allow children lots of time to explore how to use a computer: what can/cannot occur, and simple exploration of the technology without

undue anxiety about its operations. Keep in mind, the teacher gets anxious about the computer not the children.

- Integrate the computer into your instructional framework rather than using the computer labs which serves to isolate children and technology rather than bringing them together.
- Evaluate all software for developmental appropriateness and sexism, racism, violence and stereotyping and avoid use of computers for drill and skill activities. Software should be meaningful to girls and minorities, should not reinforce gender/racial stereotypes, or promote violence as an acceptable way to solve problems.
- Aim for a balance between screen time (television, computer or VCR) and activities that involve sustained attention. It's possible that flashing images or constantly moving graphics on the computer screens make it harder for children to pay attention for sustained periods. And, young children's attention seems to wander; therefore, it's important to engage students in varied activities.
- While being non-intrusive, do give information to help children understand the "if-then" sequences of computer programs. Much like a think aloud in reading, make your thinking and actions obvious to children by explaining what is happening as a result of manipulation of the hardware and software.
- Finally, set up the classroom computer center so that two children can sit comfortably so that they can share leadership, problem-solve, and interact socially. Capitalize on the computers potential to bring children together.

References

Bers, M., New, R. & Boudreau, R. (2004). Teaching and Learning when No One Is Expert: Children and Parents Explore Technology. Early Childhood Research and Practice. [Online]. . . .

Clements, D. H. (1999). Effective use of computers with young children. In J. V. Copley (Ed.), Mathematics in the Early Years. Reston, VA: National Council of Teachers of Mathematics Pages 119–128. [Online]. . . .

Clemens, D. H. & Samara, J. (2003). Strip Mining for Gold: Research and Policy in Educational Technology—A Response to **"Fool's Gold"**. **Educational Technology Review**. 11(1). [Online]. . . .

Computers and Young Children. (n.d:) Kid Source Online. [Online]. . . .

Debell M, & Chapman C. (2005). **Rates of Computer and Internet Use by Children in Nursery School and Students in Kindergarten Through Twelfth Grade**: 2003. (NCES 2005–111). U.S. Department for Education. Washington, DC: National Center for Education Statistics. [Online]. . . .

Davis, B. & Shade, D. (1994). Integrate, Don't Isolate! Computers in the Early Childhood Curriculum. ERIC Digest. ED376991. [Online]. . . .

Haugland, S. (2000). Computers and Young Children. Clearinghouse on Early Education and Parenting. No. EDO-PS-00-4. [Online]. . . .

Haugland, Susan W. (2000b). What role should technology play in young children's learning? Part 2. Early childhood classrooms for the 21st century. Using computers to maximize learning. **Young Children**, 55(1), 12–18.

Haugland, S. W. (2000c). Early childhood classrooms in the 21st century: Using computers to maximize learning. **Young Children**, 55 (1), 12–18.

Li, X. & Atkins, M. (2004). Early childhood computer experience and cognitive and motor development. Pediatrics, 113(6), 1715–1722. [Online]. . . .

Lynch, S. & Warner, L. (2004). Computer Use in Preschools: Directors' Reports of the State of the Practice. Early Childhood Research and Practice. [Online]. . . .

Murphy, K; DePasquale, R. & McNamara, E. (2003). Meaningful Connections: Using Technology in Primary Classrooms. **Young Children on the web**. [Online]. . . .

NAEYC (1996). Position statement on technology and young children—ages three through eight. Young Children, 51 (6),11–16.

Spooner, S. and American Academy of Pediatrics Steering Committee. (2004). **Preschoolers, Computers, and School Readiness: Are We On to Something? Pediatrics**, 114(3), 852–852. [Online]. . . .

Van Scoter, J., Ellis, D. & Railsback, J. (2001). Technology In Early Childhood Education: Finding the Balance. [Online]. . . .

Wardle, F. (2002). The Role of Technology in Early Childhood Programs. [Online]. . . .

Edward Miller

Less Screen Time, More Play Time

The presence of computers in early childhood classrooms is growing, despite serious doubts about whether young children really need them or benefit from using them. A recent study of child care centers in Texas found that preschool children were using computers in more than 75 percent of them. Even educators who are skeptical about the value of computer use by young children find themselves under increasing pressure from parents to incorporate advanced technologies in their classrooms, and to spend time teaching young children how to manipulate a mouse, send an e-mail, and even create PowerPoint presentations (Guernsey 2001).

Many parents today assume that the earlier a child starts to use high-tech tools, the better. As a result, software for toddlers and preschoolers is one of the fastest growing niches of the technology business.

Earlier Is Not Better

Many parents point out that their young children are fascinated by computers and other electronic gadgets, and they view technology as a powerful learning motivator. But according to most child development experts, the "earlier-the-better" assumption is incorrect. The primary work of the young child, according to Tufts University psychologist David Elkind, is to master the skills of regulating emotions; solving problems; developing flexibility, imagination, and persistence; paying attention; coordinating body movement; and negotiating social situations (Elkind 2001). There is no evidence that young children learn these skills better through high technology, and abundant evidence that they learn them best through direct interaction with other people.

Educational psychologist Jane Healy believes that starting children on computers too early is far worse than starting them too late. "The immature human brain neither needs nor profits from attempts to 'jump-start' it, and the fact that this phrase is being successfully used to sell technology for toddlers illustrates our ignorance of early childhood development" (Healy 1998).

The Decline of Imaginative Play

Computer play is different from the kind of imaginative, child-initiated play that has long been regarded as the foundation of the early childhood curriculum.

Educators report that many children that are adept at playing video games, pushing buttons, and operating a mouse show an alarming lack of imagination. Today, the average U.S. child sits in front of television, video, and computer screens for four to five hours per day, spending far less time in imaginative play. Add to this the increased emphasis on early literacy and numeracy in preschool and kindergarten, and time for open-ended play is sharply reduced—and in some cases eliminated entirely.

Early childhood education is thus in a process of radical transformation—in which play and other activities that promote social and emotional learning are being replaced by academic drills designed to improve early literacy and numeracy. Part of this push for more academic rigor in the early childhood curriculum is the requirement that schools teach "technology literacy." State and local technology education standards increasingly require teachers to integrate computers into lessons, starting at the preschool level.

For example, the model standards for "technology literacy" developed by the International Society for Technology in Education (1998) specify that children, before completing second grade, should be able to "use input devices (e.g., mouse, keyboard, remote control) and output devices (e.g., monitor, printer) to successfully operate computers, VCRs, audiotapes, and other technologies," and that, with support from adults or other students, they should be able to create "multimedia products" and gather information over the Internet.

While many technology literacy programs pay lip service to "developmentally appropriate" activities, nearly all seem guided more by what children *can* do with computers than by a deep understanding of what young children *need* to help their intellectual and emotional lives unfold and thrive. Technology education should be guided not by a focus on tools, but rather by activities that help children develop their full capacities. This, in turn, will govern what tools they should use at different ages.

A New Literacy of Technology

Last year, the Alliance for Childhood, a nonprofit partnership of educators, health professionals, and researchers, published *Tech Tonic: Towards a New Literacy of Technology* (2004), a report that questions the wisdom of infusing early education with advanced technologies. It proposed a set of basic principles—from early childhood through high school—that are solidly grounded in the developmental needs of children and based on a much broader concept of technology literacy than those included in most standards.

Current efforts to create high-tech classrooms often aim to make the technology "invisible." Our conception of technology literacy would do just the opposite—that is, it would bring technology into full visibility so that it can be closely examined and critiqued. We believe that the use of any technology for preschoolers and elementary school children should be determined by its ability to support and deepen the healthy essentials of childhood. These include:

- Close relationships with responsible adults;
- Direct knowledge of the living world of nature, developed through outdoor play, exploration, and gardening;

- Time every day for child-initiated play;
- Music, drama, puppetry, dance, painting, and the other arts, offered both as separate classes and as a kind of yeast to bring the full range of other academic subjects to life;
- Hands-on lessons, handicrafts, and other physically engaging activities that embody the most effective first lessons for young children in the sciences, mathematics, and technology;
- Rich face-to-face language experiences, including conversation, poetry, storytelling, and books read aloud; and
- Time and space for children to create meaning and experience a sense of the sacred.

Lowell Monke, a former award-winning technology teacher, argues that there is always a potential conflict between using technology tools, which extend human powers outward, and healthy child development, which is concerned with increasing the inner capacities of the child. He points out, for example, that word processors have made it possible for children to hand in long essays with no spelling errors, when they themselves are barely able to spell (Monke and Burniske 2001).

With this caution in mind, *Tech Tonic* proposes a new definition of technology literacy: "The mature capacity to participate creatively, critically, and responsibly in making technological choices that serve democracy, ecological sustainability, and a just society" (Alliance for Childhood 2004). To be technologically literate requires that we judge technology's impact on our lives according to a set of values that transcends mere technical virtuosity.

Seven Key Reforms

The Alliance for Childhood calls for seven reforms to help create a new technology literacy:

- Make human relationships and a commitment to strong communities a top priority;
- Color childhood green to emphasize children's relationships with the rest of the living world;
- Foster creativity every day, with time for the arts and play;
- Put community-based research and action at the heart of the science and technology curriculum;
- Declare one day a week an electronic entertainment-free zone;
- End marketing aimed at children; and
- Shift spending from unproven high-tech products in the classroom to children's unmet basic needs (Alliance for Childhood 2004).

We need to slow down the rush to put computer screens in front of toddlers and preschoolers and to open a wide-ranging debate about the proper role of advanced technologies in young children's lives. Reasonable people may differ about the details, but we can agree on this: All children deserve a healthy, active childhood that helps them grow into compassionate, thoughtful, courageous, and resourceful adults—willing and able to participate in the daunting technological choices that lie ahead.

References

Alliance for Childhood. *Tech Tonic: Towards a New Literacy of Technology*. College Park, Md.: Author, 2004.

Elkind, David. *The Hurried Child: Growing Up Too Fast Too Soon*, 3rd ed. New York: Perseus Books, 2001.

Guernsey, Lisa: "PowerPoint Invades the Classroom." *New York Times*, May 31, 2001.

Healy, Jane M. *Failure to Connect: How Computers Affect Our Children's Minds—and What We Can Do About It*. New York: Simon & Schuster, 1998.

International Society for Technology in Education. *National Educational Technology Standards for Students*. Washington, D.C.: Author, 1998.

Monke, Lowell and Burniske, R. W. *Breaking Down the Digital Walls: Learning to Teach in a Post-Modem World*. Albany, N.Y.: SUNY Press, 2001.

POSTSCRIPT

Should Young Children Use Computers?

Challenge Questions

1. Could young children wait to be introduced to computers and spend the early childhood years engaged in other more active forms of learning?

2. What other learning opportunities are young children missing out on while spending hours staring at a computer screen?

3. What are the principles of a truly developmentally appropriate computer program?

4. What, if any, benefits are there for children raised from infancy with computers?

5. Are children who have not been exposed to computers in their home or school setting at a greater risk of school failure?

6. Does extensive computer use by young children lead to excessive television viewing and a passive lifestyle as an adult?

7. Will young children become more frustrated by using a computer than trying to find the information another way?

Suggested Reading

Anderson, G. T. (2000). Computers in a developmentally appropriate curriculum. *Young Children*, 55(2), 90–93.

Davis, B. C., & Shade, D. D. (1997). Integrating computers into the early childhood curriculum. *Principal*, 76, 34–35.

Elkind, D. (1996). Young children and technology: A cautionary note. *Young Children*, 51(6), 22–23.

Gatewood, T. E., & Conrad, S. H. (1997). Is your school's technology up-to-date? A practical guide for assessing technology in elementary schools. *Childhood Education*, 73(4), 249–251.

Hohmann, C. (1998). Evaluating and selecting software for children. *Child Care Information Exchange*, 123, 60–62.

Kleiner, A., & Farris, E. (2002). *Internet access in U.S. public schools and classrooms: 1994–2001* (NCES 2002-018). U.S. Department of Education, Washington, D.C.: National Center for Education Statistics.

Lane, A., & Ziviani, J. (1997). The suitability of the mouse for children's use: A review of the literature. *Journal of Computing in Childhood Education*, 8(2–3), 227–245.

NAEYC. (1996). Position statement: Technology and young children ages three through eight. *Young Children*, 51(6), 11–16.

Wilhelm, T., Carman, D., & Reynolds, M. (2002). Connecting kids to technology: Challenges and opportunities. *Kids Count Snapshot*. Retrieved from http://www.aecf.org/publications/data/snapshot_june2002.pdf

ISSUE 3

Is Time-Out an Effective Guidance Technique?

YES: Lawrence Kutner, from "The Truth About Time-Out," *Parents* (April 1996)

NO: Kathy Preuesse, from "Guidance and Discipline Strategies for Young Children: Time Out Is Out," *Early Childhood News* (March/April 2002)

ISSUE SUMMARY

YES: Lawrence Kutner is a contributing editor of *Parents* and a psychologist at Harvard University Medical School. Dr. Kutner supports time-out when effectively managed by parents or teachers.

NO: Kathy Preuesse teaches at the Child and Family Study Center at the University of Wisconsin–Stout in Menomonie, Wisconsin. She finds time-out to be an antiquated practice that is not effective for helping guide the behavior of young children.

$\mathbf{T}$ ime-out, whether it occurs during a sporting event or in the course of a day's activities at a school, is a period of time for regrouping and assessing what has happened to that point. When referring to time-out in a school or home setting, it generally means one or more children are removed from a situation due to inappropriate behavior. They may have been disturbing the learning environment, been involved in a dangerous situation, or been destroying school or personal property.

Guiding the behavior of young children, or disciplining them, requires one to use a variety of management techniques. Teachers of young children have a more difficult time since preschool children are not able to reason and cannot take another person's point of view to see the situation from the other side. Whatever method is used to help children learn which behaviors are acceptable and which are unacceptable the adult must respect the dignity and self-worth of children at all times. Children must be safe and over time come to understand that other people will not be allowed to deliberately hurt them or their property, and adults cannot allow another child to hurt anyone else. Educational settings are safe places for children and adults. Teachers in schools and parents in homes often rely on the behavior management technique of removing a child from a situation and having the child sit in a chair for a period of time to reflect. This can be a safe and nonthreatening form of guiding behavior. In some early childhood classrooms one will find a special time-out chair, in other rooms a child is placed in a chair in a location away from the group, but still close enough for observation. There generally is not a designated amount of time, but the recommended amount of time is approximately one minute for each year of the child's age. Therefore, a four-year-old would be expected to be removed from the group and sit and reflect for about four minutes. The child may be isolated from an activity, other children, a particular group, the entire class, or the classroom in a school setting. The adult would make the decision based on the severity of the behavior, and how much the child may be disturbing the group while in time-out.

Observation of children given a time-out will show some young children actually look upon time-out as a positive, especially if they are removed from an unpleasant task such as cleaning-up. There are some children for whom the punishment is better than not being punished. Teachers who use time-out should also find that over the course of a school year the use should actually decrease. Teachers who are still putting as many children in time-out in April as they did in October are not making any progress toward helping children learn appropriate behavior and self-control.

Lawrence Kutner finds time-out can be effective and can help young children to gain internal control. Parents and teachers, he states, often do not know how to properly administer a time-out. Some adults think simply having a child sit in a chair will prevent future problems. He provides suggestions for adults to use when implementing a time-out with a preschool child. Kathy Preuesse writes that this is an undesirable practice teachers should not use since young children do not understand the relation between their actions and the consequences of their behavior. She provides alternatives for the use of time-out that are more effective in guiding behavior of young children.

POINT

- Time-out allows children to have a break from the activity.

- Time-out can be an effective tool for guiding behavior.

- Time-out should be used before children lose control.
- Time-out provides clear consequences to negative behavior.
- Gives children time to think about their behavior.

COUNTERPOINT

- Removing children will not help them develop the self-control for future situations.
- There are many other alternatives more effective for helping children develop self-control.
- Takes internal control of behavior away from children.
- Develops a negative self-image if used repeatedly.
- Can be rewarding for some children.

YES

Lawrence Kutner

The Truth About Time-Out

About a decade or so ago, books, magazines, and courses for parents began to hail "time-out" as the ultimate, foolproof discipline technique. However, for many parents it has seemed to work better in theory than in practice. Thrilled at first to find an alternative to yelling and spanking, they soon found themselves giving their children time-outs with ever greater frequency, often for the same problem. And when the prescribed time-out didn't correct the problem, they increased the amount of time for each infraction—but that didn't work, either.

So what's going on? Is there something fundamentally wrong with time-out? Not at all. According to child psychologists who specialize in discipline issues, it remains an extremely effective and powerful tool, especially for preschoolers. The problem is that what started out as a specific technique for stopping and changing a child's behavior has, in the hands of many parents, turned into a more general approach to punishment. That's a crucial distinction, because the goal of punishment is to make the child feel bad and pay for her mistake in the hope that she won't repeat it. The goal of discipline, on the other hand, is to help a child learn better ways of handling the situation that originally got her into trouble.

"Parents have started using time-out as a means of coercion. They put a child in time-out until she does what they want," notes Edward Christophersen, Ph.D., chief of behavioral pediatrics at Children's Mercy Hospital, in Kansas City, and author of *Beyond Discipline: Parenting That Lasts a Lifetime* (Westport). But time-out was designed as a way of helping a child learn to calm down. Therefore, it's perfectly appropriate when a preschooler is hitting or screaming, but not when she pulls the dog's ear or refuses to pick up her toys.

To make time-out effective, it's necessary to act immediately and consistently—in the original spirit of the technique (see "Get Your Child Under Control," page 42). Its primary objective is to teach children how to regain a grip on their runaway emotions. Preschoolers often find themselves getting so excited that they lose control: playful pushes turn into shoves, innocent giggles into screams. Time-outs remove children from whatever is overexciting them. Once they've had a chance to settle down, their behavior improves.

Another aspect of time-out that often confuses parents is the length of time a child should spend in it. This is a case in which a little goes a long way.

Children can calm down quite quickly if they're put in a calm environment. "For most misbehaviors, 20 minutes of time-out is far less effective than 20 seconds," says Philip C. Kendall, Ph.D., head of the division of clinical psychology at Temple University, in Philadelphia. "It also means that if you use long time-outs, you're reducing the effectiveness of future short time-outs."

In fact, isolating a child for more than a minute is likely to backfire. It gives her a chance to shift the focus of her attention from calming down to being resentful about the punishment. The anger that accompanies that resentment can lead to future misbehaviors. So how long is long enough? "As soon as the child is calm for two or three seconds, the time-out should be over," Christophersen advises. "We're now using the term *chill-out* because so many children and parents tend to equate time-out with punishment."

In fact, time-out is as much an opportunity for the parent to calm down as it is for the child. If you stay calm, your child will be able to "borrow" some of your emotional control. And showing her the behavior you'd like her to exhibit makes it easier for her to get back on track.

GET YOUR CHILD UNDER CONTROL

Sometimes you can tell by the look in your child's eyes or the rising pitch of her voice that she's emotionally wound up and quickly heading out of control. This is when, ideally, you should call a time-out. But whether or not you catch the signs in time, here's how your behavior can help improve your child's.

Keep your cool. Be as matter-of-fact as you can. Say something like, "You're losing control and need a time-out. Let's see if you can calm yourself down." Says Edward Christophersen, Ph.D., author of *Beyond Discipline: Parenting That Lasts a Lifetime* (Westport), "During a time-out, a child should be able to see that her parent is not angry, and to see what she's missing." This is more easily said than done, especially the part about the parent not being angry. But yelling at your child only adds to the emotional heat of the moment, because in this situation, your child is more likely to pay attention to the tone of your voice than to your words. Screaming at her to be quiet sends a contradictory message: you may, in fact, make the problem worse.

Bring your child to a location that's less stimulating. This doesn't need to be the same place every time. Any environment that's peaceful will help your child regain control, but you don't have to put her in isolation—she can even be in the room with you, as long as it's quiet.

Let her go as soon as both of you think she's ready. Don't be surprised if your child is able to calm down significantly within a few seconds. (And after all, isn't that just what you're hoping for?) Let her know you see the difference in her behavior by saying something like, "You're doing a good job of calming down. Ready to go back now?" If she says yes, give her a hug, let her resume her normal activities, and wipe the slate clean.

Also, whenever possible, use time-out before your child loses control. Most preschoolers become emotionally revved up, then misbehave. You can usually predict this pattern, which may start with fidgeting or some other sign of building emotional tension. If you call a time-out at that point, you can help your child become attuned to her feelings. The longer you wait, the more difficult it will be to break the pattern.

Finally, pay attention to what psychologists call time-in. "Whenever you're upset with your child, think about reinforcing 'positive opposites,'" advises Alan E. Kazdin, Ph.D., director of the Child Conduct Clinic, at Yale University. If the behavior problem involves your child screaming, praise her when she speaks calmly. If she whines, pay more attention to her when she asks for help politely.

Say you've given your four-year-old a time-out because you caught him punching his sister. That's appropriate, but the other half of the equation is to pay extra attention to the two of them when they're being nice to each other. Compliment your son on his behavior. Pat both children on the back or give them each a quick hug and tell them you're proud of them for playing without fighting.

When he sees that he gets more attention for the behavior you want than for the behavior you don't, you'll find yourself calling time-out far less often. And the less you use this technique the better it's working.

Kathy Preuesse  **NO**

Guidance and Discipline Strategies for Young Children: Time Out Is Out

In a typical early childhood classroom, children engage in a variety of behaviors—some appropriate and some inappropriate. Early childhood teachers need to deal with all behaviors, but of course it is the inappropriate ones that are the subject of so much study! And even more than the inappropriate behaviors themselves, our response to the behaviors is weighed, measured, and quantified by a wide range of early childhood experts. The question remains: how do teachers react to children's behavior, and how does that reaction impact the child in later incidents? Through the years, styles of discipline have changed. "Spare the rod and spoil the child"—the in vogue punishment over perhaps a hundred years—gave way to time out sometime in the late 1970s. And now time out, the "strategy of choice" for 20 years or so, seems to be falling out of favor. What is time out, why has it been so popular, and what strategy will replace it if indeed it is on the way out?

What Is Time Out?

Sheppard and Willoughby (1975) define time out as the "removal of an individual from a situation which contains minimal opportunity for positive reinforcement." According to Schreiber (1999) the intent of time out is to "control and extinguish undesirable behaviors." When you say time out to a classroom teacher, many times the image evoked is that of a chair in the corner of the classroom where a child is put when she has "misbehaved." The length of time that child needs to "think about what she has done wrong" is many times determined by the child's age. The rule of thumb generally has been one minute per year.

The Use of Time Out as a Discipline Strategy

Time out was originally used in institutional settings with people who had a variety of mental or emotional disorders (Marion, 2001). In that setting, time out might have been used to ensure the safety of other residents by removing a dangerous or disruptive resident from a setting. It might also have been used as a consequence, when a resident refused to comply with requests of the staff. In such a setting, time out was considered a legitimate guidance strategy.

At some point during the 1970s, time out made its way into schools as a discipline technique. As corporal punishment declined, time out arose to fill the void with what seemed as a more caring, humane, and non-violent method. In an early childhood classroom, time out has seemingly been used as a discipline strategy to control and extinguish undesirable behaviors. Well-meaning teachers might use it to cope with non-compliance in young children, or to give a consequence for unsafe behavior. In some situations time out may be viewed as a logical consequence to inappropriate behavior or the loss of self-control (Gartrell, 2001).

How effective is time out in the typical early childhood environment? *Two-and-half-year-old Ben runs over to giggling two-year-old Jack and pushes him. The teacher says, "Ben! I told you not to push Jack! Use your words!" Ben tries again to push Jack. The teacher shouts, "Ben! That is not okay! You need to sit in the time-out chair!" She leads Ben to the chair and sits him down. In the time-out chair, Ben might be thinking, "I'm sitting in the chair. . . What is that noise? . . . I'm sitting in the chair. . . I want my mommy. . . I'm sitting in the chair." Ben is probably not thinking, "Wow! I guess I'll never push Jack again! I'm really sorry I did that!" Jack might be thinking: "What happened? I was giggling and then I was pushed down!"* (Schreiber, 1999, p. 22).

Should the Use of Time Out Be Questioned?

Although many teachers view this technique as discipline, the lost opportunities and deprivation of positive interactions move this technique into the punishment category. The NAEYC Code of Ethical Conduct, P-1.1, states, "Above all, we shall not harm children. We shall not participate in practices that are disrespectful, degrading, dangerous, exploitative, intimidating, psychologically damaging, or physically harmful to children. This principle has precedence over all other in this code." Marion and Swim (2001) point out that "punishment has great potential for doing harm to children because it often serves as a model of negative, hurtful and aggressive measures."

Teachers may view time out as discipline rather than punishment, but children view these strategies as painful. When two-, three- and four-year-old children were asked in a study about time out, they expressed sadness and fear, as well as feeling alone, feeling disliked by the teacher and feeling ignored by peers (Readdick and Chapman, 2000).

Many early childhood experts agree with Readdick and Chapman. For example, Montessori (1964) sees these external controls that reward and punish as an opportunity lost to teach children how to self-regulate (Gartrell, 2001). The removal period can be confusing to the child because he lacks the cognitive ability to understand the process (Katz, 1984; Gartrell, 2001). Schreiber (1999) calls the practice of using time outs "undesirable" for five reasons: 1) external controls overshadow the need to develop internal controls; 2) adult needs are met at the expense of the child's needs; 3) a negative effect can be seen in the child's self-worth and self-confidence; 4) confusion arises over the connection between the action and the consequence; and 5) the lost opportunity for learning. These "undesirable" aspects of time out, along with the others mentioned above, make this strategy developmentally inappropriate. The needs of the child are not met, thus, causing harm to the child.

Guiding Children's Behavior

Time out needs to be revisited under the broader umbrella of guidance. Guidance can be defined as "Everything adults deliberately do and say, either directly or indirectly, to influence children's behavior, with the goal of helping them become well-adjusted, self-directed, productive adults" (Hildebrand and Hearron, p. 4, 1999). Using this definition, it is obvious that teachers have a responsibility to guide interactions towards a meaningful end. It is through positive actions or techniques that learning takes place. Today many positive techniques are available to early childhood teachers. Let's look at three areas: 1) managing the environment, 2) demonstrating developmentally appropriate practices, and 3) fostering the development of self-regulation in children.

Managing the Environment

Managing the environment must start with safety as the first priority. Consider the child who seems to be always running in the classroom. The teacher says, *"John, stop running before you hurt yourself. I've told you many times that if you run you will have to sit on a chair and slow down."* A positive alternative to this would be to take a look at the environment. Is there sufficient space for large muscle or active play? Instead of changing the child's behavior with negative consequences, add a tunnel for crawling through, steps for walking up and down or change your schedule to provide outdoor play earlier in your morning routine. Schreiber (1999) lists several ways to minimize conflicts such as keeping group sizes small so each child gets more attention and minimize crowding of play spaces to minimize disruptions. Classrooms need personal spaces and social spaces. Personal space refers to an area where children put belongings or spend time when privacy is needed. Social space refers to an area around the child that the child feels is his such as a seat at the art table, or a section of the sand box (Hildebrand & Hearron, 1999). Teachers need to provide enough social spaces in their classrooms so children feel comfortable while playing. Take a look around your room. Is there adequate play space? Consider having 50 percent more play spaces than the number of children present.

Developmentally Appropriate Practices

Developmentally appropriate practices and positive guidance strategies go hand in hand. As teachers, we must make sure our expectations are in line with the developmental levels of the children.

Giving children choices is one of Eaton's (1997) suggestions for positive guidance techniques. For example, *if a two-year-old is having difficulty coming to the snack table, the teacher can say, "It is time to sit down for snack now Jody. You may sit on the red chair or this blue chair."* Choices allow the child to have control over her environment within the boundaries set by the teacher.

Teaching expected behavior is another positive guidance strategy (Marion & Muza, 1998). As teachers we model behavior continuously. As a toddler teacher, I find myself modeling appropriate behaviors in the house area in my room especially at the beginning of the year. The children love to set the table and serve food. They also love to put everything in their mouths as they play and pretend to eat. In order to keep the toys clean (and out of the sanitizing container), I need to model how to hold the food inches from my mouth and move my lips as if I was eating. I tell them what I am doing and why. I label it by saying, "I'm pretending to eat the spaghetti." They love to watch and then repeat the modeled behavior.

Redirecting behavior takes on many forms—diverting, distracting, substituting (Marion, 1999). Consider having two of some items in your room so that substituting can easily happen such as in this example: *Sydney is playing with a doll when Michael tries to take it away. The teacher redirects by substitution when he hands Michael the second doll and replies, "Michael you may use this doll. Sydney is feeding that doll now."*

Setting limits in a preschool classroom provides boundaries for the children and teacher. Limits are set to assure the safety of children, adults, and materials. They also provide a framework in which trust, respect, equality, and accepting responsibility can flourish. Routines and transition times are ideal opportunities to apply positive guidance strategies. Use phrases such as, "It's time to (wash hands, go outside, rest quietly,)" "It's important to (use soap to remove germs, stay where a teacher can see you)," and "I need you to (wait for me before you go outside, pick up those two blocks)." (Reynolds, 2001).

Using action statements to guide behavior in young children. Telling children what to do, such as "we walk inside," takes the guesswork out of the situation. The child knows exactly what is expected of him. Hildebrand and Hearron (1999) point out that putting the action part of the statement at the beginning of the sentence is an effective method. For example, saying, "Hold on to the railing" is better than, "You might fall off the slide, so be sure to hold on." This allows the important part to be stated before it's too late or the child loses interest in your comments.

Demeo (2001) suggests when using positive guidance strategies a teacher must also take into account the variables that affect compliance. When advocating for behavior change in young children we should:

- Use statements
- Give the child time to respond
- Use a quiet voice, don't give multiple requests
- Describe the behavior we want to see
- Demonstrate and model
- Make more start requests than stop requests (do vs. don't)
- Be at the child's eye level and optimal listening distance of three feet.

Fostering the Development of Self-Regulation in Children

Self-regulation allows children to control their actions. They must develop the ability to know when to act, when to control their impulses and when to search for alternative solutions. This is a learned, ongoing process that can be fostered by teachers who use an integrated approach that considers the whole child and the developmental level of that child. "To support developing impulse control [in toddlers], caregivers can use responsive guidance techniques that emphasize individual control over behavior, provide simple cause-and-effect reasons for desired behaviors, use suggestions rather than commands, and use language to assist self-control" Bronson (2000, p. 35). When we teach problem-solving skills, we help children take responsibility for their actions, see a situation from another point of view, and develop decision-making skills (Miller, 1984). These internal processes help children think of alternative solutions and possible outcomes. As teachers we can start the thought process by asking children, "How can you . . . ?" or "What could we do to . . . ?" As children develop these skills they will soon generate their own solutions and gain control of their actions.

Conclusion

Time out is out! As early childhood professionals, we must abide by the Code of Ethical Conduct laid out by NAEYC, which states that "Above all we shall not harm children." The use of time out as a discipline strategy can harm children and must not be used in our classrooms. It is our responsibility to help "children and adults achieve their full potential in the context of relationships that are based on trust, respect, and positive regard" (NAEYC, 1990). As teachers we influence children daily. We can choose to affect children in positive ways by managing the environment, using developmentally appropriate practices, and fostering self-regulation. An effective teacher uses a mix of several techniques. One strategy may work one day while another may be best another day. It takes forethought and reflection. Positive guidance strategies help children develop into caring, respectful human beings.

References

Bronson, M. (2000). Recognizing and supporting the development of self-regulation in young children. *Young Children, 55* (2), 33–37.

Demeo, W. (2001). Time-out is out: Developing appropriate alternatives for helping difficult young children develop self-control. Presentation at NAEYC Conference, Anaheim, CA.

Eaton, M. (1997). Positive discipline: Fostering the self-esteem of young children. *Young Children, 52* (6), 43–46.

Gartrell, D. (2001). Replacing time-out: Part one—using guidance to build an encouraging classroom. *Young Children, 56* (6), 8–16.

Hildebrand V. & Hearron P. (1999). *Guiding young children.* Upper Saddle River, NJ: Prentice-Hall, Inc.

Katz, L. (1984). The professional early childhood teacher. *Young Children,* 39 (5), 3–10.

Marion, M. (1999). *Guidance of young children.* Upper Saddle River, NJ: Prentice-Hall, Inc.

Marion, M. & Muza, R. (1998). Positive discipline: Six strategies for guiding behavior. *Texas Child Care,* 22, (2), 6–11.

Marion, M. & Swim, T. (2001). First of all, do no harm: Relationship between early childhood teacher beliefs about punitive discipline practices and reported use of time out. Manuscript, under review.

Marion, M. (2001). Discussion information.

Miller C. (1984). Building self-control: Discipline for young children. *Young Children,* 39 (6), 15–19.

Montessori, M. (1964). *The Montessori method.* New York: Shocken Books.

NAEYC Code of Ethical Conduct and Statement of Commitment (1990).

Readdick & Chapman, P. (2000). Young children's perceptions of time out. *Journal of Research in Childhood Education,* 15 (1).

Reynolds, E. (2001). *Guiding young children: A problem-solving approach.* Mountain View, CA: Mayfield Publishing Company.

Schreiber, M. (1999). Time-outs for toddlers: Is our goal punishment or education? *Young Children,* 54 (4), 22–25.

Sheppard, W. & Willoughby, R. (1975). *Child behavior: Learning and development.* Chicago: Rand McNally College Publishing Company.

POSTSCRIPT

Is Time Out an Effective Guidance Technique?

Challenge Questions

1. When children get out of control and are misbehaving, who needs the break? The child or the adult?

2. Do teachers of young children have the luxury of uninterrupted time to sit and discuss the behavior with the child? Do students actually learn their behavior is unacceptable and never engage in the same behavior again after one experience with time-out?

3. Why has time-out endured for so long? Can it be used effectively with young children?

Suggested Reading

Gartrell, D. (2001). Replacing timeout: Part one—Using guidance to build an encouraging classroom. *Young Children*, 56(6), 8–16.

Hannon, J. (2002). No time for timeout. *Kappa Delta Pi Record*, 38(3), 112–114.

Johnson, R. (1999). Time-out: Can it control misbehavior? *Journal of Physical Education, Recreation and Dance*, 70(8), 32–34 & 42.

Shriver, M. D., & Allen, K. D. (1996). The time-out grid: A guide to effective discipline. *School Psychology Quarterly*, 11(1), 67–74.

Turner, H. S., & Watson, T. S. (1999). Consultant's guide for the use of time-out in the preschool and elementary classroom. *Psychology in the Schools*, 36(2), 135–148.

ISSUE 4

Does Nightly Homework Improve Academic Performance?

YES: Mary H. Sullivan and Paul V. Sequeira, from "The Impact of Purposeful Homework on Learning," *The Clearing House* (July/August 1996)

NO: Alfie Kohn, from "The Goldilocks Paradox," *American School Board Journal* (February 2007)

ISSUE SUMMARY

YES: Mary H. Sullivan from Western Connecticut State University and Paul V. Sequeira, superintendent of schools, New Britain, Connecticut, report there is sound research to support teachers assigning homework to students for the purpose of improving academic performance.

NO: Alfie Kohn, long known as a powerful advocate for education, questions the entire practice of teachers assigning homework and does not find support in the literature for the nightly ritual of children sitting at the kitchen table doing homework.

We've all struggled with it, either as a student, a parent, or both. Homework: that dreaded word in the English language. In many homes parents have replaced the traditional after-school question "How was your day?" with "What is the homework situation like for tonight?" Parents and children are stressed at home and teachers are frustrated by the lack of completed homework assignments brought in the next day.

Some children attend schools with a mandatory homework policy. All teachers in every grade level are required to assign work to be completed at home every night. For other students, homework is an option to be assigned by the individual teacher when he or she finds it appropriate. Very few college courses in teacher preparation programs address the topic of homework. Future teachers are given little guidance on the purpose of homework; whether it should be assigned or not; what constitutes an appropriate assignment; how to assign, grade, and keep track of homework; or how to use homework assignments to improve academic performance. In addition, very few teacher in-service programs address the use of homework. The beliefs teachers have about homework and its merits or perils seem to come from personal experience. For a practice that can take up to three hours of an elementary school student's evening, many believe some thought and knowledge should be given to understanding the topic.

Children today no longer arrive at home after school with a full five to six hours of unscheduled time in which to do homework. Many children are cramming sports practices, music and arts classes, community club activities, work, and care for younger siblings into those after-school and evening hours. Children whose parents' work schedules leaves little time to assist children with their homework are often left on their own to figure out complicated assignments. These children can become frustrated without assistance available to help them do their homework.

There seems to be universal acceptance among those in support of homework for what is called the "10 minute rule"—teachers assign homework they anticipate students taking approximately 10 minutes to complete multiplied by the grade. Using the rule a teacher would assign first-graders approximately 10 minutes of homework each night, second-graders approximately 20 minutes of homework, and so forth.

Mary Sullivan and Paul Sequeira find that homework can be helpful in helping students achieve academically. They discuss the three types of homework assignments typically assigned: preparation, practice, and extension. When thoughtfully assigned, Sullivan and Sequeira find homework beneficial.

Alfie Kohn, a leading spokesperson against teachers assigning homework, draws attention to what he calls the Goldilocks Paradox. Instead of asking is the homework too much, just right, or too little, he asks the question "Should there be homework at all?" He indicates homework should only be given when the assignments are beneficial and are most appropriate for completion in the home setting.

POINT

- Work at home can build on what was learned in school during the day.
- Working at home builds strong work habits.
- Homework can provide for extra practice of work introduced in class.
- Homework can involve the parents in the educational process.

COUNTERPOINT

- Students without adult assistance at home are at a disadvantage.
- Young children are more easily distracted, which could lead to less time on task.
- Not all students will complete the homework leading to a wider gap.
- Some parents can become too involved and complete the homework for their child.

YES

**Mary H. Sullivan and
Paul V. Sequeira**

The Impact of Purposeful Homework on Learning

How important is homework? Does it really contribute to a youngster's education, or is it simply meaningless repetition that the more successful students do not require and the less successful students cannot do?

Homework does have benefits to offer. It becomes an essential part of a student's total education when it provides an opportunity to integrate and expand school learning, reinforces independent work-study skills and self-discipline, and uses school and community resources.

If homework does not produce the desired results, it may be because homework practices are seldom analyzed. Problems that result from unreasonable homework assignments are all too common. Indeed, there is no evidence that teachers are provided any training for when or how to assign or to respond to homework. However, if homework is used effectively and dealt with in purposeful ways, it can be productive and rewarding. *Purposeful homework is meaningful, relevant, involving, creative, and of quality.*

Benefits of Homework

Among the desired effects of homework, the most obvious is that it can have an immediate impact on the student's retention and understanding of the material it covers (Cooper 1989). It also can improve concept formation and critical thinking and enrich the curriculum. Moreover, homework can improve students' study skills and show them that learning can take place anywhere, not just in school buildings. There are many potential nonacademic benefits as well, most of which relate to fostering independent and responsible character traits. Finally, homework can involve parents in the school process, enhancing their appreciation of education and allowing them to be aware of their children's achievements and growth.

However, homework involves an extremely complex interaction of influences. Consideration must be given to the mediating effects of student characteristics, subject matter, classroom and assignment factors, and parental influences. Homework should have different purposes for different grades. For younger students, it can foster positive attitudes, habits, and character traits. For older students, it can facilitate knowledge acquisition.

From *The Clearing House*, July/August 1996, pp. 346–248. Reprinted by permission of the Helen Dwight Reid Educational Foundation. Published by Heldref Publications, 1319 Eighteenth St., NW, Washington, DC 20036-1802. Copyright © 1996. www.heldref.org

Aspects of Homework

Individual Student Involvement

Students bring an immense diversity of levels of maturity, aptitudes, learning styles, and interests to each homework assignment. Blanket assignments of text-book exercises for homework rarely address student variation. Students need to be personally involved with what has been offered in the classroom. At home, they can proceed at their own pace to try out the skills that were presented to the entire group. That personal involvement with what has been learned during the day helps to increase retention of a skill and to increase the likelihood that the skill will be used in real life. It also prepares a student to take greater advantage of subsequent classroom presentations. In addition, purposeful connection, with variation for individual levels and styles, can assist students to master knowledge to a degree commensurate with their own potential.

Different Kinds

Three types of homework assignments are common in American schools: *preparation, practice,* and *extension* (Doyle and Barber 1990). Preparation normally refers to reading assignments given prior to class meetings. Homework of this sort involves using new material, and it should be assigned carefully to ensure that students receive sufficient guidance to begin on their own. Practice homework happens when the student repeats the same skills or concepts of the lesson after the teacher's classroom instruction. Especially valuable are practice exercises that require imaginative application of newly learned skills or concepts to student-identified situations. Extension homework occurs when the student goes beyond the classroom lesson and transfers skills or concepts into new situations. It frequently uses projects, problem solving, or individual research as a method of organization. Examples of individualized, creative homework that involve a high degree of students' participation in topic selection and method of investigation include visual representations (diorama, time line, poster, chart, board game); creative writing (radio script, newspaper article, letter, story, poem); oral reports (television interview, quiz show, song, puppets, recording others); and hands-on activities (experiments with water, food, plants, magnets, weights). All three types of homework can help facilitate learning when they are understood and properly used (Foyle 1985).

Meaningful Work vs. Busy Work

Homework as busy work can be replaced with work that has a meaningful focus (Glasser 1990). Homework, used for practice, must be the exercise of worthwhile skills with a greater emphasis placed on quality work. The purpose of homework should be explained to students; they should know the objectives of their assignments. Students do much better in learning if they believe that they can use what they learn, that it is important, and that the quality of the work really matters. Teachers must set student cooperation as a desirable goal in the quality production of homework.

Teachers who assign more original take-home projects can break away from the traditional busy-homework syndrome. Hands-on assignments arouse interest, especially those tied to real work in the real world (Vatter 1992). Business and professional people can be brought into the schools to show students the connection between assignments and jobs in the work world (Morris 1992). Youngsters are fascinated with real life problems, and many stimulating projects evolve from real work issues. Further, esteem is enhanced when a student can choose, and successfully complete, a meaningful project. Students can, for example, choose their own class pet after they estimate the cost of supplies to feed and house the pet. They can calculate the miles and time needed to travel to different possible field trips before they choose which one to go on.

The Attraction of Creativity

For study time to be effective, students must be focused and engaged (Doyle and Barber 1989). To promote positive attitudes and high motivation, teachers can assign stimulating activities, such as surveys to be given to family members or neighbors, map making of field trip locations, or critiquing of a television show. Current instructional trends focus on process teaching and increased attention to critical and creative thinking. Some creative techniques that can be employed in any classroom are affective exploration (discuss reactions to given situations); attribute listing (describe two articles and exchange adjectives); brainstorming (rapid associations); collective notebook (record the group's ideas); Delphi technique (poll absentee resources); dramatization (role playing); or futuristics (predict the future). Creative homework can be embodied in almost any assignment (Koch 1988).

To incorporate creative approaches to problems, students need to be given some of the control that teachers typically maintain (Sternberg and Lubart 1991). Students need to take more responsibility for the problems they choose to solve, and teachers need to take less. Creativity requires one to view things with flexibility. And clearly, to engender creativity, first it must be valued (Davis and Rimm 1990).

Advantages of Feedback

For homework truly to be effective, it must be checked, commented on, and returned to the students. Contrary to many teachers' beliefs, pupils appreciate feedback rather than nonresponse. The results for homework returned with teacher feedback are generally superior to assignments returned with little or no comment (Paschal, Weinstein, and Walberg 1984). It is far better to give smaller amounts of homework that a teacher can handle and check, rather than larger amounts that go unmonitored.

A simple but personalized way of making contact with the student is for the teacher to begin comments with the student's name. Recognition of student work through direct comments to each student reinforces the concern of the teacher for each individual. Remarks such as "handwriting improving," "enjoyed unusual adjectives," "fascinating analysis," "conquering long division," or "fine summary" let the students know the teacher cares.

Appropriate and positive reinforcement results when the teacher follows an assignment with a class review and resolves any difficulties experienced by the students. The teacher helps the learner comprehend the meaning of the task when the relevance to a learning objective is pointed out both *before* and *after* a homework assignment. When students are at the center of their own learning and connect with information, they are more likely to move to the higher levels of thinking: knowledge can grow to comprehension, application, analysis, synthesis, and evaluation (Bloom 1956).

Grade Level and Time Concerns

Homework can be required of all students, but the time required should differ for grade levels (Cooper 1989). For grades 1 to 3, there can be one to three assignments a week, each lasting no more than 15 minutes. For grades 4 to 6, two to four assignments a week, each lasting 15 to 45 minutes, are sufficient. For grades 7 to 9, three to five assignments a week, each lasting 45 to 75 minutes, can be handled. For grades 10 to 12, four to five assignments a week, each lasting 75 to 120 minutes, will be of advantage. These are, of course, adjustable guidelines.

Maturity does affect the amount of work that can be done profitably. Reasonable amounts for different grades must be apportioned, and a check kept on whether assignments fit appropriate time parameters. Teachers can corroborate time by asking reliable but typical students how long it has taken them to complete their homework assignment for the previous day. Sometimes the best intentioned and most sincere teachers require more of a student's time on homework than they realize or intend. However, even teachers who make an effort to give reasonable amounts of homework can be frustrated by conflicting departmental assignments. Days and amounts should be apportioned between and among different departments on the junior high and high school level.

School—Home Linkage

Homework can be particularly effective when attention is paid to the unification of school and home. A procedure that can be equally effective with all grades is to send home a weekly (or, better still, a monthly) summary of homework assignments. Both students and parents are then better able to plan their time accordingly. A resourceful teacher can assign homework by linking school and home through hands-on assignments. Many standard household materials are available and appropriate for student use, such as rulers, cups, teaspoons, half-gallon or gallon containers, and some semblance of weights. An assignment on measurement after students are taught the new skill in class can provide such a linkage.

It must be noted at this point that not all homes are able to be supportive of homework. There are an increasing number of latch-key children who return from school to empty homes, with parents or parental figures not present until late in the day. Parental help may be limited or unavailable because of economic priorities or crowded schedules. Yet, one of the positive benefits of homework is that it is an appropriate intervention for students with diverse needs, including low-ability students, minorities, the economically disadvantaged, and the learning disabled (Doyle and Barber 1990). To eliminate homework in such instances may cause some of those youngsters to fall further behind. Schools can make available the facilities and the personnel to help students who face such predicaments. A number of schools have initiated after-school programs, in which a homework cluster is provided. Senior citizens and retired teachers often are glad to be of assistance as volunteers.

A Mission Statement

It is especially helpful when the district, schools, and teachers cooperate to create a philosophy or mission statement regarding homework policy. This might state that homework can provide activities to integrate the efforts of school and home and to expand the intellectual, emotional, physical, aesthetic, social, and moral growth of every child; homework also can reinforce school learning, and provide practice, preparation, and extension of knowledge and skills according to the individual needs, capabilities, and interests of every child.

Purposeful Homework

The fact is that homework is assigned in most schools. The issue is not whether we should have homework, but rather how to make homework a viable extension of classwork and make it contribute to learning. Homework assignments should be given as carefully as any assignment in the classroom.

The aim of analyzing and organizing goals for homework certainly is not to increase the burden of teachers, parents, or students. Rather, evaluation of homework objectives can allow the time invested to have the most meaning possible for all involved—especially, of course, for the students. Support and encouragement should be an integral part of setting homework policies and guidelines. Administrators and supervisors need to energetically praise and commend those teachers who make a sincere effort to increase student motivation, participation, and relevance as a central part of homework. Encouragement must be given to the homes to reinforce their linkages with the school. To endorse self-evaluation on the part of students actively engages them in their own learning processes. When we meet the needs of students in a collaborative manner, we reinforce an appreciation for quality work done outside of school and provide the support and encouragement needed to ensure the success of homework assignments.

References

Bloom, B. 1956. *Taxonomy of educational objectives. The classification of educational goals. Handbook I: Cognitive domain.* New York: David McKay.

Cooper, H. 1989. Synthesis of research on homework. *Educational Leadership* 46(2): 85–91.

Davis, G., and S. Rimm. 1989. *Education of the gifted and talented.* Englewood Cliffs, N.J.: Prentice-Hall.

Doyle, M., and B. Barber. 1990. Homework as a learning experience. What research says to the teachers. Eric Document 319–492.

Foyle, H. 1985. Homework variety: A way to educational excellence. Eric Document 299–212.

Glasser, W. 1990. The quality school. *Phi Delta Kappan* 71(6): 424–35.

Koch, A. 1988. Creative and communicative homework. *Hispania* 71: 699–704.

Morris, B. 1992. Employability . . . Do schools have a role? *The School Administrator* 49(3): 6.

Paschal, R., T. Weinstein, and H. Walberg. 1984. The effect of homework on learning: A quantitative synthesis. *Journal of Educational Research* 78: 97–104.

Sternberg, R., and T. Lubart. 1991. Creating creative minds. *Phi Delta Kappan* 72(8): 608–14.

Vatter, T. 1992. Teaching mathematics to the at-risk secondary school student. *Mathematics Teacher* 85: 292–94.

Alfie Kohn

 **NO**

The Goldilocks Paradox

Parents frequently complain about the excessive quantity or dubious quality of their children's homework when they get together, and it's one of the first subjects to come up when they meet with teachers. There's no more reliable way to pack the house at a PTA meeting than to promise advice for dealing with homework woes. Likewise, there's a seemingly limitless demand for books that offer advice on how to get kids to do whatever they've been assigned. But the assumption that homework should, even *must,* continue to be assigned is rarely challenged.

Homework continues to be championed by policymakers, assigned by teachers, and accepted by parents in part because of our cultural aversion to digging out hidden premises, pressing for justification, and opposing practices for which justification is lacking.

Even when we regard something as objectionable, that doesn't mean we will object to it. Instead, we say we should learn to live with it, or else we focus on incidental aspects of what's going on, but not whether it should be done at all.

Thus, teachers regularly witness how many children are made miserable by homework and how many resist doing it. Some respond with Sympathy. Others reach for bribes and threats to compel students to turn in the assignments; indeed, they may insist these inducements are necessary: "If the kids weren't being graded, they'd never do it!" However, the idea that homework must be assigned is a premise rarely examined by educators or parents.

Scholars are a step removed from the classroom and therefore have the luxury of pursuing potentially uncomfortable areas of investigation. But few do. Instead they are more likely to ask, "How much time should students spend on homework?" or "How can homework completion rates be increased?" Whether students need to spend any time on it at all would be a more fundamental question, but it is apparently outside the bounds of acceptable inquiry.

Policy groups, too, are more likely to act as cheerleaders than thoughtful critics. Documents on the subject issued jointly by the National PTA and the National Education Association, for example, concede that children often complain about homework, but never consider the possibility that their complaints may be justified. Parents are exhorted to "show your children that you think homework is important"—regardless of whether it is.

The popular press does occasionally take note of the varied and virulent effects of homework, but such inquiries are rarely penetrating and their conclusions almost never rock the boat. *Time* magazine published a 2003 article entitled "The Homework Ate My Family." It opened with affecting and even alarming stories of homework's harms. Several pages later, however, it closed with a finger-wagging declaration that "both parents and students must be willing to embrace the 'work' component of homework—to recognize the quiet satisfaction that comes from practice and drill."

Homework Advice: True or False?

Countless publications provide advice about how homework ought to be done. The specifics are repeated with little variation: Students should be given clear directions about what homework they must do, and how, and when; teachers should communicate frequently with parents to let them know what is expected for each assignment; children should have well-lighted and quiet places designated for homework; and so on.

This advice, which is almost never held up for critical reflection, is problematic in three respects. First, as I've noted, paying careful attention to the details of assigning and completing homework discourages all concerned from posing more meaningful questions. Second, it's not clear that these particular suggestions even help. At least one study has found that "having a regular place for homework is not highly associated with achievement"—or, for that matter, with any other behavioral variable. Finally, an emphasis on establishing a proper homework routine is much less innocuous than it seems because it allows us to conclude that any difficulties families face are their own fault. If kids aren't getting anything out of their homework, or parents find themselves dreading the whole experience, it's just because they failed to follow the directions properly.

Sometimes parents are invited to talk to teachers about homework—providing that their concerns are "appropriate." The same is true of formal opportunities for offering feedback. A list of sample survey questions offered to principals at one school district is typical. Parents were asked to indicate whether they agreed or disagreed with statements such as "My child understands how to do his or her homework" and "The amount of homework my child receives is (choose one): too much/just right/too little."

The most striking feature of such a list is what isn't on it. Parents' feedback is earnestly sought . . . on these questions only. So, too, for the popular articles that criticize homework, or the parents who speak out: The focus is limited to how *much* is being assigned. I'm sympathetic to this concern, but I'm more struck by how it misses much of what matters. We sometimes forget that not everything that's destructive when done to excess is innocuous when done in moderation. Sometimes the problem is with what's being done, or at least the way it's being done, rather than just with how much of it is being done.

The more we are invited to think in Goldilocks terms (too much, too little, or just right?), the less likely we are to step back and ask the questions that count: What reason is there to think that any quantity of the kind of homework our kids are getting is really worth doing? What evidence exists to show that daily homework, regardless of its nature, is necessary for children to become better thinkers? Why do students rarely have the chance to participate in deciding which of their assignments ought to be taken home?

And: What if there were no homework at all?

DO WE HAVE A HOMEWORK "CRISIS"?

Despite what we hear to the contrary, the homework crisis is a bit of a bust. A new review of research on homework says that students are not overburdened with after-school assignments.

In fact, the average amount of homework across all grade levels is less than an hour per night—hardly the soul-crushing, leisure-time stealing, tears-inducing load we've heard so many stories about. Of course, that amount is an average, so it means that some students, especially those in advanced or accelerated programs, get a lot more while others get a lot less.

The review of homework's benefits and drawbacks, commissioned by the National School Boards Association's Center for Public Education, shows that the research is mixed on the effects of homework on student achievement. Some studies say that it does help raise grades and test scores. Other studies, however, say there's no connection between homework and increased student achievement, and some research even suggests that homework can have a negative effect on achievement.

Typically, according to the CPE report, older students benefit more than younger students, with some studies cautioning that homework might even be detrimental to the youngest students.

Too much homework can backfire for all groups of students, with studies showing that one-and-a-half to two-and-a-half hours is optimum for high school students; for middle schoolers, the amount is an hour or less. Any more time than that, studies suggest, lessens any academic benefits from homework.

Because the research findings on homework are inconclusive, CPE's review recommends that school boards refrain from setting an overarching homework policy for their districts. A better idea would be to have individual schools set homework guidelines, based on recommendations from teachers, administrators, and parents.

The review will be available in February on the Center for Public Education's website. . . .

—Kathleen Vail

POSTSCRIPT

Does Nightly Homework Improve Academic Performance?

Challenge Questions

1. What preparation should preservice teachers receive to assist them in assigning homework?

2. What message should school administrators and teachers send to parents about their role in assisting their child with homework?

3. Are homework help lines or Web sites effective for helping students with homework? Do all students have access to these types of assistance? What assistance should be provided for homework?

4. Under what conditions and for which students can the positive and negative effects of homework be expected to occur?

5. Does completing large amounts of homework help elementary students' academic performance? Is there a correlation between academic achievement and hours spent doing homework? Should teachers even assign homework to students?

Suggested Reading

Bennett & Kalish. (2006). *The case against homework: How homework is hurting our children and what we can do about it.* New York: Crown.

Checkley, K. (1997). Homework—A new look at an age-old practice. *Education Update*, 39(7).

Chen, C., & Stevenson, H. (1989). Homework: A cross-cultural examination. *Child Development*, 60, 551–561.

Cooper, H., Robinson, J. C., & Patall, E. A. (2006). Does homework improve academic Achievement? A synthesis of research, 1987–2003. *Review of Educational Research*, 76(1), 1–62.

Cooper, H., & Valentine, J. C. (2001). Using research to answer practical questions about homework. *Educational Psychologist*, 36(3), 143–153.

Diamond, D. (1999). Winning the homework wars. *USA Weekend*, March 5–7.

Hoover-Dempsey, K. V., Bassler, O. C., & Burow, R. (1995). Parents' reported Involvement in students' homework: Strategies and practices. *The Elementary School Journal*, 95(5), 435–450.

Kohn, A. (2006). *The homework myth: Why our kids get too much of a bad thing.* Cambridge, MA: Da Capo Press.

Kralovec & Buel. (2000). *The end of homework: How homework disrupts families, overburdens children and limits learning.* Boston: Beacon.

Internet References . . .

Association for Childhood Education International (ACEI)

This site established by the oldest professional early childhood education organization describes the association, its programs, and the services it offers to both teachers and families. Many resources for teachers of children through the elementary years are included.

http://www.acei.org

Changing the Scene on Nutrition

This is a free toolkit for parents, school administrators, and teachers to help change the attitudes toward health and nutrition in their schools.

http://www.fns.usda.gov/tn/Healthy/changing.html

International Reading Association

This organization for professionals who are interested in literacy contains information about the reading process and assist teachers in dealing with literacy issues.

http://www.reading.org

National Association for the Education of Young Children

The NAEYC Web site is a valuable tool for anyone working with young children. NAEYC is the largest professional organization for those interested and involved in the care and education of young children from birth through age eight.

http://www.naeyc.org

Teachers Helping Teachers

Basic teaching tips, new teaching methodologies, and forums for teachers to share experiences are provided on this site. Download software and participate in chats. It features educational resources on the Web, with new ones added each week.

http://www.teacherquicksource.com

Children in
Educational Programs

*E*ducational settings and the various programs available for young children vary greatly. No school experience is the same for two children. Teachers and school administrators are continuously adapting the school setting to meet the needs of all the children who attend. Many questions exist over the best way to provide for education during the early childhood years. Some decisions are made based on funds available, but others are made based on what are the best educational practices for optimal learning to occur. The issues that follow are some of the topics discussed in early care and educational settings across the country on a daily basis.

- Should Superhero or Violent Play Be Discouraged?

- Should Transition Grades Be Abolished?

- Is Being Older Better When Entering Kindergarten?

- Is Grade Retention Harmful to Children?

- Should Educators Address Students' Unhealthy Lifestyle Choices?

- Are English Language Learners Best Served in an Immersion Language Model?

- Does Learning to Read Involve More Than Phonics?

- Should Recess Be Included in a School Day?

- Are Looping Classrooms Effective Learning Settings?

ISSUE 5

Should Superhero or Violent Play Be Discouraged?

YES: Diane E. Levin, from "Beyond Banning War and Superhero Play: Meeting Children's Needs in Violent Times," *Young Children* (May 2003)

NO: Brenda J. Boyd, from "Teacher Response to Superhero Play: To Ban or Not to Ban?" *Childhood Education* (Fall 1997)

ISSUE SUMMARY

YES: Diane E. Levin is an author of eight books on the effects of violence and the media on the behavior of young children and a professor in the Department of Early Childhood at Wheelock College in Boston, Massachusetts. She describes why children find superhero and violent play attractive and how teachers can best meet children's needs for self-expression.

NO: Brenda Boyd, from Washington State University, does not view superhero play to be aggressive and believes banning this type of play will not teach children how to develop the social skills necessary for healthy living.

Marcia, a teacher of four-year-olds, calmly asked three children to remove the baby blankets draped over their shoulders to resemble capes. The three had been playing they were going to save the people from the bad guys. When she talked to the children, they told her they were gong to tie up the bad guys and then kill them dead. As the day ended, Marcia was sharing the events of the morning with her colleagues and asked in frustration if she was doing the right thing. Should she just ignore the attempts by the children to role-play superheros or other aggressive acts or should she insist there be no play that resembled good guys versus bad guys or activities that promoted aggression? Her colleagues shared similar situations they had experienced in their classrooms and a healthy discussion followed, which led to the development of a policy on superhero play for their school.

Marcia and her colleagues are not alone in their dilemma regarding superhero and violent play. The "should we or should we not allow it" quandary confronts many teachers. Children will find numerous ways to model the behaviors they see on television, in video games, and in the movies. Everything from biting graham crackers into the shape of a gun and saying pow, you're dead, to jumping off of a climber thinking they will fly can be seen in preschool programs around the country. Just as older children may pretend they are Alex Rodriguez while playing baseball or LeBron James while shooting baskets, preschoolers will role-play characters they know from their television viewing. Admittedly, Ernie, Bert, and Big Bird do not offer the excitement of the X-Men, Power Rangers, or military scenes from the news; therefore, the more glamorous characters are often the first to be imitated.

A generation ago children played cops and robbers. Today the characters are superheroes from television shows or soldiers from half way around the world they see on their televisions during the nightly news. There have always been children imitating popular heroes. Even in the times before television children would pretend they were characters from books or radio shows. The difference between the imitating of many years ago versus the twenty-first century is that children could not see what the character was actually doing prior to the invention of television. Children's imagination fueled the play. Today children imitate everything from the body slams and the high kicks to the guns and bombs. The violent terrorist attacks taking place in our country and around the world all invite children to stop and take notice of violence.

Diane Levine, in "Beyond Banning War and Superhero Play: Meeting Children's Needs in Violent Times," believes teachers should intervene and redirect play that is aggressive or violent in theme.

Brenda Boyd does not see superhero play as being violent and aggressive. She believes that in banning the play, teachers are forgoing an opportunity to teach the children pro social skills such as respect and getting along with others as well as safety. She views superhero play as important for young children in that it allows them to resolve feelings about power and control. Children live in a world dominated by adults. Role-playing a powerful individual allows them to take charge, make decisions, and be the person to whom others look. Boyd finds these all to be acceptable outcomes of superhero play.

POINT

- Violent play is not necessary for children to have a good time playing.
- Superhero play allows children to express through their play what they are thinking and feeling.
- Superhero play should be allowed as long as no one gets hurt.

- Pretend play is valuable for children.

COUNTERPOINT

- Children are simply playing what they see on television and in the movies.
- Self-expressive materials like clay and paint allow children to express what they are feeling.
- There is the potential for children to be injured in superhero play and it should not be allowed at all.
- When children pretend hurting others, they may continue hurting others as they grow older.

YES

Diane E. Levin

Beyond Banning War and Superhero Play: Meeting Children's Needs in Violent Times

Four-year-old Jules is particularly obsessed. Telling him no guns or pretend fighting just doesn't work. When he's a good guy, like a Power Ranger, he thinks it's okay to use whatever force is needed to suppress the bad guy "because that's what a superhero does!" And then someone ends up getting hurt. When we try to enforce a ban, the children say it's not superhero play, it's some other kind of play. Many children don't seem to know more positive ways to play or play the same thing over and over without having any ideas of their own. I need some new ideas.

This experienced teacher's account captures the kinds of concerns I often hear from teachers worried about how to respond to war play in their classrooms (Levin 2003). These expressions of concern about play with violence tend to increase when violent world events, like 9/11 and the war against Iraq, dominate the news.

Play, viewed for decades as an essential part of the early childhood years, has become a problem in many classrooms, something even to avoid. Teachers ask why is play deemed as being so important to children's development when it is so focused on fighting. Some are led to plan other activities that are easier to manage and appear at first glance to be more productive. Reducing playtime may seem to reduce problems in the short term, but this approach does not address the wide-ranging needs children address through play.

Why Are Children Fascinated with War Play?

There are many reasons why children bring violent content and themes into their play. They are related to the role of play in development and learning as well as to the nature of the society in which war play occurs (Cantor 1998; Carlsson-Paige & Levin 1987, 1990; Katch 2001; Levin 1998a & b, & 2003).

Exposure to Violence

From both therapeutic and cognitive perspectives, children use play to work out an understanding of experience, including the violence to which they are

From *Young Children*, 58(3) May 2003, pp. 60–63. Copyright © 2003 by the National Association for the Education of Young Children. Reprinted with permission. www.naeyc.org

exposed. Young children may see violence in their homes and communities as well as entertainment and news violence on the screen. We should not be surprised when children are intent on bringing it to their play. Children's play often focuses on the most salient and graphic, confusing or scary, and most aggressive aspects of violence. It is this content they struggle to work out and understand. Typically, the children who seem most obsessed with war play have been exposed to the most violence and have the greatest need to work it out.

Need to Feel Powerful

Most young children look for ways to feel powerful and strong. Play can be a safe way to achieve a sense of power. From a child's point of view, play with violence, especially when connected to the power and invincibility of entertainment, is very seductive. Children who use war play to help them feel powerful and safe are also the children who feel the most powerless and vulnerable.

> *Open-ended toys, like blocks, stuffed animals,*
> *and generic dinosaurs, can be used in many*
> *ways that the child controls.*

Influence of Violent, Media-Linked Toys

Children's toys give powerful messages about what and how to play. Open-ended toys, like blocks, stuffed animals, and generic dinosaurs can be used in many ways that the child controls. Highly structured toys such as play dough kits with molds to make movie characters and action figures that talk tend to have built-in features that show children how and what to play. Many of today's best selling toys are of the highly structured variety and are linked to violent media. Such toys are appealing because they promise dramatic power and excitement and then they channel children into replicating the violent stories they see on screen. Some children, like Jules, get "stuck" imitating media-linked violence instead of developing creative, imaginative, and beneficial play.

Why Are Teachers Concerned about Today's War Play?

There are many reasons why teachers are concerned about war play and why they seek help figuring out how to deal with it.

Lack of Safety in the Classroom

Play with violence tends to end up with children out of control, scared, and hurt. Managing the play and keeping everyone safe can feel like a never-ending struggle and a major diversion from the positive lessons we want children to learn.

Old Approaches Not Working

Many veteran teachers say that the bans they used to impose on war play no longer work. Children have a hard time accepting limits or controlling their intense desire or need to engage in the play. And children find ways to circumvent the ban—they deny the play is really war play (i.e., learning to lie) or sneak around conducting guerilla wars the teacher does not detect (i.e., learning to deceive).

Worries About the Limited Nature of the Play

Like Jules, some children engage in the same play with violence day after day and bring in few new or creative ideas of their own. Piaget called this kind of behavior "imitation," not "play" (Carlsson-Paige & Levin 1987). Such children are less likely to work out their needs regarding the violence they bring to their play or benefit from more sustained and elaborated play.

Concerns About Lessons Learned from the Play

When children pretend to hurt others, it is the opposite of what we hope they will learn about how to treat each other and solve problems. Children *learn* as they play—and what they play affects what they learn. When children are exposed to large amounts of violence, they learn harmful lessons about violence whether they are allowed to play it in the classroom or not.

> *When children are exposed to large amounts of violence, they learn harmful lessons about violence, whether they are allowed to play it in the classroom or not.*

At the same time, children do not think about the violence they bring into their play the same way adults do. Jules focuses on one thing at a time—the bad boy is one dimensional and bad, without thinking about what makes him bad. He thinks good guys can do whatever hurtful things they want because they are "good." Except when he gets carried away and hurts another child, Jules probably does know that at some level his play is different from the real violence he is imitating.

Reconcile Children's Needs and Adults' Concerns

In our society children are exposed to huge amounts of pretend and real violence. There are no simple or perfect solutions that simultaneously address children's needs and adults' concerns (Carlsson-Paige & Levin 1987). However, there is much teachers can do working with and outside of the play to make it better for everyone (see "Approaches to Working with Violent Play" and "Approaches to Working Outside Violent Play").

More Important Now Than Ever

There is no perfect approach for dealing with children's play with violence in these times. The best strategy is to vastly reduce the amount of violence children see. This would require adults to create a more peaceful world and limit children's exposure to media violence and toys marketed with media violence.

APPROACHES TO WORKING WITH CHILDREN'S VIOLENT PLAY

- **Address children's needs while trying to reduce play with violence.** Banning play rarely works and it denies children the opportunity to work out violence issues through play or to feel that their interests and concerns are important. Trying to ban media-controlled imitative play, or even just to contain it, can be an appropriate stopgap measure when problems become overwhelming. However, a total ban on this kind of play may leave children to work things out on their own without the guidance of adults.
- **Ensure the safety of all children.** Involve children in developing rules for indoor and outdoor play that ensure safety. Help children understand the safety issue and what they can do to prevent injuries (physical and psychological) to themselves and others. Encourage children to paint, tell stories, and write (as they get older) to deal with issues of violence in ways that are safe and easier to control than play.
- **Promote development of imaginative and creative play (rather than imitative play).** To work through deep issues and needs in a meaningful way, most children require direct help from adults. How you help depends on the nature of children's play (Levin 1998b). Take time to observe the play and learn what children are working on and how. Use this information to help children move beyond narrowly scripted play that is focused on violent actions. Help children gain skills to work out the violent content they bring to their play, learn the lessons you aim to teach, and move on to new issues.
- **Encourage children to talk with adults about media violence.** As children struggle to feel safe and make sense of violence—regardless of the source—they need to know that we are there to help them with this process (Levin 2003). Start by trying to learn what they know, the unique meanings they have made, and what confuses and scares them.

  When a child raises an issue it is helpful to start by using an open-ended question like "What have you heard about that?" Respond based on what you learn about their ideas, questions, and needs. Keep in mind that children do not understand violence in or out of play as adults do. Try to correct misconceptions ("The planes that go over our school do not carry bombs"), help sort out fantasy and reality ("In real life people can't change back and forth like the Power Rangers do"), and provide reassurance about safety ("I can't let you play like that because it's my job to make sure everyone is safe").
- **Try to reduce the impact of antisocial lessons that children learn both in and out of play.** It can be helpful to encourage children to move from imitative to creative play so they can transform violence into positive behavior. Then talk with them about what has happened in their play ("I see Spiderman did a lot of fighting today. What was the problem?"). Help children to connect their own firsthand positive experiences about how people treat each other to the violence they have seen ("I'm glad that in real life you could solve your problem with Mary by . . ."). These connections can help diffuse some of the harmful lessons children learn about violence.

Talking with children about violence is rarely easy, but it is one of our most powerful tools. It is hard to predict the directions in which children might take the conversations and teachers will often find it challenging to show respect for the differing ways families try to deal with these issues.

- **Work closely with families.** Reducing children's exposure to violence is one essential way to reduce their need to bring violence into their play. Most of young children's exposure occurs in the home, so family involvement is vital. Through parent workshops and family newsletters that include resource materials such as those listed below, teachers can help families learn more about how to protect children from violence, help children deal with the violence that still gets in, and promote play with open-ended toys and non-violent play themes (Levin 1998a, 2003). In addition, families can learn about how to resist the advertising for toys linked to violence in ways that keep the peace in the family (Levin 1998; Levin & Linn in press).

Given the state of the world, including the war against Iraq, children now more than ever need to find ways to work out the violence they see. For many, play helps them do so. We have a vital role in helping meet their needs through play. We must create an approach that addresses the unique needs of children growing up in the midst of violence as well as concerns of adults about how play with violence contributes to the harmful lessons children learn.

References

Cantor, J. 1998. *"Mommy, I'm scared!" How TV and movies frighten children and what we can do to protect them.* NY: Harcourt Brace.

Carlsson-Paige, N. & Levin, D.E. 1987. *The war play dilemma: Balancing needs and values in the early childhood classroom.* NY: Teachers College Press.

Carlsson-Paige, N. & Levin, D.E. 1990. *Who's calling the shots? How to respond effectively to children's fascination with war play and war toys.* Gabriola Island, BC, CAN: New Society.

Katch, J. 2001. *Under dead man's skin: Discovering the meaning of children's violent play.* Boston: Beacon Press.

Levin, D.E. 1998a. *Remote control childhood? Combating the hazards of media culture.* Washington, DC: NAEYC.

Levin, D.E. 1998b. Play with violence. In *Play from birth to twelve: Contexts, perspectives, and meanings,* eds. D. Fromberg & D. Bergin. New York: Garland.

Levin, D.E. 2003. *Teaching young children in violent times: Building a peaceable classroom.* 2d ed. Cambridge, MA: Educators for Social Responsibility & Washington, DC: NAEYC.

Levin, D.E. & Linn, S. In press. The commercialization of childhood. In *Psychology and the consumer culture,* eds. T. Kasser & A. Kanner. Washington, DC: American Psychological Association.

Brenda J. Boyd  **NO**

Teacher Response to Superhero Play

This kind of play is a fact of life for those of us directly responsible for young children or for the training and support of those who deal with young children. A look at a bibliographic database related to early childhood (e.g., ERIC) offers ample evidence that children's involvement in superhero play is of growing concern to early childhood educators—the number of articles classified under superhero play as a subject between 1990 and 1995 is twice that found for the years 1985–1990.

Teachers of young children have become increasingly vocal opponents of superhero play, voicing concern about the behavior in their classrooms. Articles in professional publications such as *Young Children, Child Care Information Exchange* and *Childhood Education* by such authors as Bergen (1994) and Carlsson-Paige and Levin (1995) report that more and more teachers are choosing to ban superhero play from their classrooms. Newspaper articles found in the *Seattle Times* (Henderson, 1994) and the *Wall Street Journal* (Pereira, 1994) indicate that this concern has gone beyond an academic debate about child behavior. Teachers are sincerely concerned for the safety of children and themselves; many worry about violence as children engaged in superhero play grow older.

As a former child care provider/early educator and current teacher educator, I also have concerns about reported increases in violent and aggressive behavior in preschool classrooms. I suggest, however, that banning superhero play may not be the most effective means for dealing with children's increasing exposure to inappropriate and poor quality television programming. I will suggest that 1) we do not yet have valid data on these "increases" in classroom superhero play, 2) this behavior may play some developmental function necessary for young children's healthy growth and 3) by banning superhero play, teachers may be denying themselves a powerful opportunity to teach about values, respect, safety and living in a democratic social group.

Teacher Estimates of Play and Aggression

I begin by examining the premise that aggressive, violent superhero play is on the rise in preschool classrooms. The published reports of this increase are based on anecdotal reports from teachers (Carlsson-Paige & Levin, 1991; Jennings & Gillis-Olion, 1979; Kostelnik, Whiren & Stein, 1986) and from limited surveys of teachers of young children (Carlsson-Paige & Levin, 1995). These non-random samples are often drawn from participants at conference workshops on super-hero and war play in the classroom, who may already be sensitized to and con-cerned about the issue of aggressive play. These reports lead us to believe that preschool children are spending the majority of their time karate chopping and pouncing on each other.

My own research, in which I collected time interval samples of preschool children's behavior, has led me to question this belief (Boyd, 1996). In one sample of a group of 3- to 5-year-old children at a laboratory preschool, I found that only 2 of 17 children exhibited superhero play during a 1-month observa-tion period. The time spent in superhero play accounted for less than 1 percent of the 300 minutes of play observed. In a second sample, in which children in a full-day child care program were observed, only 5 percent of play time, on the average, could be classified as superhero play. In this group of 16 children, only 4 children exhibited superhero play. In both samples, boys were the only super-hero players. Furthermore, my observers and I never witnessed a child being physically hurt by another child while involved in superhero play.

Although these findings are clearly preliminary, they suggest that teacher reports of the occurrence and nature of superhero play may not be entirely objective, and may lead to an inflated estimate of this behavior. Previous research about teachers' views of aggression offers two lines of evidence to support this hypothesis.

– First, evidence suggests that children and teachers have differing perspec-tives on "play fighting" and "aggression." In a study published in 1985, Smith and Lewis showed videotapes of play episodes to preschool children, their teacher and the assistant teacher. The children were more likely to agree with each other or with an objective observer than with their teachers in assessing behavior as play or aggression.

These results suggest that teachers rely on some perspective not shared by children to differentiate aggression and play. This perspective is reflected in the criteria teachers reportedly used for determining aggression in this study. The assistant teacher, whose assessment of behavior was least often in agreement with the children, based her remarks on her knowledge of the chil-dren's personalities, as reflected in comments such as "Well, knowing those boys, I know they can't cooperate together. Chances are it wasn't playful, it was aggressive" (Smith & Lewis, 1985, p. 180).

Second, one study (Connor, 1989) suggests that teachers' perspectives often differ not only from children's perspectives, but also from other non-teaching adults', including teachers in training. That is, teachers tend to see behavior as aggressive, rather than playful, more often than non-teachers. In this study, three preschool teachers viewed video clips of child behavior; the teachers labeled all 14 clips as examples of aggressive behavior. When the clips were shown to psy-chology students, however, the majority rated only two incidents as aggressive, two as play and the rest were rated differentially, depending on the viewer's gen-der. Men were more likely to view behavior as playful, while women more often labeled behavior as aggression. Additionally, Connor reported that preservice teachers agreed more often with female college students than with inservice teachers when rating behavior as play or aggression.

These findings suggest two points. First, some aspect of working in child care/early education may lead teachers to view play as negative behavior, in general, and as aggression in particular. Perhaps teachers' sense of responsibility for children's behavior and their safety leads them to be overly sensitive to potential disruption and physical injury. Connor's study (1989) supports this hypothesis. Teachers reported concern with the potential for injury, noting that the children "were playing too rough and someone could get hurt" (p. 217).

As I discuss superhero play with teachers, however, I find that the sense of responsibility is not only limited to concern with immediate behavior, but also includes the long-term consequences of aggressive play. I am struck by the connection teachers make between preschool play behavior and that of adolescent gangs. Early childhood educators seem to be equating young children's pretend behaviors with the actual loss of life and violence on their streets. This equation seems premature. We have too little information about the importance and/or potential harm of such fantasy play.

Second, gender socialization may also influence how teachers of young children (predominantly women) view superhero play. As Connor (1989) has suggested, women may grow up with less desire and/or opportunity to be involved in superhero and other physical play than men. This lack of involvement may lead them to be less accepting of such play. Moreover, if girls are discouraged from involvement in physical activity because they may get hurt, this may lead them to believe that rough play is dangerous and should be avoided. Taken together, the research on gender and my anecdotal information from teachers suggest that early childhood educators may be overreacting to superhero play because of their fears about an increasingly violent society, and because of gender bias about play.

The Developmental Function of Superhero Play

The possibility that superhero play may serve some developmental purpose is the essence of my second concern about banning superhero play. Early childhood educators have long held that pretend play is critical for young children's healthy emotional development. This belief has been used to defend involvement in superhero play.

Specifically, scholars suggest children have a need to resolve feelings about power and control. Some have suggested that superhero play offers a sense of power to children in a world dominated by adults, thus helping children to cope with the frustrations of limited control (Carlsson-Paige & Levin, 1990; Curry, 1971; Ritchie & Johnson, 1982; Slobin, 1976; Walder, 1976). Similarly, by playing out scenarios focused on good and evil, children can work through feelings of anxiety and fear about their own safety (Peller, 1971). Additionally, such play may help children express their anger and aggression and become comfortable with these feelings, which may otherwise be frightening to the child (Carlsson-Paige & Levin, 1990; Ritchie et al., 1982).

While this theory is well-established in the child development literature, it is a weak argument for supporting the developmental function of superhero play without empirical research that directly examines its developmental relevance. Moreover, this set of hypotheses about the role of superhero play in providing emotional security is not easily tested. Other perspectives for investigating the function of superhero play, however, are available.

Although superhero play has received limited empirical attention, a related type of play, known as "rough-and-tumble play" (R&T), has been more thoroughly researched. The term "rough-and-tumble play" is commonly used to refer to children's play fighting, wrestling and chasing behaviors, from preschool through adolescence (e.g., Costabile et al., 1991; Pellegrini, 1987). I argue that superhero play is a special case of R&T and that the similarity of these types of play allows us to develop hypotheses about the potential function of superhero play. I will describe the similarities between these types of play, outline some of the hypothesized functions of R&T and consider the implications of this work for the study of superhero play.

R&T and superhero play share several characteristics. Both types of play can involve chasing, wrestling, kicking, mock battles and feigned attacks (Kostelnik et al., 1986). In addition, R&T frequently involves fantasy enactment or pretending (Smith & Connolly, 1987; Smith & Lewis, 1985), as does superhero play. Adults often confuse both R&T and superhero play with aggression (Kostelnik et al., 1986); furthermore, R&T play is often identified as pretend play in research studies (Pellegrini, 1987). Teachers' accounts of superhero play indicate that this play is routinely marked by play fighting, kicking and martial arts moves. In fact, these types of behavior seem to be the central cause for teachers' concern (Bergen, 1994; Carlsson-Paige & Levin, 1995; Henderson, 1994). These similarities suggest to me that superhero play can be conceptualized as a special case of R&T play, in which children assume the role of a superhero character.

The similarity in these types of play led researchers to examine the function of superhero play. This body of research suggests that R&T play may serve some important developmental functions for young children, especially boys. R&T play serves three potential functions—specifically, affiliation, dominance and social skill facilitation (Smith & Boulton, 1990).

Affiliation R&T play may help children form or maintain friendships. R&T's positive social nature is underscored by the presence of children laughing and smiling, and by the absence of children inflicting pain (Blurton Jones, 1972; Smith, 1982). R&T partners are consistently found to be friends (Humphreys & Smith, 1987; Smith & Lewis, 1985). While this does not directly show that R&T play builds friendships, these results nevertheless suggest that R&T play helps children develop or maintain friendships (Smith & Boulton, 1990).

Dominance Animal researchers first used the concept of dominance to describe a hierarchical order of dominance within a species that controls access to resources such as space, food and mates (Wilson, 1975). They found that this hierarchy can reduce conflict, by clearly defining a power structure within a group (Hinde, 1974). Strayer and Strayer (1976) applied this concept to a group of children and observed a fairly stable hierarchy, with few conflicts.

Smith and Boulton (1990) suggest that through R&T play, children can maintain or improve their ranking within the hierarchy. A child can maintain her or his rank by picking worthy "opponents" who are equal in strength. Or, a child could safely improve her rank by picking a slightly stronger play partner, and suffer little if she was not successful.

Humphreys and Smith (1987) support the dominance maintenance hypothesis. When comparing class consensus rankings of 7- to 11-year-olds' strength, they found, in most cases, no consistent difference in the two participants of an R&T bout. Their findings suggest that children do select partners near to them in the dominance hierarchy.

Social skill facilitation   Some researchers have suggested that involvement in R&T offers children an opportunity to develop social skills, which consequently leads to successful peer interactions. Both parent-child play and peer play support this hypothesis. Parke, MacDonald and their colleagues report that children whose parents (especially fathers) engage in physical play with them are more likely to be popular with their peers (MacDonald, 1987; Parke, MacDonald, Beitel & Bhavnagri, 1987). Power and Parke (1981) argue that physical play with parents helps children learn to regulate and interpret emotion by serving "as context for a wide range of communicative and affectively charged social interaction" (p. 160). Indeed, in one study, physical play did correlate with girls' ability to "read" facial expressions, suggesting some relationship between physical play and skill at reading social cues (Parke et al., 1987).

While the results are more numerous in terms of peer-peer R&T, they are also more mixed. Pellegrini (1988) found that children rejected by their peers were less successful than popular children at discriminating between serious fighting and R&T. In addition, for popular children, R&T served as a precursor to rule-oriented games, yet for rejected children, it led to aggression (Pellegrini, 1991). Several other researchers' findings indicate either no relation between R&T and popularity, or a negative correlation (Dodge, 1983; Ladd, 1983; Rubin, Daniels-Bierness & Hayvren, 1982). It is difficult to compare these results, however, because there is no uniform definition of R&T (Smith, 1989).

While the connection between superhero play and R&T is clearly speculative, an examination of how R&T play functions offers a measurable perspective on superhero play's possible contribution to development. The similarity between R&T and superhero play suggests that these types of play may also serve similar developmental functions. At the very least, this examination makes clear that it is premature to deny children the opportunity for involvement in superhero play. We first need to know more about the developmental implications of such a denial.

Sending Play Underground and a Lost Opportunity

This brings us to my third and final concern about banning superhero play. As other scholars of play have noted, banning has two possible effects (Carlsson-Paige & Levin, 1995). First, banning superhero play from the classroom sends children the message that they must hide their interests from adults, and that it is wrong for them to be interested in issues of power and control, good and evil, and so on. A related consequence is that teachers may lose an important opportunity to influence children's ideas about violence and the use of power, and about managing individual needs in a social community.

My concern about children's covert involvement in superhero play stems from the observation that children have always involved themselves in play about "good guys" and "bad guys." By telling children that such play is wrong or bad, we may be communicating that it is not acceptable to be interested in issues of control, nor is it acceptable to have fears about power. At the same time, we lose an opportunity to help children feel safe in a world that may be dangerous at times. While we need not expose children to inappropriate levels of violence, danger or fear, we should not expect that young children do not share adults' fears about violence, even if it is undeveloped. Part of the human condition is to fear and to desire mastery of that fear. Should we tell children that using a natural tool to conquer that fear, such as play, is wrong?

Second, I think that if teachers are truly concerned about exposing children to televised violence and aggression (or are concerned children will likely hear about such programming from friends anyway, even if they are not allowed to watch), are they not required to help children work through these issues in their play? When we ban superhero play (or any behavior children find interesting), we ignore a powerful opportunity for helping children learn valuable lessons in a familiar and appealing context.

Resources are available for helping teachers to use superhero play effectively in the classroom. Diane Levin (1994) has published practical suggestions for helping children to learn about establishing "peaceable" classroom communities; these ideas attend to all children's safety needs without simply banning superhero play. These suggestions can help teachers address their concerns about the children who do not like to play superheroes or who are frightened by others' superhero play. In addition, Gayle Gronlund (1992) offers interesting ideas for moving children beyond the scripted narratives they see on television, which she developed from working with her kindergarten class during the Ninja Turtle days. More recently, Julie Greenberg (1995) discussed ways to "make friends with the Power Rangers." Even when teachers decide to support superhero play in their classrooms, they may not know the best way to begin. These resources offer a starting point.

I believe that banning superhero play is not the most productive manner for dealing with our concerns about increased violence in our classrooms. Instead, educators should consider the best means for making positive use of this play; some of the resources I have described can be useful in this endeavor. Be assured that I am not advocating a free-for-all without teacher input into play. Each educator must decide, on the basis of information about their students and their needs, whether this sort of play is acceptable, at what level and with what supports in place. I encourage early childhood educators to take a broad and contextual view, as we do with all the behaviors we encounter, and to offer children the best supports we can in their daily lives.

References

Bergen, D. (1994). Should teachers permit or discourage violent play themes? *Childhood Education, 70*(5), 300–301.

Blurton Jones, N. (Ed.). (1972). *Ethological studies of child behavior* (pp. 97–129). London: Cambridge University Press.

Boyd, B. J. (1996). *Superhero play in the early childhood classroom.* Unpublished manuscript.

Carlsson-Paige, N., & Levin, D. E. (1995). Can teachers resolve the war-play dilemma? *Young Children, 50*(5), 62–63.

Carlsson-Paige, N., & Levin, D. (1991). The subversion of healthy development and play: Teachers' reactions to the Teenage Mutant Ninja Turtles. *Day Care and Early Education, 19*(2), 14–20.

Carlsson-Paige, N., & Levin, D. (1990). *Who's calling the shots? How to respond effectively to children's fascination with war play and war toys.* Philadelphia, PA: New Society Publishers.

Connor, K. (1989). Aggression: Is it in the eye of the beholder? *Play and Culture, 2,* 213–217.

Costabile, A., Smith, P. K., Matheson, L., Aston, J., Hunter, T., & Boulton, M. (1991). Cross-national comparison of how children distinguish serious and playful fighting. *Developmental Psychology, 27,* 881–887.

Curry, N. E. (1971). Five-year-old play. In N. E. Curry & S. Arnaud (Eds.), *Play: The child strives toward self-realization* (pp. 10–11). Washington, DC: National Association for the Education of Young Children.

Dodge, K. A. (1983). Behavioral antecedents of peer social status. *Child Development, 54,* 1383–1399.

Greenberg, J. (1995). Making friends with the Power Rangers. *Young Children, 50*(5), 60–61.

Gronlund, G. (1992). Coping with Ninja Turtle play in my kindergarten classroom. *Young Children, 48*(1), 21–25.

Henderson, D. (1994, December 14). No "morphing" allowed in class: Power Rangers play all the rage for kids. *The Seattle Times,* pp. Al, A21.

Hinde, R. A. (1974). *A biological basis of human social behavior.* New York: McGraw-Hill.

Humphreys, A. P., & Smith, P. K. (1987). Rough and tumble, friendship, and dominance in school children: Evidence for continuity and change with age. *Child Development, 58,* 201–212.

Jennings, C. M., & Gillis-Olion, M. (1979, November). *The impact of television cartoons on child behavior.* Paper presented at the meeting of the National Association for the Education of Young Children, Atlanta, GA.

Kostelnik, M., Whiren, A., & Stein, L. (1986). Living with He-Man: Managing superhero fantasy play. *Young Children, 41*(4), 3–9.

Ladd, G. (1983). Social networks of popular, average, and rejected children in a school setting. *Merrill-Palmer Quarterly, 29,* 283–307.

Levin, D. E. (1994). *Teaching young children in violent times: Building a peaceable classroom.* Cambridge, MA: Educators for Social Responsibility.

MacDonald, K. (1987). Parent-child physical play with rejected, neglected and popular boys. *Developmental Psychology, 23,* 705–711.

Parke, R. D., MacDonald, K. B., Beitel, A., & Bhavnagri, N. (1987). The role of the family in the development of peer relationships. In R. Peters (Ed.), *Social learning and systems approaches to marriage and the family* (pp. 17–44). New York: Bruner/Mazel.

Pellegrini, A. D. (1991). A longitudinal study of popular and rejected children's rough-and-tumble play. *Early Education and Development, 2*(3), 205–213.

Pellegrini, A. D. (1988). Elementary-school children's rough-and-tumble play and social competence. *Developmental Psychology, 24*(6), 802–806.

Pellegrini, A. D. (1987). Rough-and-tumble play: Developmental and educational significance. *Educational Psychologist, 22,* 23–43.

Peller, L. (1971). Models of children's play. In R. Herron & B. Sutton-Smith (Eds.), *Child's play* (pp. 110–125). New York: Wiley.

Pereira, J. (1994, December 7). Caution: Morphing may be hazardous to your teacher. *Wall Street Journal,* pp. Al, A8.

Power, T. G., & Parke, R. D. (1981). Play as a context for early learning. In L. M. Laosa & I. E. Sigel (Eds.), *Families as learning environments for children* (pp. 147–178). New York: Plenum.

Ritchie, K. E., & Johnson, Z. M. (1982, November). *Superman comes to preschool: Superhero TV play.* Paper presented at the meeting of the National Association for the Education of Young Children, Washington, DC.

Rubin, K. H., Daniels-Bierness, T., & Hayvren, M. (1982). Social and social-cognitive correlates of sociometric status in preschool and kindergarten children. *Canadian Journal of Behavioral Science, 14,* 338–347.

Slobin, D. (1976). The role of play in childhood. In C. Shaefer (Ed.), *Therapeutic use of child's play* (pp. 95–118). New York: Aronson.

Smith, P. K. (1989). The role of rough-and-tumble play in the development of social competence: Theoretical perspectives and empirical evidence. In B. H. Schneider, G. Attili, J. Nadel & R. P. Weissberg (Eds.), *Social competence in developmental perspective* (pp. 239–258). Dordrect: Kluwer Academic Publishers.

Smith, P. K. (1982). Does play matter? Functional and evolutionary aspects of animal and human play. *The Behavioral and Brain Sciences, 5,* 139–184.

Smith, P. K., & Boulton, M. (1990). Rough-and-tumble play, aggression, and dominance: Perceptions and behavior in children's encounters. *Human Development, 33,* 271–282.

Smith, P. K., & Connolly, K. J. (1987). *The ecology of preschool behavior.* Cambridge, England: Cambridge University Press.

Smith, P. K., & Lewis, K. (1985). Rough-and-tumble play, fighting and chasing in nursery school children. *Ethology and Sociobiology, 6,* 175–181.

Strayer, F. F., & Strayer, J. (1976). An ethological analysis of social agonism and dominance relations among preschool children. *Child Development, 47,* 980–989.

Walder, R. (1976). Psychoanalytic theory of play. In C. Shaefer (Ed.), *Therapeutic use of child's play* (pp. 79–94). New York: Aronson.

Wilson, E. O. (1975). *Sociobiology. The new synthesis.* Cambridge, MA: Belknap Press of Harvard University Press.

POSTSCRIPT

Should Superhero or Violent Play Be Discouraged?

Challenge Questions

1. Are we sending children mixed messages by not allowing them to participate in superhero or violent play in their classrooms, yet condoning violent children's shows on television?

2. If teachers allow some play from television and movies to be portrayed in the classroom, at what point do they intervene and say the play has become too aggressive?

3. Are there potential benefits to aggressive play that we are missing because we do not allow children to trust their instincts and play out their fears and fantasies in the early childhood setting?

4. Are teachers in a school setting too quick to intervene when superhero or violent play is taking place?

5. At what age do children begin to say to themselves that just because I saw that on television does not mean I should do it with my friends?

Suggested Readings

Bauer, K. L., & Dettore, E. (1997). Superhero play: What's a teacher to do? *Early Childhood Education Journal,* 25(1) 17–21.

Cooper, B. S., & Speakman, S. T. (2000). Pikachu goes to school. *Teacher Magazine,* 11(7), 58–59.

Fonville, B., & Afflerbach, S. (1995). Superhero play: Making it a part of your curriculum. *Texas Child Care,* 19(2), 2–8.

Frost, J. L. (2005). Lessons from disasters: Play, work, and the creative arts. *Childhood Education,* 82(1) 2–8.

Levin, D. E., & Carlsson-Paige, N. (1995). The Mighty Morphin Power Rangers: Teachers voice concern. *Young Children,* 50(6), 67–72.

Marsh, J. (2000). "But I want to fly too!": Girls and superhero play in the infant Classroom. *Gender and Education,* 12(2), 209–220.

ISSUE 6

Should Transition Grades Be Abolished?

YES: Vera Estok, from "One District's Study on the Propriety of Transition-Grade Classrooms," *Young Children* (March 2005)

NO: Barbara S. Harris, from "'I Need Time to Grow': The Transitional Year," *Phi Delta Kappan* (April 2003)

ISSUE SUMMARY

YES: Vera Estok was a pre-first-grade teacher in Springfield, Ohio. Her district formed a committee to research their 23-year practice of offering transitional grade classrooms. After studying the literature and their program, the committee determined transitional programs were not in the best interest of the children they served. They abandoned the program and moved to full-day kindergarten classrooms.

NO: Barbara S. Harris, associate headmaster at Presbyterian Day School in Memphis, Tennessee, participates in presentations to parents and others on the benefits of giving the gift of time to young children by placing children in transition classes.

$\mathbf{T}$ here are many times in life when one-half of something is a perfect fit. Miles, shoe sizes, hours, and even the age of a preschooler are numbers we are used to hearing with 1/2 tacked on to the end. In the mid-1970s, when kindergarten classes started to become more academic, educators expanded programs for young children that were to serve as a half way or transition route for students not quite ready for the next level. These classes, or grades, are known by many names such as: developmental kindergarten, pre-kindergarten, begindergarten, junior first grade, pre-first, or extra year classes. They are most often found before kindergarten or between kindergarten and first grade. A recommendation to attend a transition class often comes from the preschool or kindergarten teacher or the school administrator at kindergarten entry screening sessions. The student is not officially retained, but spends a transition year before moving on to the next grade level. In effect, a child would take fourteen years to complete kindergarten through twelfth grade instead of thirteen. Data collected by the U.S. Department of Education found that 6 percent of children attend transition or extra-year kindergarten classes, which are available in 23 percent of U.S. schools. There is no national data on the percentage of children who attend transition first-grade classes but 72 percent of U.S. schools implement transition rooms, kindergarten retention, or both.

Supporters of transitional grades point out that the class sizes are usually lower, teachers carefully differentiate the curriculum to meet the needs of all of the students, the pace is geared to the needs of the students, there is individual attention for each student, and the teacher builds on the strengths and interests of the students in the class. Supporters also highlight the offering of extended projects and parental involvement in transitional or extra-year programs. Educators who indicate transition classes are not in the best interest of children strongly support the above mentioned practices for all young children indicating they should not be limited only to those students in transition classes. All students need curriculum that is differentiated, extended projects, and individual attention, among other support services. They also cite the fact that most transition classes are comprised of more male than female students often with birth dates near the cutoff date for kindergarten entry.

The National Association of Early Childhood Specialists in State Departments of Education (NAECS/SDE) support practices that welcome all children into regular grade classrooms and encourage teachers to provide developmentally appropriate practices for all ability levels. Often the decision to place a child in a transition class is made in March, one half year before the next school year starts.

In the following selection, Vera Estok describes how her district wanted to ensure best practices were followed. Their research did not find support for transitional grade classrooms as beneficial to children and the program was eliminated. Barbara S. Harris advocates for children attending extra-year programs comparing them to plants that don't grow as quickly as the other seeds planted at the same time and receiving the same care. She profiles three case studies of boys all recommended for transitional classes and describes their success in elementary school.

POINT

- Children are just as successful without the transitional year.
- Teachers recommend more males than females for transitional grades.
- All children deserve a curriculum adapted to meet their needs and interests.
- Any gains in academic behavior are short lived and disappear by third grade.
- The determination for attending a transitional grade is often made six months before the start of the next school year.
- Children should not be used to increase school funding.

COUNTERPOINT

- Transitional programs help children be ready for future grades.
- Provides an alternative for children not quite ready for the next grade.
- The curriculum in a transitional classroom is tailored to the ability of the students.
- Children show less behavioral problems while in transitional grades.
- Children are recommended to give them time to grow and mature.
- Brings in an extra year of funding for the school district.

YES

Vera Estok

One District's Study on the Propriety of Transition-Grade Classrooms

The end of the school year brought the usual cheers from the children, a flurry of exchanging phone numbers, and promises to keep in touch. As a pre-first teacher, I too cheered, traded phone numbers, and promised to keep in touch with my colleagues.

During the previous six months, my fellow teachers and I had become close partners in reviewing our program's approach to individualized education and the use of sound early childhood practice. We had served on a committee formed by Springfield (Ohio) Local Schools to align our district philosophy with developmentally appropriate practice to meet the individual needs of young children. Our task—now completed—was to review the district's pre-first classrooms, in which kindergartners considered developmentally unprepared for first grade attend an extra-year transitional program.

We began our six-month journey by comparing our practices with those advocated by NAEYC (Bredekamp 1987; Bredekamp & Copple 1997). Many questions arose. Committee members wanted to know what had prompted the district's adoption of pre-first 23 years earlier. They were also interested in what research shows about the academic achievement and self-esteem of children placed in pre-first classrooms. We wondered where professional organizations stand on pre-first programs. Finally, all of us wanted to examine existing alternatives, those that would best align our early childhood classes with current best practices. This article outlines the process followed by our district's teachers and administrators to improve our early childhood program.

History of Pre-first Programs

Pre-first classrooms were first introduced in the United States in the 1940s as reading readiness programs for children who lacked necessary skills for formal reading instruction (Harris 1970). Each pre-first classroom had a low teacher-child ratio, a flexible curriculum, and an interactive environment with learning centers (Horm-Wingerd, Carella, & Warford 1993; Patton & Wortham 1993). In the late 1970s, with pressure mounting for more academic emphasis in kindergarten and first grade and reliance on standardized testing for promotion and placement, interest in pre-first programs was renewed. In response

VIEWS ON GRADE RETENTION

"When individual children do not make expected learning progress, neither grade retention nor social promotion are used; instead, initiatives such as more focused time, individualized instruction, tutoring, or other individual strategies are used to accelerate children's learning."

—NAEYC

"Delaying children's entry into school and/or segregating them into extra-year classes actually labels children as failures at the outset of their school experience. These practices are simply subtle forms of retention. Not only is there a preponderance of evidence that there is no academic benefit from retention in its many forms, but there also appear to be threats to the social-emotional development of the child subjected to such practices."

—NAECS/SDE

"Students recommended for retention but advanced to the next level end up doing as well as or better academically than non-promoted peers. Children who have been retained demonstrate more social regression, display more behavior problems, suffer stress in connection with being retained, and more frequently leave high school without graduating."

—NAECS/SDE

Sources: From NAEYC position statement on developmentally appropriate practice, online pp. 16–17: www.naeyc.org/about/positions/pdf/PSDAP98.PDF; and NAECS/SDE position statement on kindergarten entry and placement, online pp. 4 and 10: www.naeyc. org/about/positions/pdf/Psunacc.pdf

to this emphasis on academics, Springfield Local Schools added a pre-first class-room. The implementation of the new class was featured in *Changing to a Developmentally Appropriate Curriculum—Successfully* (Uphoff 1989).

Today, some school districts still initiate pre-first classes as intervention programs for children who, regardless of chronological age, are considered "unready" or "immature" for placement in a regular first grade. Generally, the purpose of an additional year of instruction is to allow children to mature and develop those skills necessary for success in a regular first grade curriculum (Smith & Shepard 1987). An assumption of pre-first grade placement is that participating children will experience academic success and demonstrate higher levels of achievement than would have been possible if they had gone straight to first grade. Some studies (for example, Bohl 1984) support transitional programs based on a maturational theoretical perspective by considering them a "gift of time."

What the Research Shows

The committee weighed the research information carefully. We realized that transitional placement—a decision that requires an additional year of school life—should not be taken lightly. We turned our attention toward finding research that would support pre-first's success at promoting children's higher academic achievement and greater self-esteem.

Our investigation found the use of transition programs questionable (Shepard & Smith 1989). Gredler (1984) suggests it is counterproductive to wait for children to mature.

Academic Achievement

Three studies offer an extended and in-depth analysis of academic achievement of children in transitional programs. Shepard and Smith (1989); Mantzicopoulos and Morrison (1991); and Ferguson, Jimerson, and Dalton (2001) used recognized testing and screening measures and a host of variables to compare children in transitional classes with peers who had been promoted to first grade. The carefully designed studies show little or no improvement in achievement between children who attended extra-year programs and their peers who moved into first grade. Moreover, when placement in a transitional program did improve/increase academic achievement, the benefits prove to be short-lived. In all three studies the differences between test scores of children in transitional classes and comparison groups diminished and were nonexistent by the end of fourth grade.

Self-Esteem

While objective measures of the cognitive functioning of children are highly developed, measuring social and emotional functioning is less exact, lacking comparable reliability and validity. Still, Sandoval and Fitzgerald (1985) and Rihl (1988) document a negative or insignificant difference in the self-concept and emotional development of children assigned to extra-year classrooms.

Examination of the research was beginning to sway the committee toward an alternative to the pre-first program that would solidify our early childhood program, but what would that be? We concluded that professional organizations might offer some guidance.

What Professional Organizations Recommend

In 1987, following the release of its position statement on developmentally appropriate practice, NAEYC noted that tracking young children into ability groups is developmentally *inappropriate* practice (Bredekamp 1987). David Elkind, NAEYC past president, calls transitional classes simply "another programmatic strategy for dealing with the mismatch between children and first grade curriculum" (1987, 175). More recently, NAEYC has recommended, "Children who fall behind [should] receive individualized support, such as tutoring, personal instruction, focused time on areas of difficulty, and other strategies to accelerate learning progress" (Bredekamp & Copple 1997, 176).

The National Association of Early Childhood Specialists in State Departments of Education (NAECS/SDE) also finds transitional classes unacceptable. The NAECS/SDE states in a position paper that "all children should be welcomed into regular heterogeneous classroom settings and not be segregated into transitional programs following kindergarten" (1987, 10). In a newer, revised position statement, NAECS/SDE points out, "Reducing class size, making the curriculum less abstract and therefore more related to children's conceptual development, insisting that only the most appropriately trained, competent, child-oriented teachers are placed in kindergarten programs, and assuring every child access to a high-quality prekindergarten program are among better means to achieving the educational goal of success for all students" (2000, 14).

Our committee turned to our own state board of education for more guidance. Following a longitudinal study, the Ohio Department of Education concluded that kindergarten and first grade classrooms need developmentally appropriate programs to address children's diverse needs (Ohio Department of Education 1992). The study offers three ways to accomplish this task: (1) implement a preschool program in public schools, (2) establish Chapter 1 reading services, and (3) expand alternate-day and half-time kindergartens to full-day programs. Of the three suggestions, extension to a full-day kindergarten program is reported to reduce grade retention rates and produce the fewest remedial placements. This was the new direction we had been seeking.

Implementing Our Plan

Now that we knew what was needed to enhance our program, implementing a full-day kindergarten program was the next step. As is almost always the case, financing proved to be the most difficult part of the project. Knowing what the addition of full-day kindergarten could mean in the growth of our district, our administrative staff pulled together. They tightened the budget by eliminating the pre-first program and asked the high school and middle school to make as many cuts as they could. State funds already allocated to our district were redirected toward funding the project.

At the final school board meeting of the school year, board members were so impressed with our commitment and dedication to the project that they gave unanimous approval for full-day kindergarten. It would be implemented the next school year.

Will the addition of a full-day kindergarten experience provide added support to the children in our school system? Our committee did its homework well, and we are confident that we are following guidelines to ensure that every child has a successful school experience. We encourage any district that still has a pre-first in its early childhood program to analyze the appropriateness of such classes and find better ways to educate young children.

I am no longer a pre-first teacher but a kindergarten teacher eagerly waiting to join in as children cheer for the new school year.

References

Bohl, N. 1984. A gift of time: The transition year. *Early Years* (January): 14.

Bredekamp, S., ed. 1987. *Developmentally appropriate practice in early childhood programs serving children from birth through age 8.* Exp. ed. Washington, DC: NAEYC.

Bredekamp, S., & C. Copple, eds. 1997. *Developmentally appropriate practice in early childhood programs.* Rev. ed. Washington, DC: NAEYC.

Elkind, D. 1987. *Miseducation: Pre-schoolers at risk.* New York: Knopf.

Ferguson, P., S. Jimerson, & M. Dalton. 2001. Sorting out successful failures: Exploratory analyses of factors associated with academic and behavioral outcomes of retained students. *Psychology in the Schools* 38 (4): 327–41.

Gredler, G.R. 1984. Transition classes: A viable alternative for the at-risk child? *Psychology in the Schools* 21: 463–70.

Harris, A.J. 1970. *How to increase reading ability.* 5th ed. New York: David McKay.

Horm-Wingerd, D., P. Carella, & S. War-ford. 1993. Teacher's perceptions of the effectiveness of transition classes. *Early Education and Development* 4 (2): 130–38.

Mantzicopoulos, D., & P. Morrison. 1991. Transitional first grade referrals. *Journal of Educational Psychology* 90 (1): 122–33.

NAECS/SDE (National Association of Early Childhood Specialists in State Departments of Education). 1987. Unacceptable trends in kindergarten entry and placement. Position statement. ERIC ED 297 856.

NAECS/SDE. 2000. Still unacceptable trends in kindergarten entry and placement. Position statement. . . .

Ohio Department of Education, Division of Early Childhood Education. 1992. *Effects of pre-school attendance and kindergarten schedule: Kindergarten through grade 4. A longitudinal study.* 1992. ERIC ED 400 038.

Patton, M., & S. Wortham. 1993. Transition classes, a growing concern. *Journal of Research in Childhood Education* 8 (1): 32–40.

Rihl, J. 1988. *Pre-first: A year to grow. A follow-up study.* ERIC ED 302 332.

Sandoval, J., & P. Fitzgerald. 1985. A high school follow-up of children who were non-promoted or attended a junior first grade. *Psychology in the Schools* 22: 164–70.

Shepard, L.A., & M.L. Smith. 1989. Effects of kindergarten retention at the end of the first grade. *Psychology in the Schools* 16 (5): 346–57.

Smith, M.L., & L.A. Shepard. 1987. What doesn't work: Explaining policies of retention in the early grades. *Phi Delta Kappan* 69: 129–34.

Uphoff, J. 1989. *Changing to a developmentally appropriate curriculum—successfully.* Rosemont, NJ: Programs for Education.

Barbara S. Harris  **NO**

"I Need Time to Grow": The Transitional Year

While watering my plants near the kitchen window one morning, I noticed that one particular plant, though healthy in appearance, was not flourishing like the others I had rooted at about the same time. All had received the same amount of sunlight, well-prepared soil, water, and pruning, and since I had not moved them, the temperature was the same for all. Yet the green leaves of this plant had not matured as rapidly, the stems were not as strong, and the overall size of the plant was much smaller. As I continued to ponder these differences, it occurred to me that perhaps this one plant just needed more time before its roots took hold in that growth spurt that leads to maturity.

Isn't that just the way it is with children? When I see the kindergartners spilling into our school each fall, I'm always struck that they are alike in so many ways, yet different in so many others. We provide all of them with a bounty of care, nurturing, and attention, and it seems that they should master the social skills, soak up everything teachers can pour out for them, and mature at an ever-quickening pace. Yet, as they near the end of that kindergarten year, many of the children do not seem to possess the maturity, both academic and social, that they will need for their "replanting" in first grade.

At my school and others throughout the country, educators long ago saw the need for the transitional classroom, a place where normal children would be given the time they need to acquire maturity, to master work habits, to refine skills, and to develop the attention span that is so critical to success in the early grades.

I recently came upon an old cartoon that I had been keeping. It showed two kindergarten boys coming out of their classroom. One was saying to the other, "I plan to take a year off between kindergarten and first grade to find myself." I suspect that more than just a few kindergartners need to "find themselves" during an extra year's time between kindergarten and first grade—a year that can stimulate them to further learning and support their development of positive self-esteem.

When I think back over the years about the students I've known who seemed to succeed with ease in the early years and compare them to those who struggled, the major difference that I see has to do with readiness—developmental

From *Phi Delta Kappan*, by Barbara S. Harris, vol. 84, no. 8, April 2003, pp. 624–627. Copyright © 2003 by Phi Delta Kappan. Reprinted by permission of the publisher and Barbara S. Harris.

readiness. In *All Grown Up and No Place to Go,* David Elkind writes, "In New Hampshire children are not hurried. It is one of the few states in the nation that provides 'readiness' classes for children who have completed kindergarten but who are not yet ready for first grade."[1]

Yes, we are a society that is in a hurry, but where are we going, and what will we get there with, if our young children are not fortified and nurtured in the early years of growth? As Nancy Bohl so clearly put it many years ago in her special message to parents, the step between kindergarten and first grade is a *giant* one, and for those who are not developmentally ready, it can lead to frustration and failure.[2]

I recently participated in a panel discussion with several kindergarten teachers who bear the responsibility of recommending (or requiring) that students in their classes attend a transitional class for a year rather than passing directly into first grade. In the case of *recommending* transition, parents have the option of choosing whether the student moves on to first grade or goes to the transitional year. If a student is *required* to attend the transitional class, there is no option, and the child must be enrolled in the transition program.

These are not easy decisions that teachers make overnight. They think long and hard and observe the children in their kindergarten classes closely as they work throughout the entire year to evaluate each child's readiness for first grade. That readiness is measured in several ways:

- using handwriting samples for assessment,
- testing letter/sound recognition,
- using checklists for mastery of skills in reading and math,
- evaluating journal writing,
- observing the student and peer group,
- judging the student's ability to work in groups versus independently,
- evaluating how well students listen to and follow directions,
- assessing work habits and organizational skills,
- using one-on-one testing, and
- using standardized testing.

Of course, as any kindergarten teacher would recognize, this list is just a partial one. We know that the most important evaluative tool is the teacher, who must work patiently each day as he or she interacts continually with each young child.

The kindergarten teachers with whom I spoke mentioned several factors that influence their decision to recommend students to the transition program. All agreed that a lack of maturity is one factor that is usually noted early in the school year. Other factors that they felt are important in identifying readiness for first grade include attentiveness, ability to focus, listening skills, blending sounds, understanding math concepts, ability to process skills, responsiveness, developmental readiness in written work, independence, and skill mastery. The kindergarten teachers unequivocally determined that poor behavior related solely to conduct would *not* be a reason to recommend a student to the transition program. Reading readiness was the number-one academic area that most influenced their decision to require a student to move into a transitional class.

Ever since the late 1950s, there has been considerable debate in the education community as to whether the transitional class is a valuable program that actually improves academic performance. It does seem clear that transitional classes have a beneficial effect on social growth and the growth of self-esteem. Anthony Coletta argues that "supporters [of transitional classrooms] view them favorably because they help children who might do poorly in a rigid, academic curriculum by providing instead the opportunity to be successful in a more relaxed, developmentally appropriate environment. Extra-year programs are therefore seen as a clear alternative to grade retention."[3]

I recently interviewed Laurel Childs, teacher of a successful transitional class in an all-boys elementary school. Years before, she had also been a kindergarten teacher who evaluated students in her own class and recommended to transitional classes those students who needed an extra year. I asked her to identify some of the specific strengths that make her transitional class so successful. Here are some of the factors that she mentioned:

- smaller class size (between 11 and 13 students),
- individual attention to meet the specific needs of students,
- time for extra reinforcement of skills,
- building on the successes and strengths of students,
- whole-language exposure, as well as a strong phonics approach, and
- extra patience on the part of the teacher in dealing with students' repeated mistakes.

Childs mentioned that the slower-paced curriculum of the transitional class allows students to move at their own rate. One of her goals is building character and self-esteem. She said that she makes a great effort to develop a team whose members work with and for one another. Each child has a basic individualized plan to help work on strengths and weaknesses. "My classroom is set up to be a place that is nonjudgmental. Students can make mistakes in a safe and trusting environment. Administration and special-area personnel give much attention to the students, giving praise and reinforcement. Enrichment activities include special field trips, unique projects, and lots of parent involvement. Parental concerns and needs are recognized and addressed through extra communication," says Childs. I asked her to share some of the feedback that she has received from parents, teachers, and children.

Former parents praise the program and testify to what it has done for their children. Last year, one mother told me that they came in "kicking and screaming" and did not want this transitional year, but now she feels that it has been a wonderful year. I have seen former students go on to become successful because of that gift of another year. Current students often want to stay in the same classroom and not move on to a new grade because it is a safe and successful place for them. Teachers who teach the transition child the following year praise the program because they feel it gives the child a boost that is needed for the child to be successful in first grade.

Anthony Coletta describes published research in which Jonathan Sandoval of the University of California studied high school students who years earlier had completed the transitional (junior) first grade. Students placed in the transitional class were superior to a control group on three out of four indicators of academic progress. The students exhibited positive attitudes about having been in the program and stated that the experience helped them to do better socially and emotionally, as well as academically.

In three case studies that I conducted on former transitional class students, I found some similarities regarding their progress following the transitional year.

Case study A.   A boy was recommended for an extra year because he had difficulty writing letters and numbers, cutting, and coloring, and he was unable to follow a story silently while another child read. He also exhibited a lack of self-control, as well as an inability to complete work carefully within a reasonable period of time. By the end of the transitional year, reading, math, and language development showed marked improvement, and the student had received an "E" for excellence in his ability to complete work.

Case study B.   A boy was recommended for the transitional class because he had difficulty with his work habits. He was unable to complete work in a reasonable period of time, could not follow directions, and was unable to continue an activity without constant help. The lack of reading readiness became a concern as the year progressed. He was unable to blend sounds; sequence objects, pictures, and events; and follow a story silently while another child read. He was also unable to solve number sentences in math by the end of the kindergarten year. However, reading skills were the main focus of the transitional year for this student, and he made marked improvement in all areas.

Case study C.   This boy had difficulty following directions, listening, and working independently. Some reversals were noted in numbers and letters throughout the year. Following the year in the transitional class, he exhibited marked improvement in all areas.

All three students appeared to have benefited from the transitional class. At the time that these case studies were completed, student A had completed the first grade, student B was finishing his third-grade year, and student C was finishing fifth grade in a departmentalized setting. Student B was the only one who appeared to be leveling off academically. It is interesting to note that all three of the students had a positive feeling about having been in the transitional class. They exuded confidence, and their self-esteem was strong.

Educators need to remember that each child has his or her own time line. Even though schools use chronological age to determine a child's legal readiness for school, age is not always a reliable indicator of readiness for learning. Giving students the opportunity to mature physically, socially, and emotionally in a nurturing environment that is intellectually stimulating, relatively free of stress, and has a low pupil/teacher ratio can provide them with the opportunity to build their developmental readiness and so offer a better chance for academic success.

Notes

1. David Elkind, *All Grown Up and No Place to Go* (New York: Addison Wesley, 1996).
2. Nancy Bohl, "A Gift of Time: The Transition Year," *Early Years,* January 1984, p. 14.
3. Anthony Coletta, *What's Best for Kids* (Rosemont, N.J.: Modern Learning Press, 1991).

POSTSCRIPT

Should Transitional Grades Be Abolished?

Challenge Questions

1. List some factors in a child's development that would lead some teachers to recommend a transitional year program.

2. How would you respond to those who indicate support for transitional programs because they offer curriculum that is modified to meet the needs of the individual children in the class?

3. What would be some alternatives to a school offering transitional grades?

4. How has the question, "Is this child ready for kindergarten?" fueled the debate around transitional classrooms?

5. What are the effects on self-esteem for children placed in transitional classrooms or promoted to the next grade?

Suggested Readings

Buntaine, R., & Costenbader, V. (1997). The effectiveness of a transitional prekindergarten program on later academic achievement. *Psychology in the Schools,* 34(1), 41–50.

Clifford, R., Barbarin, O., Change, F., Early, D., Bryant, D., Howes, C., Burchinal, M., & Pianta, R. (2005). What is pre-kindergarten? Characteristics of public pre-kindergarten programs. *Applied Developmental Science,* 9(3), 126–143.

Dennebaum, J., & Kulerg, J. (1994). Kindergarten retention and transition classrooms: Their relationship to achievement. *Psychology on the Schools,* 31(1), 5–12.

Karweit, N., & Wasik, B. (1992). A review of the effects of extra-year kindergarten programs and transitional first grades. Center for Research on Effective Schooling for Disadvantaged Students, pp. 1–18 (ED 357-894).

Mantzicoppoulos, P. (2003). Academic and school adjustment outcomes following placement in a developmental first-grade program. *Journal of Educational Research,* 97(2), 90–105.

National Association of Early Childhood Specialists in State Departments of Education. (2000). Still! Unacceptable trends in kindergarten entry and placement.

Nelson, R. (2000). Which is the best kindergarten? *Principal,* 79(5), 38–41.

Pagani, L., Larocque, D., Tremblay, R., & Lapointe, P. (2003). The impact of junior kindergarten on behaviour in elementary school children. *International Journal of Behavioral Development,* 27(3), 423–427.

ISSUE 7

Is Being Older Better When Entering Kindergarten?

YES: Nancie L. Katz, from "Too Young for Kindergarten?" *The Christian Science Monitor* (July 21, 1997)

NO: Hermine H. Marshall, from "Opportunity Deferred or Opportunity Taken? An Updated Look at Delaying Kindergarten Entry," *Young Children* (September 2003)

ISSUE SUMMARY

YES: Nancie Katz, a writer for *The Christian Science Monitor*, examines families who chose to keep their children out of kindergarten for a year and are pleased with the decision. She cites research that found children with later birthdays were retained at a higher rate.

NO: Hermine Marshall, a professor emerita at San Francisco State University in California, presents arguments to dispel any myths about older students performing better and suggests children should attend kindergarten when they are age eligible.

Unless children live in New Zealand, where kindergartners start school on their fifth birthday, parents and teachers routinely have discussions about when a child should begin kindergarten. Cutoff dates for kindergarten entry around the country vary from the earliest of a child must be five years of age by July 1 before they can start kindergarten in the fall to the latest being January 1 of the school year in which they start kindergarten. There are at least 12 different dates in-between those two dates not counting the six states that leave the entrance-age decision up to local district decision. There will always be children who are up to one year apart in age in any given class no matter when the cutoff date is for kindergarten entry. When parents keep children from starting kindergarten when they are age eligible, they create an even wider age discrepancy among the children. Instead of having children all of whom within 12 months of age in the same class, there are children who can vary by as much as 24 months in the same class. Additionally, 27 states allow children to enter kindergarten before they reach age eligibility, which could make the age span even greater.

John Locke stated in the early 1600s, "Accommodate the educational program to fit the child, don't change the child to fit the program." When programs for young children are developmentally appropriate, there are experiences that will meet the ability levels of all the children in the room. All children with the same birth date are not necessarily able to learn at the same time or rate. Teachers of young children need to provide a learning environment that can accommodate the diverse learning styles in their classroom. Teachers of preschool age children are adept at adapting the environment since it is not uncommon to have a preschool class of children from 2 1/2 through five years of age in the same room. The hallmark of good early childhood teachers is making the various learning experiences easier or more challenging based on the developmental abilities of the children in the class.

The trend to keep children from entering kindergarten for a year is particularly popular in middle- and upper middle-class neighborhoods. These parents want to give their child a social and academic boost by being one of the older students in the class. Children whose parents decided to send them to kindergarten when they were age eligible may find themselves being significantly younger than their peers.

It has been reported that approximately 15 percent of children are kept from attending kindergarten each year when they are age eligible. In one midwestern state 21 percent of first-graders in 2006–2007 were old enough to be in second grade. Whether these children had their entry to school delayed, spent a year in a transitional program, or repeated a grade, they were in a grade with other children greatly different in age. The age factor can also be an issue at the other end when children who are 19 years of age are still in high school. There are reports of increased behavior problems and higher school dropout rates for those older students. Many state high school athletic associations have rules stating 19-year-olds cannot compete in high school sports, leaving older high school students on the sidelines instead of participating.

In the first selection, Nancie Katz found parents viewed holding their child out of kindergarten as giving their child a gift of time.

Hermine Marshall argues that there are many factors, other than age, which determine success in kindergarten, and throughout school for that matter. She strongly believes that simply by raising the kindergarten age there will not be a guarantee that all children will be successful in school. It takes much more than older children to have successful learning experiences.

The National Association for the Education of Young Children recommends that children enroll in a kindergarten when they are age eligible. There is a need for teachers of young children to adapt activities to the range of developmental levels in the group.

POINT	COUNTERPOINT
• Older children have an advantage over younger peers.	• There will always be a minimum of a one year age difference in students in any grade.
• Children need to enter school with abilities to peers.	• Teachers should get schools ready for children.
• Older students bring a level of maturity to the classroom.	• Older does not mean better.
• Older children will learn more quickly.	• Keeping some age eligible children out only exacerbates the ability difference.

YES

Nancie L. Katz

Too Young for Kindergarten?

When it came time to put her son in kindergarten, Holly Hankins faced a tough choice: Should he enter as one of the youngest in the class, or should he wait a year?

Like many other parents in 1985, she chose the latter. And she's glad she did.

"It was one of those years that everyone did that with boys [because they say they develop later than girls]," says Mrs. Hankins, mother of three in Washington. "He's been bored on and off, but I think he would have been bored regardless. At least now he's more mature."

A similar decision, however, left Cheryl Flax-Davidson with mixed feelings. "In the early grades, it seemed fine, because it gave her confidence," she says of her youngest child. "But lately, I think some of her friends are less mature and she's having trouble finding kids she can play with."

It's an age-old question: When is a child ready to start formal schooling? Kindergarten is widely viewed as key preparation for first grade, when a child needs to have mastered social skills so as to be able to concentrate on reading and math. Traditionally, school districts have dictated that any child who turns 5 before Dec. 31 should be in kindergarten.

But over the years, support has been growing for delaying entry into kindergarten. Today only four states—Maryland, Connecticut, Hawaii, Rhode Island—and the District of Columbia still have the end of the calendar year as an entrance cut-off date. In an attempt to ensure the child's readiness to learn, most of the others now require children to turn five by September, or earlier. And many parents are voluntarily holding children back.

Some consider it insurance against repeating kindergarten or future grades. But in an increasingly competitive era, many parents simply like the idea of giving their child an academic and social boost by being older. The popularity of doing so, particularly among well-educated, middle-class Americans, has some questioning whether it really produces benefits.

Nancy Elbin, a Montgomery County, Md., guidance counselor who taught first grade for 26 years and has researched retention issues, says studies have found no evidence that holding a child back is "a positive thing to do. Those who repeat don't generally outperform the others."

Look Before You Leap

Indeed, experts caution parents against rash judgments.

"If you have a child on the younger side . . . don't use the child's reading or math ability [or] the child's size, if they're tall," says Stanley Greenspan, a child psychiatrist at George Washington University Medical School in Washington.

What parents should do, he says, is "look at how well the child is able to reason, how quick he is to think on his feet, his ability to read social cues, and his analytical reading and problem solving. Look at the ability to follow instructions and ideas."

If children appear "sluggish" in those areas, he notes, "you might want to buy them another year. Otherwise, they can move on."

He says parents can help children prepare for school—and gauge their readiness—by reading aloud, ensuring play with peers, and playing in inventive ways. He suggests daily "floor time," where parents follow the child's lead, "reading, imagining, and problem-solving" and helping them catch nonverbal social cues.

Is Bigger Really Better?

Ultimately, the evidence is mixed as to whether a delay can help children. In Fairfax County, Va., Douglas Holmes, the director of student services, says his state chose to hold back children who turn 5 after Sept. 30 because of "concern by educators that the kids who were most unsuccessful academically were younger kids."

"What we know is that kids who came in with October to December birthdays were retained at a higher rate," he says.

But, he notes, "What's missing in that is the many [as many as two-thirds] who were successful." Nevertheless, the view persists that children may have a cutting edge by being older, more articulate, and just plain larger. That assumption may be redefining the kindergarten year. Not only do teachers have students as much as a year apart in age, but they are facing more demands from parents, especially in more affluent areas, who want a curriculum that incorporates academics.

Timothy Welsh, a veteran teacher at Murch Elementary in Washington, says kindergarten should help children to learn to work in groups, to shed the egocentricity of earlier childhood, and gain skills to sort out conflict.

"They have to be able to share, to delay gratification, to treat each other with respect," he says. "It's being able to walk away from another child instead of knocking the blocks down. And it's laying that foundation so they're not dealing with these issues when they're buckling down to make those test scores that are so important."

Hermine H. Marshall

 **NO**

Opportunity Deferred or Opportunity Taken? An Updated Look at Delaying Kindergarten Entry

Many families find themselves in a quandary about whether their child is ready for kindergarten, even though he or she is legally eligible to enroll. They often seek the advice of the preschool or kindergarten teacher concerning their child's readiness. One family may wonder whether their child is mature enough. Another family may consider keeping their child out of school an extra year because the family wants to give the child an extra advantage. This practice has been labeled *redshirting*, analogous to the deferment procedure in high school and college sports. Teachers themselves may have concerns about certain children in their class, and therefore need to be aware of the latest research regarding the consequences of keeping eligible children out of school an extra year.

Parent concerns often are based on outdated beliefs and assumptions about the meaning of readiness. In the following sections, I discuss these assumptions and accompanying pressures as well as teachers' and parents' beliefs about prerequisites for kindergarten success. Then I summarize recent research on the effects on both the academic and social domains of delaying children's entry into school.

To ensure the quality of the research reviewed, I began with research that was published only in peer-reviewed journals. I then eliminated studies that were inadequate in terms of such factors as (a) reliability, validity, meaningfulness, and bias of the measures and (b) equivalency of control groups. I added a book-length interview study of the meaning of readiness (Graue 1993b) that provides insights regarding beliefs not available from other sources. I conclude the article with suggestions for early childhood educators to help families in their decisions.

Assumptions and Pressures

Unexamined assumptions about the meaning of readiness held by families and teachers as well as pressures on administrators for accountability influence decisions about whether to recommend holding children out of kindergarten.

From Young Children, September 2003, pp. 84–93. Copyright © 2003 by National Association for the Education of Young Children. Reprinted by permission. www.naeyc.org

Assumptions based on beliefs about the relative importance to development and learning of maturation versus interactive stimulation and teaching are elaborated below, followed by a discussion of the effects of accountability pressures on kindergarten entry decisions.

The Meaning of Readiness

Maturationist assumptions.   For many years readiness for school was conceptualized in terms of the maturation of cognitive, social, and physical abilities. These abilities were perceived as developing essentially on their own according to a child's own time clock, without regard to stimulation from the outside environment. The idea that development proceeds in a linear and automatic manner has been interpreted to mean that certain levels of maturity need to be reached before children can succeed in school.

Maturationists believe that the passage of time will produce readiness. They generally advise delaying school entry for some children, especially those whose birthdays occur near the cutoff date and those considered not ready for kindergarten by teachers, caregivers, and parents who believe that with the simple passage of time, children will achieve higher levels of development and greater readiness to participate in kindergarten.

Interactionist assumptions.   An alternate conception of readiness derives from interactionist and constructivist views. The work of Piaget is often mistakenly interpreted as supporting the view that children must reach a certain level of development before they are ready to learn new strategies or skills. Frequently overlooked, however, is Piaget's view that development results from the interaction between a child and the physical and social world (see Liben 1987).

Piaget did not believe that development is automatic. Rather, he believed that development must be stimulated by children's interactions with the world around them and the people with whom they come in contact. A child may handle an object in a new way and make new discoveries that lead to higher levels of thinking. Or children may watch other children do something they had not thought of, and this may cause them to try new actions. Or a peer or teacher might ask a question that stimulates new ways of thinking. According to this interactionist view, interactive stimulation rather than age or maturation alone contributes to development and to readiness for new tasks.

Extending this view further, Vygotsky (1978) described how learning, development, and readiness for new learning often require guidance and instruction, not just the passage of time. In Vygotsky's view, learning and often teaching precede development. New knowledge and skills result from support or *scaffolding* by an adult or a more expert peer. According to this view, the point is not that children need to be ready for school, but that schools need to be ready to guide, support, and instruct each child, regardless of the skills or knowledge a child brings. Age is largely irrelevant. In fact, research in countries with different age requirements for school entry shows that the oldest entrants in one country would be the youngest in another (Shepard & Smith 1986).

Countering a maturationist perspective, the National Association for the Education of Young Children (NAEYC) points out that believing that children need basic skills before they can proceed is a misconception. For example, children can compose stories that are far more complex than those they can read. In other words, learning does not occur according to a rigid sequence of skills (NAEYC 1990).

Pressures

Accountability pressures have led some school districts to raise the age of school entry, with the goal of ensuring that children are ready for tasks formerly found in first grade. With older, supposedly more mature children at each grade, administrators in districts in which children enter at an older age hope for higher average achievement scores. However, raising the entrance age provides only a temporary solution. A more academic kindergarten curriculum increases the number of families who hold out their children (Cosden, Zimmer, & Tuss 1993). When families delay their children's school entry, the children who have been redshirted require a more advanced curriculum—thereby boosting the spiral upward.

The need for appropriate support and stimulation for children and the futility of increasing school entry age form the basis for the position of NAEYC: "The only legally and ethically defensible criterion for determining school entry is whether the child has reached the legal chronological age of school entry" (NAEYC 1990, 22). Kagan (1992) adds that in addition to "a clear defensible standard, the flexibility to individualize . . . services according to children's needs after entry" (p. 51) is necessary. It is the school's responsibility to meet the needs of the children who are legally eligible. Similar concerns are expressed in the position statement on kindergarten trends developed by the National Association of Early Childhood Specialists in State Departments of Education, and endorsed by NAEYC, "Not only is there a preponderance of evidence that there is no academic benefit from retention in its many forms, but there also appear to be threats to the social-emotional development of the child subjected to such practices" (NAECS/SDE 2000).

Beliefs

The beliefs of families, preschool and kindergarten teachers, school administrators, and pediatricians concerning the prerequisites for kindergarten influence decisions about school entry. These include beliefs concerning skills and attitudes important to school success and beliefs underlying families' consideration of delaying kindergarten for their children.

Beliefs About Prerequisite Resources and Skills

For children to start school ready to learn, experts on the National Education Goals Panel emphasized five interrelated dimensions of development:

WHAT TEACHERS CAN DO

What can you do if you are concerned about the readiness of any of the children in your preschool or kindergarten class?

Explore resources for screening for suspected problems in speech, hearing, vision, communication, or motor development. Discuss your concern with the family, prefacing your remarks with the caveat that children develop at different rates. Emphasize that to avoid problems in the future, it might be wise to have expert guidance.

Be sure your program includes opportunities for children to develop social and communication skills along with cognitive and motor skills. Model appropriate ways to enter a group, to ask for a desired object, to solve problems. Use stories and puppets to raise social dilemmas. Have the children suggest ways to solve the dilemma. Discuss with the family ways to enhance their child's social and communication skills.

If your concerns relate to parenting skills, include good parenting practices in your parent education meetings or recommend parenting classes.

- physical well-being and motor development
- social and emotional development
- approaches to learning
- language use
- cognition and general knowledge (Kagan, Moore, & Bredekamp 1995)

On a more specific level, in the National Household Education Survey—a nationally representative sample of families of four- to six-year-olds not yet in school—parents rated taking turns, sitting still and paying attention, and knowing letters as important (Diamond, Reagan, & Bandik 2000).

In a mostly African American and Latino urban district that had high rates of poverty as well as high drop-out, grade retention, and special education placement rates, parents of both ethnicities agreed with teachers that health and social competence were important prerequisites (Piotrkowski, Botsko, & Matthews 2000). However, parents of both ethnicities emphasized academic skills and compliance with teacher authority to a greater extent than did teachers. Regardless of their educational level, parents believed that children's knowledge was more important than their approach to learning. Preschool teachers in this study, like those in a sample from a less impoverished community (Hains et al. 1989), had higher expectations for entry level skills than did kindergarten teachers.

Teachers' Beliefs, Program Implementation, and Effects on Parents

Teachers' and administrators' beliefs as well as pressures from other teachers affect teachers' perceptions of children's readiness for school. These beliefs also affect how they deliver programs for children. Graue's (1993b) fascinating study of conceptions of readiness in kindergarten classrooms in three different schools within the same school district shows contrasting views and practices.

Fulton.   The kindergarten teacher at Fulton, a school in a working class community, saw readiness as comprised of both the child's maturational level and an environmental component that the teacher provided through appropriate activities and feedback. The teachers in this school "tended to work on an interventionist model of readiness . . . [to] allow precise remediation of problems" (Graue 1993b, 236). For example, an extended-day kindergarten program was developed with the goal of encouraging all children to learn the skills needed to leave kindergarten on an equal level. Families in this school relied on the staff to gain an understanding of the meaning of readiness. Consistent with an interactionist approach in which teachers see their role as providing needed learning materials and stimulation, holding children out was not a popular idea at Fulton.

Rochester.   An interventionist approach was also in place in one kindergarten at Rochester, a school with children from different socioeconomic backgrounds and ethnicities in a community with a large bilingual population. The teacher in the extended-day bilingual class that Graue studied believed that provision of environmental stimulation was critical to enhancing the readiness of the children because they lacked the kinds of preschool experiences from which other children benefited. The bilingual families in this class, like the families at Fulton, counted on the teacher to interpret the meaning of readiness for them. They entered their children when they were eligible, whereas affluent families at Rochester were more likely to hold their children out.

Norwood.   In contrast, the teachers at Norwood, a school in a primarily Anglo, middle-class community, held a maturationist model of readiness. As opposed to schools where teachers worked together to understand and meet the needs of individual children, the kindergarten teachers at Norwood felt pressured by the first grade teachers to produce students who could meet fairly rigid standards for first grade entry. The kindergarten teacher in the class studied believed that readiness was related to age. She expected younger children to be less ready.

Not surprisingly, the parents at Norwood also conceived of readiness "in terms of age, maturity, and social behaviors necessary to do well in school" (Graue 1993b, 230). They worried about whether their children had the necessary skills for kindergarten success. They were also aware of the expectations of the first grade teachers.

More parents at Norwood delayed kindergarten entry for their children, especially boys, apparently to ensure success—although these parents were not necessarily concerned about their children's academic readiness. Fourteen percent of kindergarten boys in the school and close to 40 percent of the boys in the class studied had been held out an extra year. (Other studies, e.g., Graue &

DiPerna 2000, also show that boys are more frequently held out.) Various extra-year programs were tried in attempts to provide children with more time to develop readiness.

Clearly, the beliefs and practices of the Norwood administration and teachers influenced not only their practices, but also the beliefs and decisions of parents. The beliefs in this school were similar to those of parents and teachers in another high achieving school studied by Graue (1993a).

Parents' Beliefs Related to Delaying Kindergarten Entry

Very little research is available about parents' reasons for delaying kindergarten entry. In making their decisions, parents of four- to six-year-olds in the National Household Education Survey expressed concern about their children's preacademic skills rather than about reports of their behavior (Diamond, Reagan, & Bandik 2000). Although Anglo parents were less likely than other parents to be concerned about their children's readiness (however, 13.5 percent were)—even with level of parent education controlled—these parents and parents with higher education levels were more likely to suggest delaying their child's kindergarten entry.

Only the study by Graue (1993b), noted earlier, specifically sought information about parents' actual decisions prior to the beginning of school. Graue conducted interviews with the parents of the five or six oldest and youngest children scheduled to enter kindergarten in each school about what they thought about kindergarten entrance. Parents at all three schools expressed concerns about maturity, which they saw in terms of personal and social characteristics, rather than academic knowledge. Many also emphasized wanting their children to have a good start.

The culture at Norwood and of the more affluent parents at Rochester seemed to encourage parents to hold their children out. For example, of the six parents interviewed at Norwood, three had kept their age-eligible children (two boys and one girl) out the previous year. Greg's mother wondered about his emotional readiness. She was the only parent to state that the major reason for holding her child out was to give him an advantage in high school sports (reflecting the traditional meaning of redshirting). She commented, "Plus, everyone says how boys are so much later blooming in a lot of ways" (Graue 1993b, 128). The decision of one parent at Rochester to hold out her son was influenced by the fact that her own brother had been held back in third grade and did better following retention.

Even among those whose children entered Norwood when eligible, parents expressed reservations. Typical was Alyson's mother, who worried that Alyson's September birth date put her at a disadvantage, although both mother and preschool teacher thought she was ready. However, the mother's desire for her child to be at the top of her class made her consider keeping her out an additional year. Families of older children often stated that they were glad their children were more mature and would feel stronger about themselves.

WHAT WE DO KNOW ABOUT HOLDING CHILDREN OUT

1. Some families delay their child's kindergarten entry because of maturity concerns. Often these concerns are influenced by the culture of the school or community.
2. On average, delaying kindergarten entry has no long-term effect on academic achievement. By about third grade, any early differences disappear. However, the combination of youngness and low ability may have negative consequences for achievement.
3. Holding children out deprives them of instruction that, regardless of age, promotes learning of many skills.
4. Holding children out does not result in any social advantage. There are no differences in peer acceptance or self-concept. On the contrary, some children who are redshirted worry that they have failed and develop poor attitudes toward school. They are more likely later to have behavior problems and to drop out.
5. Children who have been held out are more likely to receive special education services later. Enrolling children when they are eligible may lead to their receiving help earlier.
6. In developmentally appropriate kindergartens, children's age or maturity should make no difference. In kindergartens that are pressure-cookers influenced by the demands of achievement-oriented teachers, families may have greater cause for concern.

Effects of Delaying School Entry

Maturationists predict that children whose kindergarten entry is delayed will fare better in school. However, as we will see, research does not substantiate the predicted beneficial effects on achievement, self-concept, or social development. The research results are summarized below according to their focus on academic or social effects.

Academic Effects

The classic review of the literature by Shepard and Smith (1986) indicates that although the oldest children in a class on average are more successful than their younger peers in the first few grades (in first grade by about 7–8 percentile points), these differences are of little practical significance and usually disappear by grade three. Most of the differences are almost entirely attributable to children who fall below the 25th percentile in ability. That is, it seems that the combination of young age and low ability has negative consequences for achievement. Moreover, the validity of those studies in which differences were found can be questioned on the basis of criteria that are subject to teacher bias. The influence of teacher expectations regarding age can also be seen in teachers' tendencies to retain more younger than older students even if their skills are equally deficient.

WHAT WE DON'T KNOW ABOUT HOLDING CHILDREN OUT

1. Little information is available about why parents hold their children out. The one interview study included only a small number of families. We do not know if parents suspect that their child has some problems, which they hope will disappear with the passage of time, that could prevent him (or occasionally her) from being successful in kindergarten.
2. There are no longitudinal studies that follow individual children over their school career that include information about why each child was held out and whether they received special services during the extra year. The research results reported are based on averages. Therefore, we cannot predict under what circumstances which children might encounter negative consequences nor which children might benefit from being held out and provided with what types of special services.
3. We do not know whether children's progress differs depending on whether the decision to delay was based on family concerns or whether it was the result of district screening.
4. There is no way of knowing whether children who were held out might have fared more poorly if they had not been held out (Stipek 2002). Controlled studies to investigate this possibility would be difficult to conduct.

Many studies have been conducted over the past 15 years that shed further light on the issue but essentially uphold Shepard and Smith's basic findings. For example, in a study of African American and Caucasian urban children, older children performed slightly but significantly better academically in grade one, but these differences disappeared four years later (Bickel, Zigmond, & Staghorn 1991; see also Cameron & Wilson 1990). In a study of children in families with very low incomes from a predominantly Anglo rural community, a predominantly African American urban community, and a predominantly Latino urban community, the oldest children scored higher than the youngest in reading and math in kindergarten, but these differences disappeared by grade three. Similarly, for upper-middle-class children, performance differences decreased by grade five (Sweetland & DeSimone 1987).

A comparison of children in a transitional (readiness) first grade classroom with children who were selected but not placed in that classroom, remaining in first grade, showed no significant differences in second grade achievement (Ferguson 1991). That is, having an extra year with a "dumbed-down curriculum" and attaining an older age had no positive effect on children's achievement or need for other services. A recent review of the empirical literature concludes that delayed entry as well as retention and transition class practices are not effective (Carlton & Winsler 1999).

Schooling vs. allowing time to mature. Among the advantages of children entering when eligible is that some skills, such as those needed for reading readiness, require instruction. A well-controlled study of more than 500 children in a district with developmentally appropriate kindergartens compared young first-graders (whose birthdays fell within two months of the cutoff date) with older kindergartners (whose birthdays fell within two months following the cutoff date) and older first-graders (who were one year older than the older kindergartners). At pretest, the reading and math achievement scores of younger first-graders were lower than those of older first-graders but higher than those of older kindergartners. The same was true at post-test. The differences between older kindergartners and younger first-graders on pretest indicate that a year in kindergarten has instructional benefits.

Moreover, there was no difference in the progress of younger and older first-graders from fall to spring. That is, each group achieved one year's growth. In addition, younger first-graders' progress exceeded that of older kindergartners, suggesting that age is an insufficient criterion for benefiting from reading and math instruction in first grade (Morrison, Griffith, & Alberts 1997).

Other studies comparing same-age children in different grades showed that by the end of first grade, younger children's reading ability was no different from their older classmates' (Crone & Whitehurst 1999), and math achievement scores were higher than those of their same-age peers who were still in kindergarten (Stipek & Byler 2001; see also Morrison, Smith, & Dow-Ehrensberger 1995). After reviewing the research literature, Stipek (2002) concluded that for math and most reading and literacy skills, the effects of schooling seem to be more potent than the effects of time to mature; whereas for certain tasks, such as conservation and story recall and production, general maturation and experience are likely to contribute to skill acquisition. Other work suggests that instruction in school may contribute to the development of children's working-memory strategies (Ferreira & Morrison 1994).

Factors other than age.   An additional point to consider is that a substantial number of redshirted and retained children have above average IQ scores (Morrison, Griffith, & Alberts 1997). The number of younger and older students who qualified for a gifted program was similar, although more older students were sent to be evaluated (De Meis & Stearn 1992)—perhaps exemplifying teacher expectations. Even though the oldest children in a large nationally representative study were more likely than the youngest to score in the highest quartile in reading, math, and general knowledge, some of the youngest also scored in the highest quartile and some of the older children scored in the lowest quartile (West, Denton, & Germino-Hausken 2000). Many other factors, such as mother's education and marital status, had similar relationships. Hence, it is not age alone that contributes to children's achievement.

It is important to note that parents who hold their children out for social reasons may be disappointed by the lack of academic content and challenge in some kindergartens. They often discover that their children encounter what appears to be largely a repeat of preschool (Graue 1993a).

Social Effects

Contrary to popular belief, children whose entry into school has been delayed do not seem to gain an advantage socially. In fact, more drawbacks than advantages

WHAT TO ADVISE FAMILIES

What advice can preschool teachers and early childhood caregivers give to families who question whether their child is ready for kindergarten?

First, it is wise to become familiar with what the kindergartens in your area expect in terms of abilities and whether they are prepared to meet the needs of all children. If kindergartens are overly academic and competitive, advocate for developmentally appropriate classes. Help families understand what this means so they also can advocate for kindergartens that are prepared to receive, support, and stimulate all children.

Second, find out why families are considering holding their child out. If it is due only to a late birthday, tell them that although we cannot predict for individual children, research shows that any early achievement differences generally disappear by third grade and that children who are held out may worry that they have failed. These children are also more likely to have behavior problems by high school and to drop out of school. Some evidence suggests that children placed in readiness programs are also more likely to drop out. Encourage families to take the long view and think about what they would like their child to be like in 10 to 15 years.

For families concerned about their child's social skills, let them know that delaying kindergarten does not provide children with a social advantage. Focus on finding ways to enhance children's social skills through your curriculum. Suggest things that a family can do, like arranging for the child to play with another compatible child.

If a family is concerned about communication skills, suggest activities the family can do with the child or refer them to a specialist. Tell them that if special services are needed, the child's entry at the eligible age might provide these services earlier.

Although parents are unlikely to admit it, some may want to keep their child out because of their own needs and fears of separation. If you suspect that this is the case, reassure them that this is not uncommon. Refocus them on their long-term goals for their child.

You can also present information about readiness concerns and the development of skills at a parent education meeting.

---

are evident. Many children who have been redshirted worry that they have failed or been held back (Graue 1993b) and often have poor attitudes toward school (Shepard & Smith 1989; Graue & DiPerna 2000). Furthermore, students who are too old for grade are less likely to graduate from high school. However, according to Meisels (1992), "[i]t is possible that middle- to upper-income students who have been held out will form a subgroup of overage students who will not be at risk for dropping out in the same way as other students, but this is yet to be demonstrated" (p. 167).

Social development. Reviews of the literature have found no difference in self-concept, peer acceptance, or teacher ratings of behavior (Graue & DiPerna

2000; see also Stipek & Byler 2001). In one study of social adjustment and self-perceptions in a mostly Anglo and Latino sample, the few correlations found between social functioning and age were subject to teacher bias; and most of these differences disappeared by grade one (Spitzer, Cupp, & Parke 1995). No differences were found in self-reported school adjustment, loneliness, perceptions of competence, or acceptance. However, although younger children were no more likely than older children to be rejected or neglected, they were less likely to be nominated by peers as well liked and as showing prosocial behavior.

Children who were deemed unready according to the Gesell Test (Ilg & Ames 1965) and placed in a developmental kindergarten or pre-first-grade class showed no difference in ratings for social development in first grade when compared to a matched control group (Matthews, May, & Kundert 1999). Those who were identified as immature but who did not attend readiness programs were no more likely to miss school or receive poor social development ratings in grade one than those who had attended the readiness classes. However, a greater number of students identified as unready to enter school but who were not placed in readiness programs were retained at some point in their school career, and half of these retentions were made in kindergarten.

These results raise several questions: How many of the decisions to retain children have been based on a screening test with questionable reliability and validity? Were kindergarten teachers more likely to retain those children whose parents did not follow through on recommendations? Or were parents and teachers reluctant to retain those already overage from earlier developmental placement? More important, would special help during the kindergarten year have obviated the need for retention?

Challenging behaviors.   Those who advocate the benefits of delaying kindergarten entry predict fewer behavior problems for children who are unready and whose entry is delayed. With the exception of a study by Bickel, Zigmond, and Staghorn (1991), studies have found an increase in behavior problems for children held out or those placed in a transition class (Ferguson 1991; Graue & DiPerna 2000). Note, however, that although the study of urban African American and Caucasian children by Bickel and associates found no difference in report card ratings of conduct, referrals, and retentions when controlled for socioeconomic level, preschool attendance, and race, the measure used in the study is subject to teacher bias.

Moreover, a large cross-sectional survey of more than nine thousand children at different ages shows that by adolescence, the overage children, even those who had not been retained, had higher rates of parent-reported behavior problems, such as bullying, trouble getting along with others, depression, losing temper, feeling inferior; and after age twelve, hanging out with kids who get in trouble—even though these children had low scores for being at risk when they were younger (Byrd, Weitzman, & Auinger 1997). This was especially true for the Caucasian youth. Children who have been redshirted were also found to need more special services, not fewer (Graue & DiPerna 2000; see also Matthews, May, & Kundert 1999).

These findings suggest that there may be adverse behavioral consequences associated with the decision to delay kindergarten entry that may not appear until later years. It is not clear whether these problems derive from the effects of holding children out or from some preexisting condition that influenced parents' decisions; however, the latter is unlikely since many problems do not emerge until adolescence.

Influenced by maturationist thinking, parents often believe that with additional time, their child will outgrow a possible problem. What they fail to realize is that the sooner the nature of the problem is identified, the sooner the child can receive special services that may help the child overcome the problem (see also Maxwell & Eller 1994). When children who may have problems enter at the eligible age, they may actually benefit—assuming the school district makes services available and that their teachers refer them for these services rather than advising families to keep these children out an extra year.

Suggestions for Advising Families

Many families are under the mistaken impression that holding their child out will be beneficial, that it will give the child the gift of time. But families need to be aware of the possibility of too little challenge and the potential negative effects of holding children out. They need to know about the advantages of enrolling children when they are eligible.

In the cases of children whose entries were not delayed and who were later retained, it is important to consider whether the stimulation provided by the next year's teacher and/or remediation would have allowed the child to catch up without retention. Families also need to consider what would have happened had the child received extra help during the year before he or she was retained. Growth and skill learning are not linear.

Some teachers and administrators encourage families to delay kindergarten entry for a number of reasons. Not only might they be unaware of current research on the negative effects of delaying school entry, but they often see only the progress children make during an extra year. They do not consider that similar or greater progress might occur if the child were to enter school and receive stimulation, instruction, and intervention services.

Nor do teachers see the negative consequences, which might not appear until high school. Moreover, pressured administrators frequently believe that if younger children are held out, the achievement scores of the older children remaining will be higher.

Conclusions

Families concerned about their child's maturity and whether to enroll their child in kindergarten when he or she is eligible have often been advised to give the child the gift of time. Research does not support this practice. In fact, delaying kindergarten entry often has negative effects. Families need to consider that by holding their child out, they may in fact be depriving the child of important opportunities for learning—what Graue and DiPerna (2000) refer to as *theft of opportunity.*

References

Bickel, D., N. Zigmond, & J. Straghorn. 1991. The effect of school entrance age to first grade: Effects on elementary school success. *Early Childhood Research Quarterly* 6 (2): 105–17.

Byrd, R., M. Weitzman, & P. Auinger. 1997. Increased behavior problems associated with delayed school entry and delayed school progress. *Pediatrics* 100 (4): 651–61.

Cameron, M.B., & B.J. Wilson. 1990. The effects of chronological age, gender, and delay of entry on academic achievement and retention: Implications for academic redshirting. *Psychology in the Schools* 27 (3): 260–63.

Carlton, M., & A. Winsler. 1999. School readiness: The need for a paradigm shift. *School Psychology Review* 28 (3): 338–52.

Cosden, M., J. Zimmer, & P. Tuss. 1993. The impact of age, sex, and ethnicity on kindergarten entry and retention decisions. *Educational Evaluation and Policy Analysis* 15 (2): 209–22.

Crone, D.A., & G.J. Whitehurst. 1999. Age and schooling effects on emergent literacy and early reading skills. *Journal of Educational Psychology* 91 (4): 604–14.

Diamond, K.E., A.J. Reagan, & J.E. Bandyk. 2000. Parents' conceptions of kindergarten readiness: Relationships with race, ethnicity, and development. *Journal of Educational Research* 94 (2): 93–100.

Ferguson, P.C. 1991. Longitudinal outcome differences among promoted and transitional at-risk kindergarten students. *Psychology in the Schools* 28 (2): 139–46.

Ferreira, F., & F.J. Morrison. 1994. Children's metalinguistic knowledge of syntactic constituents: Effects of age and schooling. *Developmental Psychology* 30 (5): 663–78.

Graue, M.E. 1993a. Expectations and ideas coming to school. *Early Childhood Research Quarterly* 8 (1): 53–75.

Graue, M.E. 1993b. *Ready for what? Constructing meanings of readiness for kindergarten.* Albany: State University of New York Press.

Graue, M.E., & J. DiPerna. 2000. Redshirting and early retention: Who gets the "gift of time" and what are its outcomes? *American Educational Research Journal* 37 (2): 509–34.

Ilg, F.L., & L.G. Ames. 1965. *School readiness: Behavior tests used at Gesell Institute.* New York: Harper & Row.

Hains, A.H., S.A. Fowler, I.S. Schwartz, E. Kottwitz, & S. Rosenkotter. 1989. A comparison of preschool and kindergarten teacher expectations for school readiness. *Early Childhood Research Quarterly* 4 (1): 75–88.

Kagan, S.L. 1992. Readiness past, present, and future: Shaping the agenda. *Young Children* 48 (1): 48–53.

Kagan, S.L., E. Moore, & S. Bredekamp, eds. 1995. *Reconsidering children's early development and learning: Toward common views and vocabulary.* National Educational Goals Panel. Goal 1 Technical Planning Group. Washington, DC: U.S. Government Printing Office.

Liben, L.S. 1987. *Development and learning: Conflict or congruence.* Hillsdale, NJ: Erlbaum.

Matthews, L.L., D.C. May, & D.K. Kundert. 1999. Adjustment outcomes of developmental placement: A longitudinal study. *Psychology in the Schools* 36 (6): 495–504.

Maxwell, K.L., & S.K. Eller. 1994. Children's transition to kindergarten. *Young Children* 49 (6): 56–63.

Meisels, S.J. 1992. Doing harm by doing good: Iatrogenic effects of early childhood enrollment and promotion policies. *Early Childhood Research Quarterly* 7 (2): 55–74.

Morrison, F.J., E.M. Griffith, & D.M. Alberts. 1997. Nature-nurture in the classroom: Entrance age, school readiness, and learning in children. *Developmental Psychology* 33 (2): 254–62.

Morrison, F.J., L.K. Smith, & M. Dow-Ehrensberger. 1995. Education and cognitive development: A naturalistic experiment. *Developmental Psychology* 31 (5): 789–99.

NAECS/SDE (National Association of Early Childhood Specialists in State Departments of Education). 2000. Still unacceptable trends in kindergarten entry and placement. . . .

NAEYC. 1990. Position statement on school readiness. *Young Children* 46 (1): 21–23.

Piotrkowski, C.S., M. Botsko, & E. Matthews. 2000. Parents' and teachers' beliefs about children's school readiness in a high need community. *Early Childhood Research Quarterly* 15 (4): 537–58.

Shepard, L.A., & M.L. Smith. 1986. Synthesis of research on school readiness and kindergarten retention. *Educational Leadership* 44 (3): 78–86.

Spitzer, S., R. Cupp, & R.D. Parke. 1995. School entrance age, social acceptance, and self-perception in kindergarten and first grade. *Early Childhood Research Quarterly* 10 (4): 433–50.

Stipek, D. 2002. At what age should children enter kindergarten? A question for policy makers and parents. *Social Policy Report* 16 (2): 3–17.

Stipek, D., & P. Byler. 2001. Academic achievement and social behaviors associated with age of entry into kindergarten. *Journal of Applied Developmental Psychology* 22 (2): 175–89.

Sweetland, J.D., & P.S. DeSimone. 1987. Age of entry, sex, and academic achievement in elementary school children. *Psychology in the Schools* 24 (4): 406–12.

Vygotsky, L. [1930–35] 1978. *Mind in society: The development of higher psychological processes,* eds. & trans. M. Cole, V. John-Steiner, S. Scriber, & E. Souberman. Cambridge, MA: Harvard University Press.

West, J., K. Denton, & E. Germino-Hausken. 2000. America's kindergartners: Findings from the early childhood longitudinal study, kindergarten class of 1998–99: Fall 1998. *Education Statistics Quarterly* 2 (1): 7–13.

POSTSCRIPT

Is Being Older Better When Entering Kindergarten?

Challenge Questions

1. How can teachers work to ensure all children will be successful in school?
2. What is the purpose of kindergarten?
3. Is kindergarten the only grade when one's birth date is important?
4. Would a high school teacher take a child's birth date into consideration when looking at the child's academic performance? Are there problems associated with being the oldest among one's peers at the secondary level?
5. What should parents consider when making a decision about their child's kindergarten entry? Are factors such as the height of the child's parents and the child at age four, peers attending kindergarten, or changes in the family issues to also be considered when making the decision?
6. What can be done to better meet the needs of all students? Instead of working hard to change the children before or during their attendance in kindergarten, are there other alternatives that would be more successful for all involved?

Suggested Reading

Byrd, R., Weitzman, M., & Auinger, P. (1997). Increased behavior problems associated with delayed school entry and delayed school progress. *Pediatrics*, 100 (4), 654–661.

Connecticut Early Childhood Education Council. (1996). Coming to school in Connecticut: Accepting children as they are. ERIC Document Reproduction Service, ED410063.

Crosser, S. L. (2001). Enter early or hold out: The kindergarten age dilemma. *Early Childhood News*, 13(2), 16–21.

Morrison, F., Griffith, E., & Alberts, D. (1997). Nature-nurture in the classroom: Entrance age, school readiness, and learning in children. *Developmental Psychology*, 33(2), 254–262.

National Association for the Education of Young Children. (1995). *NAEYC position statement on school readiness.* http://www.naeyc.org/about/position/psredy98.htm

Spitzer, S. Cupp, R., & Parke, R. D. (1995). School entrance age, social acceptance, and self-perceptions in kindergarten and first grade. *Early Childhood Research Quarterly*, 10, 433–450.

ISSUE 8

Is Grade Retention
Harmful to Children?

YES: **Susan Black**, from "Second Time Around," *American School Board Journal* (November 2004)

NO: **Joellen Perry**, from "What, Ms. Crabapple Again?" *U.S. News & World Report* (May 24, 1999)

ISSUE SUMMARY

YES: Susan Black, a contributing editor for the *American School Board Journal*, reports that grade retention has never been a positive experience for children when it happens, later in their schooling or well into their adult life. She finds little, if any, benefits for the well-entrenched practice.

NO: To many parents and children, the only solution for getting back on the right track in school is to start again. For these children, repeating a grade offers the student a chance at a positive experience. Joellen Perry, a writer for *U.S. News & World·Report*, shares stories from families for whom retention was successful.

$\mathbf{G}$rade retention was not used when public education first began. Students of different ages and ability levels were educated in a one-room school containing many grades. When content was mastered, the student received work at the next level. The growth of public schools necessitated a more manageable system and individual grades were established. Students deemed not ready for the next grade level were told they failed and had to be held back or repeat their current grade the next school year. Retention is so popular today it has risen nearly 40 percent over the past 20 years supporters say. Retention allows a child having difficulty keeping up with his or her peers time to catch up and feel comfortable in a school setting.

Teachers are often told in October to begin keeping a list of those children they think might be candidates for retention at the end of the school year. Approximately 2.5 million students are retained each year. The numbers are especially high for males and minorities in urban areas. By ninth grade, approximately 50 percent of all students have been retained at least once. It is not always readily accepted by parents, but is sold to them as a solution for the constant struggle their child is undergoing. The children have the summer to accept the idea, and by September they usually begin to embrace attending the same grade again. They gain new respect being older, and are more experienced than the rest of the class.

Just what is the criteria teachers use to determine if a student is a candidate to be retained? The list varies among teachers and school districts, but some of the most frequently occurring characteristics include younger than peers; small for size; poor self-concept or social skills; poor academic performance, especially in reading; and if in kindergarten, lack of previous school experience. These are the most common characteristics of retained children, yet students' problems with school are just as likely caused by undiagnosed health problems, the need for eyeglasses, frequent moves, high absenteeism, lack of routines in the home, speakers of a language other than English in the home, and not being read to at home. All of these issues require family support services that go beyond a child simply spending another year in the same grade.

Research-based practices strongly support not retaining students but instead offering additional support services. Such as summer school after school help, small-group tutoring or information and assistance for the families to help the child at home. To be proactive, a school district can implement a quality pre-school program along with family school and community partnership programs starting at an early age. The challenge is having school districts pay for additional services when the extra year of funding from the state that the district would receive for a retained student would not materialize.

Susan Black presents an overview of the research on retention, which indicates little, if any, support for this widely used practice. The practice of failing students receives a failing mark in all categories. She argues that it may seem like a good short-term solution to a problem, but looking long range at the total educational experience, she finds it does not help a child be more successful and can in fact cause more harm than good.

Joellen Perry found many parents who saw retention as an ideal solution and are pleased they decided to retain their child. For certain children and families, retention can be a successful experience and should be presented as a viable option for school success.

POINT

- Retention is discriminatory since more boys, younger children, and minorities are retained.
- There are many ways school districts can help students, such as after-school tutoring sessions, smaller class size, summer programs homework help, etc., that will help the student more than spending another year in the same grade.
- There are limited short-term academic gains when children are retained and no long-term benefits.
- Retention caries a lifelong stigma.

COUNTERPOINT

- Retention gives children extra time to grow and develop.
- Promoting students (social promotion) does not help them academically.
- The extra year in the same grade is worth it to help students academically.
- Always being behind one's peers is challenging.

 **YES**

Susan Black

Second Time Around

Making students repeat a grade hasn't worked for 100 years, so why is it still happening? And why do government officials, school leaders, and teachers persist in recommending retention as a remedy for low student achievement—even when researchers call it a failed intervention?

Linda Darling-Hammond, executive director of Columbia University's National Center for Restructuring Education, Schools, and Teaching, has a one-word answer: assumptions. Many schools, she says, operate on the assumption that failing students motivates them to try harder, gives them another chance to "get it right," and raises their self-esteem.

Those claims aren't true, Darling-Hammond maintains. The widespread trust in retention is uncritical and unwarranted, she says. It ignores several decades of research showing that, for most children, retention:

- Fails to improve low achievement in reading, math, and other subjects.
- Fails to inspire students to buckle down and behave better.
- Fails to develop students' social adjustment and self-concept.

Darling-Hammond concedes that grade retention might benefit some students in the short term, but in the long term, holding students back puts them at risk. More often than not, students who are retained never catch up academically. Many eventually drop out, and some end up in the juvenile justice system.

The belief that students, as well as their parents, are to blame for low achievement plays into most retention decisions. But teachers and principals seldom accept their share of blame for inept instruction, lackluster lessons, low expectations, and other school factors that contribute to students' academic disengagement and behavior problems, Darling-Hammond says.

As a result, most retained students are just recycled. But as Darling-Hammond points out, simply giving students more of what didn't work the first time around is an exercise in futility.

Teachers' Power to Retain

It's easy to see why teachers believe retention works. But it's less easy to understand why schools allow teachers to hold so much power over this practice.

Gwendolyn Malone, a fifth-grade teacher in Virginia and president of her local teachers union, writes in *NEA Today* that retention offers students the chance to "refresh, relearn, and acquire new skills," as well as to gain self-confidence and become good students. She urges schools to "nip problems in the bud by retaining students early in their school careers"—as early as kindergarten and first grade.

Malone believes the threat of retention is an incentive for students to study so they'll be promoted with their same-age classmates. Weak students who are promoted, she says, end up feeling ashamed, angry, and defensive about their so-called deficiencies.

In most schools, classroom teachers determine which students will pass or fail. At the end of the 2003–04 school year, for instance, one New York City teacher identified 17 of her 28 third-graders for retention. The high numbers didn't trouble her—although she told a reporter that "there would be no fourth grade if all struggling children were held back."

Shane Jimerson of the University of California-Santa Barbara says teachers play a key role in deciding which students will be retained, even though most teachers are unfamiliar with research that casts a dubious light on this practice. School psychologists should study the research and present it to school staffs, Jimerson recommends, and they should head teams consisting of counselors, teachers, and administrators who will make pass/fail decisions.

But before they make those decisions, he says, team members should know these research findings:

- Retaining elementary-age students may provide an achievement "bounce," but gains tend to be slight and temporary; once the bounce tapers off, students either level off or again fall behind their classmates.
- Retaining kindergarten and first-grade students as a preventive intervention is no better for students than retaining them in upper grades.
- Retaining students without providing specific remedial strategies and attending to students' risk factors has little or no value.

Team decision making might help avoid a problem RMC Research Corporation's Beckie Anderson has identified. She reports that teachers often retain students to avoid criticism from teachers in the next grade for promoting poorly prepared students. Many principals, it turns out, are quietly complicit in this practice by giving teachers complete authority over retention decisions.

A Troubling Process

Over the years I've watched a number of schools, both rural and urban, retain more students each year, especially in kindergarten, first grade, and ninth grade. Many of the schools I've studied now hold back 30 to 40 percent of their youngest students, but a handful of schools retain close to 50 percent.

And many of the teachers and principals I've interviewed think of retention as standard practice. A first-grade teacher told me, "By November, I know which half of my class will pass and which half will fail."

The retention ritual doesn't begin in earnest until April or May, however, when teachers submit a list of students for retention to their principals, who generally approve their recommendations.

Here's how one such decision played out a few weeks before the close of school in 2004. A third-grade teacher called in a 10-year-old boy's mother to discuss retention, and I sat in on the conversation. The teacher admitted that the boy—I'll call him Ryan—was "quite smart," especially in science and math. But, she insisted, Ryan, who is small for his age, needed another year to "grow into third grade."

The mother balked—Ryan had already repeated first grade for the same reason—but the teacher overruled her objection. The principal was nowhere to be seen, and neither were the school's counselor or psychologist.

At the end of the meeting the teacher brought a signed form to the office, and Ryan was officially retained. I thought of Lorrie Shepard and Mary Smith's 1989 book *Flunking Grades* in which they write that "teachers consistently underplay the extent of conflict with parents over the decision to retain and underestimate the degree of parents' active resistance or passive but unhappy compliance."

Teachers may believe retention does no harm, but Anderson says researchers' interviews with children who were held back in elementary school tell a different story. More than 25 percent of the children were too ashamed to admit that they had failed a grade. Almost without exception, the retained children said staying back made them feel "sad," "bad," and "upset," and they thought repeating a grade was "punishment."

When I met with Ryan over the summer, he told me, "I'll never be smart in school. I'm only smart at things we don't do in school—like inventing mazes and drawing." When I asked why he thought he had to repeat third grade he replied, without hesitation, "I got in lots of trouble for not walking on the red line." In this school, I learned, teachers drill students on walking silently and ramrod straight on a narrow red line that runs the length of the school's corridor.

Retention's Long Reach

According to best estimates, nearly 2.5 million students are retained each year in U.S. schools, with the highest rates found among boys—especially minorities, special education students, and those who come from low-income families and live in the inner city.

University of Wisconsin-Madison's Robert Hauser, who recorded national retention rates for the National Research Council, found that 25 percent of 6- to 8-year-olds and 30 percent of 9- to 11-year-olds have been retained at least once. By ages 15 to 17, retention rates for black and Hispanic students are 40 to 50 percent, compared with 35 percent for white students.

Retention rates in some metropolitan schools are even higher. In Baltimore, for instance, a nine-year study shows that 41 percent of white students and 56 percent of black students were retained by grade three, and up to a third of those students were retained again before entering middle school.

Schools often retain students on the basis of a shortsighted belief that repeating a grade will give kids a boost that will last through 12th grade. It's true that retention reaches far into students' futures, but often the long-term effects are devastating. Jimerson's studies show that students who are retained once are 40 to 50 percent more likely to drop out than promoted students. Retaining students twice doubles their chances of dropping out, raising the risk to 90 percent.

Retention is a *predictor* of dropping out, not a *cause*, he says. Achievement, behavior, and home and school environments also factor into the equation. Still, retained students run a high risk of developing problems with self-esteem, social and emotional adjustment, peer relations, and school engagement—and such problems substantially increase the likelihood of giving up on school.

A Better Plan

But if retention isn't working, neither is promoting students who aren't learning. As Darling-Hammond puts it. "The negative effects of retention should not become an argument for social promotion."

The solution, say Richard Allington and Sean Walmsley, authors of *No Quick Fix*, requires whole-school reform, beginning with the school's "institutional ethos."

In schools with an adversarial climate (teachers against parents and students), Allington and Walmsley found that two out of three children were retained, assigned to transitional classes, or placed in special education. But schools with a respectful and professional climate retained only 1 or 2 percent of their students.

How can school leaders halt runaway retention? Darling-Hammond recommends four strategies:

1. Teach teachers how to instruct all students according to the ways they learn.
2. Redesign schools to give students more intensive learning opportunities through multiage classes, cross-grade grouping, and block scheduling.
3. Give struggling students support and services as soon as they're needed.
4. Use student assessments to monitor and adjust teaching content and strategies.

For his part, Jimerson suggests "constructive discussions" on prevention and intervention techniques that keep students from failing in the first place. In addition, he recommends:

1. Train school psychologists to be well-informed about retention research and serve as advocates for children as soon as they show problems learning.
2. Promote students' social competence as a counterpart to academic competence.

3. Establish protective factors, such as parent involvement programs and school-community partnerships that offer support to needy children.
4. Sponsor high-quality preschool programs that focus on child development.

These researchers layout a tough mission for schools. But perhaps the toughest job will be confronting and dismantling ungrounded assumptions about retention.

Selected References

Allington, Richard, and Sean Walmsley. *No Quick Fix*. New York: Teachers College Press/International Reading Association, 1995.

Anderson, Beckie. "Retention in the Early Grades: A Review of the Research." Learning Disabilities Online, Winter 1998. . . .

Darling-Hammond, Linda "Alternatives to Grade Retention." *The School Administrator Web Edition*, August 1998. . . .

Hauser, Robert, and others. "Race-Ethnicity, Social Background, and Grade Retention." Paper presented at the Laboratory for Student Success at Temple University, October 2000.

Jimerson, Shane. "A Synthesis of Grade Retention Research: Looking Backward and Moving Forward." *The California School Psychologist*, 2001. . . .

Jimerson, Shane, and others. "Grade Retention: Achievement and Mental Health Outcomes." National Association of School Psychologists, July 2002. . . .

Jimerson, Shane, and others. "Winning the Battle and Losing the War: Examining the Relation between Grade Retention and Dropping out of High School." *Psychology in the Schools*, 2002. . . .

Malone, Gwendolyn, and Philip Bowser. "Debate: Can Retention Be Good for a Student" *NEA Today*, 1998. . . .

Shepard, Lorrie and Mary Smith. *Flunking Grades: Research and Policies on Retention*. London: Folmer Press, 1989.

What, Ms. Crabapple Again?

To kids, the only thing worse than repeating a grade is the thought of losing a parent or going blind. That's the finding of a classic 1980 study on childhood stress. Academics tend to agree, and not only because of the stigma. Research shows that repeaters rarely catch up with classmates and are more likely to drop out of school.

Tell that to the Yee family in Kailua, Hawaii. Last year, Luana Yee's daughter Keolamau struggled as the youngest, smallest first grader at Punahou School. Academically, the 6-year-old held her own, but older classmates drowned her out of discussions and teased her. Keolamau's self-confidence crumbled; she began squinting excessively and urinating nearly 15 times a day. When academic and medical testing ruled out a mental or physical disability, Keolamau's parents requested that she repeat first grade. Keolamau accepted the decision reluctantly—at first. But as she finishes her second year of first grade, her physical symptoms have disappeared and she is a well-liked class leader.

Like the Yees, a significant number of parents are using voluntary retention as a way to aid a failing or flailing child. The trend has not been quantified, but based on anecdotal evidence, repeating a grade is clearly becoming part of a parent's arsenal of school-management tools.

What about studies showing that retention doesn't work? Educators argue that retention is not a solution for academic failure. Neither, according to research, is "social promotion"—pushing kids through school to buoy their self-esteem. But the cautionary studies don't distinguish between students forced to repeat a failed grade and those who voluntarily stay back for developmental reasons, and children who voluntarily repeat a year. The latter group is but a tiny minority among the nearly 20 percent of students held back each year. In addition, classrooms can have a wide age spread to the clear disadvantage of the young and the immature. Nearly 1 in 10 children enters kindergarten a year late, redshirted by parents hoping to hone an academic or athletic edge. As a result, a child with a birth date right before the cutoff for entering kindergarten may be a year or more younger than at least a few classmates.

There is no sure-fire way for parents to know if a child will benefit from being retained, but certain signs may help identify a potential candidate. Children who feel developmentally out of sync with classmates might form

From Joellen Perry, "What, Ms. Crabapple Again?" *U.S. News & World Report* (May 24, 1999).

close bonds with youngsters in the grade below. Second or third graders with late-blooming fine motor skills, lacking the hand-eye coordination to deftly maneuver a pencil, can struggle with writing. Other students may find the school day physically exhausting. Kindergarten wiped out Christine Morris by midweek. "By Wednesday," recalls her mother, Valerie, "she just didn't want to go." Christine attended a yearlong transitional program before first grade; today she is in the top 5 percent of her junior class at a metropolitan Atlanta high school.

Gift of time   Preparing children to repeat a year is perhaps the most dreaded hurdle of the retention process. Presenting the second year as a "gift of extra time" helps kids view repeating as an issue of development, rather than personal failure, educators say. "Reassure children that some people just need more time than others," counsels Lilian Katz, professor of education at the University of Illinois. Parents of children born prematurely, and of those who are chronologically young for their grade, or physically small for their age, have tangible reference points for why children might need more time. Luana Yee recalls that her daughter Keolamau, born three months prematurely and two months before her school's entrance cutoff date, accepted the logic that her brain and body simply needed time to catch up to those of her older classmates.

Some parents do a public-to-private switch that eliminates the debate over retention. While public schools often have a fall birth date as a cutoff for entering a grade, private schools frequently use a spring date. If the retention is engineered within the confines of the public school system, parents might consider switching teachers, or even schools, to lessen the stigma or allay fears that the coming school year will be a boring rehash of the past year.

If a child remains "unalterably opposed" to repeating, though, counsels Garry Walz, professor emeritus of education at the University of Michigan, a second year in the same grade could be disastrous. Parents should consider promotion coupled with intensive tutoring or counseling to give the child both self-confidence and strategies for succeeding in school.

Other difficulties   The results of retention should be clear after just a few months, says James Uphoff, professor emeritus of education at Wright State University in Dayton, Ohio. A child whose academic or social struggles intensify or plateau in the repeated year likely has issues that run deeper than developmental immaturity. Perhaps the problem is an undiagnosed learning disability or a chemical imbalance triggering, for instance, depression or an attention disorder. But a midyear switch up a grade is not recommended, says Uphoff, as the child will have missed months of crucial material. He suggests that students remain in the repeated grade while parents and school staff continue to seek the true source of the difficulties.

But when a child simply needs extra time, retention can work wonders. In 1993, third grade overwhelmed Sterling Collins-Hill of Oakland, Maine. Tough math problems could reduce him to tears. Even sloppily tied shoelaces might upset him. "He was hanging on by his fingernails," says his father, Steven Collins. Sterling recalls feeling "pretty alone" returning to third grade while his friends went ahead, but the feeling faded fast. Now 15 and a freshman on the honor roll and lacrosse team at Messalonskee High School, he says, "When I look back, I see it turned out for the best."

The Risks of Retention

Academics point out that there are many reasons not to retain, starting with the stigma. Slow learners or students with attention disorders will encounter the same difficulties the second time around, while enduring the shame of repeating a grade. Educators also warn of a lingering, powerful "should be" syndrome. Years later, many retained children believe their rightful place is in the grade above.

For these reasons, most experts advise parents to consider retention as a last resort. They recommend testing first to rule out learning disabilities, then exploring other interventions—tutoring, therapy, or medication, for example—suggested by teachers, administrators, school counselors, and doctors.

POSTSCRIPT

Is Grade Retention Harmful to Children?

Challenge Questions

1. Is retention the answer for children who are not able to keep up with their peers?
2. Would another year in the same grade yield more success the second time around?
3. What are the short-term and long-term academic effects of retention?
4. Would it be better to promote the child, in what many call a social promotion, just so the student can be with his or her peers?
5. What memories do you have of people you knew who were retained?
6. What are some alternatives to retention?

Suggested Reading

Bergin, D. A., Osburn, V. L., & Cryan, J. R. (1996). Influence of child independence, gender, and birth date on kindergarten teachers' recommendations for retention. *Journal of Research in Childhood Education*, 10, 152–159.

Grant, J., & Johnson, B. (1997). Preventing retention in an era of high standards. *Principal*, 76, 20–22.

Jimerson, S., Carlson, E., Rotert, M., Egeland, B., & Sroufe, L. A. (1997). A prospective, longitudinal study of the correlates and consequences of early grade retention. *Journal of School Psychology*, 35, 3–25.

Mantizcopoulos, P. Y. (1997). Do certain groups of children profit from early retention? A follow-up study of kindergartners with attention problems. *Psychology in the Schools*, 34(2), 115–127.

Mohr, K. (1997), Seth's story: The tale of a self-determined retention. *Childhood Education*, 74(1), 36–38.

Owings, W. A., & Magliaro, S. (1998). Grade retention: A history of failure. *Educational Leadership*, 56 (1), 86–88.

Peel, B. (1997). Research vs. practice: Kindergarten retention and student readiness for first grade. *Reading Improvement*, 34, 146–153.

Potter, L. (1996). Examining the negative effects of retention in our schools. *Education*, 117(2), 268–270.

Shepard, L., & Smith, M. (1990). Synthesis of research on grade retention. *Educational Leadership*, 47(8), 84–88.

ISSUE 9

Should Educators Address Students' Unhealthy Lifestyle Choices?

YES: **Sheree Crute**, from "Growing Pains," *NEA Today* (March 2005)

NO: **Michael I. Loewy**, from "Suggestions for Working with Fat Children in Schools," *Professional School Counseling* (April 1998)

ISSUE SUMMARY

YES: Sheree Crute, a freelance health and medical writer and editor, reports on what many call an epidemic in overweight children and the urgent need to have children make immediate changes in their eating habits and activity choices. Crute provides statistics on the possible causes for the increase in overweight and obese children.

NO: Michael I. Loewy is a professor in the Department of Counseling and School Psychology at San Diego State University, San Diego, California. He contends we need to stop being obsessed with weight and instead focus on having children feel positive about their body.

One of the first statistics reported on a newborn, after the sex, is the weight. Throughout his or her life, weight could play a role in everything from clothes worn and participation in leisure-time activities to employment opportunities as an adult. Images of perfect bodies and statistics about healthy lifestyles related to food choices and levels of activity are found daily in the media. Educators are unsure of their role related to education about healthy lifestyle versus forming a positive attitude about body types.

Body image starts forming at an early age and is developed over many years as the child interacts with peers, participates in activities, and views media images. It can be found in the increasing numbers of second-graders on diets and the 70 percent of high school girls wanting to lose weight. Overweight boys can find solace when they are compared to large, but very successful, professional athletes. Girls, on the other hand, don't have positive overweight role models, which may be one reason more girls than boys are diagnosed with eating disorders.

With over 9 million children overweight or obese the issue is front and center every day in America's classrooms. Overweight is defined as weighing more than is recommended for a given height, and obesity is defined as having excess body fat over 20 percent of recommended weight for height, age, and sex. The numbers of overweight children are increasing, especially for our youngest children with 10 percent of two- to five-year-olds overweight. The numbers of overweight children from six to eleven has doubled in the past 20 years and it is reported that 25 percent of all children are obese.

Teachers are finding standard school desks and chairs are too small for overweight students and physical education instructors report less participation of overweight children in class activities. The exact responsibility of educators related to teaching about healthy food choices and appropriate levels of physical activity has caused many to shy away from the topic completely and revert to just feeling sorry for students who sit alone at the snack or lunch table or are left on the sideline while other students participate in games on the playground.

School administrators and school board members are addressing the issue of healthy lifestyles by enacting policies prohibiting the sale of carbonated beverages in schools, banning trans fats from school cafeterias, and offering healthy food choices. Administrators facing financial challenges are forgoing the large incentives from soft drink companies to sell carbonated beverages. School districts are recognizing the need to work with families to have conversations about healthy lifestyle choices and acceptance of body types begin at home and continue throughout school.

An individual's race, disability, marital status, or sex are not allowed to be considered in job situations; yet an individual's weight is used as a discriminatory factor. Overweight children and adults want their body type accepted by others without attempts to ridicule or change. Those overweight encourage teachers to help children accept their body type and learn to be proud of who they are as a person.

In the following two selections Sheree Crute reports on what many call an epidemic in overweight children and the urgent need to have children make immediate changes in their eating habits and activity choices.

In "Suggestions for Working with Fat Children in Schools," Michael Loewy contends we need to stop being obsessed with weight and instead focus on having children feel positive about their body.

POINT

- Being overweight can be a barrier to student learning.
- Families are responsible for children's diets.

- Through education, children can change lifestyle behaviors to become more health conscious.
- Being overweight is a major risk factor for a healthy lifestyle.

- Parents and educators should not let children get overweight.

COUNTERPOINT

- Students of all sizes can learn if in a caring and supportive environment.
- School food service programs are as much to blame as homes and restaurants for serving unhealthy food options.
- Stop trying to change children and instead focus on nurturing all children and accept them as they are.
- A negative self-esteem as a result of perception about body type is more harmful to children.
- Heredity and emotional factors play a key role in an individual's weight and are difficult to change.

YES

Sheree Crute

Growing Pains

Deborah Morris began seeing the telltale signs in her Oakland, California, classroom years ago. "The kids came to school every morning with soda, a bag of Doritos, and a candy bar—that was their breakfast of champions," says this resource specialist for special education students at Fremont's Youth Empowerment High School. A stickler for healthy eating, she knew it was all wrong—and the impact became evident the longer she taught. "Their diet was affecting their energy levels and ability to concentrate"—not to mention their waistlines, she says. Now, Morris is facing this stark reality every day: "Almost one-third of the kids in our school," she says, "are overweight."

Disturbing, yes. But Morris knows her students are not alone. Nationally, some 9 million children are overweight or obese, and the numbers are growing so fast that some health experts are calling it a national crisis.

"Epidemic is absolutely the correct word for what we're seeing," says David Ludwig, M.D., director of the obesity program and the Children's Optimal Weight for Life (OWL) program, at Children's Hospital in Boston, Massachusetts. "In children ages 6 to 19, of all genders and races, we've seen a three-fold increase [since the late 1970s] in the number who are overweight or obese," says Ludwig. And in children 8 to 10 years old, he says, there's been an "extraordinary" increase in type II diabetes—once, but no longer, called adult-onset diabetes.

While the epidemic touches children of all cultures, a disproportionately high number of Hispanic and African-American children are overweight, and now even the youngest of children appear to be at risk. In December 2004, the American Heart Association reported 10 percent of American children ages 2 to 5 are also overweight, a 7 percent increase since 1994.

The situation has become so dire that across the country, school districts like Oakland and educators like Morris are taking matters into their own hands—banning junk food, starting new fitness and nutrition programs, and saying no to high-fat cafeteria fare. What they understand: the unhealthier students are, the more vulnerable their chances for academic success.

A High Price

"If kids aren't healthy, their learning suffers," says Jerry Newberry, executive director of the NEA Health Information Network, "and research shows that

From *NEA TODAY*, March 2005, pp. 22–24, 26–31. Copyright © 2005 by National Education Association. Reprinted by permission.

128

sedentary kids who eat high-sugar, high-fat meals may have poorer cognitive skills, higher anxiety levels, and problems with hyperactivity."

Not surprisingly, unhealthy kids also miss school more. Action for Healthy Kids, a group of 40 health and education agencies (including NEA) that partners with schools in every state, recently reported that "tens of millions of dollars" are lost because of absenteeism caused by inactivity and poor nutrition.

Then there are the emotional downsides: overweight children who can't play sports, who can barely fit in their chairs at school, who can't get through a school day without being bullied and ostracized by their peers. "The psychological risks of obesity can be as great as the physical risks," warns Ted Feinberg, assistant executive director of the National Association of School Psychologists. "Low self-esteem and depression can undermine children's learning, behavior, and well-being."

A Cultural Shift

Unfortunately, say health experts, the current crisis only portends graver days ahead. "The rate of obesity in childhood predicts adult obesity," explains David Katz, M.D., a nutrition expert and director of the Yale Prevention Research Center at the Yale School of Medicine. And that, he says, can spell a lifetime of ill-health—in the form of heart disease, high blood pressure, diabetes, and other diseases. Indeed, some experts estimate that children in the nation's youngest generation may be the first to have shorter lives than their parents.

It all begs the question: How did it come to this? Experts say there are several factors—and for educators, many are obvious. "Genetics may play a role for some," says Ludwig, "but there's the lowering of physical activity and the loosening of family ties. Fewer kids are sitting down to a family dinner with a parental supervisor."

With working parents busier than ever, he says, fast, processed, and prepackaged foods have become the gastronomical delight of choice—but at a price. A 15-year study by Ludwig and Mark Perreira at the Minnesota School of Public Health found that fast food increases the risk of obesity and type II diabetes and that people who chowed down on fast food two or three times a week gained 10 more pounds than those who ate fast food less than once a week.

Over the years, schools have been hard-pressed to help. Cash-strapped, many have cut vending deals with soda companies and brought high-fat, high-revenue fare into cafeterias to balance shaky budgets. Even where schools have tried to buck the trend, it's a financial struggle. It still costs a school district more than twice as much to provide a high-fiber, low-fat, veggie burger than it does to provide a higher-fat, fiber-free hamburger, according to a report by the Physicians Committee for Responsible Medicine, a Washington-based group that promotes healthy eating. That's because the federal government subsidizes hamburger and other meats but not alternatives like soy, or in the case of milk, calcium-rich, non-dairy beverages.

Kicked to the Curb: Exercise

It hasn't helped that kids are getting less physical activity—at home and at school. Video games have replaced the playground as kids' favorite pastime, and more than 50 percent of the nation's schools have eliminated physical education classes altogether. Once a regular part of nearly every school day, P.E. programs have become rare to nonexistent in many parts or the country, even though researchers have found that just one additional hour of P.E. per week is significant in addressing obesity for 5- and 6-year-olds, especially girls.

Kids in Trouble

- **8 percent** of elementary schools, 6.4 percent of middle schools, and 5.8 percent of high schools have daily physical education.*
- **60 percent** of children ages 5 to 10 had at least one risk factor for cardiovascular disease.**
- **9 million** children over age 6 are obese. Another 15 percent are borderline and at risk.***
- **13 percent** of white children ages 12 to 19 are overweight, 21 percent of African-American children ages 12 to 19 are overweight, and 23 percent of Mexican-American adolescents are overweight.***

---

*National Association of State Boards of Education.

**2004 data from the Institute of Medicine report, *Childhood Obesity: Health in the Balance, 2004.*

***The National Center for Health Statistics.

Bruce Hanson, a physical education teacher at Fairview Elementary School in Westminster, Colorado, says he's seeing the results of inactivity every day: many of his kids can't run a minute around the track without stopping. "They could do it a decade ago but today's kids can't handle it," he says. "They're struggling."

Compounding matters: the so-called No Child Left Behind law, which has put pressure on schools to spend less time on P.E. and more time preparing students for make-or-break standardized tests. Educators say the shift is ironic given the link between fitness and academic success. A University of Miami survey, for example, found that fit high school seniors had higher grade point averages and less depression than their peers.

Junk-free Heaven

Luckily, many educators are getting the message, and have begun doing battle to reclaim the health of their students. Several years ago, Deborah Morris' Oakland school district, along with Berkeley and San Francisco, began tackling the problem with innovative—some would say even revolutionary—ideas.

Declaring its schools junk-free zones, Oakland banned the sale of sugary drinks and candy in vending machines. It even outlawed that staple of every school fundraiser, the half-pound chocolate bar. Not everyone was ecstatic about the changes, officials there note. The students wanted their soda, candy, ice cream, and cookies back. And the sports coaches and art teachers worried about losing the vending machine funds that paid for P.E. and art classes.

But at Morris' school, Freemont High, the staff got on board. Teachers chatted with students about the connection between their health and their diets and modeled healthy eating habits. Now, Morris says, "When I eat my tofu salad in front of the kids, they ask 'What's that?' They're really fascinated. It gives them something to think about. I've even heard kids say—gasp!—they're sick of McDonald's."

A Discipline Fix?

But change comes slowly, Morris found, and when she realized some of her students were still clinging to their old habits, she decided to open The School Store. "I started out with my own money and stocked it with water, low-fat granola bars, and other healthy snacks." She charges 50 cents for snacks but extends, credit to any kid who needs it. "I give away a lot of food," she concedes, but notes that the store turns enough of a profit for her to buy more food, help fund the school's art club, and buy other books and supplies.

Still, the real benefit has been in the classroom.

"Since we've opened the store and given the kids healthy nutrition breaks in the morning and afternoon, we have fewer discipline issues," says principal and former teacher Maureen Benson. "Teacher referrals for problems are down 10 to 12 percent." The connection may not be coincidental. A Brooklyn College study found that children with behavior problems, especially attention deficit/hyperactivity disorder, could be sensitive to certain foods, including refined sugars and food additives that cause them to act out even more.

And so, at Oakland's Roosevelt Middle School, students trained as peer health educators talk to their classmates about topics like fat and sugar in a cool

---

Fit for Life

"Even small steps in the classroom can contribute to healthier students and school environments," says Alicia Moag-Stahlberg, executive director of Action for Healthy Kids. She offers these **tips for teachers:**

BE ROLE MODELS FOR HEALTHY HABITS. Talk to students about the physical activities they enjoy, such as walking or riding a bike. Be aware of foods and drinks you consume in front of students. Are you sending healthy messages?

USE HEALTHY INCENTIVES. Use a walk or playtime outside as a reward for individual students or an entire class. Take a break for movement (stretching, running, or jumping in place) to rekindle energy on a stressful day.

BRING BRAIN FOOD. Incorporate healthy snacks (for example, veggie sticks, whole grain crackers and cheese, fruit, low-sugar cereal) into test-day regimens. And party smart by replacing soft drinks with flavored milk or 100 percent juice at pizza parties. Bring carrot and celery sticks with dip to offer on the side.

STAGE A CHALLENGE. Have students track their activity and meals daily, challenging each other to increase the number of minutes they are active.

STAY COMMITTED. Helping students develop healthy habits now will benefit them for life. Research shows that healthy habits translate into more success in the classroom right now: better attendance, better behavior, and overall better performance.

way. "They talk about things teenagers can relate to," says Samantha Blackburn, school nurse and director of the school-based health center, "like making healthier choices at fast food restaurants or the corner convenience store."

Across the bridge in the San Francisco school district, a tough "no more empty calories" policy sets maximum levels for sugar, fat, and saturated fat and allows only snacks with a minimum of 5 percent of eight essential nutrients in the schools' vending machines and à la carte cafeteria selections. Suspensions have dropped 50 percent since the policy was implemented, officials say.

In the nearby Berkeley Unified School District, the nutrition policy includes organic gardens, salad bars, and cooking classes. And as part of a pilot program that will be the first of its kind in the country, the district will revise its curriculum to integrate lessons on farming, cooking, and nutrition into core subject areas.

In other parts of the country, some school districts are taking the controversial step of including students' body mass index (a measure of body fat) on their report cards—an effort to involve parents. . . .

Food for Thought

Food service workers often find themselves in the eye of the storm when the alarm is sounded for better cafeteria fare, but often their hands are tied by district food policies. Rest easy. "Food service personnel have more power than they might think," says Amy Joy Lanou, nutrition director for the Physicians Committee for Responsible Medicine. She offers some hands-on **tips for cafeteria workers:**

ENCOURAGE CHILDREN to choose the healthiest options—fresh fruit rather than gelatin and carrots rather than french fries.

SPEAK POSITIVELY about healthy food choices such as whole grains, bean dishes, fruits, and vegetables and avoid glamorizing less healthful choices such as ice cream, fried foods, sweets, and meaty, cheesy dishes.

WHEN YOU CAN, cook with less oil. When possible bake or grill rather than fry or pan-fry. Serve fresh foods rather than canned, breaded, or sweetened. Test recipes that have lower fat, sugar, and salt content.

KEEP YOUR SALAD BAR well-stocked, attractive, and encourage kids to choose meals from it.

Michael I. Loewy

 **NO**

Suggestions for Working with Fat Children in the Schools

Sandy McBrayer, the 1995 national teacher of the year, tells of visiting an elementary school that was proud of its ethnic diversity and the integration of many racial groups in the school's social milieu. The principal walked her to the newly built multipurpose "cafetorium" and ceremoniously pulled open the doors to reveal children of all colors and ethnicities eating, talking, and laughing together.

As she entered, a contrasting scene near the door caught her eye. Separated from the rest of the student body were two obese children sitting at a table eating their lunch in silence, staring directly ahead. They were not laughing. They were not talking. They were just bringing their forks to their mouths and down again, trying to be inconspicuous and to finish quickly. This day they were too slow.

As other children finished their meals and exited the cafetorium, they threw their uneaten food at the two children. The fat children appeared oblivious as food hit their table and slid to the floor or hit their hands and fell onto their plates. They just kept eating and staring directly ahead. They behaved as if they did not know what was happening or that there was no reason to react because it was a normal occurrence—and nobody was going to intervene on their behalf.

The ridicule and torment of fat children by others is a story told again and again by fat children and by adults who were fat children. What effect does such ridicule—often accepted and endorsed by society—have on its young victims? How can educators and counselors intervene to support fat children? The purposes of this article are to create awareness of the issues faced by fat children in the schools and to provide strategies for meeting their social and emotional needs. The article begins with a review of literature on prejudice toward fat kids and its detrimental effects on their lives. Prevailing efforts to control children's eating habits and weight are then critiqued. The article concludes with suggestions that teachers and counselors can use to enhance all students' self-esteem and good health through self-acceptance and embracing diversity of body type.

From *Professional School Counseling*, April 1998, pp. 18–22. Copyright © 1998 by American School Counselor Association—ASCA. Reprinted by permission.

Prejudice and Its Effects

A review of the literature reveals that fat children are the target of prejudice, ridicule, and disgust by both their peers and the adults in their lives such as teachers, counselors, and parents. This is no small problem in schools since, according to the Centers for Disease Control (1994), 21% of people aged 12 to 19 years are overweight. As early as preschool age, children have accepted the stereotypes about and developed prejudice against fat people. Given the opportunity to play with fat or thin dolls, all children, even those who could correctly identify that the fat dolls looked more like them, preferred to play with thin dolls (Dyrenforth, Freeman & Wooley, 1978; Rothblum, 1992). Given pictures of children who were in a wheelchair, missing a limb, on crutches, facially disfigured, or obese, most children said they would least like to play with the fat child (Rothblum, 1993).

By elementary school, children are describing fat children as lazy, sloppy, dirty, stupid, and ugly (Levine, 1987). Fat children are less likely than other children to receive "best friend" ratings from their classmates (Rothblum, 1992). When shown silhouettes of fat and thin males and females, 9-year-old children rated the fat figures as having significantly fewer friends, as less liked by their parents, doing less well at school, being less content with their appearance, and as wanting to be thinner (Hill & Silver, 1995). A group of boys ages 6 to 10 rated fat children as most likely to be teased (Staffieri, 1967).

By adolescence, the subjective importance of physical appearance is particularly great among girls (Wadden & Stunkard, 1987). A longitudinal study of 1,000 high school students revealed that more than 50% of girls wanted smaller hips, thighs, and/or waists. Sixty-three percent of 9th-grade and 70% of 10th and 12th-grade girls wanted to lose weight (Huenemann, Shapiro, Hampton, & Mitchell, 1966). Canning and Mayer (1966) found lower acceptance rates into prestigious colleges for obese high school students compared to normal-weight students, even though the two groups did not differ in high school performance, academic qualifications, or application rates to colleges.

Teachers and counselors are subject to the same stereotypes and biases as parents and children. In a study of more than 200 pre-service and in-service teachers, it was found that for such characteristics as attractiveness, energy level, leadership ability, self-esteem, and the ability to be socially outgoing, obese children are consistently perceived more negatively than average weight children (Schroer, 1985). In a study of 599 Texas education professionals, a picture of an average-sized, teenage girl received higher ratings on scholarship, while the picture of a fat girl was rated highest on risk for personal problems and recommendation for psychological referral (Quinn, 1987). A study of 52 mental health professionals indicated that counselors have the same biases as the general public; they tend to stereotype fat people negatively and thin people positively (Loewy, 1994/1995).

Parents have a strong impact on children's self-image and esteem. Crandall (1991) found that girls were less likely to receive support from their parents for college education if they were fatter than average. Controlling for income, ethnicity, family size, and number of children attending college did not change the results. Upon further examination it was found that the reluctance to pay for heavier daughters' education is a matter of parental choice, not ability (Crandall, 1995).

According to Ronald Kleinman (1994), M.D., chief of the Pediatric Gastroenterology and Nutrition Unit, Massachusetts General Hospital, and associate professor of Pediatrics at Harvard Medical School:

> Many parents are unnecessarily concerned with their children's weight. They badger their high-achieving, happy kids for generally unfounded reasons. We need to communicate to parents [and other responsible adults] that a fat child does not have any more medical problems than other children the same age. Over the long term, these kids do quite well (p. 70).

Parents and educators often project their dissatisfaction with their own bodies on the children over whom they have influence. It cannot be stressed enough that adults must deal with their own negative body image and fear, loathing, and disgust of fat before they can stop teaching children to hate their bodies.

This cultural obsession with thinness and the stigma attached to obesity take a toll on the mental health of obese people. Although they show no greater disturbance on conventional measures of psychopathology, many fat people suffer from poor body image (Wadden & Stunkard, 1987). Fat people characteristically view their own bodies as grotesque and loathsome and believe that others view them with hostility and contempt (Stunkard & Mendelson, 1967). Since poor body image is an internalization of parental and peer criticism (Wadden & Stunkard, 1987), only a cultural shift in parental concern regarding obesity, and acceptance of fat children by peers and adults, can alleviate the resulting internalized self hatred.

Critique of Common Strategies

Several perceptions encourage well-meaning parents and teachers to be concerned with childhood obesity. First, it is commonly believed that obesity is a health hazard. Second, it is generally accepted that fat children grow into fat adults (Stunkard & Berkowitz, 1990). Third, no one wants one's child to be the target of oppression and discrimination. Fourth, we know that being overweight during adolescence has important social and economic consequences. For example, overweight adolescents and young adults remain single more often and have lower household incomes in early adult life than their non-overweight counterparts, regardless of their socioeconomic origins and aptitude-test scores (Gortmaker, Must, Perrin, Sobol, & Dietz, 1993).

As a result of these perceptions, many parents subject their overweight children to commonly prescribed strategies for weight loss, including caloric restriction, behavior modification, and commercial weight-loss programs. Most attempts at weight loss will result in short-term success (Bennett & Gurin, 1982). Yet current research demonstrates that for many children, such methods result in increased frustration and lower self-esteem.

What is not generally accepted or understood is that efforts to control or limit the food intake of children and adults through diets (or the euphemistic term, "lifestyle change") do not work in the long term. There is overwhelming evidence that obesity is primarily genetically determined (Price et al., 1990; Stunkard et al., 1986; Stunkard, Harris, Pedersen, & McClearn, 1990). In a study of same-sex, monozygotic and dizygotic twin pairs, estimated heritability of obesity was 88% (Borjeson, 1976). Price, Cadoret, Stunkard, and Troughton (1987) found a strong relationship between body mass index (BMI) of adoptees and their biological parents, whereas no relationship was found in the BMI of adoptees and their adoptive parents.

Research has shown that metabolic rate has a familial pattern. The metabolic rate of the 4-year-old children of obese parents was 10% lower than the rate of the 4-year-old children of nonobese parents (Griffiths & Payne, 1976). At 3 months of age, the BMIs of infants of lean and obese mothers were indistinguishable. However, the energy expenditure was more than 20% lower in the infants who later became overweight (Roberts, Savage, Coward, Chew, & Lucas, 1988). The findings of Ravussin et al. (1988), who studied energy expenditure among Southwest American Indians, indicate that, absent of differences in caloric intake between obese and lean children, the children of obese parents became obese later in life.

Fat children, as a group, do not eat more than average size children. Withholding or restricting someone else's food is the same as starving that person; and it feels the same—torturous. When one withholds or restricts one's own food intake, we call it a diet. In reality, it is self-starvation. In fact, in their effort to lose weight or maintain weight loss, many people eat less or feed their children less than prisoners who are subjected to starvation as a form of torture.

Several reviews of behavioral and dietary treatments of obesity have revealed the dismal failure of these methods (Bennett & Gurin, 1982; Garner & Wooley, 1991; Wadden, Stunkard, & Liebschutz, 1988). Although almost all weight-loss programs appear to demonstrate moderate success in promoting at least some short-term weight loss, there is virtually no evidence that clinically significant weight loss can be maintained over the long term by the vast majority of people.

The most successful weight loss programs studied have incorporated behavior management techniques, exercise, social influence, longer treatment duration, and continued therapeutic contact after the end of formal treatment. These strategies have been found to promote greater weight loss and improved maintenance during the first 18 months after treatment. However, over and over again the initial encouraging findings have eroded with time (Garner & Wooley, 1991). Based on long-term follow-up studies it is evident that weight is gradually regained over time, with many participants weighing more than they did when they started.

For example, in a 5-year, follow-up study, Stalonas, Perri, and Kerzner (1984) reported that the average participant had gained 11.9 pounds since the end of treatment, making him or her 1.49 pounds heavier than when treatment began. Researchers studying 114 men and 38 women who had successfully completed a 15-week behavioral weight loss program reported that less than 3% maintained their posttreatment weight loss after 4 years (Kramer, Jeffery, Forster, & Snell, 1989). Weight rebound seems to be almost as reliable a consequence of treatment as initial weight loss (Garner & Wooley, 1991).

Not only do these methods fail to produce lasting results, but there is strong evidence that continued attempts at dieting result in increased biological resistance to weight loss. Young people are often advised to lose weight now because it gets harder to lose as one gets older. However, the earlier one starts this cycle of losing and regaining, the heavier one will be as an adult.

Teachers, parents, and other caregivers who lack understanding of the variations in growth patterns that occur during childhood may do more harm than good. Poor role modeling and attempts to limit children's food intake are ineffective and can even be harmful in dealing with children's body size issues. (Ikeda & Naworski, 1992, p. x) The more pressure we put on children and adolescents to conform to the ideal body type, the more we perpetuate the myth that this ideal can be achieved by everyone. Furthermore, we are sending children the message that they are damaged and need to change in order to be acceptable.

In reality, it seems that body weight is regulated by physiological mechanisms that oppose the displacement of weight caused by either over or underfeeding. This concept, known as *set point,* accounts for the data from human and animal studies showing that there is a remarkable stability and homeostasis of body weight over time (Bennett & Gurin, 1982). Set point accounts not only for the difficulty people have in losing weight, but also for the extreme difficulty some people have in gaining and maintaining gained weight.

In essence, as body weight is reduced, the resting metabolic rate is also reduced. Therefore, it takes increased restriction of caloric intake to maintain any weight loss. Furthermore, when food intake is normalized after a period of food restriction, there is a tendency for energy to be redeposited preferentially as body fat (Dulloo & Girardier, 1990).

In sum, a small percentage of children will slim down as they physically mature, and for some very few, weight loss programs may have long-term benefits. However, the vast majority of children and adolescents who attempt to artificially control their weight will experience failure and frustration, which leads to weight gain and lower self-esteem.

Recommendations for Support

Counselors, psychologists, physicians, and other experts suggest that a strategy more beneficial to the social and emotional well being of fat children would be to accept them at any size and support them in building self-esteem and positive body image (Ikeda & Naworski, 1992; Kleinman, 1994; Loewy, 1994/1995). I believe this is possible by adopting an attitude of admiration, appreciation, and nurturance of fat children.

Fat children should be admired because being fat in our society takes tremendous strength. For fat children to face teasing, rejection, and discrimination on a daily basis and still thrive takes great strength of character. It is amazing that so many fat children survive adolescence, given the hatred and meanness directed at them. Indeed, some do not make it, as evidenced by the 15-year-old high school student in Alabama who shot and killed himself in the classroom last year because he could no longer take the torment.

To appreciate fat children is to value the diversity of people and to see fat children as a valid part of that diversity. When we think of diversity in the classroom, we usually think in terms of race, ethnicity, and gender. Some of us may include physical ability and sexual orientation in our view of the diverse classroom. Fat children often have a unique perspective on life and society. It is important to validate that perspective and appreciate the richness that different perspectives bring to the classroom.

Fat children need to be nurtured, not changed. To nurture a fat child one must see that child as indispensable in our society. If we see fat children as indispensable, we will view them with genuine affection and delight. We will then be willing to advocate for them, love them, and nurture them just as they are.

Following are some specific suggestions that we can apply on a daily basis to make sure fat children have a nurturing—not hostile—educational environment:

1. Educational materials and instruction should be free of derogatory representations of fat people. Avoid using materials with text or illustrations that endorse negative stereotypes about fat people such as lazy, sloppy, stupid, mean, or eating too much. Material should not depict fat people whose problems are solved because or when they lose weight. To the contrary, there should be positive images of fat people of all ages, genders, and ethnicity in educational materials. As educators, we must demand that the publishers of educational material provide us with unbiased tools. (See box Classroom and Library Materials Supportive of Fat Children.)

2. It is important to help all children learn to critically analyze stereotypes presented by the media. Educators and parents must point out to children when the media are endorsing negative stereotypes about fat people. The diet industry pumps billions of dollars into media advertising each year. The media risks losing those dollars if they do not promote the unrealistic and harmful thin ideal. It is our job to educate children about the financial incentive for television and magazines to perpetuate these myths.

3. Teachers, school counselors, and other school employees should be sensitive to students who are using derogatory remarks about size as a weapon against other children. Neither physical violence nor harassing language against fat children should be tolerated. The word fat is a neutral word. It is not derogatory and should not be used as such. Use ugly and hurtful incidents as an educable moment, just as one would with racial slurs or sexist remarks. We all know when words are used to hurt, and such action should not be tolerated.

4. However, it should not be assumed that the word fat is always used to hurt. We can take the sting out of the word by using it in a positive way. Look it up in the dictionary. Readers will be surprised to find so many positive connotations. We can begin to teach this to

our children by example. Fat can be paired with words like attractive, strong, proud, healthy, and loving. Beautiful and healthy bodies come in all shapes: fat, thin, and muscular.

5. Encourage healthy eating and exercise for health's sake, not to reach some ideal goal. Children of all sizes should be encouraged to eat a healthy and varied diet. They can be taught to trust their own satiety signals. As long as a healthy variety of foods are available, children will eat as much as their bodies require. We should not coax children to eat more or less or deny them foods that others get to eat because they are a different size.

6. Movement should be fun and desirable for all children. As long as physical activity is competition based, some will succeed and others will fail, often the fat kid. All children should be encouraged and given the opportunity to be as physically active as they desire to be. One of the obstacles to physical activity for big kids is the unavailability of physical education uniforms in their size. Insist that the school provide all students with uniforms that fit. It is not the child's responsibility to fit their bodies into the uniforms.

7. Not only should the child's physical education uniform fit the child, but so should the rest of the child's environment. Make sure that the child has clothes that fit. Have resources available for parents who do not know where to find large-size children's clothing. (JC Penney's catalogue, 800-222-6161, has clothes that will fit most fat children.) Ensure that classroom desks comfortably accommodate all children. Not all children can fit into the desks provided in most classrooms. It is hard to learn when one is squeezed into a desk that is causing physical pain. Be aware of the seating in the lunch room, auditorium, bathroom, and other school environments. Tables and sturdy armless chairs work best for very large people.

8. Perhaps most important is for educators, counselors, and parents to confront our own prejudice and disgust toward fat people. Working through our fear of fat will allow us to accept and love our own bodies just as they are. Too many of us hate our bodies and are constantly concerned with our shapes and eating habits. Hearing adult role models complain about their bodies, discuss the success of their latest diet, or refuse to eat a special treat in the class because they are watching their weight or worried about getting bigger is an indication to children that large bodies are not acceptable. Stop supporting people in their weight-loss efforts. Stop complimenting people about the success of their latest diet. These actions are neither supportive nor complimentary. It is inappropriate to comment on another's body unless asked. It is important for children to have role models who affirm that their self-worth is not based on their weight. We cannot be effective, positive role models if we have not confronted our own fat phobia.

Conclusion

All children deserve love and respect regardless of the size of their bodies. By teaching children the value of respecting fat people and enforcing that value, we are teaching fat children to love and respect themselves. We are also teaching average-size children the importance of embracing and including in their lives people who may be different from them. As school personnel, we must advocate for all youth, especially those who need our advocacy most.

We do not need to single out fat children or ask them directly if they are having a problem being fat. Chances are, they are having a problem but will not trust anyone to be on their side. We need to speak to all children about our appreciation for fat children. In this way, fat kids will know that we are approachable, and trust will begin to build. At the same time, average-size kids are learning an important lesson about the value of people outside the dominant culture.

The first step in confronting any prejudice is always the most difficult. We must take a hard look at our own prejudices and confront them directly. It is very difficult to rid ourselves of long-held beliefs and stereotypes. However, by becoming more aware of them, we can stop ourselves from acting on those prejudices.

Our goal as child educators and advocates is to produce healthy children who feel good about themselves. Let us take the focus off size, food, and eating, and put it back on health and self-esteem. Our children can only benefit.

References

Bennett, W. I., & Gurin, J. (1982). *The dieter's dilemma*. New York: Basic Books.

Borjeson, M. (1976). The etiology of obesity in children. *Acta Pediatrica Scandinavia, 65,* 279–287.

Canning, H., & Mayer, J. (1966). Obesity: Its possible effects on college admissions. *New England Journal of Medicine, 275,* 1172–1174.

Centers for Disease Control. (1994). Prevalence of overweight among adolescents United States 1988–1991. *Morbidity and Mortality Weekly Report, 43,* 818–821.

Crandall, C. S. (1991). Do heavyweight students have more difficulty paying for college? *Personality and Social Psychology Bulletin, 17,* 606–611.

Crandall, C. S. (1995). Do parents discriminate against their heavyweight daughters? *Personality, and Social Psychology Bulletin, 21,* 724–735.

Dulloo, A., & Girardier, L. (1990). Adaptive changes in energy expenditure during refeeding following low-calorie intake: Evidence for a specific metabolic component favoring fat storage. *American Journal of Clinical Nutrition, 52,* 415–420.

Dyrenforth, S. R., Freeman, D., & Wooley, S. C. (1978). *Self esteem, body type preference, and sociometric ratings of peers in pre-school children.* Unpublished manuscript, Department of Psychiatry, University of Cincinnati College of Medicine.

Garner, D. M., & Wooley, S. C. (1991). Confronting the failure of behavioral and dietary treatments for obesity. *Clinical Psychology Review, 11,* 729–780.

Gortmaker, S. L., Must, A. V., Perrin, J. M., Sobol, A. M., & Dietz, W. H. (1993). Social and economic consequences of overweight in adolescence and young adulthood. *New England Journal of Medicine, 14,* 1008–1012.

Griffiths, M., & Payne, P. R. (1976). Energy expenditure in small children of obese and nonobese parents. *Nature, 26,* 698–700.

Hill, A. J., & Silver, E. K. (1995). Fat, friendless and unhealthy: 9-year old children's perceptions of body shape stereotypes. *International Journal of Obesity, 19,* 423–430.

Huenemann, R. C, Shapiro, L. R., Hampton, M. C., & Mitchell, B. W. (1966). A longitudinal study of gross body composition and body conformation and their association with food and activity in a teenage population. *American Journal of Clinical Nutrition, 18,* 325–338.

Ikeda, J., & Naworski, P. (1992). *Am I fat? Helping young children accept differences in body size.* Santa Cruz: ETR Associates.

Kleinman, R. (1994). Today's kids are no worse for weight. *Education Digest, 59*(8), 69–71.

Kramer, E. M., Jeffery, R. W., Forster, J. L., & Snell, M. K. (1989). Long-term follow up of behavioral treatment for obesity: Patterns of weight regain among men and women. *International Journal of Obesity, 13,* 123–136.

Levine, M. P. (1987). *How schools can help combat student eating disorders: Anorexia nervosa and bulimia.* Washington DC: National Education Association of the United States.

Loewy, M. I. (1995). Size bias by mental health professionals: Use of the illusory correlation paradigm (Doctoral dissertation, University of California, Santa Barbara, 1994). *Dissertation Abstracts International, 56/03,* 1704-B.

Price, R. A., Cadoret, R. J., Stunkard, A. J., & Troughton, E. (1987). Genetic contributions to human fatness: An adoption study. *American Journal of Psychiatry, 144,* 1003–1008.

Price, R. A., Stunkard, A. J., Ness, R., Wadden, T., Heshka, S., Kanders, B., & Cormillot, A. (1990). Childhood onset (age<10) obesity has high familial risk. *International Journal of Obesity, 14,* 185–196.

Quinn, B. H. (1987). Attitudinal ratings of educators toward normal weight, overweight, and obese teenage girls. (Doctoral dissertation, Texas Women's University, 1987). *Dissertation Abstracts International, 48/10-B,* 3156-B.

Ravussin, E., Lillioja, S., Knowler, W. C., Christen, L., Freymond, D., Abbott, W. G. H., Boyce, V., Howard, B. V., & Bogardus, C. (1988). Reduced rate of energy expenditure as a risk factor for body-weight gain. *New England Journal of Medicine, 318,* 467–472.

Roberts, S. B., Savage, B. A., Coward, W. A., Chew, B., & Lucas, A. (1988). Energy expenditure and intake in infants born to lean and overweight mothers. *New England Journal of Medicine, 318,* 464–466.

Rothblum, E. D. (1992). The stigma of women's weight: Social and economic realities. *Feminism & Psychology, 2*(1). Newbury Park: Sage Publications.

Rothblum, E. D. (1993). I'll die for the revolution but don't ask me not to diet: Feminism and the continuing stigmatization of obesity. In S. Wooley, M. Katzman, & P. Fallon (Eds.), *Feminist perspectives on eating disorders,* (pp. 53–76). New York: Guilford Press.

Schroer, N. A. (1985). Perceptions of in-service teachers and pre-service teachers toward obese and normal weight children. (Doctoral dissertation, Texas A&M University, 1985). *Dissertation Abstracts International, 47/01-B,* 434-B.

Staffieri, J. R. (1967). A study of social stereotype of body image in children. *Journal of Personal and Social Psychology, 7,* 101–104.

Stalonas, P. M., Perri, M. G., & Kerzner, A. B. (1984). Do behavioral treatments of obesity last? A five year follow-up investigation. *Addictive Behaviors, 9,* 175–183.

Stimson, K. W. (Ed.). (1996). *Size positive resources for children and adolescents.* (Available from Largesse: The Network for Size Esteem, PO Box 9404, New Haven, CT 06534-0404. . . .

Stunkard, A. J., & Berkowitz, R. I. (1990). Treatment of obesity in children. *Journal of the American Medical Association, 264,* 2550–2551.

Stunkard, A. J., Harris, J. R., Pedersen, N. L., & McClearn, G. E. (1990). The body-mass index of twins who have been reared apart. *New England Journal of Medicine, 322,* 1483–1487.

Stunkard, A. J., & Mendelson, M. (1967). Obesity and the body image: Characteristics of disturbances in the body image of some obese persons. *American Journal of Psychiatry, 123,* 1296–1300.

Stunkard, A. J., Sorenson, T. I. A., Hanis, C., Teasdale, T. W., Chakraborty, R., Schull, W. J., & Schulsinger, E (1986). An adoption study of human obesity. *New England Journal of Medicine, 314,* 193–198.

Wadden, T. A., & Stunkard, A. J. (1987). Psychopathology and obesity. *Annals of the New York Academy of Sciences, 499,* 55–65.

Wadden, T. A., Stunkard, A. J., & Liebschutz, J. (1988). Three year follow up of the treatment of obesity by very low calorie diet, behavior therapy, and their combination. *Journal of Consulting and Clinical Psychology, 56,* 925–928.

POSTSCRIPT

Should Educators Address Students' Unhealthy Lifestyle Choices?

Challenge Questions

1. What are some of the basic needs that must be met before children can learn?
2. How can school personnel work to meet those needs?
3. How can teachers best address bullying related to size and weight?
4. What images of body types do young children see?

Suggested Reading

Aronson, D. (1997). No laughing matter: Young people who are over-weight can face a lifetime of discrimination. *Teaching Tolerance*, 6 (2), 21–23.

Christie, K. (2005). Setting food and exercise standards for kids. *Phi Delta Kappan*, 87, 5–7.

Cooper, P. (2005). A coordinated school health plan. *Educational Leadership*, 63, 32–36.

Froschl, M., Sprung, B., & Mullin-Rindler, N. (1998). *A teacher's guide on teasing and bullying for use with students in grades K–3*. New York: Educational Equity Concepts.

Ikeda, J. (1990). *If my child is too fat, what should I do about it?* Berkeley, CA: California University Cooperative Extension Service.

Jalongo, M. R. (1999). Matters of size: Obesity as a diversity issue in the field of early childhood. *Early Childhood Education Journal*, 27 (2), 95–103.

Ogden, C. L., Trooiano, R. P., Briefel, R. R., Kuczmarski, K. M., and Johnson C. L. (1997). Prevalence of overweight among preschool children in the United States, 1971–1994. *Pediatrics*, 99 (4), 1–7.

U.S. Department of Health and Human Services, Centers for Disease Control and Prevention. (2000). *CDC's guidelines for school health programs promoting lifelong healthy eating* (ED 460-103).

ISSUE 10

Are English Language Learners Best Served in an Immersion Language Model?

YES: Christine Rossell, from "Teaching English Through English," *Educational Leadership* (December 2004/January 2005)

NO: Jill Wu, from "A View from the Classroom," *Educational Leadership* (December 2004/January 2005)

ISSUE SUMMARY

YES: Christine Rossell, a professor of political science at Boston University in Massachusetts, found English language immersion programs best for students learning English.

NO: Jill Wu, a graduate student at the University of Colorado, supports programs that first teach students basic skills in their native language prior to teaching them English.

The issue of English language learners (ELL) in schools is more complicated than simply what is the best way for children to learn English when it is not their primary language. Some of the subparts to this complicated issue are:

1. Can ELL continue to master the content expected of them for their grade while they are also learning English and continuing to progress at speaking their primary language?
2. For how long should students receive instruction in either their primary language or in English in a setting separate from other students?
3. At what pace and in what type of classroom and with what type of teacher will children best acquire proficiency and grade level content?
4. How is proficiency in English defined?
5. How will the students' families be involved in the process?

There are endless questions that surround this issue. The topic becomes even more complicated when a school has English language learners from many different countries and from families with different English skills. According to 2000 U.S. Census data, 18.4 percent of children older than five speak a language other than English and 6.6 percent of those students have difficulty speaking English.

English language immersion programs, sometimes called Structured or Sheltered English Immersion (SEI), are classrooms taught solely in English for instruction in all subject areas. Students with a variety of English skills are taught in English, only usually at a slower pace. The most successful of these programs have smaller class size, with eight students the most commonly recommended class size. English language learners are sometimes placed in a classroom together if the numbers warrant a separate classroom. In school settings where there are not enough students for a separate ELL classroom, students are placed in a regular grade-level classroom. Immersion programs may also include English as a second language (ESL) classes or other services in a pull-out format.

Students new to a school who all speak the same non-English language are often placed in bilingual classrooms. These classes are most prominent in areas of the country where there are numbers of people speaking a language and the size of the group warrants a special classroom with a dedicated bilingual teacher who speaks English and the children's primary language. Spanish is the most commonly found bilingual setting in the United States. The instruction in bilingual classrooms gradually progresses from speaking the first language only to English over the course of several years. The goal is to eventually move students to the regular all English-speaking classrooms.

There are very limited studies of this issue in controlled settings. The programs studied have for the most part been existing classrooms and varied in many ways including location, the size of the ELL population, the income level of the families, and the resources available to support the new students.

In the following selections chosen for this issue Christine Rossell supports sheltered English immersion programs for children learning English. Jill Wu finds it is very challenging for students to learn subject matter as well as English simultaneously. She advocates for children to be in bilingual programs while they are learning content, especially reading, prior to moving into regular English-only classrooms.

POINT

- Immersion language programs allow students to learn English in a supportive environment.
- Immersion language programs help students move to regular classrooms after a year in a sheltered English immersion classroom.
- Approximately one half of ELL students are in English immersion classrooms.
- Students' scores in math and reading increased when they were removed from bilingual classrooms.

COUNTERPOINT

- Students may miss some content if it is not in their primary language.
- Students need more than a year of English instruction before they are ready for a regular classroom.
- Bilingual programs are still popular in many areas.
- Students in bilingual classrooms are able to ask questions about content in their primary language.

YES

Christine Rossell

Teaching English Through English

During the last 25 years, U.S. public schools have developed six different instructional approaches to support students learning English as a second language:

- *Structured immersion*—or *sheltered English immersion*—provides instruction almost entirely in English, but in a self-contained classroom consisting only of English language learners (ELLs).
- *ESL pullout* programs supplement regular, mainstream classroom instruction with instruction in a small-group setting outside the mainstream classroom aimed at developing English language skills.
- The *sink-or-swim* approach provides mainstream classroom instruction with no special help or scaffolding.
- *Transitional bilingual education* initially delivers instruction and develops students' literacy in the students' native language but puts a priority on developing students' English language skills.
- *Two-way bilingual education* (also known as *two-way immersion*) is designed to develop fluency in both the students' first language and a second language; teachers deliver instruction in both languages to classes consisting of both native English speakers and speakers of another language (most commonly Spanish).
- *Bilingual maintenance* programs generally consist of non-English speakers and, like two-way bilingual education programs, place equal emphasis on maintaining students' primary language and developing their English proficiency.

Notice the order in which I have listed these programs. According to my own research and my reading of others' research, this list proceeds from the most effective to the least effective approaches in terms of helping students become proficient at speaking, writing, and learning in English. This research indicates that in general, the most effective way for students to learn a second language and to learn subject matter in that second language is to learn *in* the second language—as in the first three programs—rather than learn in the students' native language, as in the last three programs (see Baker & de Kanter, 1981, 1983; Genesee, 1976, 1987; Gersten, Baker, & Otterstedt, 1998; Lambert & Tucker, 1972; Rossell, 2002, 2003, 2004; Rossell & Baker, 1996a, 1996b).

I am aware that this conclusion is highly controversial. In the past, bilingual education has enjoyed enormous support among many researchers and educators. But the apparently successful implementation of sheltered English immersion in California, Arizona, and Massachusetts may change the common perception.

When Is "Bilingual" Not Bilingual?

Despite the common belief in the effectiveness of bilingual education, my observations and my analyses of data from state department of education Web sites indicate that only a minority of immigrant children in the United States are enrolled in bilingual programs in any form. In California, only about 29 percent of English language learners were enrolled in bilingual education in 1998, the year in which this approach was voted out as the default assignment for such students. Approximately 71 percent of California's English language learners participated in programs that used English as the dominant language of instruction—most of them in sink-or-swim or near-sink-or-swim situations (Rossell, 2002). Similarly, in Arizona in 2000 and in Massachusetts in 2002—the years in which these states mandated a switch to structured immersion—only 40 percent of English language learners at most were enrolled in bilingual education (Arizona Department of Education, 2004; Massachusetts Department of Education, personal communications, 2004).

Indeed, despite the lack of intellectual support for the sink-or-swim method, it seems to be the dominant approach to educating English language learners throughout the United States—perhaps because educators believe that the benefits of integration and language role modeling by fluent English speakers outweigh the disadvantages of students' initial noncomprehension of the curriculum, or perhaps because it is simply easier.

Another approach, sheltered English immersion (also called structured immersion), similarly predominates in more schools than one would assume from looking at statistical reports. A sheltered English immersion classroom differs from a mainstream, sink-or-swim classroom because the class is composed entirely of English language learners and is taught by a teacher trained in second-language acquisition techniques. The teacher conducts instruction almost exclusively in English, but at a pace students can keep up with.

Many programs throughout the United States identified as "bilingual education" can be more accurately described as sheltered English immersion because they are actually taught completely or almost completely in English. For example, during the two decades I have spent observing bilingual classrooms across the country, I have observed many Chinese "bilingual education" programs—but have never seen one taught in Chinese. Teachers in these classes believe that Chinese reading and writing skills are not transferable to English because the two written languages are so different. Teachers seldom even teach orally in Chinese because spoken Chinese encompasses many dialects, and it is rare that all students in a classroom speak the same one.

In fact, after observing numerous Russian, Vietnamese, Chinese, Khmer, Haitian, Cape Verdean, Spanish, Japanese, Hebrew, and Portuguese "bilingual education" classrooms and talking with their teachers, I have concluded that schools almost never offer bilingual education that fits the theoretical model, in which students learn to read and write initially as well as learn subject matter in their native language. The sole exception is in languages that use a Roman alphabet. If the primary language doesn't use the Roman alphabet, teachers perceive the transferability of reading skills as too small to justify the effort.

These practical reasons—ignored in the theoretical literature—account for the fact that in the United States, non-Spanish "bilingual education" programs are actually sheltered English immersion programs. This also means that statistics on bilingual education enrollment consistently overestimate the number of students who actually receive native language instruction.

Sheltered English immersion also travels under other labels, such as *content ESL* and, at the secondary level, *sheltered subjects*. I once visited a school in New York City that, according to the board of education Web site, had a Bengali bilingual program. When I arrived at the classroom door, however, I found a sign that said *Content ESL*. In this classroom, Bengali-speaking English language learners were taught by a teacher who was fluent in Bengali. Students who had little English fluency spent most of the day in this class learning English and learning subjects through English. The teacher taught no Bengali at all; he claimed that he did not even use it orally to clarify or explain. These students were actually in a sheltered English immersion class that tailored instruction to their needs.

At the secondary level, many students receive sheltered English immersion in the form of *sheltered subject* classes (such as sheltered algebra and sheltered U.S. history). Sheltered subject classes have been around for decades, but they often go unnoticed because the language of instruction is English and the curriculum is similar to that of a mainstream classroom. In a sheltered algebra class, for example, the teacher would teach algebra in English to a class composed solely of English language learners.

Although the literature specifies a number of ways in which sheltered English immersion classes differ from mainstream classes (Echevarria & Graves, 2002; Haver, 2002), I have observed many of these classrooms and have seen little difference between the two. Teachers in sheltered English immersion classes seem to speak no more slowly than those in mainstream classes do, and they do not use more visual props. The teachers tell me that the major difference is that they cover less material and use more repetition. Some of these sheltered classes are called "bilingual" if all the students have the same country of origin, but only Spanish speakers in secondary bilingual classes ever hear more than a minimal amount of their native language used in instruction.

Lessons from California

Although sheltered English immersion has been around for decades under various labels, it became the default assignment for English language learners by state mandate in California in 1998, in Arizona in 2000, and in Massachusetts in 2002. Research and observation in California yield some valuable insights about the ways in which teachers implement instruction for their English language learners and the relative effects of the bilingual education and sheltered immersion approaches.

Responding to the Research

In response to the California law (Proposition 227), schools developed two structured immersion models that differ by the ethnic composition of the classrooms and by the amount of sheltering provided. Programs serving English language learners from a variety of linguistic backgrounds provide instruction and conversation in English only. Programs serving exclusively Spanish-speaking students, however, often use Spanish to explain or clarify concepts.

Because the school districts do not reliably distinguish between these different models, evaluating the academic impact of sheltered English immersion is difficult, if not impossible. We can, however, compare with some confidence the academic outcomes of keeping or dismantling transitional bilingual education because the California, Arizona, and Massachusetts laws all allow a school to offer bilingual education to students if the students' parents sign a waiver and if the school can justify using this approach on pedagogical or psychological grounds.

Approximately 10 percent of English language learners in California are still enrolled in bilingual education. My analyses (Rossell, 2002, 2003) show that after controlling for student and school characteristics, the average score increased by six points in reading and by three points in mathematics in schools that eliminated bilingual education. This is a .56 standard deviation gain in reading (a large effect) and a .21 standard deviation gain in math (a small effect). Bali (2001) found that taking Pasadena students out of bilingual education increased their reading scores by two points (.18 standard deviation) and their math scores by one-half point (.03 standard deviation) compared with ELLs who had always been in English immersion classes.

Testing rates are another measure of the effectiveness of alternative programs because a lower testing rate means that the school considers more students unready to take the test. My research (Rossell, 2002) found that schools with more than 240 ELLs enrolled in bilingual education had lower testing rates in reading and math than did those with no ELLs enrolled in bilingual education, after controlling for student and school characteristics. Bali (2000) found that prior to 1998, the rate of testing for English language learners enrolled in bilingual education was 50 percent, compared with 89 percent for those enrolled in English language classrooms. Los Angeles Unified School District found that after five years of participating in the program, only 61 percent of ELLs enrolled in bilingual education were tested, compared with 97 percent of those in English language classrooms (1998).

Unfortunately, there is no scientific research that directly compares the success rates of English language learners in a sheltered English immersion classroom with the success rates of ELLs in a mainstream classroom with ESL pullout. Nevertheless, I believe that at least for the first year, a sheltered classroom is a better environment for most English language learners than a mainstream classroom. My interviews in California indicated that teachers who formerly taught bilingual education but who now teach in sheltered English immersion programs believe the same.

After the first year, however, most English language learners are probably better off in a mainstream classroom with some extra help. Most of them will know English well enough that a sheltered English immersion classroom would slow them down unnecessarily, particularly when new students without any English skills enter the class. The one-year time limit ("not normally intended to exceed one year") is part of the sheltered English immersion laws in California, Arizona, and Massachusetts and is a provision my fellow researcher and I recommended in our writing (Rossell & Baker, 1996a, 1996b).

Teacher Implementation

My observations of almost 200 classrooms in California from spring 1999 through fall 2004 identified several themes that provide insight into the effectiveness of sheltered English immersion in the state.

Former Spanish bilingual education teachers were impressed by how quickly and eagerly their Spanish-speaking English language learners in kindergarten and 1st grade learned to speak and read in English and how proud the students were of this accomplishment. The teachers were also surprised at how much they themselves liked teaching in sheltered English immersion classrooms, although they had never worked harder (see Haager, Gersten, Baker, & Graves, 2001).

When I asked the teachers in 2001 whether they would ever want to return to teaching in a bilingual education classroom, all of them said no (Rossell, 2002). Bilingual education was a good theory, they claimed, but in practice it had too many problems. They attributed these problems to a lack of materials, teachers, and support.

Interestingly, Chinese bilingual teachers saw Proposition 227 as a non-event. Because they had already been teaching in English, nothing had changed for them except that Proposition 227 justified their practices.

Besides moving most English language learners into sheltered immersion programs, Proposition 227 also changed the way Spanish bilingual education programs operated. The teachers with whom I spoke in the remaining Spanish bilingual education classes in spring 1999 said that they were using more English for instruction than they had in the past. They gave two reasons. First, the Proposition 227 vote expressed California's citizens' preference for a greater emphasis on English, and teachers believed that they should respond to the wishes of the people they served. Second, because the law greatly reduced the demand for bilingual classes, there was no guarantee in any specific school that a bilingual class could be assembled for the next grade in the following year. Accordingly, teachers felt the need to prepare their students for the possibility that they could soon be in an English language classroom. Thus, the task of comparing the effectiveness of bilingual education with that of sheltered immersion is further complicated by the fact that the former is less bilingual than it has been in the past.

Instruction in the Target Language Is Key

Despite the strong support for sheltered English immersion that now exists among educators, policymakers, and the public in California, only about half of all English language learners are actually enrolled in such programs. Most of the other half are in mainstream classrooms, and about 10 percent are still in bilingual education, albeit with more use of English than before.

My classroom observations in California indicate that most educators base decisions about how to teach not just on state mandates but also on their assessment of what their English language learners need, the numbers of English language learners in their classes, and their own philosophy. Most teachers with whom I have talked believe that teaching students in English is more important than ensuring that the students are in a sheltered environment (although the state law requires both).

In general, a mainstream classroom that provides extra help seems to be more practical for many schools, and any academic harm caused by such classrooms is apparently not significant enough to be noticeable to most educators or to offset the relative ease with which schools can form such classrooms. After all, most immigrant children in the United States and throughout the world are in mainstream classrooms, and most of them seem to swim, not sink.

References

Arizona Department of Education. (2004). . . .

Baker, K., & de Kanter, A. (1981). *The effectiveness of bilingual education programs: A review of the literature*. Washington, DC: U.S. Department of Education.

Baker, K., & de Kanter, A. (1983). Federal policy and the effectiveness of bilingual education. In K. Baker & A. de Kanter (Eds.), *Bilingual education*. Lexington, MA: D. C. Heath & Company.

Bali, V. (2000). *"Sink or swim": What happened to California's bilingual students after Proposition 227?* Unpublished paper, California Institute of Technology, Pasadena, CA.

Bali, V. (2001). "Sink or swim": What happened to California's bilingual students after Proposition 227? *State Politics and Policy Quarterly, 1*(3), 295–317.

Echevarria, J., & Graves, A. (2002). *Sheltered content instruction: Teaching English-language learners with diverse abilities* (2nd ed.). Upper Saddle River, NJ: Pearson Education.

Genesee, F. (1976). The suitability of immersion programs for all children. *Canadian Modern Language Review, 32*(5), 494–515.

Genesee, F. (1987). *Learning through two languages: Studies of immersion and bilingual education*. Rowley, MA: Newbury House.

Gersten, R., Baker, S., & Otterstedt, J. (1998). *Further analysis of "A meta-analysis of the effectiveness of bilingual education," by J. P. Greene (1998)*. Unpublished report. Eugene, OR: Eugene Research Institute.

Haager, D., Gersten, R., Baker, S., & Graves, A. (2001, February). *An observational study of first grade reading instruction for English language learners using sheltered immersion methodology*. Paper presented at the Pacific Coast Research Conference, La Jolla, California.

Haver, J. (2002). *Structured English immersion: A step-by-step guide for K-6 teachers and administrators*. Thousand Oaks, CA: Corwin.

Lambert, W. E., & Tucker, G. R. (1972). *Bilingual education of children: The St. Lambert experience*. Rowley, MA: Newbury House.

Los Angeles Unified School District. (1998). *Clarification of English academic testing results for Spanish-speaking LEP fifth graders*. Unpublished report.

Rossell, C. H. (2002). *Dismantling bilingual education, implementing English immersion: The California initiative*. Unpublished report. Boston: Boston University.

Rossell, C. H. (2003). The near end of bilingual education. *Education Next, 3*(4), 44–52.

Rossell, C. H. (2004). *Meta-murkiness: A critique of meta-analyses of bilingual education*. Unpublished paper. Boston: Boston University.

Rossell, C. H., & Baker, K. (1996a). *Bilingual education in Massachusetts: The emperor has no clothes*. Boston: Pioneer Institute.

Rossell, C. H., & Baker, K. (1996b). The educational effectiveness of bilingual education. *Research in the Teaching of English, 30*(1), 7–74.

 **NO**

A View from the Classroom

As the number of English language learners in U.S. schools increases, experts continue to seek ways to effectively educate these students. Those who argue for English immersion and for other practices emphasizing English-only instruction believe that this approach avoids segregating language learners, promotes assimilation of immigrants, and helps students learn English as quickly as possible. Bilingual education, they feel, divides society and limits Latinos' opportunities. These supporters cite evidence of ineffective bilingual programs and stories of immigrant children who have succeeded in immersion programs (Chavez, 2000; Duignan, n.d.).

Many second-language acquisition experts and others counter that immersion programs have not been proven effective. They believe that bilingual education programs, which provide initial instruction in students' first language, are more successful in helping students acquire English (Krashen, 2000; Mora, 2002; Slavin & Cheung, 2004). For example, Crawford (1998) found that students in programs that stressed native language instruction had much larger increases in English reading and math skills than did students in English immersion programs or programs that stressed early transition to English.

My experiences teaching English language learners in three different settings help to explain why bilingual education programs sometimes work and sometimes do not. These experiences demonstrate what advocates on both sides of the issue often fail to realize: that not all bilingual programs are the same; that no program will guarantee success for all students in all settings; and that English language learners often receive confusing and inconsistent instruction whether their program is called bilingual or immersion.

A Dual Language Classroom

My first experience with bilingual education was in a dual language immersion school in Wisconsin. In this setting, native English speakers and native Spanish speakers learned together in the same classroom. Instruction began in Spanish for both English and Spanish speakers. As students acquired a good reading base in Spanish, we gradually incorporated English. By 5th grade, students received half of their instruction in each language.

Unlike transitional bilingual education, which views native language instruction as a means to learn English, dual language programs aim to produce students who are fluent in both languages. According to speech-language experts Roseberry-McKibbin and Brice (2004), studies have shown that English language learners in dual immersion programs have higher academic achievement than do those taught in English immersion programs. By taking an enrichment approach rather than a remedial approach, dual language immersion produces bilingual and biliterate students who can switch effortlessly from one language to the other.

As I worked in this school, I realized why the dual language immersion approach was successful. No one group had the dominant language—the language of power. The native Spanish speakers felt empowered, not only because they acquired literacy and found success in their own language, but also because they were models for the English-speaking students. The English-speaking students also benefited by acquiring a second language at an early age.

In 1st grade, these students were exciting to teach. They spurred one another on. Classroom discourse naturally alternated between English and Spanish, unlike the conversation in many bilingual classrooms where students never speak English except when talking to the teacher.

Socially, this approach had powerful implications. At the beginning of the year, I saw many shy Spanish speakers who congregated together. As I taught these students to read in Spanish, they became more confident in their Spanish literacy skills, but they were still reluctant to use English. Slowly, however, the native Spanish speakers and the native English speakers began to communicate with one another. As students interacted, they learned English and Spanish in meaningful ways, communicating with their peers on the playground and in the classroom. When one of the English speakers had a birthday party at her house, I had the opportunity to see the children interact outside the classroom. I was surprised when Leah, a native Spanish speaker whom I had never heard use English, spoke in fluent English as she communicated with her English-speaking friends at the party.

Bilingual Education Inconsistently Applied

When I left Wisconsin, I was enthusiastic about dual immersion bilingual education and all that it could accomplish. My next school district, in Colorado, had recently adopted a transitional bilingual model in which Spanish-speaking students would acquire literacy in their primary language and then gradually achieve literacy in English.

I took a job as a 1st grade bilingual teacher. Most of my students were Spanish speakers who did not know any English. I was surprised to discover that they had no letter-recognition skills—in fact, no literacy skills at all. I soon figured out that the problem stemmed from their kindergarten experience the year before.

The district-adopted transitional bilingual policy had not yet filtered down from the central office to the school level, so my 1st grade students had not received reading readiness instruction in their primary language. Instead, the school had placed all of the native Spanish speakers in one kindergarten class with an English-speaking teacher who made little effort to make English comprehensible to them. These students spoke Spanish in almost all settings of their lives. But for a few hours each day, they came to school and listened to a lady speak English. The input they received was similar to what we might hear from Charlie Brown's teacher—"wa, wa, wa, wa." Although some of my students had learned their colors and how to say words like *bathroom*, they had no phonemic awareness or letter-recognition skills in either language.

When I tested the students' knowledge of letter-sound correlation, I got another shock. I asked students which words started with the *A* sound and gave them some examples of Spanish words from alphabet posters with corresponding pictures. The students insisted that *manzana* started with an *A* sound, *abeja* started with a *B* sound, *helado* started with an *I* sound, and so on. I was confused. Why couldn't the students hear the beginning sounds of these words?

Then I realized what had happened. *Manzana* means *apple* in English; *abeja* means *bee*; and *helado* means *ice cream*. In kindergarten, the students had memorized the pictures that go with the letters in the English alphabet. They had never learned how to say *apple*, *bee*, or *ice cream* in English; they had translated the words into Spanish. They had never learned to hear the sounds; they had merely learned that the picture of a *manzana* somehow matches the symbol *A*.

Although the students' kindergarten instruction had given them almost no prereading skills, I was eager to teach them to read in Spanish, as directed by the district's new bilingual policy. We spent hours every day working on letter sounds. Simultaneously, I taught other core subjects (math, social studies, and science) in Spanish, gradually incorporating more English and developing the students' oral English skills as we discussed concepts from these subjects.

As the students and I struggled through the first four months, I began to wonder when they would make progress learning to read in any language. Many of them still struggled with blending letters. Eventually, however, it all seemed to click. A few students started to read, and the rest soon followed.

Because Spanish is a completely phonetic language, when students know how to decipher syllables they can decode almost anything. Learning how to read in Spanish empowered my students. After their Spanish literacy skills became more solid and their oral English skills improved, many of them began to read in English. This time, the goal seemed easily attainable because all their reading skills from Spanish transferred to English. This experience confirmed the views of language experts who have found that once we can read in one language, we do not need to learn how to read all over again (August, Calderon, & Carlo, 2001; Krashen, 2000). In addition, my students had the English vocabulary to comprehend what they read; they were delighted when they could sound out *C-O-W* and know what the word meant.

Although this method of teaching was not quite as natural or easy as teaching in the dual language school in Wisconsin, it still worked and gave me many reasons to support transitional bilingual education. If I had taught the students to read in English initially, it would have taken much longer for them to acquire literacy. Because I taught core subjects in Spanish, students could keep up with grade-level content because they could understand what they were learning. Their success learning in one language motivated them to succeed in the second.

Another 1st grade class of English language learners in the school that year had a different experience. After their bilingual teacher left early in the year, they received instruction from a full-time substitute who spoke no Spanish. When my students went on to 2nd grade, their teachers told me that they were much better prepared and spoke and wrote better English than the students who had been taught in an English-only class. My students had acquired English in a natural way, and they had transferred their Spanish reading skills smoothly to English.

Incoherent Programs

Later, I moved to 4th grade at a different school in the same district. I was excited by the change; I wanted to see firsthand how older students were gaining English literacy skills.

To meet the needs of the bilingual students, the school had decided to group the 4th and 5th grade English language learners for reading. Two teachers would teach a group of 4th and 5th graders who were performing on or near grade level, which included many native Spanish speakers who had transitioned to English. Another teacher would teach a group of Spanish-speaking students who had just moved to the United States and were not ready to transition. I would teach the group of students who were just beginning to transition to English literacy. I was excited about teaching these students, assuming that like my 1st graders, they would just need a little push to master learning and reading in English.

Unfortunately, the reality soon became clear. All the students in my reading group were performing far below grade level and lacked many reading skills. They did not have the same motivation that the 1st graders had displayed. How had the bilingual program failed them? Why, by the time they reached 4th grade, were these 30 kids still reading at the 1st grade level or below?

Ineffective Grouping

At first, I thought that the practice of grouping our students by language level for reading instruction sounded wonderful; the students' needs would be similar and I would be able to teach them more effectively. Unfortunately, my group included not just the bilingual students, but all students who came into 4th or 5th grade reading at the 1st grade level or below. This meant that the class contained struggling English readers who spoke Spanish, the school's few Vietnamese and Cambodian students, and many of the special education and emotionally disturbed students.

A class that could have helped students transition into reading in English became the class to dump all the students with "needs." But just because these students struggled to read did not mean that they struggled to read for the same reasons. Effective instruction for the class's English language learners would not necessarily address the needs of other struggling students with different needs.

Even the English language learners in the group had experienced many different instructional environments. Some had attended the same school since kindergarten and had received Spanish language reading instruction through 1st grade, with a transition to English in 2nd grade. Others were new immigrants to the United States. Some had recently moved from other districts or from other schools in the same district that were unable to staff bilingual classes. Because of high mobility rates, some students had switched several times between Spanish language and English language instruction.

Reading Skills and Background Knowledge

Reading involves many complex processes, and learning to read presents extra challenges for second-language learners. August and colleagues (2001, 2003) discovered that English language learners acquire decoding skills easily, but they struggle more than native English speakers in their reading comprehension. By the time these students read to the end of a sentence or a book, they may have no idea what either means. They have a hard time monitoring their comprehension.

My 4th and 5th graders' struggles confirmed August's observations. My students' biggest challenge was their lack of background knowledge and vocabulary. They had no frame of reference to understand the books we studied. I often heard such questions as "What is the ocean?", "What is a zoo?", and "Do we really have mountains near here?" Because many of the students had never left their neighborhoods, a book about life under the sea posed difficulties for them. They not only had to work on their decoding, fluency, and vocabulary, but they also had to comprehend content that was outside their realm of experience.

Second-language acquisition experts say that developing students' first language gives them subject-matter knowledge that enables them to comprehend what they read and hear in English (Krashen, 2000). I found that many of my students had not been given the opportunity to develop skills in any language. Perhaps the students had been transitioned too quickly, before they developed solid reading skills and background knowledge in Spanish, and thus they did not have fully formed skills to transfer over to English. Consequently, they had not experienced success that would motivate them. Instead of creating bilingual students, we had created students who could speak two languages to some degree but who could not read or comprehend academic material in either.

Success in Spite of Frustration

In spite of the barriers that the system had put in their way, many of my students learned and progressed. Hard work and belief in students can accomplish a lot. And a few students far exceeded expectations. What accounted for their success?

Maria and Marcos, two 5th graders in my reading class, had only been in the United States a little more than a year, but they were ready to transition to reading in English. Both progressed to near grade-level proficiency in one year, surpassing other students who had been in the country longer.

One of the reasons Maria and Marcos succeeded was that they had a solid education in their native language. They were fluent readers in Spanish and had strong background knowledge. Researchers have found that the amount of formal schooling a student receives in the first language is the strongest predictor of how that student will perform academically in the second (Thomas & Collier, 2002) and that the most successful English language learners are those who have maintained bilingualism and a strong connection with their family's culture (Rumbaut & Portes, 2001). Marcos and Maria could connect whatever they read about in English with knowledge and concepts that they had learned in Spanish. Thus, they felt successful and motivated.

Experience Supports Research

For English language learners, becoming fluent in English is a challenging process that cannot be accomplished in a single year. Because of accountability pressures, the debate that surrounds bilingual education, and the panic to get students on grade level, schools often push students rapidly into English-only instruction, where they flounder or get labeled as needing special education.

My experience suggests that students acquire a second language most easily when they develop literacy skills and content knowledge in their native language, have opportunities to interact with English-speaking peers, and learn with students of different ability levels. We need to remember that the fastest way is not necessarily the most effective way. When advocates push for English fluency at any cost, they fail to realize that the cost may be students' literacy and academic development.

References

August, D. (2003, February). *Supporting the development of English literacy in English language learners*. Baltimore: Johns Hopkins University. . . .

August, D., Calderon, M., & Carlo, M. (2001, February). *Transfer of skills from Spanish to English: A study of young learners*. Washington, DC: Center for Applied Linguistics. . . .

Chavez, L. (2000, October). Uneducated bilingualism. *Hispanic, 13*(10), 106.

Crawford, J. (1998). *Issues in U.S. language policy: Bilingual education* [Online]. . . .

Duignan, P. (n.d.). *Bilingual education: A critique*. Hoover Essay. Stanford, CA: Hoover Institution.

Krashen, S. (2000). Bilingual education, the acquisition of English, and the retention and loss of Spanish. In A. Roca (Ed.), *Research on Spanish in the U.S.: Linguistic issues and challenges*. Somerville, MA: Casadilla Press.

Mora, J. K. (2002). *Debunking English-only ideology: Bilingual educators are not the enemy* [Online]. . . .

Roseberry-McKibbin, C., & Brice, A. (2004). *Acquiring English as a second language: What's normal, what's not*. Rockville, MD: American Speech-Language-Hearing Association [Online]. . . .

Rumbaut, R. G., & Portes, A. (Eds.). (2001). *Ethnicities: Children of immigrants in America*. Berkeley, CA: University of California Press.

Slavin, R. E., & Cheung, A. (2004, March). How do English language learners learn to read? *Educational Leadership, 61*(6), 52–57.

Thomas, W. P., & Collier, V. P. (2002). *A national study of school effectiveness for language minority students' long-term academic achievement. Final Report Executive Summary*. Santa Cruz, CA: Center for Research on Education, Diversity & Excellence. . . .

POSTSCRIPT

Are English Language Learners Best Served in an Immersion Language Model?

Challenge Questions

1. How did the passage of Proposition 227 affect English language learners in the state of California?

2. What are some of the strengths of an English immersion program?

3. How can teachers involve the families in helping children learn English while continuing to become proficient in their primary language?

Suggested Reading

Coppola, J. (2005). English language learners: Language and literacy development during the preschool years. *The New England Reading Association Journal*, 41(2), 18–23.

Espinosa, L. M. (2005). Curriculum and assessment considerations for young children from culturally, linguistically, and economically diverse backgrounds. *Psychology in the Schools*, 42(8), 203–210.

Glenn, C. L. (2002). One language or two? *Principal*, 82(2), 29–31.

Mora, J. K. (2000). Policy shifts in language-minority education: A mismatch between politics and pedagogy. *The Educational Forum*, 64(3), 204–214.

Senesac, B. V. K. (2002). Two-way bilingual immersion: A portrait of quality schooling. *Bilingual Research Journal*, 26(1), 1–17.

Thomas, W. P., & Collier, V. P. (2003). The multiple benefits of dual language. *Educational Leadership*, 61(2), 61–64.

ISSUE 11

Does Learning to Read Involve More Than Phonics?

YES: Judy Willis, from "The Gully in the 'Brain Glitch' Theory," *Educational Leadership* (February 2007)

NO: National Reading Panel, from "Teaching Children to Read: An Evidence-Based Assessment of the Scientific Research Literature on Reading and Its Implications for Reading Instruction," http://www.nichd.nih.gov/publications/nrp/smallbook.htm (April 13, 2000)

ISSUE SUMMARY

YES: Judy Willis is a board-certified neurologist who specialized in clinical research prior to becoming a classroom teacher. Dr. Willis found that enjoyment and understanding of the reading process is more important than phonics when learning to read.

NO: Members of the National Reading Panel concluded that students need a strong foundation in systematic phonics instruction in kindergarten through sixth grade to be successful readers.

Learning to read has been the cornerstone of education for hundreds of years. One hotly contested debate raging in public schools today centers around the issue of the best way to teach children to read. With the marketing of reading materials and children's books reaching in the billions of dollars in sales, it is clear to see why the battle rages. Reading is a measurable item that can be assessed and used to determine the success of a school system in teaching its pupils to learn. Legislators and administrators can say children will leave third grade knowing how to read, and assess that skill to determine a success rate.

Faculty at colleges that prepare teachers to teach pre-kindergarten through third grade, and teachers and administrators in schools that actually educate those children, are participating in a mad scramble to find the best method of teaching and learning to read. Best has not yet been defined; does it mean fastest, most long lasting, easiest, or less expensive way to teach children to read? What ever it is, the battle rages on and on and shows no sign of easing. There are basically two camps in what has been called by many the reading wars. First, there is the side that supports phonics instruction. Phonics focus on the way letters and sounds correspond to each other and how they are used by a reader to successfully read and spell. Phonics helps beginning readers learn how the twenty-six letters of the English alphabet are linked to sounds, also called phonemes. The philosophy behind the phonics approach to teaching reading is when children learn to blend or segment the sounds in words using the letters, they can learn to read words, any word, in print. Teachers who provide early literacy experiences not solely based on phonics instruction use what has been called by a number of names such as literature-based instruction, whole language, phonics-embedded instruction, and the current name of balanced literacy. When children learn to read in a classroom using balanced literacy instead of phonics only, they are initially exposed to high-quality children's literature by being read to a great deal. They hear books many times, and as they learn letter sounds, they learn to distinguish words in context to make sense of the story. Phonics in a classroom using this approach are presented in what is called incidental phonics instruction. The teacher uses the teachable moment to bring to the students' attention certain components of phonics as they appear in material being read at the time. Proponents of balanced literacy believe if children are exposed to good literature, are interested in and enjoy what they are reading, and have knowledgeable teachers, they will master the technique of reading. In the past twenty-five years, excellent children's books have been published that make the presentation of high-quality, appropriate literature easier than it was a generation ago. The debate rages on.

To examine the issue more closely, two articles have been chosen that represent each side of the teaching debate. First, Dr. Judy Wills in "The Gully in the 'Brain Glitch' Theory" discusses the misinterpretations of neurological research, which have not totally studied the complex process of learning to read. The National Reading Panel released a 35-page Summary Report on the five key areas examined of which phonics was one. The panel concluded that systematic, explicit phonics should be taught to all elementary students. They determined that beginning in kindergarten children who are taught phonics will read more proficiently later in school. Due to the length of the panel's report, only the portion that addressed alphabetics, including phonics, is presented here.

POINT

- Phonics is just one piece of the learning-to-read puzzle.

- Enjoyment of the reading process is critical to learning to read.

- A one-size-fits-all phonics heavy approach to teaching reading is not in the best interest of all students.

- Learning to read is a very complicated process involving a number of complex components.

COUNTERPOINT

- Phonics is the base upon which understanding the reading process is built.

- Learning to read involves more than having fun.

- Phonemic awareness instruction teaches all students to understand how letters are linked to sounds.

- Phonics is a concrete tool that students can use in learning to read.

YES

Judy Willis

The Gully in the "Brain Glitch" Theory

$\mathbf{L}$earning to read is not a natural part of human development. Unlike speech, reading does not follow from observation and imitation of other people (Jacobs, Schall, & Scheibel, 1993) and has no specific regions of the human brain dedicated to it. Reading requires multiple areas of the brain to operate together through intricate networks of neurons; thus, many different brain dysfunctions can interfere with the complex process of learning to access, comprehend, and use information from text. Knowing how interdependent these areas of the brain are, we should hardly be surprised that an estimated 20 to 35 percent of students experience significant reading difficulties (Schneider & Chein, 2003). In fact, it is wonderful that anyone learns to read at all.

Unfortunately, misinterpretations of recent neurological research have ignored the complexity of the cognitive processes involved in learning to read. Some education policymakers have used the conclusions of this research to claim that neuroscience proves the necessity of intensive phonics instruction for students who struggle with reading. This oversimplified interpretation of the cognitive research harms students and schools.

An Oversimplified Picture of the Brain

During more than 20 years of practicing neurology and conducting electron microscope research analyses of the neurophysiology of the cerebral cortex, I have been fascinated by the connections among many parts of the brain that neuroimaging revealed. Since leaving my medical neurology practice to become a classroom teacher, I have felt compelled to respond to research analyses that oversimplify and misinterpret the results of neuroimaging scans.

Unfortunately, federal policymakers are currently using flawed research analyses to advance a narrow approach to reading instruction. When President George W. Bush promoted the Reading First program and introduced Head Start legislation that heavily favored phonics reading instruction, he assured the nation that "scientific" brain research had produced definitive data proving the merits of this approach. To support such claims, phonics advocates often cite research conducted by Shaywitz and colleagues (1998, 2002, 2003)— research that falls far short of the medical scientific model. I have read this

From *Educational Leadership*, February 2007, pp. 68–73. Copyright © 2007 by ASCD. Reprinted by permission. The Association for Supervision and Curriculum Development is a worldwide community of educators advocating sound policies and sharing best practices to achieve the success of each learner. To learn more, visit ASCD at www.ascd.org

research, and I believe that its conclusions are based on flawed studies and misinterpretations of the findings.

Shaywitz and colleagues used functional magnetic resonance imaging (fMRI) to measure differences in the brain activity of normal and dyslexic readers as they performed such tasks as reading a list of rhyming nonsense words. Because the dyslexic readers' brains showed a disruption at the rear area of the brain, where visual and sound identifications are made during reading, the researchers concluded that a "glitch" in the brain circuitry holds the key to reading difficulties.

The major flaw in the brain glitch research was its assumption that subjects were actually *reading* during the fMRI scans. The reading tasks evaluated were not authentic reading. Rather, they were phonics-based sound-and-symbol tasks.

The researchers' interpretations of the fMRI scans considered only one portion of the brain's complex—and still not completely defined—reading network, focusing on a brain region known to be more active during phonics processing. Predictably, this brain region became more metabolically active when the test subjects performed phonics processing activities. Also predictably, when students receive intensive phonics instruction, this region of the brain shows more activity, and the students' performance on tests designed to measure phonics skills improves. But we cannot generalize from these findings that all reading improves when the so-called phonics center becomes more active.

Such a conclusion would be like taking a patient who has suffered permanent right-arm paralysis that has spared, but weakened the right pinky finger and treating the patient by performing intensive physical therapy on that one finger. If the patient moves that finger during an fMRI scan, the brain region with neurons dedicated to movement of the right pinky finger (there is such a place in the left frontal lobe) will show an increase in metabolic activity, use more glucose and oxygen, and light up the colors of the fMRI scan. If the patient receives physical therapy exercising that finger, a subsequent fMRI scan could show that the brain has responded by building more cellular connections around the neurons in that dedicated section. Yet, no improvement would necessarily occur in the movement of any other part of the patient's arm; the therapy would not affect the damaged neurons that control the whole arm.

In the same way, it is faulty science to conclude that reading ability has improved just because phonics-intense instruction has produced changes in phonics-functioning brain regions and improved performance on phonics-weighted post-tests. Nevertheless, researchers have used the brain glitch theory to lump diverse reading differences and learning styles under a single label of phonics impairment. And policymakers have used that label to promote one-size-fits-all, phonics-heavy reading instruction (Coles, 2004). A generation of students is paying the price.

Limitations of Neuroimaging

Functional magnetic resonance imaging and other neuroimaging technologies—which show increased blood flow and blood oxygenation in parts of the brain that are activated during various cognitive tasks—are exciting tools for studying what happens in the human brain as people learn. But it's important that we use caution in drawing conclusions from the results of brain scans. The brain glitch researchers' conclusions reached far beyond the current limitations of neuroimaging.

As an example of one such limitation, the observation that a brain area is metabolically active *during* a reading task does not prove that it is active explicitly in the reading task. . . .

Another problem with current neuroimaging technology is speed. Both fMRI and positron emission tomography (PET) neuroimaging scans show changes in metabolism over seconds, but many parts of the reading process take place during the 20 to 200 milliseconds before the eyes move from one word to the next. To "see" cognitive events occurring that rapidly, such as individual word identification or naming, some research has used time-precise neuro-electric monitoring systems that measure the activation of small clusters of cells (Kail, Hall, & Caskey, 1999). The brain glitch scanning studies did not use such technology and thus relied on the gross metabolic activations of fMRI scans to represent the complex brain activity that occurs as children read.

The Complex Brain

Although the brain glitch theory treats learning to read as an isolated, independent cognitive process, reading is actually a complex process connecting multiple learning and association centers in the brain. Neuroimaging shows that specific sensory inputs (sound, visual images, and so on) are received in the brain lobes specialized to accept them. Any new information en route to its designated lobe passes through a type of alerting system in the limbic system (parts of the temporal lobe, hippocampus, and amygdala). Here, the sensory information is linked to previously learned memory, connecting new data with the prior information and thus forming long-lasting relational memory. After the initial response to the new input, feedback goes back to the medial temporal lobe where the relational memory is sent along neural circuits to long-term memory storage areas. This process both reinforces and expands brain neurodendritic circuits that connect the multiple brain lobes.

Just because fMRI scans during sound-and-symbol phonics activities show activation in one brain center, that does not prove that other brain areas are not equally or more metabolically active during other types of reading tasks or for children with different learning styles. Regardless of which center shows initial activation or even sustained activation, all brain operations are complex and involve communication among multiple lobes. At the minimum, reading stimulates the limbic system, occipital cortex, associational subcortical frontal lobe centers, and medial temporal lobe. Reading instruction that stimulates multiple brain areas is likely to be more successful for different styles of learners and more efficient in facilitating the multicentric, dynamic process of reading.

Combining Science with the Art of Teaching

The implications of neuroimaging for education and learning research are still largely suggestive. Researchers have not yet established a solid link between how the brain learns and how it metabolizes oxygen or glucose. It is premature to claim that any instructional strategies are firmly validated by a solid combination of cognitive studies, neuroimaging, and classroom research. For now, educators must be guided by a combination of the art of teaching and the science of how the brain responds metabolically and electrically to stimuli. Here are some promising areas of research and practice.

The Amygdala—Where Heart Meets Mind

The education literature has included theories about the effects of emotion on language acquisition for decades. Dulay and Burt (1977) and Krashen (1982) proposed that strong positive emotion reinforces learning, whereas excessive levels of stress and anxiety interfere with learning. Educators know from subsequent cognitive psychology studies and firsthand classroom experience that high stress, boredom, confusion, low motivation, and anxiety can hinder students' learning (Christianson, 1992).

Research using neuroimaging and neuroelectrical brain wave monitoring supports the connection between emotion and learning, enabling us to see what happens in the brain during stress (Introini-Collison, Miyazaki, & McGaugh, 1991). The amygdala, part of the limbic system in the temporal lobe, senses threat and becomes overactive, delaying or blocking electrical activity conduction through the higher cognitive centers of the brain. When the amygdala is in the overactive metabolic state associated with stress, the rest of the brain's cortex does not show the usual fMRI or PET scan activation that represents the processing of data (Chugani, 1998; Pawlak, Magarinos, Melchor, McEwen, & Strickland, 2003). New information coming through the sensory intake areas of the brain cannot pass as efficiently through the amygdala's affective filter to gain access to the brain's cognitive processing and memory storage areas, such as the left prefrontal cortex. . . .

This brain research supports educators' firsthand experience, which tells us that superior learning takes place when learning activities are enjoyable and relevant to students' lives, interests, and experiences (Puca & Schmalt, 1999). Teachers recognize the state of anxiety that occurs when students feel alienated from their reading experiences or anxious about their lack of understanding. I witnessed this response when, as a student teacher, I worked in a school district that had implemented time-and-page synchronization of its phonics-heavy reading program (Open Court). All teachers were required to cover material at a mandated pace, so that students at each grade level were on the same page of the program each day. Second graders were brought to tears or outbursts of frustration when they were confused; their requests for help went unheeded as teachers struggled to keep to the timetable. Students were told, "Don't worry. If you don't understand or finish now, you'll be taught this same material in a lesson some time in the future."

Neurochemical, neuroimaging, and neuroelectric research support a learning model in which reading experiences are enjoyable and relevant. The brain research evidence reinforces the need for classrooms to become places where students' imaginations and spirits are embraced when reading time begins.

The Chemistry of Motivation

Research on neurochemistry also supports the benefits of intrinsically reward-ing, positive experiences associated with the learning process. Chemical impulses in the brain enable information to travel across nerve synapses—the gaps between neurons. (Information travels along the nerve cells' branching and communicating sprouts—axons and dendrites—as electrical impulses and is temporarily converted from an electrical impulse into a chemical one to travel across the synapses.) Neurotransmitters, such as dopamine, are brain proteins that are released by the electrical impulse on one side of the synapse and then float across the synaptic gap, carrying the information with them to stimulate the next nerve ending in the pathway.

Neurochemical neuroimaging analyses show that dopamine release increases in response to pleasurable and positive experiences (Brembs, Lorenzetti, Reyes, Baxter, & Byrne, 2002). Early studies suggested that when an individual engages in certain activities (for example, playing, laughing, exercising, being read to, and recognizing personal achievements), the amount of dopamine released by the brain increases. Later studies discovered that neuron circuits going from the limbic system into the frontal lobe and other parts of the cere-brum, rich in dopamine receptors, respond to this dopamine release (Wunderlich, Bell, & Ford, 2005). Follow-up research has also shown increased release of dopamine even when subjects *anticipated* pleasurable states (Nader et al., 2002).

Because dopamine is the neurotransmitter associated with attention, memory, learning, and executive function, it follows that when the brain releases dopamine in expectation of pleasurable experience, this dopamine will be available to increase the processing of new information.

Unfortunately, most phonics-based reading curriculums do not place a priority on providing enjoyable reading materials that induce pleasurable states in the brain, pacing lessons at comfortable speeds, giving students opportunities for self-satisfaction, and acknowledging authentic achievement. The decodable reading books in phonics-heavy reading systems are often overly simplistic, and their language sounds unnatural because of the limitations of phonetically decodable vocabulary. Such books lack personal relevance or interest to many young readers. They do not stimulate a student's intrinsic interest in reading. . . .

Where Are We Now?

The stated goal of much education legislation is for all students to learn to read. The goal of most educators extends beyond that—for students not only to learn the mechanics of reading, but also to develop a love of reading. We can begin to achieve these goals when we teach students to read in nonthreatening, engaging, and effective ways.

Cognitive psychology, affective filter data, and neuroimaging, neuro-electric, and neurochemical evidence do not support an approach that puts phonics first at the expense of intrinsic appeal and significance to the young reader. They do support a phonics-embedded approach that uses literature as a medium through which motivated, engaged students can enjoyably learn reading skills and strategies.

Although valid neurological research offers exciting possibilities and must continue, we should not be fooled by policymakers or program developers who use the term *brain-based learning* in ways that many medical and teaching professionals consider irresponsible. Until there is a direct connection between double-blind, variable-controlled analysis and confirmed results, interpretations of data to "prove" that certain instructional strategies are superior fall into the realm of speculation. As educators, we can only evaluate the research, read objective evaluations by neutral third-party reviewers, and create or use strategies that are compatible with what we know about the brain. Teaching reading is still far from being pure science, and educators need to call on their training and experience as well as consider the findings of neurological research to shape their instruction.

References

Andreasen, N. C., O'Leary, D. S., Paradiso, S., Cizadlo, T., Arndt, S., & Watkins, G. L. (1999). The cerebellum plays a role in conscious episodic memory retrieval. *Human brain mapping, 8*(4), 226–234. Iowa City, IA: Wiley-Liss.

Brembs, B., Lorenzetti, F., Reyes, F., Baxter, D., & Byrne. J. (2002). Operant reward learning in aplysia: Neuronal correlates and mechanisms. *Science, 31,* 1706–1709.

Christianson, S. A. (1992). Emotional stress and memory: A critical review. *Psychological Bulletin, 112*(2), 284–309.

Chugani, H. (1998). Biological basis of emotions: Brain systems and brain development. *Pediatrics, 102,* 1225–1229.

Coles, G. (2004). Danger in the classroom: "Brain glitch" research and learning to read. *Phi Delta Kappan, 85*(5), 344–351.

Dulay, H., & Burt, M. (1977). Remarks on creativity in language acquisition. In M. Burt, H. Dulay, & M. Finocchiaro (Eds.), *Viewpoints on English as a Second Language* (pp. 74–83). New York: Regents.

Friston, K. J., Zarahn, E., Joseph, O., Henson, R. N. A., & Dale, A. (1999). Stochastic designs in event-related fMRI. *NeuroImage, 10*(5), 609–619.

Guthrie, J., Wigfield, A., Barbosa, P., & Perencevich, K. C. (2004). Increasing reading comprehension and engagement through concept-oriented reading instruction. *Journal of Educational Psychology, 96*(3), 403–423.

Introini-Collison, I., Miyazaki, B., & McGaugh, J. (1991). Involvement of the amygdala in the memory-enhancing effects of denbuteral. *Psychopharmacology, 104*(4), 541–544.

Jacobs, B., Schall, M., & Scheibel, A. B. (1993). A quantitative dendritic analysis of Wernicke's area in humans: Gender, hemispheric, and environmental factors. *Journal of Comparative Neurology, 327*(1), 91–111.

Kail, R., Hall, L., & Caskey, B. (1999). Processing speed, exposure to print, and naming speed. *Applied Psycholinguistics, 20,* 303–314.

Krashen, S. (1982). Theory versus practice in language training. In R. W. Blair (Ed.), *Innovative Approaches to Language Teaching* (p. 25). Rowley, MA: Newbury House.

Nader, M. A., Daunais, J. B., Moore, T., Nader, S. H., Moore, R. J., Smith, H. R., et al. (2002). Effects of cocaine self-administration on striatal dopamine systems in rhesus monkeys: Initial and chronic exposure. *Neuropsychopharmacology, 27*(1), 35–46.

Pawlak, R., Magarinos, A. M., Melchor, J., McEwen, B., & Strickland, S. (2003). Tissue plasminogen activator in the amygdala is critical for stress-induced anxiety-like behavior. *Nature Neuroscience, 6*(2), 168–174.

Puca, M., & Schmalt, H. (1999). Task enjoyment: A mediator between achievement motives and performance. *Motivation and Emotion, 23*(1), 15–29.

Schneider, W., & Chein, J. M. (2003). Controlled and automatic processing: Behavior, theory, and biological mechanisms. *Cognitive Science, 27,* 525–559.

Shadmehr, R., & Holcomb, H., (1997). Neural correlates of motor memory consolidation, *Science, 277*(5327), 821.

Shaywitz, S. E. (2003). *Overcoming dyslexia: A new and complete science-based program for reading problems at any level.* New York: Knopf.

Shaywitz, S. E., Shaywitz, B. A., Pugh, K. R., Fulbright, R. K., Constable, R. T., Menci, W. E., et al. (1998). Functional disruption in the organization of the brain for reading in dyslexia. *Proceedings of the National Academy of Sciences, 95,* 2636–2641.

Shaywitz, B. A., Shaywitz, S. E., Pugh, K. R., Mencl, W. E., Fulbright, R. K., Skudlarskie, P., et al. (2002). Disruption of posterior brain systems of reading in children with developmental dyslexia. *Biological Psychiatry, 52,* 101–110.

Sowell, E. R., Peterson, B. S., & Thompson, P. M. (2003). Mapping cortical change across the human life span. *Nature Neuroscience, 6,* 309–315.

Wunderlich, K., Bell, A., & Ford, L. (2005). Improving learning through understanding of brain science research. *Learning Abstracts, 8*(1), 41–43.

Teaching Children to Read

Introduction

Congressional Charge

In 1997, Congress asked the "Director of the National Institute of Child Health and Human Development (NICHD), in consultation with the Secretary of Education, to convene a national panel to assess the status of research-based knowledge, including the effectiveness of various approaches to teaching children to read." This panel was charged with providing a report that "should present the panel's conclusions, an indication of the readiness for application in the classroom of the results of this research, and, if appropriate, a strategy for rapidly disseminating this information to facilitate effective reading instruction in the schools. If found warranted, the panel should also recommend a plan for additional research regarding early reading development and instruction."

Establishment of the National Reading Panel

In response to this Congressional request, the Director of NICHD, in consultation with the Secretary of Education, constituted and charged a National Reading Panel (the NRP or the Panel). The NRP comprised 14 individuals, including (as specified by Congress) "leading scientists in reading research, representatives of colleges of education, reading teachers, educational administrators, and parents." . . .

NRP Approach to Achieving the Objectives of Its Charge and Initial Topic Selection

The charge to the NRP took into account the foundational work of the National Research Council (NRC) Committee on *Preventing Reading Difficulties in Young Children* (Snow, Burns, & Griffin, 1998). The NRC report is a consensus document based on the best judgments of a diverse group of experts in reading research and reading instruction. The NRC Committee identified and summarized research literature relevant to the critical skills, environments, and early developmental

From National Reading Panel, "Teaching Children to Read: An Evidence-Based Assessment of the Scientific Research Literature on Reading and Its Implications for Reading Instruction," A Report of the National Reading Panel, http://www.nichd.nih.gov/publications/nrp/smallbook.htm (April 12, 2000). National Institute of Child Health and Human Development (NIH Publication No. 00-4769). Washington, DC: U.S. Government Printing Office, 2000. References omitted.

interactions that are instrumental in the acquisition of beginning reading skills. The NRC Committee did not specifically address "how" critical reading skills are most effectively taught and what instructional methods, materials, and approaches are most beneficial for students of varying abilities.

In order to build upon and expand the work of the NRC Committee, the NRP first developed an objective research review methodology. The Panel then applied this methodology to undertake comprehensive, formal, evidence-based analyses of the experimental and quasi-experimental research literature relevant to a set of selected topics judged to be of central importance in teaching children to read. An examination of a variety of public databases by Panel staff revealed that approximately 100,000 research studies on reading have been published since 1966, with perhaps another 15,000 appearing before that time. Obviously, it was not possible for a panel of volunteers to examine critically this entire body of research literature. Selection of prioritized topics was necessitated by the large amount of published reading research literature relevant to the Panel's charge to determine the effectiveness of reading instructional methods and approaches. A screening process was therefore essential.

The Panel's initial screening task involved selection of the set of topics to be addressed. Recognizing that this selection would require the use of informed judgment, the Panel chose to begin its work by broadening its understanding of reading issues through a thorough analysis of the findings of the NRC report, *Preventing Reading Difficulties in Young Children* (Snow, Burns, & Griffin, 1998). Early in its deliberations the Panel made a tentative decision to establish subgroups of its members and to assign to each of them one of the major topic areas designated by the NRC Committee as central to learning to read—Alphabetics, Fluency, and Comprehension.

Regional Public Hearings

. . . The Panel believed that it would not have been possible to accomplish the mandate of Congress without first hearing directly from consumers of this information—teachers, parents, students, and policymakers—about their needs and their understanding of the research. Although the regional hearings were not intended as a substitute for scientific research, the hearings gave the Panel an opportunity to listen to the voices of those who will need to consider implementation of the Panel's findings and determinations. The regional hearings gave members a clearer understanding of the issues important to the public. . . .

Adoption of Topics to Be Studied

Following the regional hearings, the Panel considered, discussed, and debated several dozen possible topic areas and then settled on the following topics for intensive study:

- Alphabetics

    — Phonemic Awareness Instruction
    — Phonics Instruction

- Fluency
- Comprehension

    — Vocabulary Instruction
    — Text Comprehension Instruction
    — Teacher Preparation and Comprehension Strategies Instruction

- Teacher Education and Reading Instruction
- Computer Technology and Reading Instruction

In addition, because of the concern voiced by the public at the regional hearings that the highest standards of scientific evidence be applied in the research review process, the methodology subgroup was tasked to develop a research review process including specific review criteria.

Each topic and subtopic became the subject of the work of a subgroup composed of one or more Panel members. Some Panel members served on more than one subgroup. The subgroups formulated seven broad questions to guide their efforts in meeting the Congressional charge of identifying effective instructional reading approaches and determining their readiness for application in the classroom:

1. Does instruction in phonemic awareness improve reading? If so, how is this instruction best provided?
2. Does phonics instruction improve reading achievement? If so, how is this instruction best provided?
3. Does guided oral reading instruction improve fluency and reading comprehension? If so, how is this instruction best provided?
4. Does vocabulary instruction improve reading achievement? If so, how is this instruction best provided?
5. Does comprehension strategy instruction improve reading? If so, how is this instruction best provided?
6. Do programs that increase the amount of children's independent reading improve reading achievement and motivation? If so, how is this instruction best provided?
7. Does teacher education influence how effective teachers are at teaching children to read? If so, how is this instruction best provided? . . .

Methodological Overview

In what may be its most important action, the Panel then developed and adopted a set of rigorous research methodological standards. . . . These standards guided the screening of the research literature relevant to each topic area addressed by the Panel. This screening process identified a final set of experimental or quasi-experimental research studies that were then subjected to detailed analysis. . . .

It is the view of the Panel that the efficacy of materials and methodologies used in the teaching of reading and in the prevention or treatment of reading disabilities should be tested . . . rigorously. However, such standards have not been universally accepted or used in reading education research. Unfortunately, only a small fraction of the total reading research literature met the Panel's standards for use in the topic analyses. . . .

Findings and Determinations of the National Reading Panel by Topic Areas

Alphabetics

Phonemic Awareness Instruction

Phonemes are the smallest units composing spoken language. For example, the words "go" and "she" each consist of two sounds or phonemes. Phonemes are different from letters that represent phonemes in the spellings of words. Instruction in phonemic awareness (PA) involves teaching children to focus on and manipulate phonemes in spoken syllables and words. PA instruction is frequently confused with phonics instruction, which entails teaching students how to use letter-sound relations to read or spell words. PA instruction qualifies as phonics instruction when it involves teaching children to blend or segment the sounds in words using letters. However, children may be taught to manipulate sounds in speech without any letters as well; this does not qualify as phonics instruction. PA is also frequently confused with auditory discrimination, which refers to the ability to recognize whether two spoken words are the same or different. . . .

Findings and determinations The results of the meta-analysis were impressive. Overall, the findings showed that teaching children to manipulate phonemes in words was highly effective under a variety of teaching conditions with a variety of learners across a range of grade and age levels and that teaching phonemic awareness to children significantly improves their reading more than instruction that lacks any attention to PA.

Specifically, the results of the experimental studies led the Panel to conclude that PA training was the cause of improvement in students' phonemic awareness, reading, and spelling following training. The findings were replicated repeatedly across multiple experiments and thus provide converging evidence for causal claims. While PA training exerted strong and significant effects on reading and spelling development, it did not have an impact on children's performance on math tests. This indicates that halo/Hawthorne (novelty) effects did not explain the findings and that indeed the training effects were directly connected with and limited to the targeted domain under study. Importantly, the effects of PA instruction on reading lasted well beyond the end of training. Children of varying abilities improved their PA and their reading skills as a function of PA training.

PA instruction also helped normally achieving children learn to spell, and the effects lasted well beyond the end of training. However, the instruction was not effective for improving spelling in disabled readers. This is consistent with other research showing that disabled readers have difficulty learning how to spell.

Programs in all of the studies provided explicit instruction in phonemic awareness. Specifically, the characteristics of PA training found to be most effective in enhancing PA, reading, and spelling skills included explicitly and systematically teaching children to manipulate phonemes with letters, focusing the instruction on one or two types of phoneme manipulations rather than multiple types, and teaching children in small groups. . . .

Phonics Instruction

Phonics instruction is a way of teaching reading that stresses the acquisition of letter-sound correspondences and their use in reading and spelling. The primary focus of phonics instruction is to help beginning readers understand how letters are linked to sounds (phonemes) to form letter-sound correspondences and spelling patterns and to help them learn how to apply this knowledge in their reading. Phonics instruction may be provided systematically or incidentally. The hallmark of a systematic phonics approach or program is that a sequential set of phonics elements is delineated and these elements are taught along a dimension of explicitness depending on the type of phonics method employed. Conversely, with incidental phonics instruction, the teacher does not follow a planned sequence of phonics elements to guide instruction but highlights particular elements opportunistically when they appear in text. . . .

Questions guiding the NRP analysis of phonics instruction   The NRP examined the research literature concerning phonics instruction to answer the following questions: Does phonics instruction enhance children's success in learning to read? Is phonics instruction more effective at some grade levels than others? Is it beneficial for children who are having difficulties learning to read? Does phonics instruction improve all aspects of reading or just decoding and word-level reading skills? Are some types of phonics instruction more effective than others and for which children? Does phonics instruction have an impact on children's spelling?

To address these questions the NRP performed a literature search to identify studies published since 1970 that compared phonics instruction to other forms of instruction for their impact on reading ability. The initial electronic and manual searches identified 1,373 studies that appeared relevant to phonics instruction. Evaluation of these studies to determine adherence to the general and specific NRP research methodology criteria identified 38 studies from which 66 treatment-control group comparisons were derived. Data from these studies were used in a meta-analysis, including the calculation of effect sizes.

The meta-analysis indicated that systematic phonics instruction enhances children's success in learning to read and that systematic phonics instruction is significantly more effective than instruction that teaches little or no phonics.

Findings and determinations   The meta-analysis revealed that systematic phonics instruction produces significant benefits for students in kindergarten through 6th grade and for children having difficulty learning to read. The ability to read and spell words was enhanced in kindergartners who received systematic beginning phonics instruction. First graders who were taught phonics systematically were better able to decode and spell, and they showed significant improvement in their ability to comprehend text. Older children receiving phonics instruction were better able to decode and spell words and to read text orally, but their comprehension of text was not significantly improved.

POSTSCRIPT

Does Learning How to Read Involve More Than Phonics?

Challenging Questions

1. Is the push to teach phonics rooted in the belief of adults that they learned to read using phonics so it must be an acceptable method for children today?
2. Do adults today have positive or negative images of learning to read based upon the approach under which they were taught?
3. What roles does the enjoyment of literature play in learning to read?

Suggested Reading

Butler, J., Liss, C., & Sterner, P. (1999). Starting on the write foot: Helping parents understand how children learn to read and write. *Texas Child Care,* Winter, 2–9.

Cunningham, A., & Shagoury, R. (2005). The sweet work of reading. *Educational Leadership,* 63(2) 53–57.

Manzo, K. K. (1999). Whole language lives. . . *Teacher Magazine,* 10, 11–13.

Palmaffy, T. (1997). See Dick flunk. *Policy Review,* 86, 76–88.

Parlakian, R. (2004). Early literacy and very young children. *Zero to Three,* September, 34–37.

Reisner, T. (2001). Learning to teach reading in a developmentally appropriate kindergarten. *Young Children,* 56(2) 44–48.

Tunnell, M. O., & Jacobs, J. S. (1989). Using "real" books: Research findings of literature based reading instruction. *The Reading Teacher,* 42, 470–477.

ISSUE 12

Should Recess Be Included in a School Day?

YES: Tom Jambor, from "Recess and Social Development," *Early Childhood News,* http://www.earlychildhoodnews.com/earlychildhood/contact.aspx

NO: Kelly King Alexander, from "Playtime Is Cancelled," *Parents* (November 1999)

ISSUE SUMMARY

YES: Tom Jambor, an associate professor of early childhood development at the University of Alabama at Birmingham, strongly supports daily recess for young children. He cites many benefits and ways to advocate for recess.

NO: Kelly King Alexander writes about the required additions to state-mandated curricula. Many school administrators have no choice but to eliminate nonacademic time from the schedule. With life and times changing rapidly she raises questions having free time scheduled into the school day.

Recess had become such a part of the American education landscape that it was often referred to as the fourth "R," along with "reading, riting, and rithmetic." The fourth "R" is now being dropped with many school districts implementing a no recess policy and some going as far as to build new schools without playgrounds. This means those schools are serious about their no recess policy and have no plans to change in the near future.

Although no specific studies exist on the academic disadvantages for children who do have recess, teachers cite reasons such as difficulty in getting the students settled down after being outside, students are more likely to get into fights on a playground, physical education provides exercise, and there are so many academic subjects to cover there is no time for recess. The lack of time in the schedule appears to be the most consistent reason for recess being limited or eliminated nationwide.

Just as adults welcome a break from their daily routine, those in support of recess argue that children need time to relax and regroup for more intense work. By allowing children time to socially interact, think about the work just completed, and exercise large muscles, we are sending the message that work hard and you will be rewarded with a break. Expecting young children to sit and be quiet, to retain large amounts of information, or to focus on writing tasks for a three-hour block of time is asking a great deal of a small body.

Jambor provides strategies for advocating to those parents, legislators, and taxpayers for recess and provides information on the pro social implications of children participating in recess. He reports the greatest academic gains occurred after there were breaks between intellectual activities. Kelly Alexander quotes Mike Jordan, principal of Magellan Charter School in Raleigh, North Carolina. He states that, "We're here to educate children. To take thirty minutes out of our instructional day just to let kids play doesn't sound good—to parents, to legislators, or to taxpayers."

POINT

- Children, like adults, perform more effectively after a break.
- Recess gives children an opportunity to develop social skills.
- Fights most often occurred not on the playground, but as children lined up after recess.

COUNTERPOINT

- Breaks during the school day are a luxury school districts cannot afford.
- Children can develop social skills after school.
- It is difficult for adults to monitor all areas of the playground and calm the students down after recess.

YES

Tom Jambor

Recess and Social Development

Although nearly four decades have passed, this writer can still vividly remember the joys and experiences of play and socializing during the primary school years. For my friends and me, the opportunity to play together was an important reason to come to school.

We played on the formal playground and in general open areas before the school bell rang or the teacher signaled us to come in to start our lessons. We were given a 20-minute outdoor recess in the morning, a like 20 minutes in the afternoon, and a full "lunch hour"-gulping food down as quickly as possible so we could get out to our ball games, jump-rope partners, games of chase, cliques, or just to wander around solo.

Although teachers watched over us, they seldom told us what to play or with whom to play. They seemed to enjoy the break as well. It was a time for all of us to get away from academic tasks and recharge. I enjoyed my teachers in that informal context. They were different there. They seemed just like regular people. They laughed at our silly jokes and behavior, they hugged us in joy or after a bump or bruise, and it wasn't hard to consider them friends. Younger kids watched and learned from older kids. It was a time to figure out who we were, to deal with the justices and injustices of social involvement, and to practice the skills that round out what is now referred to as "the whole child."

Growing up is not easy. There are so many disappointments, challenges, and important decisions, all of which can hammer away at one's self-esteem and tug hard on emotions. But it is all part of growing into a responsible, caring, secure, autonomous young adult. Social time with peers each day helped my childhood friends and me put life's challenges into perspective and allowed us to assert our own personal identities.

Recess is simply a break in what one is engaged in. It is a period of time away from the task at hand: an interlude, a change of pace. For example, a judge may call a recess if courtroom participants are tired, frustrated, or unfocused because of too much on-task activity. Congressional sessions recess for similar reasons. An office worker may remove herself from the tedium at her desk to stretch, walk around, get a cup of coffee, or socialize with a colleague.

"Recess," then, is not an alien word in our adult vocabulary, nor an abnormal response to physical and mental needs. Ask any adult; we need recess periods! It helps our sanity, our nerves, our need to move, converse, change pace, etc. It helps us to get through the work day; to reduce fatigue and burnout; to enhance on-task behavior, enthusiasm and energy; and to develop a more positive outlook on our work.

If adults have this daily need to recess from prolonged confinement, then it is not difficult to understand the child having, at the very least, similar needs. Although short on scientific credibility, the surplus energy theory has been seen by psychologists as a means for justifying the need for children to release excess energy, or "blow off steam" after a long time in the classroom (Pellegrini and Davis, 1993). For both adults and children, on-task attention can, then, be increased by providing opportunities for diversion. This is the basis for novelty theory:

> Children need recess because they are temporarily bored with their immediate classroom environment. When they go outdoors for recess they seek novelty by interacting with different peers in different situations. But, when the novelty of the recess environment begins to wane, they again need to change. At this point, the classroom becomes a novelty and children actually pay closer attention (Pellegrini, 1991, p. 40).

While adults can better inhibit their needs to move and socialize during work hours, it is difficult for children to do so. The child is a natural mover, doer and shaker. It is natural that a child who must tolerate repeated periods of "seat work" will feel mental fatigue and restlessness. Yet we all too often force children through stretches of time and tedium that would tax many adults. Prolonged confinement of children in elementary classrooms has been found to result in a high probability of fidgeting, restlessness, and subsequent reduction in concentration (Pellegrini and Davis, 1993).

Tomporowski and Ellis (1988) have suggested that vigorous playground behavior is related to attention to seat work after recess and that exercise increases attention to various cognitive tasks. According to Pellegrini and Glickman (1989), "the longer young children spend in classrooms, the longer and more vigorous is their play outdoors. . . . [and] such a release period for them (not to mention the teachers) may facilitate their subsequent attention to more academic tasks and minimize fidgeting and squirming in their seats once they return from recess" (p. 23). Stevenson (1992) also found that "attention is more likely to falter after several hours of classes than it is if opportunities for play and relaxation precede each class" (p. 75). Recess then, is an important element of classroom management and behavior guidance.

Recess and Social Implications

Recess encourages all areas of children's development. As children interact, they use language and nonverbal communications; they make decisions and solve problems, and they deal with the emotional trials and tribulations of their interactions (Jambor, 1986; Jambor & Gargiulo, 1987). According to Pellegrini and Glickman (1989, p. 24):

Recess is one of the few times during the school day when children are free to exhibit a wide range of social competencies—sharing, cooperation, negative and passive language—in the context that they see meaningful. Only at recess does the playground become one of the few places where children can actually define and enforce meaningful social interaction during the day. Without recess, the children lose an important educational experience.

Pellegrini's and Davis' (1993) research suggests that there is a significant relationship between classroom behavior and recess. For example, children engaged in recess may be practicing cognitive skills they already possess and are using when doing seat work. This would be consistent with Groos's (1901) notion of play as practice. Pellegrini and Davis (1993) also offer a more liberal interpretation of this practice theory: "children on the playground, through social interaction with peers, are learning skills which are transferred to the classroom. This is consistent with Piaget's (1970) notions of the facilitative effects of peer interaction on cognition" (p. 95).

The educational role of recess for both social and cognitive development is becoming increasingly clear. Children must function in both the social and the cognitive domains if they are to successfully adapt to school and societal norms.

These domains are empirically related and should be considered intertwined and separable (Pellegrini, 1992; Pellegrini and Smith, 1993). In other words, social interaction facilitates cognition; recess (indoor and out) offers the opportunity for this growth.

The playground during recess is one of the few places where today's children can actively confront, interpret, and learn from meaningful social experiences. Interactive games such as "chase," where both boys and girls are able to compromise and negotiate roles through language forms, can, for example, predict academic success. Random chase often turns into the organized game of "tag" (Pellegrini and Glickman, 1989). These social experiences become quite educational: "First, they help the children learn to cooperate to the extent that the play requires cooperation. Second, children learn to solve problems in such forms of play. They realize that in order to sustain their chase play with peers they must take turns being the chaser or the chased. If they refuse to change roles, play ends. This reciprocating role is a powerful predictor of the ability to cooperate and view events from different perspectives" (p. 24). This valuable educational experience is lost for those who do not have recess opportunities. Sluckin (1981) and Sutton-Smith (1971) have long considered social skills learned and practiced on the playground during recess as important to later development. Groos (1901), Piaget (1932), Vygotsky (1978), and Sluckin (1981) all viewed children's play as practice and preparation for adulthood. The school playground was the practice site that encouraged games of competition, allowed experimentation with new and novel social strategies, and accommodated family-oriented dramatic play. Each child could find a spot that fit along the play continuum, from rough-and-tumble play (Pellegrini and Perlmutter, 1988) to sedentary play.

Recess is a rich opportunity for assessment of social development through informal observations. Teachers observing children on the playground during recess can assess peer popularity, a proven predictor of school adjustment (Pellegrini and Glickman, 1989). For example, boys who engage in solitary play during recess, even if vigorous (e.g. climbing, running, jumping), may be rejected by their peers, because they do "not have necessary social skills to interact cooperatively with their peers. . . . Children who consistently spend their recess sitting alone or with playground supervisors, and not participating with their peers, may be at risk for personality disorders and need help" (p. 24). Rejection from or being disliked by peers also appears to be linked to risk of juvenile delinquency later on.

Teachers also can observe whether boys and girls have equal opportunities to join competitive and noncompetitive types of play. A socialization model (Sluckin, 1981; Lever, 1976; Finnan, 1982) characterizes children's roles as being the product of adult roles, and children's play as a reflection of these roles. Thus, recess play has been seen as a training ground for development of gender roles and the preparation for adulthood. Although adult gender roles have changed over the years, play patterns based on traditional gender roles persist. Informal observations of play during recess allow teachers to monitor whether they are effectively offering both types of play to both sexes.

Changing Attitudes toward Recess

Recess, once a reliable part of American children's school life, now is absent or only an afterthought in many schools. As a result, opportunities for social interchange are minimal. All too many schools now greatly restrict talking among children before class, during class, during lunch, and when standing in line to go anywhere. Indeed, recess may be the only time when children can interact without adult intervention or restriction. This makes school recess more vital than ever to social development.

Once upon a time, the vast majority of children came home from school and played in backyards and neighborhoods with friends. This supported the argument that children had plenty of time after school and on weekends for play and the subsequent social experiences that promote total development. Today, however too many children have restricted play experiences after school because they indulge in excessive television viewing and sedentary electronic game playing. Many are home alone in the afternoons and restricted to solitary indoor activity, and, when allowed outside, are not allowed to wander because of parental fears (often justified) of violence. In addition, over the last 20 years, a growing urbanization has slowly and methodically squeezed out the natural play spaces used by children, while "formal" play spaces, such as park and community school playgrounds, are often considered unappealing and/or unsafe because of antiquated equipment and the lack of consistent maintenance (Jambor and Guddemi, 1993).

The children of today should have the same opportunities for frequent, free play and the accompanying social development, as did children of past generations. Our children are at risk of losing their right to play. School recess (indoor as well as outdoor) is the best time for guaranteeing all children time to play.

Unfortunately, too many adults who influence early childhood curricula and school schedules do not understand the value and importance of recess as a time to play. Many teachers, administrators, and parents consider recess wasted time. They believe that recess is, at best, peripheral to children's learning experiences and that children learn best in school when they focus on basic skills and stay on task (Pelligrini and Glickman, 1989). They fear that our children are not keeping up with the academic successes of Asian children and argue for us to get back to basics (as if play is not basic) and academics and to improve test scores. In this view, recess takes children away from academic curriculum on which they will be tested. Education policy makers are so obsessed with academic attainment that they have eliminated or drastically reduced other activities which are important in children's total growth, development and learning. Curriculum is weighted too heavily towards cognitive development. There is nothing wrong with cognitive gain, unless its emphasis becomes so overwhelming that children's other developmental domains, including social development, become stifled. Today's education policy makers have too little understanding of how powerful recess and related experiences can be to the child's overall growth, development, and educational program.

If we must compare the academic successes of American children with Asian children, it might be beneficial to look at the Asian academic program within the context of their total school day. Granted, Chinese, Taiwanese, and Japanese children spend long hours at school, but their eight-hour school day includes frequent recesses, long lunch periods, and afterschool activities and clubs. These add up to one-fourth of their school day. The Asian school day is longer because so much time is devoted to these non-academic opportunities (Stevenson, 1992). Elementary schools that alternate studying with frequent periods of play and physical activity help children maintain attention, make learning easier and more enjoyable, and create cooperative and positive attitudes toward academics. While play, social interaction and extracurricular activity may not contribute directly to academic success, they make school more interesting and pleasant. Asian elementary schools appear to strive for a balance among academic curriculum, play, social interaction, and extracurricular activities (Stevenson, 1992). Recess is also a part of school life for most primary schools in Great Britain. It is not uncommon to find British school children with 15-minute periods of outdoor play in both the morning and afternoon, and an 80–90 minute play period at dinner time (Pelligrini and Smith 1993). That these countries value recess is another argument for reexamining the value of recess.

Strategies for Advocating Recess

But how can early childhood teachers and caregivers advance the case for recess? Here are some ideas. The following suggestions for the classroom teacher promote both recess advocacy and curriculum content:

- **Educate administrators.** Provide your principal with articles that advocate the virtues of recess. Highlight important points and ask to talk with your principal later about your school's recesses.
- **Educate the faculty.** Talk with them about the issue. When you think a good number of teachers are sympathetic, ask to put the topic on the agenda of a faculty meeting.
- **Educate parents.** Parents have a tremendous influence on what is acceptable or unacceptable within your curriculum. To gain parent allies who also advocate recess time within the child's daily schedule, hold a parent meeting armed with dialogue and literature to convince them of the value of play and the recess play experience. A motivating, knowledgeable outside speaker on recess, play and children's development may also have strong audience impact. Parent understanding of the principles of play, and of children's total development through play, can affect both support for recess and the level of assistance and commitment for developing a safer, more stimulating playground.
- **Provide in-class recesses.** While you may be unable to change school schedules, you probably can change your classroom's schedule to provide more indoor recess. The "free play" or "choice time" of the preschool classroom is easy to adapt for primary children. To encourage children's social development, allow them plenty of space and freedom to play in small groups. Give them regular opportunities to choose their own activities in the classroom and let them talk!
- **Write letters and opinion pieces.** Share ideas about the value of recess in newsletters to parents and letters to the editors of local newspapers. Write to school board members, legislators, and the superintendent. Children can write their own letters, too.
- **Speak out!** Talking one-on-one with parents, other teachers, and administrators, and writing letters and opinion pieces, will give you the experience and confidence you need to become a spokesperson for recess! Try this tactic: Invite a television feature reporter to experience recess with your children. Practice conversational, positive, persuasive comments about the value of recess so that you will be ready to give an on-camera interview. You might also prepare a fact sheet with some basic points about the value of recess to give to the reporter.

When children participate, the process of advocacy for recess can have several educational benefits. Like any topic, recess can be woven into the sociocognitive environment of the classroom. Children who think, talk, create art, and write about the value of recess will practice critical thinking, problem-solving, decision-making, verbal and written language, and motivational and persuasion strategies.

Conclusion

Both school day memories and recent research support the need and value of recess. Recess sets the occasion for play and subsequent social encounters that influence and nurture all other areas of development. Recess is an important counter to rigorous academic curricula and expectations for on-task behavior.

Recess allows teachers to observe and evaluate children's social interactions and behavior and to respond accordingly. Recess offers children a chance to be children; to do child-like things; to claim a time during the day to call their own. I can still hear that predictable question by the visiting relative, "What do you like best about school?" The inevitable reply, "recess!"

References

Finnan, C. (1982). The ethnography of children's spontaneous play. In G. Spindler (Ed.), *Doing the ethnography of schooling* (pp. 355–387). New York: Holt, Rinehart & Winston.

Groos, K. (1909). *The play of man*. New York: Appleton.

Jambor, T. (1986). Risk-taking needs in children: An accommodating play environment. *Children's Environments Quarterly* 3(4) 22–25.

Jambor, T., & Gargiulo, R. (1987). The playground: A social entity for mainstreaming. *Journal of Physical Education, Recreation and Dance* 58(8) 18–23.

Jambor, T., & Guddemi, M. (1993). Can our children play? In M. Guddemi & T. Jambor (Eds.), *A right to play: Proceedings of the American Affiliate of the International Association for the Child's Right to Play*, Sept. 17–20, 1992, Denton, Texas (pp. 3–5). Little Rock, Ark.: Southern Early Childhood Association.

Lever, J. (1976). Sex differences in the games children play. *Social Problems* 23, 478–487.

Pellegrini, A. D. (1991). Outdoor recess: Is it really necessary? *Principal*, 70(5) 40.

Pellegrini, A. D. (1992). Kindergarten children's social cognitive status as a predictor of first grade achievement. *Early Childhood Research Quarterly* 7, 565–577.

Pellegrini, A. D., & Davis, P. D. (1993). Relations between children's playground and classroom behavior. *British Journal of Educational Psychology*, 63, 88–95.

Pellegrini, A. D., & Glickman, C. D. (1989). *Principal* 62(5) 23–24.

Pellegrini, A. D., & Perlmutter, J. C. (1988). Rough-and-tumble play on the elementary school playground. *Young Children* 43(2) 14–47.

Pellegrini, A. D., & Smith, P. K. (1993). School recess: Implications for education and development. *Review of Educational Research* 63(1) 51–57.

Piaget, J. (1932). *Play, dreams and imitation*. New York: Norton.

Piaget, J. (1970). Piaget's theory. In P. H. Mussen (Ed.), *Carmichael's manual of child psychology Vol. 1*, 703–732. New York: Wiley.

Sluckin, A. (1981). *Growing up in the playground*. London: Routledge & Kegan Paul.

Stevenson, H. W. (1992). Learning from Asian schools. *Scientific American* 267(6) 70–76.

Sutton-Smith, B. (1971). A syntax for play and games. In R. Herron & B. Sutton-Smith (Eds.), *Child's play* (pp. 298–310). New York: Wiley.

Tomporowski, P., & Ellis, N. (1988). Effects of exercise on cognitive processes: a review. *Psychological Bulletin*, 99, 338–346.

Vygotsky, L. (1978). *Mind in society*. Cambridge, Mass.: Harvard Press. University

Playtime Is Cancelled

At first, Julie Moorhead, of Algiers, Louisiana, was unfazed when her four children came home from elementary school complaining that they weren't having recess. "Give it a couple of days," she reassured her kids. "Things may be disorganized because it's the first week."

But Moorhead soon received a bulletin from the principal of Alice M. Harte Elementary School explaining that recess had, in fact, been cut to comply with a state mandate increasing the amount of time students must spend on academics. "No time for recess?" asked Moorhead, a former teacher. "How could this happen?"

Parents across the country have been similarly shocked by the elimination of what many fondly remember as the best part of the school day. In the scramble to improve standardized test scores, as many as 40 percent of the country's school districts are considering doing away with recess or modifying it in some way, according to an informal poll conducted by the American Association for the Child's Right to Play.

And the no-recess movement may be more than just a passing educational fad. In Atlanta, which scrapped recess in all of its 69 elementary schools more than a decade ago, at least two elementary schools have been constructed without playgrounds, and a third is on the drawing board. This makes it unlikely, if not impossible, for these schools to one day reverse their policies. "It's sad," says Rhonda Clements, Ed.D., author of *The Case for Elementary School Recess* (American Press, 1999). "An entire generation may never experience games like jump rope, hopscotch, or freeze tag."

Until recently, recess was almost the fourth "R" in American education. In colonial times, educators had a "religious duty" to give students breaks from their studies, and healthy play in fresh air was considered an essential counterbalance to the confinement of one-room schoolhouses. Recess periods were much longer—a typical lunch break might last 90 minutes—as children played in nearby woods or meadows.

By the turn of the 20th century, most American schools held 15- to 20-minute morning and afternoon recesses in addition to hour-long lunch breaks. Until the 1950s, three daily recesses were still the norm; then, as fine arts, physical education, and other specialty areas were added to the curriculum, the afternoon break began to disappear. Since the 1970s, the lunch hour has been cut in half, and the length of the periods devoted to traditional academics has increased.

All Work and No Play

In the 1990s, American students' poor showings on standardized tests have spawned a back-to-basics movement that regards recess as frivolous. Although concerns such as school-yard safety, liability for injuries, and teachers' unwillingness to supervise are sometimes cited, the overwhelming reason for the decline of recess is the intense pressure on schools to improve test scores.

"We're here to educate children," says Mike Jordan, principal of Magellan Charter School, a middle school with no formal recess, in Raleigh, North Carolina. "To take thirty minutes out of our instructional day just to let kids play doesn't sound good—to parents, to legislators, or to taxpayers."

Child-development experts, who are unanimous in their belief that play is an essential part of a child's day, don't have much say in the matter. Nor do kids themselves. Certainly no one asked Julie Moorhead's son David, 7, an active first-grader who began returning home from first grade every afternoon with a headache, or Nicholas Maxwell, 10, a straight-A fourth-grader at Ashworth Elementary, in Arlington, Texas, who often complains of being exhausted after a seven-hour recessless school day followed by two hours of homework.

But such a rigid emphasis on work, not play, along with the force-feeding of academics, could backfire, experts say, creating kids who despise school and misbehave more often. After all, if adults need coffee breaks and lunch hours, don't kids as well? "It really isn't normal for children to sit quietly in chairs all day," says Jane McGrath, M.D., school health officer for the state of New Mexico.

There is also growing evidence that the dramatic increase over the past two decades of children with attention disorders may be related to the decline in physical activity. "We have an epidemic of attention-deficit disorder (ADD) in this country," says educational psychologist Jane M. Healy, Ph.D., author of *Failure to Connect* (Simon and Schuster, 1999). "This is partly because children lack the physical and emotional outlets found in active play."

Keli Strain, of Arlington, doesn't believe that lack of recess caused her 10-year-old son Benjamin's ADD, but she's convinced that his sitting for seven hours a day without a play break has made it worse. In fact, Benjamin's ADD was not diagnosed until he was in the fourth grade, when his class suspended recess in order to buckle down for state standardized tests.

Even children who do not have attention disorders will struggle to stay focused when they go for long periods without a break, says Olga Jarrett, Ph.D., an assistant professor of early-childhood education at Georgia State University, in Atlanta. Dr. Jarrett and her colleagues found that kids who have regular recesses were less fidgety and spent more time "on task"—teacher-speak for being engaged in schoolwork—than kids who did not. "There's this misguided idea that you can just pump information into kids all day," says Dr. Jarrett. "Learning doesn't happen that way."

Let's Get Physical

In many ways, however, child burnout is the least of it. In an era when childhood obesity is at an all-time high, and many kids are enrolled in before- and after-school day-care programs (which are usually indoors and highly structured), or return home from school only to spend several latchkey hours in front of the TV or computer, Dr. McGrath believes that outdoor free play at school is more essential than ever.

Indeed, last year, the National Association for Sport and Physical Education (NASPE) released its first-ever guidelines for elementary-school children, recommending that young kids be physically active for at least one hour a day. No-recess proponents often argue that kids move around in the classroom during group work or as they change classes. But a brief episode of controlled movement, such as "walking quietly to the library, finger on your lips, does not constitute physical activity," says Judy Young, NASPE's executive director.

Similarly, some school administrators maintain that their students don't need recess because they run around in physical-education [PE] class. But even Young, whose Virginia-based group represents over 25,000 PE teachers, coaches, and sports professionals, rejects that argument. PE is to recess, she says, what phonics drills are to reading comic books at home: The former teaches a structured curriculum, while the latter gives kids a chance to practice what they've learned in ways of their own choosing.

The views of children themselves highlight another critical difference between recess and PE. In another study by Dr. Jarrett and Darlene Maxwell, of Mercer University, in Atlanta, fourth-graders said they needed a time in the day when they had choices about what to play and whom to play with. Or as Elisabeth Bayer, a freckle-faced 8-year-old, puts it, "In PE, you have to do certain things. At recess, you do whatever you want."

New research suggests that 10- to 15-minute bursts of varied activity throughout the day aren't just good for the body, they actually stimulate brain development, especially in children. Other studies suggest that aerobic exercise pumps oxygen into the brain, thereby improving alertness and memory. "We are about to see an upsurge in research about the connection between motor development and brain development that will make recess critics look even more foolish," says Dr. Healy, who also notes that in countries where students academically outperform those in the United States, recess has not been sacrificed. Even the highly rigorous Japanese system offers more outdoor recess time than the average American elementary school.

Playing to Learn

Anyone harboring doubts that play spurs learning need only listen in on a group of kindergartners engrossed in sculpting a hamlet out of pea gravel during morning recess at St. George School, in Baton Rouge. "We're reptiles, and this is our reptile village," says Bradley, 6, who will not formally study cold-blooded vertebrates for at least another two years. "This is our bridge, this is our lake, and these are our houses. We're snakes and alligators and Tasmanian devils."

"Sometimes we build a volcano and turn it into a castle," adds Paige, 5, "or pretend were unicorns."

As important as the flights of imagination gleaned from this quarter hour of play is the socialization taking place. During the freedom of recess, children figure out how to get along. Bradley and the other kids settle a dispute over who will be the reptilian king. Paige and two other girls agree on a game without interference from their teacher, who observes from a distance.

"Recess is sort of like the sandlot of life before kids go to the major leagues," says June Lange Prewitt, state developer for the Parkway School District, in Missouri. "It allows them to develop emotional and social skills. To learn to say, 'Can I play?' is an important skill. And so is being able to handle the answer when it's no."

Ironically, kids 'difficulty in getting along has been the reason for some principals' decisions to revoke recess. As many of us remember, recess is often the time when bullies hold sway. Annette Maiden, principal of Ames Elementary School, in Marrero, Louisiana, declined to talk to *Parents* but told *The Times-Picayune,* a New Orleans newspaper, that the number of fights and disciplinary infractions of her school has dropped by 80 to 90 percent since recess was cut. Many of Philadelphia's 176 public elementary schools have implemented "socialized recess" periods—a kind of cross between free play and PE class—to reduce bullying and another playground violence.

Yet most experts believe that such statistics only point to a greater, rather than lesser, need for recess. Children who have little free play lose not only a positive outlet for excess energy but also, gradually, the ability to entertain themselves. "In my neighborhood, kids don't know how to go out and organize a game," says NASPE's Young. "A fight breaks out in five minutes. We referee every minute of our children's lives, and then we wonder why they're bored' and out of control when they reach adolescence."

Of course, few educators disagree with the myriad benefits of recess. But, they ask defensively, how can they fulfill all their responsibilities to the children in a six- or seven-hour day? Although the length of the American school day has changed very little in 30 years, much has been squeezed into the curriculum, including mandated courses in everything from self-esteem and sex education to character building and conflict resolution.

"Because so much has been heaped on the curriculum, teachers struggle to fit everything in," says Judy Linderman, principal of Ashworth Elementary, in Arlington. "We're constantly forced to choose what's more or less important." Linderman has left the recess decision up to the discretion of individual teachers, but recent complaints from parents whose kids miss recess have prompted her to reexamine the policy.

There has been no research to determine whether kids without recess perform better academically, but past studies have shown a link between higher scores and more time spent on schoolwork. One solution might be to lengthen the school day or year to allow time for play and rest as well as for the teaching of core courses and enrichment programs. Proponents cite the success of some European schools with extended days and add that the change would relieve many working parents of the burden of securing child care during latchkey hours, as well as cut down on crime by unsupervised minors. Opponents include teachers' groups, which worry that longer hours will mean additional responsibilities without commensurate pay.

In the meantime, a counterrevolution is afoot. The National Education Association and the National Association of Elementary School Principals have adopted resolutions encouraging members to preserve recess at their schools. Private and parochial schools, which have traditionally put a high premium on recess, have strengthened that commitment by extending free-play periods, according to Rhonda Clements.

And some districts and individual schools have actually retracted their no-recess policies. Last year, the superintendent of elementary schools in the Evanston and Skokie, Illinois, district reinstated recess within months of its elimination because of parental outrage. Recess has also returned to Alice M. Harte Elementary—thanks to Julie Moorhead and other parents who believe so strongly in its value that they have volunteered to supervise kids during lunch and for one 15-minute recess per day. Student conduct has since improved in the cafeteria and on the playground, says principal Stacy Rockwood, because kids don't want to waste valuable free time misbehaving.

Moorhead fondly recalls the day students first got their freedom back. "One little boy was standing in line as we were preparing to leave the cafeteria," she says. 'I know what we have to do now,' he said in a monotone. 'Walk in a straight line back to class.' I looked at him and said, 'No, we don't. It's recess now. Go play.'

"I wish I'd had a video camera," Moorhead says, laughing. "The kids were whooping and running around the playground. You'd have thought I'd given them a million bucks. In fact, I gave them something better."

POSTSCRIPT

Should Recess Be Included in a School Day?

Challenge Questions

1. Has the need for recess increased or decreased due to the changes in society?
2. Would adults tolerate a day with no breaks, other than the twenty minutes allowed for lunch? How can the attitude in workplace environments be transferred to schools for young children?
3. Could classroom instruction time be increased if schools eliminated recess during the school day?

Suggested Reading

Bishop, J. C., & Curtis, M. (Eds.). (2001). *Play today in the primary school playground.* Philadelphia: Open University Press.

Chmelynski, C. (1998). Is recess needed? *Education Digest,* 64(4), 67–68.

Jarrett, O. S., & Maxwell, D. M. (2000). What research says about the need for recess. In Clements, R. (Ed.), *Elementary school recess: Selected readings, games, and activities for teachers and parents* (pp. 12–23). Boston: American Press.

Johnson, D. (1998). Many schools putting an end to child's play. *The New York Times,* April 7, 1998, p. A1.

Pelligrini, A. D., & Smith, P. (1993). School recess: Implications for educational development. *Review of Educational Research,* 63(1), 51–67.

Schultz, K. (1997). On the elimination of recess. *Education Week,* 17, 38–40.

ISSUE 13

Are Looping Classrooms Effective Learning Settings?

YES: Mary M. Hitz, Mary Catherine Somers, and Christee L. Jenlink, from "The Looping Classroom: Benefits for Children, Families, and Teachers," *Young Children* (March 2007)

NO: Allan S. Vann, from "Looping: Looking Beyond the Hype," *Principal* (May 1997)

ISSUE SUMMARY

YES: Mary M. Hitz, Mary Catherine Somers, and Christee L. Jenlink, all educators in the state of Oklahoma, encourage teachers to loop with their students to the next grade and see many positive benefits to the practice.

NO: Allan S. Vann, a principal at the James H. Boyd Intermediate School in Huntington, New York, cautions teachers to think carefully about looping. He states it is not for everyone and there may be disadvantages of having a child stay with the same teacher or peers for two years.

We all remember teachers in whose class we would love to spend another year. They were caring, passionate teachers who made learning come alive and meaningful. Then we also remember teachers from our past we were not sad to say goodbye to at the end of the school year. How long should each teacher have to influence young children? If one year is too short of time, are two or more years too much time for one teacher? Looping, or having the teacher move up to the next grade with his or her class, is an educational practice gaining in popularity in recent years.

Staying with the same teacher for more than one year is not uncommon, especially in early childhood settings. Preschool children are often enrolled in a multiage three- and four-year-old classroom and have the same teacher throughout their preschool years. The teacher has two years to developing a strong working relationship with the children and families.

As school populations grew, children typically spent one year with each teacher as they progressed through the grades in an elementary school. Teachers across the nation have been challenging that tradition by requesting that they be allowed to move up to teach the next grade and keep their class in tact for the following year. This may occur when enrollments increase and a teacher needs to be added to the next grade level. It is also often prompted by a teacher who has had an extremely successful year with a group of students and wants to continue the progress into the next year.

Generally, every school has teachers who are known by the parents and students to be the good teachers, the teachers they would request or hope to have as a teacher. Conversely, there are also teachers whom students and parents feel would not be the best match for their family.

Teachers who feel confident about their abilities and who want to be challenged as professionals are those who most often volunteer for looping. Taking on new responsibilities and work is usually a trait found in high-performance teachers.

Looping has not been found to have significant advantages to academic performance; neither has it been found to be harmful. The question then becomes, should we endorse educational practices that have not been found to improve performance? Are we just throwing more twists and turns into the academic setting without any concrete improvement?

Hitz, Somers, and Jenlink view looping as an opportunity to buy extra time to learn. The beginning of the second year together allows a teacher and class to delve right into the curriculum of that grade, having already established a relationship over the past year. The rules are known and familiarity with the families has taken place. Allan Vann sees more disadvantages than advantages with looping. He reports on the disadvantages to looping including students being exposed to teachers' weaknesses and the ridicule students may face from the same peers for two consecutive years. Although he does list some advantages, he prefaces those by saying if he were to advocate looping it would be for those reasons. He has concerns about children being placed for a second year in a setting that has not been productive to their growth and development.

POINT	COUNTERPOINT
• Two or more years with the same teacher allows students the opportunity to get to know the teacher and the teacher to know his or her students.	• Children may spend two years with an ineffective teacher and fall far behind other students.
• Continuity and consistency is beneficial for young children.	• Children are flexible and can learn to adapt to different adults.
• Relationships with families develop over time.	• Families may not want the same teacher for two years.

YES
Mary M. Hitz, Mary Catherine Somers, and Christee L. Jenlink

The Looping Classroom Benefits for Children, Families, and Teachers

The second week of school, the second-graders work intently in small groups or individually. They require little direct teacher instruction and clearly understand their responsibilities and the teacher's expectations. How did this independence develop so early? What did the teacher do?

Welcome to a Looping Classroom! "Looping—which is sometimes called multiyear teaching or multiyear placement—occurs when a teacher is promoted with her students to the next grade level and stays with the same group of children for two or three years" (Rasmussen 1998, 1). What results is a continuity of relationship with their teacher that enables children to flourish (Wynne & Walberg 1994).

Looping Origins

The practice of looping is not a new concept in education. America's one-room schoolhouse was a looping classroom, with the teacher teaching the same children over a period of several years. In Germany in 1919 Rudolf Steiner developed the Waldorf School model. Oppenheimer suggests that one unusual aspect of education in the Waldorf School "Is a system called looping, whereby a homeroom teacher stays with a class for more than a year . . . from first through eighth grade" (1999, 82). Also in the early 1900s, Italian pediatrician Maria Montessori introduced the Montessori Method, characterized by relationship development over several years on the part of the teacher, child, and parents (Seldin n.d).

Generally, in modern Germany, student groups formed in first grade remain together over the next four years (Zahorik & Dichanz 1994). In China, grouping is by grade level, with a homeroom teacher who stays with students two to three years in elementary school and for three years in both junior and senior high schools. Many subject area teachers also choose to teach the same students for two to three years (Liu 1997).

In 1974 Deborah Meier founded the Central Park East Elementary School in New York City. Because she believed it takes time to build relationships, in this school the children and teachers stayed together for two years (Meier 1995).

THE MULTIAGE CLASSROOM

Two or more grade levels are intentionally placed in a single classroom. Children are taught as a class and regrouped as necessary for different activities based on interests and/or abilities rather than on chronological age or grade level. At the end of each year, the older students move to a new class, and a group of younger students joins the class. In a multiage grouping, children can experience being both younger and older among the students in their class.

In other instances, U.S. schools developed looping classrooms to solve scheduling problems or manage the significant population shifts in enrollment numbers per grade. This led to teachers being assigned to different or combined grades especially in small rural schools where school populations fluctuate each year. The multiage model is another popular form of looping (see "The Multiage Classroom").

Introducing Looping Today

It is not expensive or difficult to begin a school looping program. Two teachers volunteer for the assignment in any two contiguous grade levels. For example, teacher A teaches first grade and teacher B teaches second grade. The next year, teacher A moves with her class to teach second grade, and teacher B cycles back to begin with a group of new first-graders. Prior to looping, the two teachers and their administrator thoughtfully plan for this structural change (see "Starting a Looping Program," p. 82).

Benefits of Looping for Children

In today's rapidly altering world, many children's lives are filled with change: of residence, in family structure, in economic status. Numerous children come from single parent homes or have two parents both working full-time away from home. Children can benefit from the looping classroom's stability and teacher continuity (Nichols & Nichols 2002).

Children in typical settings. Because children typically attend school six or more hours a day, five days a week, the teacher is a significant adult in their lives. Staying together two years or longer enhances the bonding and trust established between children and teacher (Grant, Johnson, & Richardson 1996). Pianta and LaParo, in discussing how to improve early school success, conclude that "relationships that children have with adults and other children in families, child care, and school programs provide the foundation for their success in school" (2003, 27). When children form secure relationships with teachers and other caregivers, both social and cognitive competence show improvement (Kontos & Wilcox-Herzog 1997; Gallagher & Mayer 2006).

In the looping classroom children build relationships over time with an adult confidant. Grant and Johnson suggest, "For a lot of children today, their teacher is often the most stable, predictable adult in their life" (1995, 34). Several examples of benefits follow from two coauthors' (Hitz and Somers) primary grades looping classrooms.

> Makayla, an eight-year-old, was one of four children, including a sister who was very bright and two brothers with cognitive disabilities. She brought a great deal of pent-up anger to school. During the first year in the looping class, her many angry outbursts involved lashing out at anyone nearby. By her second year in the looping class, she trusted us enough to tell us what was happening. When necessary, Makayla could choose to move to a more isolated area to work alone or, with teacher permission, could go to the office to talk with the assistant principal. Makayla's aggressive expressions lessened, and she gained a sense of control over her emotions.

With additional time together, teachers can become more familiar with each child's learning style, interests, strengths, and needs and respond with individualized learning experiences (Seldin n.d.). In a looping classroom children are not apprehensive about their second or next years; they already know their teacher and classmates (Lacina-Gifford 2001). The familiar environment also allows a shy child to blossom. For example,

> At the beginning of his first looping year, Eric cried when called upon during any kind of discussion. Later in the year he would raise his hand to volunteer, only to shrink inside himself at being recognized. Once in a while he worked with another child.
>
> Knowing we would have Eric for two years, we did not feel the pressure to force participation in the first year. We offered support and encouragement when he attempted to participate but also allowed him needed time to mature.
>
> Although Eric struggled in reading all that first year, during the second year he volunteered more often and answered questions. Eric was on grade level at the end of the year. His mother was glad he was in a looping classroom. He was still quiet, but he knew he could do well in a new third grade classroom.

In a looping classroom, the teacher and the children experience a sense of community. The bonds between children grow strong; they share achievements and disappointments, resolve problems, and learn to trust each other. Teachers personalize their teaching and talk about their individual interests and their families.

One of the most positive elements of looping is that it allows a child to grow at his or her own pace, not at an arbitrary fixed-grade rate. John Goodlad reminds us that children "don't fit into a nice, neat age-grade package, either collectively or individually. Each individual child differs in regard to the various areas of accomplishment" (Stone 1999, 265). An example from our classroom follows:

> Austin, a young first-grader, worked hard in class and at home with his parents. By the end of the year, however, he was barely able to read at the preprimary level. His mother asked if we should retain Austin in first grade. We

STARTING A LOOPING PROGRAM

- Form a proposal study group
- Read about looping programs
- Enlist and build support from administrators and other teachers
- Involve parents in the planning
- Design the program to allow for change
- Provide time for staff development
- Visit other looping programs
- Invite teachers to volunteer for looping classrooms
- Work with administrators on the careful selection of teachers for looping

suggested waiting, since as a looping class we could monitor Austin's progress in the coming year.

Austin bloomed that second year. Reading became his favorite activity, and by the end of the year he was reading above grade level. In third grade he moved into the gifted program. Had Austin been in a nonlooping classroom, he might have been retained.

English-language learners.   The looping classroom supports children and their families for whom English is a second language. As English-language learners (ELLs) adjust to a new school and become comfortable with their teacher, they develop confidence in practicing their new language. Eventually they may help others who are new to the class or have little knowledge of U.S. culture. When children who are ELLs are members of a class, the other children can learn firsthand from a peer about another culture and country. The experience results in respect and understanding among all the students (Haslinger, Kelly, & O'Lare 1996).

> Maritza uses both English and Spanish. One day, in her second year, she and three other Spanish-speaking friends chose a book to read to the class and designed follow-up activities. They read the story aloud—in Spanish. The other children gained an idea of what ELL students experience when learning a second language. Because Maritza and her friends felt safe and secure in their classroom, they could make this presentation to their peers.

Looping Pluses for Others

Looping provides time for teachers to get to know each child and family in a personal way, and it fosters stronger bonds between teachers and families.

Teachers.   In nonlooping classrooms, each year teachers spend the first four to six weeks determining each child's skills, abilities, and interests. In contrast, in the second year of a looping classroom cycle, the teacher already knows the students and is able to immediately support their learning, thus making better use of instructional time (Little & Dacus 1999). Effective teaching and learning can begin on the first day of the second year after a brief review of rules and procedures (Burke 1996).

Many teachers provide summer learning packets to help children bridge from one year to the next. In looping classrooms the children are returning to the same classroom and teacher, and it is easy to design packets and follow up with them the second year. Children are excited to share journals kept over the summer, stories they wrote, or special books they read. The looping teacher can build on children's previous year's experiences and use the summer packets to lead into the second year's curriculum.

Usually teachers choose to loop because they believe in developmentally appropriate practices, including the importance of encouraging emotional development (Dunn & Kontos 1997). Such teachers understand young children's need for stability and how the looping classroom addresses that need.

In looping classrooms, collaborating teachers learn new skills and curriculum (Albrecht et al. 2000) by sharing materials and ideas. They have a chance to know more about the children—where they live, who needs extra motivation, who works best with whom (Burke 2000). Units of study can extend into the next year. Looping gives teachers an extra year to consider high-stakes decisions regarding retention or referral for testing for special services (Jacobson 1997; Liu 1997; Bracey 1999).

Families.   Looping classrooms foster stronger bonds between families and teachers. "Because parents are the most significant people in a child's life, the relationship between the teacher and the parents is paramount" (Albrecht et al. 2000, 24). Parents tend to place more trust in a teacher the second year, with the development of a relaxed relationship conducive to a positive attitude toward the teacher (Nichols & Nichols 2002). Conversely, the teacher values input from the home, a direct result of the collaborative relationship that has been forged in this type of classroom setting.

Parents get to know the teacher's philosophy of education and how it relates to their child. Because a trusting relationship builds over the long span of a looping classroom, families may be more willing to accept a teacher's constructive suggestions (Chirichello & Chirichello 2001) and tend to be comfortable sharing the challenges they face with their child at home. Our looping classroom provides this example:

> Zach had difficulty completing classroom assignments on time. At home, his family reported he was never ready on time and every morning was a fight to get dressed for school. Zach's mother called one morning to say he would be at school on time, but in his pajamas. We were proud of the other children for not making fun of Zach or teasing him. But ever after, Zach was always ready for school.

For the families of children who are English-language learners, the stability of having the same teacher for a span of two years helps them gain confidence in talking with the teacher about their children's progress. The teacher can also smooth this transition by having materials translated as frequently as possible into the family's home language and arranging for translators to attend conferences.

What Concerns Might Arise in Looping?

While the advantages of a looping classroom are many, some concerns do arise. One issue parents express is a fear of their child being locked in for two years with a possibly ineffective teacher. Other potential problems include a teacher-child personality conflict, a child who simply does not get along with the other children, or a parent who does not get along with the teacher. Although looping teachers report that these occurrences are rare; each school needs to have procedures for reviewing class placements. The school principal plays an important role in identifying teacher-child personality conflicts as well as ensuring that teachers have the skills and work ethic necessary to create a successful looping classroom.

In our looping classroom two sets of parents came to us with concerns about their children. In both instances the issues reflected differences about teaching philosophy. After discussions, with both sets of parents, we jointly decided to place each child in a traditional classroom. Involvement of the school principal is essential in such situations to ensure making the best decision for the child.

Another challenge involves a new child entering the program, especially in the second year when children are already familiar with each other and the classroom. The looping teacher must prepare and encourage the children to welcome and accept the new student and help the child become part of the community.

Conclusion

At the end of the school year, it is always difficult to say good-bye, but when a teacher and children have been together for two years, it is doubly difficult. The class is a learning community that has shared joys as well as the sadness of departure. Some teachers plan special events to highlight their two years together. The children outline their advice to the incoming group of younger students and write letters to their future teachers to introduce themselves. Receiving teachers visit the looping class to be introduced to their new students when possible.

Good-bye is a bittersweet time. Sometimes it's harder for parents. Not only do looping teachers have to reassure the children that they will succeed, but also they have to reassure the families.

The concept of a looping classroom is being revisited by many teachers today. It favors both the child and the teacher and adds stability to children's lives. It provides time—time for children to grow and develop at their own rates and time for teachers to get to know each child and family in a personal way.

Looping may not be a good fit for everyone nor solve all the problems in education. But teacher proponents express it this way: Looping provides the most rewarding opportunity for helping children succeed (Rasmussen 1998).

References

Albrecht, K., M. Banks, G. Calhoun, L. Dziadul, C. Gwinn, B. Harrington, B. Kerr, M. Mizukami, A. Morris, C. Peterson, & R. R. Summers. 2000. The good, the bad and the wonderful! Keeping children and teachers together. *Child Care Information Exchange* (136): 24–28.

Bracey, G.W. 1999. Going loopy for looping. *Phi Delta Kappan* 81 (2): 169–70.

Burke, D.L. 1996. Multi-year teacher/student relationships are a long-overdue arrangement. *Phi Delta Kappan* 77 (5): 360–61.

Burke, D.L. 2000. Learning to loop and loving it. *The School Administrator Web Edition.* . . .

Chirichello, M., & C. Chirichello. 2001. A standing ovation for looping: The critics respond. *Childhood Education* 78 (1): 2–10.

Dunn, L., & S. Kontos. 1997. What have we learned about developmentally appropriate practice? *Young Children* 52 (5): 4–13.

Gallagher, K.C., & K. Mayer. 2006. Teacher-child relationships at the forefront of effective practice. *Young Children* 61 (6): 44–49.

Grant, J., & B. Johnson. 1995. *A common sense guide to multiage practices, primary level.* Columbus, OH: Teachers' Publishing Group.

Grant, J., B. Johnson, & I. Richardson. 1996. *Our best advice: The multiage problem solving handbook.* Petersborough, NH: Crystal Springs Books.

Haslinger, J., P. Kelley, & L. O'Lare. 1996. Countering absenteeism, anonymity, and apathy. *Educational Leadership* 54 (1): 47–49.

Jacobson, L. 1997. 'Looping' catches on as a way to build strong ties. *Education Week* 17 (7): 1–3.

Kontos, S., & A. Wilcox-Herzog. 1997. Teachers' interactions with children: Why are they so important? *Young Children* 52 (2): 4–12.

Lacina-Gifford, L. J. 2001. The squeaky wheel gets the oil, but what about the shy student? *Education* 122 (2): 320–21.

Little, T.S., & N.B. Dacus. 1999. Looping: Moving up with the class. *Educational Leadership* 57 (1): 42–45.

Liu, J. 1997. The emotional bond between teachers and students: Multi-year relationships. *Phi Delta Kappan* 78 (2): 156–57.

Meier, D. 1995. *The power of their ideas: Lessons for America from a small school in Harlem.* Boston, MA: Beacon.

Nichols, J.D., & G.W. Nichols. 2002. The impact of looping classroom environments on parental attitudes. *Preventing School Failure* 47 (1): 18–25.

Oppenheimer, T. 1999. Schooling the imagination. *The Atlantic Monthly* 284 (2): 71–83.

Planta, R.C., & K. LaParo. 2003. Improving early school success. *Educational Leadership* 60 (7): 24–29.

Rasmussen, K. 1998. Looping: Discovering the benefits of multiyear teaching. *Education Update* 40 (2): 41–44.

Selden, T.N.d. Montessori 101: Some basic information that every Montessori parent should know. . . .

Stone, S.J. 1999. A conversation with John Goodlad. *Childhood Education* 75 (5): 264–68.

Wynne, E.A., & H.J. Walberg. 1994. Persisting groups: An overlooked force for learning. *Phi Delta Kappan* 75 (7): 527–30.

Zahorik, J.A., & H. Dichanz. 1994. Teaching for understanding in German schools. *Educational Leadership* 51 (5): 75–77.

Allan S. Vann

 **NO**

Looping: Looking Beyond the Hype

Looping," the practice of having teachers stay with the same class for two consecutive grade levels, has been getting a lot of favorable attention lately in professional publications and at educators' conferences. What looping advocates often don't mention, however, is that this grouping strategy has been around since the one-room schoolhouse, and that while looping has been successfully implemented in many schools, there is no body of research supporting greater cognitive or affective growth in children who have experienced it. . . .

Advantages of Looping

If I were to advocate looping, I would probably cite three reasons for implementing such a practice:

1. If teachers move up with their classes, the first weeks of the second year will probably be more productive because the teachers will not need the days or weeks usually taken to become familiar with each child's learning style, strengths, weaknesses, interests, or home situation.
2. For the many children coming to school from fragile homes, looping teachers provide familiar and welcome "significant others" in their lives, giving them a greater sense of security.
3. If teachers believe that looping is beneficial, the "Hawthorne effect" may prevail—i.e., when people feel strongly about a concept and are willing to work hard to make it succeed, it probably will.

Disadvantages of Looping

Looping is not for everyone, however, and certainly should not be mandated or forced on an unwilling staff. Even with enthusiastic participation, there may be disadvantages in having a child remain with the same peers and teacher for a second year, such as:

1. Time may be lost at the beginning and throughout the school year as the looping teacher strives to master the new curriculum. The higher the grade level, the more curriculum content there is to be mastered.

2. Despite the best efforts to match teaching styles with children's learning styles, there will always be mismatches. Continuing those mismatches for a second year is unfair to both teacher and child.
3. Every teacher has strengths and weaknesses. As children move from grade to grade in the traditional system, they may go from a teacher who is gifted at teaching one subject to a teacher who is strong in a different subject. But looping relegates children to two consecutive years with an instructor who may not teach an important curriculum area as well as other grade-level teachers, or who may not be able to bring out the best in a particular child's area of special interest.
4. Each year, there are some children who are ridiculed or even ostracized by peers who perceive them as too smart, too dumb, too tall, too short, too fat, too thin, or too this or that. Looping extends the negative consequences for both those children and their classmates. Also, remaining with the same class for a second year limits a child's opportunities to make new friends in the classroom setting. . . .

Two Pitfalls to Avoid

Some advocates argue that looping teachers should view their curriculum as a two-year course of instruction. Such an approach, however, can have negative outcomes for children who opt out, and for new children placed in the class the second year. The scope and sequence of their instruction will have serious gaps if the looping teacher omits certain topics from the customary grade-level curriculum the first year in the expectation of teaching them the second year. It may be prudent for the teacher to cover the graded curriculum one year at a time.

Some looping proponents also feel that teachers must implement nontraditional teaching strategies to ensure success. However, looping is essentially a grouping strategy and its success or failure has not been shown to be dependent on its environment, be it structured or unstructured, teacher-centered or child-centered. Attempts to wed looping to a particular learning environment should be discouraged, as this may limit the number of available teachers, as well as the ability of principals to match student learning styles with teaching styles. It may also create unfair expectations in the minds of parents.

I see no outstanding advantages for looping, nor do I see any insurmountable disadvantages.

POSTSCRIPT

Are Looping Classrooms Effective Learning Settings?

Challenge Questions

1. Are we asking too much to have teachers teach a different curriculum every year?

2. What grades would be best to loop?

3. Are there greater advantages or disadvantages for being with the same teacher and peers for two or more years?

4. Would students whose parents feel it is not in their child's best interest to be with a certain teacher for a second year feel alienated from their peers for leaving the group?

5. When a school district allows looping, as an option, are those teachers who are most often classified as the good teachers placed into looping grades leaving the teachers with less favorable ratings for those students who do not loop?

Suggested Reading

Bellis, M. (1999). Look before you loop. *Young Children*, 54(3), 70–73.

Bracey, G. W. 1999. Going loopy for looping. *Phi Delta Kappan*, 81(2), 169–170.

Chapman, J. (1999). A looping journey. *Young Children*, 54(3), 80–83.

Chirichello, M., & Chirichello C. (2001). A standing ovation for looping: The critics respond. *Childhood Education*, 78(1), 2–10.

Forsten, C., Grant, J., & Richardson, I. (1999). Multiage and looping: Borrowing from the past. *Principal*, 78(4), 15–18.

Hanson, B. J. (1995). Getting to know you—Multiyear teaching. *Educational Leadership*, 53(3), 42–43.

Nichols, G. W., & Nichols, J. D. (1999). Looping: The impact on parental attitudes in the educational environment. *International Journal of Educational Reform*, 8(3), 274–279.

Internet References . . .

Center for Effective Discipline

This organization supports guiding the behavior of children at home and in school without the use of corporal punishment. The site includes statistics on laws around the world related to corporal punishment.

http://www.stophitting.com

Complementary Learning Approach to the Achievement Gap

Complementary learning provides a variety of support services for all children to be successful. These supports reach beyond the school and work toward consistent learning and developmental outcomes for children.

http://www.gse.harvard.edu/hfrp/projects/

complementary-learning.html

National Association of School Boards (NASB)

The NASB provides information for the thousands of elected school board members throughout the country. The organization provides resources for board members that assist them in making decisions affecting thousands of students in their district.

http://nsba.org/site/index.asp

National Center for Education Statistics

The National Center for Education Statistics (NCES), located within the U.S. Department of Education and the Institute of Education Sciences, is the primary federal entity for collecting and analyzing data related to education.

http://nces.ed.gov

Phi Delta Kappa

This important organization publishes articles about all facets of education. By clicking on the links in this site you can check out the journal's online archive. There are many excellent articles about assessment.

http://www.pdkintl.org/

Educational Policies

*T*here are decisions made by others in Washington, D.C., in the many *state legislatures throughout the country, or at local school board meetings that affect what happens in individual schools and classrooms. Many of these policies are a result of No Child Left Behind (NCLB) and require educators to implement practices or follow specific guidelines. Individual educators can become advocates for their students by sharing with others how policies they enact affect young children.*

- Should Public Money Be Spent on Universal Preschool?

- Is Regular Testing the Best Way to Improve Academic Performance?

- Will School Improvement Efforts Alone Narrow the Racial/Ethnic Achievement Gap?

- Should Corporal Punishment in Schools Be Outlawed?

- Are Boys in Crisis in Our Schools?

ISSUE 14

Should Public Money Be Spent on Universal Preschool?

YES: Julie Poppe and Steffanie Clothier, from "The Preschool Promise," *State Legislatures* (June 2005)

NO: Darcy Ann Olsen, from "Universal Preschool Is No Golden Ticket: Why Government Should Not Enter the Preschool Business," *Policy Analysis Cato Institute,* February 9, 1999 (ERIC ED 427-875)

ISSUE SUMMARY

YES: Both Julie Poppe and Steffanie Clothier are policy researchers in areas related to child care and early childhood education for the National Conference of State Legislatures in Washington, D.C. They see preschool education as extremely important for all young children and urge state legislatures to become involved in supporting preschool education.

NO: Darcy Ann Olsen, an entitlements policy analyst at the Cato Institute, argues that government should not pay for education of preschool children. She finds that public schools cannot provide education for the children for whom they are responsible now; to add younger children would be a poor decision.

We can go back over 150 years in this country to find the beginnings of public acceptance of the age of five as appropriate for public school entry. The first nonpublic kindergartens served children as young as two and a half years all the way through five years of age. When the St. Louis Public Schools were the first to offer kindergarten, the board of education established five as the entry age. Over the years various states have approved laws both making public school available for all children starting around the age of five and requiring school attendance by five or six years of age. Recently, state legislatures have started to make school available, in the form of preschool, for all three- and/or four-year-olds in the state. These universal preschool offerings are causing many to carefully examine the initial public school experiences for our youngest learners.

Public school districts are often criticized for not fully educating all of their students so they will be successful graduates. This causes many to question public schools entering the business of educating children at a younger age.

Is three or four years of age the best time to start public school education, skeptics of universal preschool ask?

One of the initial concerns when the subject of universal preschool was first explored centered on the private preschool operators already in business. Their concern was the offering of a state-supported program would drive the private programs out of business. Successful states have managed to carefully provide a variety of options for parents, some private and some public but all supported by state funding. Supporters of universal preschool would say the purpose is not to close the private programs already successfully operating, but to make preschool attendance available and, in many cases, required for all students.

In the following two selections, Poppe and Clothier wrote one of the many articles currently out in both education journals as well as in the general press related to the rapid growth of preschools funded by state government. Universal preschool, available and/or required for all children, is already happening in North Carolina, Georgia, and New York. Thirty-seven states currently offer state-funded preschool, but in most states there are eligibility requirements that must be met for attendance. States offering universal preschool agree to pay the full cost of attending for all children, regardless of whether they meet the eligibility requirements, which usually include criteria such as low-income level, an incarcerated parent, a non-English-speaking parent, a child with a speech or hearing problem, a child born to teenage parents, and so on. Children meeting usually one or two of the criteria are eligible to enroll in the state-funded half- or full-day preschool. Universal preschool programs are those preschool programs paid for by the state that are available for all children residing in that state. These programs are usually a combination of private and public programs that all receive the same funding.

Darcy Ann Olsen, an entitlements policy analyst at the Cato Institute, reviews the literature looking at how universal preschool would benefit all children, not just those who are economically disadvantaged. She writes, if the benefits of preschool attendance for children across all income levels is not as significant as it is for low-income children, then the cost of offering preschool programs is not a wise investment of public funds. She also contends that public schools have failed to properly educate the children currently attending, therefore the concept of states offering universal preschool and adding even more children is one that should not be adopted.

POINT	COUNTERPOINT
• Preschool is an important first step in a child's education.	• Children can learn just as much at home with their mothers.
• There are significant benefits for at-risk children who attend quality preschool programs.	• The government shouldn't pay for all children if the gains are not significant for middle-income children.
• The effects of attending a quality preschool are long lasting well into adulthood.	• The benefits of attending preschool are short term.
• Young children have the capacity to learn during the preschool years.	• The government should not have to pay for preschool children to play at school.

YES

Julie Poppe and
Steffanie Clothier

The Preschool Promise

If you walk into a good preschool classroom, you might see a teacher reading to a group of kids, children immersed in an art project, little ones playing on a computer or getting ready for a field trip to a nearby museum or public library.

Those children, mounting research shows, will do better in school and are more likely to attend college. As adults they will have better jobs and pay more taxes. They will even be better parents.

The good news is that more and more children go to preschool; in 2002, 66 percent of 4-year-olds attended. Some schools are government supported, others are private. Today, at least 40 states provide state funding for preschool programs, compared to only 10 in 1980.

Parents from all income ranges send their children to preschool, although better educated parents with higher incomes have the highest participation rate.

Preschools are designed to provide education and a safe caring environment. Some states fund programs that incorporate the needs of working parents, sometimes by coordinating their programs with Head Start and child care subsidy programs to ensure full-day services.

Ready for School

One of the striking findings in early education is the size of the achievement gap at the start of kindergarten between children who have gone to preschool and those who have not. That difference hardly ever goes away. It continues in reading and math achievement in the early grades and throughout school and into the job market. Steve Barnett from the National Institute for Early Education Research—an independent, nonpartisan organization that conducts research and follows state early education policy—says that kids living in poverty are 18 months behind the average kid when they start kindergarten. "This is an incredible amount of time for a school to catch up," Barnett says. But the achievement gap isn't just a poverty issue. "The gap continues up the income ladder," he says. Because of these findings and recent brain research showing that almost 90 percent of brain growth occurs in children by age 5, more lawmakers, economists, business leaders and parents are supporting early education.

The Right Programs Are Key

What makes a good preschool program? Proper teacher qualifications and training, small class sizes and teacher-to-student ratios, stimulating curriculum and other services that support families. A good program can improve a child's achievement over the short and long term. Recent focus on quality has prompted states to consider enhancements. For example, 23 now require preschool teachers to have a bachelor's degree with additional certification and license.

Most states target their state-funded initiatives to children who are in low-income families or at risk of school failure. Some states are looking to expand their preschool programs in response to state litigation, the need to improve test scores due to No Child Left Behind, and the latest research showing early education improves children's school success. Some states have different goals in mind, such as funding and expanding early education programs to reach more working families.

Paying for Quality Preschool

Arkansas has a state-funded preschool program that started in 1991 for low-income children. In recent years, $40 million in funding has allowed more children to attend. Representative LeRoy Dangeau carried a bill this session that resulted in an additional $20 million over the next two years for the continued expansion of the state's program.

Figure 1

The Achievement Gap at Kindergarten Family Income Has a Great Deal to Do with How Well a Child Does on Readiness Tests When Entering Kindergarten. The School Readiness Gap is Steepest for Children from Families with the Lowest Incomes and Continues Through Middle Income Families, Gradually Decreasing as Income Rises.

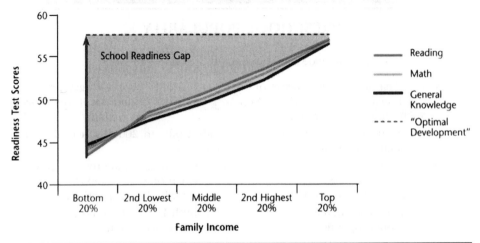

Source: Preschool Policy Matters, April 2004, National Institute for Early Education Research.

Other preschool funding comes from a beer tax (since 2001) that raises about 18 cents on every six-pack, generating $8 million annually for early education. This April, the Legislature passed a bill to extend the beer tax until June 2007.

Dangeau hopes that by the summer of 2007 there will be a total of $100 million dedicated for voluntary preschool for all 3- and 4-year-olds.

"When I became a legislator four years ago," says Dangeau, "I had no clue about the importance of early childhood. But I saw the research, including the benefits of preschool over time, and how it is the best investment of our money," he says.

In a recent Arkansas Supreme Court case on school funding inequity, the court recognized the importance of preschool (but didn't mandate it) as part of its ruling. "I think that the court case had an impact on how the Legislature views preschool," says Dangeau. "We see it as the quickest way to improve test scores. The issue is not whether or not to have preschool. The question is how much money to put into it."

Last year, the National Institute for Early Education Research ranked the quality of Arkansas' preschool program very high.

"I am very proud to say that Arkansas ranked best in terms of quality," says Dangeau. He believes the success is directly tied to legislation passed in 2003 that puts preschool teachers on the same pay scale as K–12 teachers. Any program or school may provide preschool services as long as they meet the state's quality standards, such as one certified teacher per 10 students.

Supporting Working Families

In the mid-'80s, the Illinois legislature established a preschool program for at-risk children. To support working families, the state allows child care centers and Head Start programs that meet standards to provide full-day early education services along with public schools. Local communities determine eligibility; there are an estimated 64,000 3- and 4-year-olds enrolled statewide.

PRESCHOOL POPULARITY

At least 40 states provide state funding for preschool programs.

- The first to expand preschool to all 4-year-olds were Georgia and then Oklahoma. Florida, Maryland, New York and West Virginia are in the process of phasing in their programs.
- Thirty-six states considered early education bills in 2005. At least 28 states considered expanding preschool programs.
- Florida legislators, responding to a state ballot measure, approved legislation for a voluntary preschool program for all 4-year-olds. New Mexico legislators passed a pilot preschool bill with a $5 million initial appropriation.
- Mississippi, Montana, North Dakota and South Dakota have no state-funded preschool programs, but did consider legislation this session.

Figure 2

Kindergarten and Preschool Participation 1965–2002. Over the Last Several Decades, Preschool and Kindergarten Participation Has Increased Steadily for Children Ages 3 to 5.

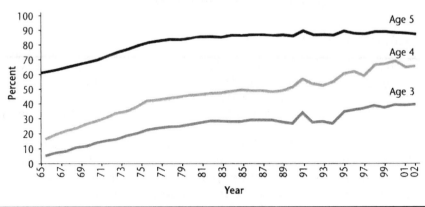

Source: National Institute for Early Education Research.

The state has significantly increased funding over the past few years. Since 2003, lawmakers have appropriated $30 million annually for early education and are looking to do the same this legislative session.

The National Institute for Early Education Research gave the state high marks for quality. Teachers participating in the program must hold an early childhood teaching certificate to be on the same pay scale as K–12 teachers.

In 2003, lawmakers created the Illinois Early Learning Council. It builds on the work the state has already done to develop a high-quality early learning system available to all Illinois children up to age 5. Four legislators currently are members of the council, including Representative Elizabeth Coulson.

Coulson, who has a business background, sits on two of the House Appropriation Committee's subcommittees, Human Services and Education, which make funding decisions for early education. She is also a member of the House Human Services Committee. "I'm a link between key committees that focus on early childhood," she says.

She says that Illinois has been concerned for some time about supporting working families and making sure a strong birth-to-age-5 system is in place that nurtures children. In 2003, the legislature increased the percentage of funding for birth-to-age-3 programs from 8 percent to 11 percent of the state's early childhood education block grant. The block grant makes up the state's funding for preschool education, parental training and prevention initiatives. "The formative years have the most impact on education. This is not just a women's issue, but it's also a children's issue and [in terms of economics and business] an important issue for the whole state," she says.

Nearly a third of all Illinois 4-year-olds are in a state-funded preschool program and the number is up from the year before. Coulson says early care is a thriving industry that has an impact on Illinois' economy, and businesses need to be aware of the benefits. Recent research shows that every tax dollar invested in preschool produces $17 for the economy.

"This session, we continue to focus on quality and funding," Coulson says, in the last two years, the state has increased preschool spending by $60 million. "This is a bad budget year for Illinois, but I am optimistic we will find a way to fund another $30 million for early childhood," she says.

Legislative Involvement

During the mid-'80s, Massachusetts set up a state-funded early education program in public schools. Since then, the state has allowed community partnership providers who meet early childhood standards to participate in programs targeting at-risk 3- and 4-year-olds from working families serving almost 16,000 children last year.

During the 2004 session, more than 100 legislators, including leadership in both houses, signed on to a proposal for preschool for all 3-to-5-year-olds to be phased-in over 10 years, at an estimated cost of $1 billion. Two bills that were eventually enacted laid the groundwork for the expansion by reworking state governance of early childhood programs. One law creates a single department to streamline early childhood programs and to expand preschool to all 3- and 4-year-olds. "Hopefully, we will see less duplication of services," says Representative Patricia Haddad.

She co-chairs the legislature's Joint Committee on Education and the state's legislatively created Advisory Committee on Early Education and Care. Nine other legislators participate. They have conducted five public hearings throughout the state. "We had to be a part of the hearings ourselves, because it is nice to read a report, but the passion is different when you are involved," says Haddad. State early childhood advocates also held meetings throughout the state to educate the public on the importance of early childhood education and full-day kindergarten for all.

Last December, the advisory committee completed a report that identified four key components: developing a workforce, defining quality, delivering the system and evaluating progress. Haddad says the next step is providing a good workforce development program for teachers and providers.

The 2004 legislation also created a new board of early education and care, which will start this July. The commissioners from the boards of Higher Education, Education, and Early Education and Care will each sit on each other's boards. "We want the commissioners to be talking to one another, which will lead to better communication between these three entities," says Haddad.

Representative Haddad says people in Massachusetts are starting to realize the importance of preschool and the role that it might possibly play with No Child Left Behind. "If you do not provide the very best for children in the early years, you will continue to see gaps," she says.

Darcy Ann Olsen

 **NO**

Universal Preschool Is No Golden Ticket: Why Government Should Not Enter the Preschool Business

Introduction

Should legislators expand the public school system to include three- and four-year-old children? Should schooling for preschool-aged children be compulsory as it is for most five- and six-year-olds? Legislators across the country are debating those questions, and several states have already made decisions.

Georgia and New York legislators implemented universal preschool for four-year-olds in 1993 and 1997, respectively, and Massachusetts, New Jersey, and Kentucky have taken steps in that direction. The California Department of Education has recommended that public preschool be made available to all three- and four-year-olds, and appropriate legislation has been introduced. And in 1998 Vermont state legislator Bill Suchmann proposed a study of the cost of compulsory preschool for all three- and four-year-olds, saying that compulsion is the only way to guarantee that children have an equal opportunity for education.[1]

Supporters of universal preschool frequently argue that most parents fail to provide their children with the experiences and environment necessary to promote their healthy development. Suchmann explains, "Many children do not have parents available at home or even capable of appropriate intellectual stimulation."[2] The result is that many children are not "ready to learn" when they enter kindergarten. Consequently, those children perform at a substandard academic level, which leads to long-term problems including low educational attainment and juvenile delinquency. Proponents of preschool believe they can prevent those problems by intervening before children enter kindergarten. The California Department of Education's Universal Preschool Task Force puts it this way: "The concept of universal preschool recognizes that before children enter kindergarten, much of their potential for learning and healthy growth has already been determined. . . . Effective early childhood education is crucial to children's later success and well-being."[3]

From *Policy Analysis*, no. 333, February 9, 1999, pp. 3–23. Copyright © 1999 by Cato Institute. Reprinted by permission.

Whether or not one agrees with the advocates' premises, experience shows that there is little reason to believe universal preschool would significantly benefit children. Since the 1960s hundreds of privately and publicly funded early intervention programs have failed to significantly benefit participating children. The largest and best known early intervention program, Head Start, has been a failure. The U.S. Department of Health and Human Services synthesized the findings from the impact studies on Head Start and concluded that the program had no meaningful, long-term effects on the cognitive, social, or emotional development of participating children: "In the long run, cognitive and socioemotional test scores of former Head Start students do not remain superior to those of disadvantaged children who did not attend Head Start."[4]

Furthermore, evidence shows that middle-class children stand to gain little, if anything, from early education. In fact, many child development experts have argued that formal schooling can actually be harmful to young children. Finally, it is simply irresponsible to expand public schools when so many are failing to educate the children already enrolled. For those reasons, legislators would be wise to reject proposals for universal preschool.

Proposals for Universal Preschool

Proposals for universal preschool vary from state to state and from person to person. Advocates of universal preschool differ on such things as whether preschool should include infants and toddlers, whether parents should be charged an income-based fee, whether preschool should be formal and highly structured or informal and casual, whether programs should be school based or community-wide, and whether attendance should be voluntary or compulsory. Nevertheless, there is general agreement among advocates that preschool programs should be made available, at a minimum, to all three- and four-year-olds regardless of family income.

Universal preschool plans are not aimed solely at children who have traditionally been labeled "disadvantaged"—that is, those from low-income families.[5] The Carnegie Corporation explains, "Make no mistake about it: underachievement is not a crisis of certain groups: it is not limited to the poor; it is not a problem afflicting *other* people's children. Many middle- and upper-income children are also falling behind intellectually."[6] As Sharon L. Kagan, president of the National Association for the Education of Young Children and senior associate at the Bush Center in Child Development and Social Policy at Yale University, and Nancy E. Cohen, a graduate student in the Department of Psychology at the University of California at Berkeley, put it: "The problems in early care and education are legion for poor children and families, but they impact all young children."[7]

A majority of preschool proponents claim that such programs can ensure a child's healthy development. In addition, they claim that early schooling can inoculate children against problems during adolescence and early adulthood, such as low academic achievement, drug use, teenage pregnancy, juvenile delinquency, and unemployment. For example, the California Department of

Education's Universal Preschool Task Force wrote, "Extensive research in recent years has demonstrated the undeniable influence of preschool education on children's later success in school. When children experience success in school, numerous other problems, such as dropping out of school, delinquency, crime, and teenage pregnancy, are prevented."[8]

Other advocates of universal preschool simply see it as a way to provide daycare. For example, Edward F. Zigler, director of the Bush Center in Child Development and Social Policy at Yale University and a cofounder of Head Start, supports universal preschool for three- and four-year-olds as a school-based approach to child care.[9] It is important to note that Zigler has spoken against mandatory participation, and he has also argued that formal schooling per se may be premature and dangerous for many young children. In short, Zigler argues, "Our four-year-olds do have a place in school, but it is not at a school desk."[10]

Still other advocates see universal preschool as having a dual purpose. For example, Lisbeth Schorr, director of the Project on Effective Interventions at Harvard University, argues that federal-state and public-private agencies must commit to "first, a universal preschool program, providing all 3- and 4-year-olds with access to a setting offering both a high-quality preschool experience and child care during the hours that parents work . . . [and, second, a] universal system of supports to ensure that infants and toddlers get the best possible start on life."[11]

Many advocates share Schorr's desire to provide universal preschool or daycare for infants and toddlers. For example, in "Not by Chance," Kagan and Cohen write, "Stated most simply, the 'Not By Chance' mission is that by the year 2010, high-quality early care and education programs will be available and accessible to all children from birth to age five whose parents choose to enroll them."[12]

Kagan and Cohen conservatively estimate the cost of such a program at $116 billion a year.[13] They arrived at that estimate by multiplying the number of eligible children, 20 million, by the average per child cost of public education in 1994, $5,800. Kagan and Cohen say that in some ways the figure is too high, since not all parents would enroll their children. In other ways, however, they believe the figure is too low. For example, they say that "quality" early care and education programs would likely cost more than $5,800 per child per year. Indeed, that seems probable considering the lower student-teacher ratios that would almost certainly be required to care for infants and toddlers and the cost of capital expansion, among other things.

Proponents of universal preschool have various ideas for funding such programs, but there seems to be a consensus that all taxpayers, rather than parents themselves, should have to pay for the programs. According to Kagan and Cohen, "The public must acknowledge its role and pick up more of the tab for early care and education. . . . The public—not simply the direct consumers—should be responsible for funding American early care and education."[14] They suggest possible mechanisms for funding, including individual and corporate income taxes, federal payroll taxes, trust funds, and new sales or excise taxes.

Preschool and Public Education Today

New York and Georgia have implemented universal preschool programs, and Massachusetts, New Jersey, and Kentucky have taken significant steps in that direction.[15] All told, 37 states fund prekindergarten programs.[16] Fourteen of those states target four-year-olds only, and 13 target both three- and four-year-olds. Only 10 of the 37 states have established specific family income levels as required criteria for child eligibility, and not all of the remaining states plan to serve all children. A vast majority of programs use public schools to provide services, and some include parenting education and home-based components.[17]

Twenty-four states fund statewide, comprehensive programs for infants and toddlers.[18] Those programs typically include home visits to parents with newborns, parenting education, and limited child care. The National Center for Children in Poverty reports, "In many states there is a deepening commitment to comprehensive programs and planning for young children and families." In fact, since 1996, 10 states have started or expanded programs for infants and toddlers.[19] Per state spending on those programs ranges from $300,000 to over $200 million.[20]

In addition, states supplement state funds with federal funds. In 1997 approximately $11.5 billion in federal funds was available for child care and early education activities through five major programs: Head Start, the Child Care and Development Fund, the Child and Dependent Care Tax Credit, the Child and Adult Care Food Program, and the Social Services Block Grant.[21] That estimate does not include funds for more than 85 other federal preschool and child-care programs for children from birth through age five.[22] Most federal funds can be used at the states' discretion to pay for child-care and early education programs such as public preschool. As more and more states open public preschools, it is likely that there will be more pressure on federal legislators to increase the amount of federal funds available for that purpose.

Few legislators, thus far, have proposed mandatory attendance. However, if the history of public education is any indicator, it is likely that such mandates will appear in time. For example, in 1898 only 10 states had compulsory school attendance laws, and they generally applied to children between the ages of 8 and 14 and required attendance for a few months per year.[23] Today all 50 states have compulsory attendance laws, and many apply to children between the ages of 5 and 18 and require attendance for at least eight months per year.[24] The trend has been to expand the duration of required attendance to include both younger (age 5 and below) and older (age 18) students.[25] At present, the U.S. Department of Education reports, "The notion of transforming schools into all-day, year-round learning centers appears to be a popular one."[26] Given historic and current trends, it seems likely that the mandatory participation of three- and four-year-old children in preschool could be required by many states in the early part of the next century.

The trend of expanding the responsibilities of the public school system does not bode well for America's youngsters, particularly given the gross failure of the public school system to educate the children who are currently enrolled. Although we're spending five times more per pupil than we did in the 1940s and more than twice what we spent in the 1960s (adjusted for inflation), student achievement scores on a variety of competency exams have plummeted. Results of the 1994 National Assessment of Educational Progress showed that 57 percent of high school seniors scored below the "basic" level of history achievement, that is, they answered fewer than 42 percent of the questions correctly. The Third International Mathematics and Science Study, released in 1996, found that U.S. eighth-graders scored below the average of students from 40 nations on math and just above the average on science. Scholastic Aptitude Test scores have fallen from 978 in 1963 to 904 today.[27] The public schools' failings have forced colleges and businesses to do the work of the high schools: by the late 1980s, 21 percent of U.S. college freshmen were taking remedial writing courses and 16 percent were taking remedial reading courses. And a recent survey of 200 major corporations found that 22 percent of them teach employees reading and 41 percent teach writing.[28]

In addition, the poor quality of public schools has been faulted as a primary reason for the growing disparity between "haves" and "have-nots." As Cato's executive vice president David Boaz argues in *Liberating Schools: Education in the Inner City,*

> Education used to be a poor child's ticket out of the slums; now it is part of the system that traps people in the underclass. In a modern society a child who never learns to read adequately—much less to add and subtract, to write, to think logically and creatively—will never be able to lead a fully human life. He or she will be left behind by the rest of society. Our huge school systems, controlled by politics and bureaucracies, are increasingly unable to meet the needs of individual children. Too many children leave school uneducated, unprepared, and unnoticed by the bureaucracy.[29]

Given the relentless failure of the public school system to educate child after child, year after year, the downward extension of public schooling to three- and four-year-olds is ill-conceived and exceedingly irresponsible.[30]. . .

Conclusion

Whether or not early intervention enhances a child's development, the government should remain neutral with regard to the provision of early intervention programs. The state should not encourage early intervention programs by subsidizing them, nor should it, on the other hand, discourage early intervention programs by tinkering with the tax code to favor stay-at-home parenting. Put simply, it is not the province of the state to educate young children.

To be sure, the provision or funding for early education programs by the federal government cannot be squared with the notion of a national government whose powers are enumerated and thus limited by the Constitution. But equally important is the recognition that few issues are more important or personal than a young child's well-being, including her early education. You don't need a Ph.D. in political science to understand that parents, not 535 politicians in Washington and a handful of local officials, are best equipped to make decisions about early education—decisions that require keeping the unique needs of each child and family in mind. . . .

It is a truism that politicians relish the opportunity to be photographed with children—it isn't easy to say no to anything with a child attached to it, be it a politician or a program. Perhaps that is one reason why preschool programs have been so widely embraced. But we should be careful to scrutinize the facts behind these programs. Anything less would be a disservice to children whose welfare is dependent on the decisions adults make on their behalf. Given the facts—that preschool does not provide lasting benefits to disadvantaged or mainstream children—Congress and state legislators should resist calls to support or implement universal preschool for toddlers and young children.

Notes

1. See Anne Geggis, "Mandatory Preschool?" *Burlington Free Press*, February 16, 1998.

2. Bill Suchmann, "Not 'Mandatory,'" Letter to the editor, *Burlington Free Press*, March 8, 1998.

3. Superintendent's Universal Preschool Task Force, California Department of Education, "Ready to Learn: Quality Preschool Programs for California's Young Children," Draft, December 24, 1997, pp. 3–4, . . .

4. Ruth McKey et al., "The Impact of Head Start on Children, Families, and Communities," U.S. Department of Health and Human Services, HHS 85-31193, June 1985, Executive Summary, p. 1.

5. It is appropriate that advocates have stopped using the terms "low-income" and "disadvantaged" interchangeably, given the mounds of empirical evidence showing that family income does not determine a child's outcome. See, for example, Susan E. Mayer, *What Money Can't Buy: Family Income and Children's Life Chances* (Cambridge, Mass.: Harvard University Press, 1997); and Paul R. Amato and Alan Booth, *A Generation at Risk* (Cambridge, Mass.: Harvard University Press, 1997). However; that assumption appears to have been replaced by the equally untested assumption that *most* parents do not provide for their children's healthy development.

6. Carnegie Corporation of New York, "Years of Promise: A Comprehensive Learning Strategy for America's Children," September 1996, p. viii, . . . Emphasis in the original.

7. Sharon L. Kagan and Nancy E. Cohen, "Not by Chance: Creating an Early Care and Education System for America's Children," Bush Center in Child Development and Social Policy, Yale University, 1997, p. 3.

8. Superintendent's Universal Preschool Task Force, California Department of Education, "Universal Preschool: Urgent Education Priority," March 15, 1998, http://www. cde.ca.gov/preschool/priority.htm.

9. Edward F. Zigler, "School-Based Daycare for All Children," Testimony to the U.S. House Education and Labor Committee, February 9, 1989.

10. Edward F. Zigler, "Formal Schooling for Four-Year- Olds? No" in *Early Schooling: the National Debate*, ed. Sharon L. Kagan and Edward F. Zigler (New Haven, Conn.: Yale University Press, 1987), p. 40.

11. American Political Network Inc., "Spotlight: Early Childhood Conundrum," *Daily Report Card* 42, no. 7 (May 12, 1997). . . .

12. Kagan and Cohen, "Not by Chance," p. ix.

13. Sharon L. Kagan and Nancy E. Cohen, "Funding and Financing Early Care and Education: A Review of Issues and Strategies," Bush Center in Child Development and Social Policy, Yale University, 1997, p. 10.

14. Kagan and Cohen, "Not by Chance," p. 35.

15. Anne Mitchell, Carol Ripple, and Nina Chanana, "Prekindergarten Programs Funded by the States: Essential Elements for Policy Makers," Families and Work Institute, New York, July 1998, pp. 28–29, 36–37, 44–46, 56–58, 61–62.

16. Not included are city and county investments or state actions that direct federal funds to specific projects to benefit preschoolers, such as Head Start programs. See ibid., pp. 3–6.

17. Jane Knitzer and Stephen Page, "Map and Track: State Initiatives for Young Children and Families," National Center for Children in Poverty, New York, 1998.

18. Ibid., pp. 34, 45.

19. Ibid., p. 7.

20. Ibid., p. 15.

21. General Accounting Office, "Federal Child Care Funding," GAO/HEHS-98-70R, January 23, 1998, pp. 3, 8–9.

22. The General Accounting Office could not report a precise figure for total federal spending because many program administrators were unable to determine how much they spent on children under age five. See General Accounting Office, "Early Childhood Programs and Overlapping Target Groups," GAO/HEHS-95-4FS, October 1994, pp. 2–5.

23. Mary K. Novello, "A Case against Compulsion," Washington Institute Foundation, Seattle, Policy Brief, March 1998, p. 3.

24. Education Commission of the States Information Clearinghouse, "Compulsory School Age Requirements," *Clearinghouse Notes*, March 1994; and Education Commission of the States Information Clearinghouse, "State Characteristics: Kindergarten," April 1997. . . .

25. Kenneth Duckworth, *Encyclopedia of Educational Research*, 6th ed. (New York: Macmillan, 1992), vol. 1, p. 100.

26. Office of Educational Research and Improvement, U.S. Department of Education, "Dramatic Expansion Proposed for After-School Programs," *OERI Bulletin*, Fall 1998, p. 3. See also Ron Haskins, "Beyond Metaphor: The Efficacy of Early Childhood Education," *American Psychologist* 44, no 2 (February 1989): 280.

27. See David Boaz and R. Morris Barrett, "What Would a School Voucher Buy? The Real Cost of Private Schools," Cato Institute Briefing Paper no. 25, March 26, 1996, pp. 1–4, . . .; and David Boaz, "Department of Education" in *Cato Handbook for Congress: 106th Congress* (Washington: Cato Institute, 1999), pp. 123–31.

28. Boaz and Barrett, p. 2.

29. David Boaz, "The Public School Monopoly: America's Berlin Wall," in *Liberating Schools: Education in the Inner City* (Washington: Cato Institute, 1991), pp. 11–12.

30. For more information on public schools and ideas for reform, see Bruce Goldberg, *Why Schools Fail* (Washington: Cato Institute, 1996); David Harmer, *School Choice: Why You Need It, How You Get It* (Washington: Cato Institute, 1994); Daniel McGroarty, *Break These Chains: The Battle for School Choice* (Rocklin, Calif.: Prima, 1994), pp. 14–32; and Myron Lieberman, *Public Education: An Autopsy* (Cambridge, Mass.: Harvard University Press, 1993).

POSTSCRIPT

Should Public Money Be Spent on Universal Preschool?

Challenge Questions

1. Are there long lasting benefits to preschool attendance?
2. Should public funds support the education of children prior to kindergarten entry age?
3. What changes in society have brought about the need for preschool programs?
4. What are the long-term economic consequences for universal preschool?

Suggested Reading

Bowman, B. T. (2000). *Eager to learn: Educating our preschoolers.* Washington, D.C.: National Research Council.

Galinsky, E. (2006). *The economic benefits of high-quality early childhood programs: What makes the difference?* New York: Committee for Economic Development.

Gormley, W. T. (2005). Is it time for universal pre-k? *Phi Delta Kappan, 87,* 246–249.

Karoly, L. A., Greenwood, P. W., Everingham, S. S., Hoube, J., Kilburn, M. R., Rydell, et al. (1998). *Investing in our children: What we know and don't know about the costs and benefits of early childhood interventions.* Santa Monica, CA: RAND Corporation.

Masse, L. N., & Barnett, W. S. (2002). *A benefit-cost analysis of the Abecedarian early childhood intervention.* New Brunswick, NJ: National Institute for Early Education Research.

Schweinart, L. J., Montie, J., Xiang, Z., Barnett, W. S., Belfield, C. R., & Nores, M. (2005). *Lifetime effects: The High/Scope perry preschool study through age 40.* Ypsilanti, MI: High-Scope Press.

ISSUE 15

Is Regular Testing the Best Way to Improve Academic Performance?

YES: Matthew Gandal and Laura McGiffert, from "The Power of Testing," *Educational Leadership* (2003)

NO: Kenneth A. Wesson, from "The 'Volvo Effect'—Questioning Standardized Tests," *Young Children* (2001)

ISSUE SUMMARY

YES: Matthew Gandal and Laura McGiffert are on staff at Achieve, Inc., an organization whose goal is to raise academic standards and improve schools. They make the analogy that teachers testing students is similar to the medical tests doctors run on patients to determine what needs to be done to improve the patient.

NO: Kenneth A. Wesson, from San Jose/Evergreen Community College District in San Jose, California, also works as a consultant with educators in preschool through university level. He fears that tests do not adequately demonstrate what children have learned and may lead to teaching a narrow set of tested skills.

There seems to be no more intensely charged issue in education today than that of testing. The who, what, where, when, and why questions all good journalism 101 students are told to ask certainly apply to the testing issue. Let's take a look at these five important questions as they relate to the testing dilemma.

1. *Who should be tested?* Some say all students should be tested starting in preschool, and in fact Head Start does test four-year-olds. Others indicate only students who are showing signs of difficulties need testing to determine where additional help is required.
2. *What exactly should be tested?* What teachers teach varies greatly from classroom to classroom within a school, from district to district, from state to state, and from country to country. The fear is that teachers will teach a very narrow curriculum only including content upon which the students will be tested.
3. *Where should testing occur?* Teachers with a strong background in child development and observational skills say they are able to assess

children in a variety of ways both in informal learning situations inside the classroom and out and do not have to rely solely on formal in-class testing situations.

4. *When should testing occur?* Currently, No Child Left Behind requires annual testing for all students from third through eighth grades and once in high school. Some schools are starting formal testing earlier to prepare students for what they will face when it really counts toward Adequate Yearly Progress. The time spent on testing, many argue, could be much better spent actually having the students engaged in meaningful learning experiences. Proponents of testing say practice makes perfect and only through consistent formal testing will students learn to perform consistently and not allow stress to affect the results.

5. *Why is the test critical?* Why are assessments used and how will the results be received in a timely manner? Teachers should use the information gained to monitor and adjust teaching to meet the needs of individual students.

One of the other key issues related to testing is often centered around the phrase, "high stakes." When students have more than one opportunity to demonstrate they understand a particular skill or content then testing is effective.

Matthew Gandal and Laura McGiffert compare the need for school personnel to consistently test to the need that medical professionals have to test patients before they begin treatment. They insist that teachers use the data to inform practice just as physicians use these results to devise a treatment plan for the patient. Kenneth A. Wesson's fear is school personnel so concerned over the ramifications of their students doing poorly on the tests will narrowly focus the curriculum to only teach what is tested. Children will not be exposed to any subjects other than what they are required to know for the test. He also describes the failure of tests to adequately measure what students have learned, especially young children.

POINT

- Teachers rely on test results to understand what students are learning.

- Students should learn early in their schooling how to take tests.

- Formal assessments provide an accurate picture of how the student is progressing.

- Teachers can use test results to change their teaching to better help students.

- Standardized tests provide administrators with accurate information on student performance.

- Consistent testing will require teachers to teach the basics.

- Testing is an effective way of identifying gifted students.

COUNTERPOINT

- There are many authentic or meaningful assessment tools teachers can use.

- Time is wasted taking tests that could be better spent learning.

- A one-time picture may not be an accurate measure of students' learning.

- Test results often take months to be returned to teachers.

- The use of standardized tests assumes all students of a certain grade level are proficient in the same skills at the same time.

- Curriculum will become narrowed and only focused on the basics.

- Some students are tested constantly throughout their educational career.

YES

**Matthew Gandal
and Laura McGiffert**

The Power of Testing

Our society relies on testing. We expect tests to tell us whether our water is safe to drink, our cholesterol is too high, or the dishwasher we want to buy is the best value. These tests help us ensure our safety, take care of our health, and spend money wisely.

In medicine, no one seriously questions the connection between testing and appropriate medical treatment. A patient may present certain obvious symptoms, but before making a diagnosis, a doctor will routinely order a battery of tests to isolate the specific condition causing those symptoms. Once these tests have identified the problem, the doctor can offer a treatment plan.

We may complain about the quantity, cost, or inconvenience of these tests, but we do not question their basic value. We expect our doctors to stay up-to-date on the latest testing methods, and we demand that our health plans provide coverage for the tests that we need.

When it comes to education, testing holds the same power to bring about the result we all want—academically healthy students. Although some may raise legitimate concerns about the adequacy of some tests now in use, we should not discount the validity or utility of testing altogether.

Imagine that every child had an annual education checkup—a set of assessments created to measure agreed-on expectations. The results of this checkup would help teachers chart a course for individual student improvement. The federal No Child Left Behind Act offers exactly this sort of checkup to U.S. schools and teachers. By the 2005–2006 school year, schools in every state will assess students in reading and math annually in grades 3–8, and again before they graduate from high school. Science assessments in key grades will follow in 2007–2008.

No Child Left Behind puts tremendous pressure on states to create new assessments within a tight timeline. At least 36 states will have to develop more than 200 new tests within the next few years to comply with the federal law. If the end result is quantity without quality, little value will be added. If these assessments are of high quality, however, they have the potential to add significant value to school improvement efforts.

High Expectations for All

Doctors treat each patient differently on the basis of his or her individual needs, yet they base their judgments on conventions widely held across the profession. A thermometer is the same in Indianapolis or Miami, as are a blood pressure gauge and a scale. What do these measures have in common? Each reports results against a common standard. A fever is a fever, regardless of where you live.

Similarly, we should hold students to the same achievement standards regardless of their race, their socioeconomic status, or where they attend school. Unfortunately, this does not always happen. Teachers' expectations for their students differ; an *A* awarded in one school can mean something very different in another school. And students in disadvantaged communities are disproportionately held to lower standards.

Challenging all students to meet common standards should be non-negotiable. These standards must be more than just minimum requirements; they must be anchored in the challenging content and skills that students need to succeed. The highest-performing school systems around the world use this formula of common standards and assessments. Students in these countries routinely outperform U.S. students on international assessments, not because they have more talent, but because their schools expect more from them (TIMSS International Study Center, n.d.).

If these international comparisons are not convincing enough, we can find plenty of other evidence of the need for common, high standards. Too many students graduate from high school unprepared for the challenges that lie ahead. Increasing numbers of students at four-year colleges need remedial education in reading, writing, or mathematics. Employers tell a similar story: 34 percent of job applicants tested by major U.S. firms in 2001 lacked sufficient reading and math skills to do the jobs that they sought (American Management Association, 2001).

It Matters What We Measure

Useful medical tests must provide relevant and reliable information. A doctor would not order an X-ray to determine treatment for a sore throat, or a throat culture to treat a broken ankle. Doctors need tests that reveal information about a patient's particular condition.

Similarly, useful education assessments must make clear what they measure, and they must measure what we value most. In other words, states must tightly align assessments and standards to provide valid and meaningful information to educators.

Many states have found it difficult to accomplish this goal. Such alignment requires states to rely less on off-the-shelf, norm-referenced tests. These tests are not well aligned with most states' standards, and they report results against a norm, or average, rather than show whether students have met standards.

But even states that have developed their own tests have had trouble measuring their standards well. Our analyses of more than a dozen state tests designed to support standards-based instruction found that many tests are unbalanced, over-sampling some standards and under-sampling others. The more advanced content and skills usually get short shrift. For example,

Achieve's research has found that although most states' middle school math standards emphasize the foundations of algebra and geometry, more than 60 percent of the questions on their 8th grade tests dealt with computation, whole-number operations, and fractions.

In contrast, Massachusetts is an encouraging example of a state that has established a well-aligned system of standards and tests. The state's 10th grade exams in English and math are among the most robust assessments in the United States. They are based on clear and challenging standards, and they measure the depth and breadth of those standards well. Students must read and write thoughtfully to do well on the Massachusetts English language arts tests, and they must demonstrate their understanding of both basic and advanced mathematics to do well on the mathematics tests. These exams will count for graduation this year for the first time, and although this requirement has engendered some debate, most people in the state agree that the tests measure what matters most (Achieve, 2002a).

Using Data to Inform Practice

The patient's examination is over, the relevant tests have been completed, and the results have come back. Now, with all the information in hand, the doctor can offer a diagnosis and prescribe treatment. He or she may pronounce that the patient is in perfect health, or may recommend antibiotics, physical therapy, or even surgery. The important question is what happens after the results come back.

Just as in medicine, assessments in education are a means to an end. Assessments provide information on where students and schools need to improve, and they may provide incentives for students and schools to make the necessary improvements. But tests alone cannot create improvement. Educators, parents, and students must do the work of raising student achievement.

To make this possible, schools must get test results in a timely and useful manner. Waiting six months to see how students scored is of little value in helping those students improve. In addition, states must provide the test data in a form that educators can understand and use, with a freer degree of specificity than just a number on a scale. For example, a particular score in phonemic awareness conveys more to a teacher than an overall score in reading and certainly more than a score in English language arts. Specific results that identify students' particular strengths and weaknesses enable teachers to target instruction to meet the needs of each student.

New York City has dramatically altered how it reports results on state assessments in order to make them useful in classrooms. Partnering with the Grow Network, the city provides every parent, teacher, and principal with clear reports and instructional tools linking the data to state standards. Innovative technology can disaggregate the data to the individual level, allowing teachers to identify which students need help with which concepts, instead of requiring the entire class to review all topics. This approach has met with remarkable approval from educators and parents, who now find the data from the state tests much more useful (Grow Network, n.d.).

Meaningful data turn a diagnosis into action, thereby enabling educators to respond to individual student needs. They also make assessments a helpful tool for educators rather than simply an accountability hammer.

Beyond Large-Scale Tests

Doctors routinely pair their own clinical observations with an objective test—like a blood cell count—to identify an illness. This practice allows them to get the most coherent and complete information and make an accurate diagnosis.

Educators, too, get the best information about their students when they compile data from a number of sources, including classroom assignments, quizzes, diagnostic tests, and large-scale assessments. Together, these tools paint a fuller picture of student performance than a single assessment can.

Large-scale state tests play a crucial role in monitoring and encouraging school improvement, but they are not enough. To tap the power of testing, schools and teachers need access to diagnostic assessments that give them immediate feedback on student performance throughout the school year. As states add new large-scale tests to meet the requirements of No Child Left Behind, school districts have the chance to drop duplicative tests and invest instead in diagnostic tools. Spring Branch Independent School District in Texas has done this to great effect by developing lessons, quizzes, and tests directly aligned to the standards that teachers can use in their classrooms at any time (Achieve, 2002b).

The Real High Stakes

With the results of medical tests in hand, doctors have an ethical duty to give their patients the best possible care, regardless of the complexity of the disease. In fact, they can be held responsible if they do not provide appropriate treatment.

We, too, must provide the best education for all students—not just those who are easy to educate. Indeed, we are delinquent if we pass students through the grades and award them diplomas even if they are unprepared for the opportunities and challenges that await them. The real high stakes for these youngsters will come when they arrive at college or the workplace and lack the skills to succeed.

Like doctors who do not act responsibly, schools whose students consistently fail to meet expectations should face consequences. Rather than just a heavy stick, these consequences should include a combination of assistance and sanctions. In Kentucky and North Carolina, for example, the state assigns teams of distinguished educators to help low-performing schools develop and implement improvement plans that often focus on boosting the ability of teachers to teach to the state standards. Both states have seen a dramatic decline in the number of low-performing schools (Mandel, 2000). But ultimately, if assistance does not lead to improved performance, states must take stronger actions—including reconstitution or state takeover.

The Challenge Ahead

Standards, testing, and accountability have become the policy framework within which schools in every state must operate. For schools and students to reap the benefits of standards-based reform, we need clear and rigorous standards, assessments aligned to those standards, results reported in meaningful ways, and appropriate incentives and consequences. States and districts also must work in tandem to align curriculum, diagnostic assessments, and high-quality professional development for teachers.

A few critics will always condemn the use of testing in schools. However, with students' futures at stake, we must not abandon the very tools that have the power to transform teaching and learning. We must make our education assessments stronger and take advantage of the information they provide to ensure that all of our graduates are academically healthy.

References

Achieve, Inc. (2002a). *Three paths, one destination: Standards-based reform in Maryland, Massachusetts, and Texas.* Washington, DC: Author.

Achieve, Inc. (2002b). *Aiming higher: Meeting the challenges of education reform in Texas.* Washington, DC: Author.

American Management Association. (2001). *AMA survey on workplace testing: Basic skills, job skills, psychological measurement.* New York: Author.

Grow Network. (n.d.). *About the Grow Network* [Online]. . . .

Mandel, D. R. (2000). *Transforming underperforming schools: A strategy for Tennessee 2000.* Berkeley, CA: MPR Associates.

TIMSS International Study Center. (n.d.). *Third international mathematics and science study—1995* [Online]. . . .

Kenneth A. Wesson

 **NO**

The "Volvo Effect"—Questioning Standardized Tests

Several overarching and critically important points should be understood concerning the basic underpinnings of many of the standardized assessment tools that are increasingly being used by too many of our schools, as well as by those who evaluate our pre-K through college institutions.

As one of the founding members of the Association of Black Psychologists, the group largely responsible for minimizing the use of IQ tests in our nation's schools, I continue to find the testing debate both frustrating and fascinating. It has taken several politically irresponsible turns of late. Why is it, for example, that those who know the least about child development and learning are the most vocal about the value of standardized tests—and often are those most listened to? Why is it that those parents whose children have most often been declared the "winners" on such tests continue to pressure schools and politicians with demands to expand the use and importance (so-called merits) of standardized tests? Several factors that warrant inclusion in this discussion will help answer some of the more crucial elements concerning standardized tests.

Standardized Tests are Not Divine Creations

Standardized tests were not brought down from the mountaintop tucked under Moses' arm next to the Ten Commandments. They are not divine creations, contrary to the beliefs held by some. Commercial testing companies develop them with several clearly stated objectives driving their structure and architecture. Standardized tests were never intended to measure educational quality nor to serve as gauges of teaching excellence. Even the companies responsible for producing these tests will concede these facts. In numerous ways, standardized tests are grossly inappropriate evidence-seeking instruments for evaluating the quality of any school. This is a clear case of educational mistaken identity. There are several fallacies in the rationalizations behind high-stakes testing. The predictive value of the SAT is one example.

As one of the most influential standardized tests, the SAT was initially designed to measure college preparedness of one particular kind. The goal was

From *Young Children*, vol. 20, no. 12, November 22, 2000, pp. 34–36. Copyright © 2001 by NAEYC. Reprinted with permission from the National Association for the Education of Young Children. www.naeyc.org

to correlate an assessment tool with success during the freshman year of college only, not over one's entire college career. Instruction in the mostly New England-based, college-preparatory, males-only schools for which the test was devised aligned perfectly with the first-year coursework in Ivy League colleges, so these tests received wide acceptance as predictors of college success (albeit for an extremely small segment of the population). In many ways, the Ivy League freshman year was intended to be the logical next step for these young privileged students, and the very purpose behind their college-preparatory education; the Ivy League schools were precisely the colleges to which the college preparation for these boys had been directed.

Moreover, the SAT results regularly overpredicted college success for young men in general and underpredicted the college performance of young women. Although boys commonly earned higher SAT scores, their female counterparts regularly received significantly higher grade point averages in both high school and later in college than these same boys. Yet the higher SAT test scores determined college admissions, unfairly eliminating two generations of well-qualified young women from the opportunity to attend many of the nation's most elite institutions of higher education. Impartial educators, as well as any parents of girls, should find these facts quite troubling.

High Scores Correlate Best with High Family Income

Seldom was it mentioned that these test scores were more accurately mirror reflections of the economic advantages and disadvantages seen throughout American society. Test scores have typically had a high correlation to socio-economic characteristics such as the parents' occupations, levels of education, the family's income bracket, and the location of a student's elementary and secondary school (the highly predictable "ZIP code factor"). The highly touted Academic Performance Index (API) is more accurately an "Affluence-Poverty Index" with an extremely high and predictable correlation between standardized test scores and socioeconomic position. Family income plays such a dominant role in test scores that some testing analysts have facetiously proposed gauging something they call the "Volvo Effect" as a way to save vast amounts of money on standardized tests. Simply count the number of Volvos, sport utility vehicles, and comparably priced luxury cars used to transport students to and from a given school, and use that figure to measure "school quality."

"Leave No Child Behind"? Or Label a Few "Failures" and Leave Just *Them* Behind?

Let's be honest. If poor, Inner-city children consistently outscored children from wealthy suburban homes on standardized tests, is anyone naive enough to believe that we would still insist on using these tests as indicators of success? Would we continue to advocate the use of such tests if there were evidence that they presented inner-city students with a sizable advantage in the distribution of future opportunities in the United States? We would either abandon such a test or drastically modify it until it generated more "acceptable" results. This is one of the saddest realities underscoring the disingenuous positions taken in support of academic "merit."

Worst of all, we have tacitly agreed *which* children we will *allow* to fall into the lower end of this sorting process. Even as we announce that we will "leave no child behind," we are aware that many children will be left far behind by the very design of the standardized tests, and that we have made a settlement in advance as to who they will be and where they should live.

Before the first bubble is filled in, we know by historical data and, of course, by ZIP code how certain schools and children will stack up in the standardized-testing process. We can predict these general test results with fairly high degrees or accuracy.

America—A Land in Which "All Children are Above Average"?

Statistically, *some* schools and students must fall toward the lower end of any distributed performance range. Yet, in low-performing schools, administrators and teachers are now being unfairly and unwisely threatened with job termination. Many of us are asking, "Why would we use tests that are carefully and deliberately designed to produce performance variances, and then punish schools that help prove that these tests have indeed met their prestated design goals?" Only in Garrison Keillor's fictitious Lake Wobegon will one find a place "where all the kids are above average." Notwithstanding the rhetoric of many politicians, critics of public education, and other modestly informed contributors to this debate, a goal of 100% of the students scoring above the statistical average is impossible on any test.

Producing a wide range of student scores is essential on standardized tests. If most scores were bunched together in one single area, there would be no way to make any judgments about the hundreds of thousands of test-takers. Variations in test scores are vitally important; standardized tests must produce differences that can be interpreted as achievement, intelligence, or performance distinctions, otherwise students and their schools cannot be assigned a place or rank—the tests' ultimate purpose. Precisely what those differences truly indicate is a better question to ask.

These Tests Aren't Designed to Show What We Know Children Have Learned

Another factor to consider is this: test items that can *prove* that they are almost impervious to high-quality classroom instruction have a higher probability of remaining on a standardized test. Only those items that scatter youngsters across the performance spectrum are allowed to survive the question-pruning process. Important content and skills that appear to be mastered by most kids at a given grade level will invariably be replaced by "better" items that some children will get right and many others will get wrong. Test developers are well aware of the fact that standardized test scores reflect as much of what a child has learned *outside* of the classroom as what he or she has learned while *in* school. The question-pruning procedure renders test items that fall into the first group far more valuable during test construction, but then tests become, more honestly, measures of environmental enrichment and not indicators of teacher or school effectiveness.

Suppose, for example, that all of the country's third-grade educators did an excellent job of teaching a particular mathematical concept, and consequently all third-grade children gave the correct response to a test item representing that concept. That particular test item would be eliminated from the test because it does not sponsor the further distribution of the student respondents.

If masterful teachers achieved a high level of efficiency in teaching a target skill and 98% of their students responded with correct answers, that test item would be removed during test revision. It simply does not contribute to the goal of score variations. By the same token, if 98% of the children gave an incorrect response, that item would also have little testing value.

If 50% or fewer of the children responded correctly, then the item would help in dispersing children along the performance continuum. A 98% rate of correct responses would tell us that our teachers have indeed been engaged in some exceptionally successful instruction. However, these results ironically would backfire on the educators. Once the tests were modified, the newer version of the test would omit that success indicator. At that point, the test would again consist of only those items that continue to distribute youngsters, often reflecting what the students have yet to be taught, rather than rewarding them and their schools for actually learning what they were supposed to learn.

Limited English Proficiency Lowers Test Scores and Does Not Reflect Abilities

Likewise, children from limited-English backgrounds invariably score lower on reading and language fluency tests given in English. On mathematics tests they often perform well on the computational portions but demonstrate more difficulty with word problems. When children cannot convert a word problem into an algorithm (computational format) when tested for a particular skill in which they have already demonstrated proficiency, it is clear that language background interferes with favorable performance.

Spanish-speaking children in most states typically perform better on mathematics test items that are less dependent on language background. There is a distinct and obvious language advantage when a child lives in a home where he regularly hears his parents and family members express ideas and use language in a manner consistent with the language used by the teachers during classroom instruction and the language found in the textbooks, and the language later encountered on standardized tests. Language proficiency in many ways dictates the final testing outcome.

For most Americans, when a passage to be read in French on a standardized test is followed by questions that are also in French, and the correct answers are arrived at by understanding and processing fine-line language distinctions in French, that is the point at which the French language has become a key element in their success on this hypothetical test. Language fluency would constitute either a contributing or a determining factor in student performance, which would clearly be attributed in part to familiarity with and fluency in French.

America's Spanish-speaking kids would be at a distinct advantage if standardized tests were all administered in Spanish only, but that would constitute an intolerable circumstance due to the socially unacceptable results it would produce and such a practice would be put to a very quick end.

Our overexpanded preoccupation with multiple-choice, fill-in-the-bubble standardized tests has taken on dangerous new dimensions with our deceptive claims of being in pursuit of accountability and educational quality justifying their usage. Can any truly meaningful concept be reduced to a bubble response? Should a concept reduced to its most diminished form be used as a valid indicator of superior levels of intelligence, acquisition, or cognition? If a significant notion can be intellectually downgraded to a bubble, then legitimate questions should be raised concerning its ability to reflect the higher levels of thinking (far better examples of quality) that we seek to teach.

Louis Albert, the former vice president of the American Association of Higher Education, said, "It is deep and long-lasting learning that we are after." Such learning is not to be found on a standardized test. Much of what *is* found on many standardized assessment tools would not at all suggest deep understandings of the important principles that underlie the very essence of any significant content area or discipline. High ideational complexity, inventiveness, applying one's ingenuity and creativity in a problem-solving situation (genuinely high standards) cannot be converted into the "bubblized" format of standardized tests.

What about the cultivation of important talents such as perseverance, intuition, adaptability, responsibility, sensitivity, empathy, self-control, honesty, trustworthiness, confidence, motivation, effective communication skills, open-mindedness, generosity, originality, cooperation, kindness, commitment, loyalty, friendliness, emotional maturity, and inventiveness? While none of these can be measured via the current standardized testing strategies, any parent, prospective employer, or educator would gladly exchange 100 individuals who tested high in, say, long division for one who exhibited these other more valuable characteristics. Indeed, there are worthy purposes in educating our children. American educator Susan Kovalic describes the primary goal of education as the careful development of intelligent, fully functioning citizens who in many ways will determine the future of our civilization.

That which is quantifiable is sometimes devoid of genuinely significant educational, personal, or social value. And the assessment tools currently being used are not adequately capturing the best indicators of those traits, characteristics, and skills we need to develop in today's young people. Although these may defy easy or precise calibration, they are of far greater educational value for all children regardless of where in the world their learning takes place. Let's give more time and attention in our schools to the many other talents that matter in the long run in an enlightened society. It's time for a serious reexamination of our unbridled faith in standardized tests.

NAEYC VIEWPOINT . . .

Standardized Tests *Do Not Equal* Assessment or Accountability!

As demands for educational accountability grow, inappropriate uses of standardized testing are all too common. But it is important that concerns about the misuse of testing not be extended to argue against assessment or greater accountability.

The following *principles* are drawn from the 1990 NAEYC joint position statement with the National Association of Early Childhood Specialists in State Departments of Education (NAECS/SDE) regarding program evaluation and accountability.

1. No principle of appropriate curriculum are violated in constructing assessment procedures to evaluate programs or determine their accountability.

2. Children's performance data collected by teachers to aid in planning instruction are used to evaluate *how well a program is meeting its goals* for children and families.

3. Programs use multiple indicators of progress in all developmental domains to evaluate the programs' effect on children's development and learning. Standardized achievement tests are prohibited before third grade, preferably the fourth.

4. To judge program effectiveness, all components of a program are considered within the overall context of opportunities for children and families, including staff development/evaluation, parent satisfaction, program administration, physical environment, and health and safety. Outside, independent evaluation such as program accreditation is useful.

5. Programs employ sampling methods whenever feasible if they are mandated to use standardized tests of children's progress for program evaluation/accountability. This sampling approach eliminates subjecting all children to testing, which can consume large blocks of time, cause children undue stress, and result in unwarranted decisions about individual children.

Greater accountability is helpful, especially if we consider how well schools and communities are fully supporting *each* child's educational achievement.

Guidelines for Appropriate Curriculum Content and Assessment in Programs Serving Children Ages 3 through 8—NAEYC and NAECS/SDE position statement is available online . . .

POSTSCRIPT

Is Regular Testing the Best Way to Improve Academic Performance?

Challenge Questions

1. What are some signs of test anxiety children may display?
2. What are some alternatives to formal testing that may be used to gather information on student performance?
3. What does Mr. Wesson mean by the "Volvo Effect" and do you think this happens?

Suggested Reading

Black, S. (2003). Too soon to test. *American School Board Journal*, 190(1), 38–40.

Craig, C. (June 2004). The dragon in school backyards: The influence of mandated testing on school contexts and educators' narrative knowing. *Teachers College Record*, 106(6), 1229–1257.

Guskey, T. R. (2003). How classroom assessments improve learning. *Educational Leadership*, 60(5), 6–11.

Haladyna, T., Haas, N., & Allison, J. (1998). Continuing tensions in standardized testing. *Childhood Education*, 7(5), 262–273.

Kohn, A. (2001). Fighting the tests: Turning frustration into action. *Young Children*, 56(2), 19–24.

McCaw, D. S. (2007). Dangerous intersection ahead. *The School Administrator*, 2(64), 32–34.

Neill, M. (2003). The dangers of testing. *Educational Leadership*, 60(5), 43–46.

Sloane, F. C., & Kelly, A. E. (2003). Issues in high-stakes testing programs. *Theory into Practice*, 42(1), 12–17.

ISSUE 16

Will School Improvement Efforts Alone Narrow the Racial/Ethnic Achievement Gap?

YES: Kati Haycock, from "Closing the Achievement Gap," *Educational Leadership* (March 2001)

NO: Richard Rothstein, from "Class and the Classroom: Even the Best Schools Can't Close the Race Achievement Gap," *American School Board Journal* (October 2004)

ISSUE SUMMARY

YES: Kati Haycock is the executive director of Education Trust and follows the belief that adequate funding and high standards will improve academic achievement.

NO: Richard Rothstein is a research associate of the Economic Policy Institute and a visiting professor at Teachers College, Columbia University in New York City. Rothstein believes the achievement gap will be narrowed when collaboration occurs from a number of outside groups, not just those functioning within the schools.

There is a lot riding on this debate. Can schools make a difference in the lives of children to the point that any deficiencies that are a result of either the home environment, race, or economic level be negated by the school curriculum? Do the events in the early years before a child starts school and the hours after entry before and after school affect academic achievement? The Education Trust defines the achievement gap as the difference in school achievement between groups of students, such as racial/ethnic groups, family income levels, or special needs. This issue will focus on the racial/ethnic achievement gap in America.

The dental profession would not want to be rated based on the number of cavities their patients have if they have no control over early dental care practices or daily oral hygiene. School personnel are facing a similar situation when they are being rated based on academic achievement of students who may or may not have quality preschool experiences, receive proper nutrition, or have access to early literacy materials in the home. Others say anything can be achieved if the goal is important and work is focused and purposeful. If all students have access to teachers who are knowledgeable, caring, and set high standards for their students, then the students will achieve.

The racial/ethnic achievement gap appears early in a child's schooling. Black children enter school one to three years behind white students. One third to one half of black and Latino kindergartners have math, reading, and general achievement test scores in the bottom quarter, whereas only a sixth of white kindergartners had test scores that low.

The gap continues to widen during the summer months when minority families may not be able to afford summer tutors, camps, or other enrichment programs for their children. Students affected the most by the racial/ethnic achievement gap are often attending schools least prepared to help these students. Funding for supplemental programs is nonexistent in schools serving predominately minority or urban students. These schools often have large class sizes and teachers who meet minimal standards, and may lack resources to fully assist the students who most need help.

Under No Child Left Behind (NCLB), schools must report test results by race. Will this bring more attention to the gap or will it cause more talk and little action over a viable solution?

Kati Haycock contends the only way to really close the ethnic and racial achievement gap is to fix underperforming schools. More resources must be devoted to the schools that need the most help. Only after we put great effort, funds, and expertise in our weakest schools will the students attending these schools succeed.

Richard Rothstein wants to bring more players to the table when it comes to improving academic achievement. He says educators alone can't bring about change and families and community groups must be involved and become partners in education. Training parents on the importance of their job is crucial for success to occur. He believes there are income, health, safety, along with other gaps that contribute to the academic achievement gap.

POINT

- Educators must provide a challenging curriculum for all students.

- Student expectations must be raised.

- Quality teachers are critical to improving academic achievement.

COUNTERPOINT

- Teachers alone can't bring about a change in the achievement gap simply by teaching better.

- Telling students they must do better without helping them get there is not the answer.

- Parents and other family members must be more involved in student achievement.

YES

Kati Haycock

Closing the Achievement Gap

There's been a lot of talk lately about the achievement gap that separates low-income and minority youngsters from other young Americans. For more than a generation, we focused on improving the education of poor and minority students. Not surprisingly, we made real gains. Between 1970 and 1988, the achievement gap between African American and white students was cut in half, and the gap separating Latinos and whites declined by one-third. That progress came to a halt around 1988, however, and since that time, the gaps have widened.

Although everybody wanted to take credit for narrowing the gap, nobody wanted to take responsibility for widening it. So, for a while, there was mostly silence.

But that is changing. Good. Because if we don't get the numbers out on the table and talk about them, we're never going to close the gap once and for all. I worry, though, about how many people head into discussions without accurate data. And I worry even more about how many education leaders have antiquated—and downright wrong—notions about the whys beneath the achievement gap.

I want to respond to both these worries by putting some crucial data on the table and by sharing what both research and experience teach us about how schools can close the gaps between groups of students. Most of the data are from standard national sources, including the National Center for Education Statistics (NCES) and the National Assessment of Education Progress (NAEP), as well as from states and local school districts that have been unusually successful at educating poor and minority students.[1]

Understanding Achievement Patterns

The performance of African American and Latino youngsters improved dramatically during the 1970s and 1980s. The 1990s, however, were another matter. In some subjects and at some grade levels, the gaps started growing; in others, they were stagnant (National Center for Education Statistics, 2001).

- Reading achievement among 17-year-old African Americans and Latinos climbed substantially through the 1970s and 1980s, but gaps separating them from other students widened somewhat during the 1990s.

- The patterns in mathematics achievement look similar for 13-year-olds, with the African American and white gap reaching its narrowest in 1990 and the Latino and white gap narrowing until 1992, and the gaps widening thereafter.

In 1999, by the end of high school

- Only 1 in 50 Latinos and 1 in 100 African American 17-year-olds can read and gain information from specialized text—such as the science section in the newspaper (compared to about 1 in 12 whites), and
- Fewer than one-quarter of Latinos and one-fifth of African Americans can read the complicated but less specialized text that more than half of white students can read.

The same patterns hold in math.

- About 1 in 30 Latinos and 1 in 100 African Americans can comfortably do multistep problem solving and elementary algebra, compared to about 1 in 10 white students.
- Only 3 in 10 African American and 4 in 10 Latino 17-year-olds have mastered the usage and computation of fractions, commonly used percents, and averages, compared to 7 in 10 white students.

By the end of high school, in fact, African American and Latino students have skills in both reading and mathematics that are the same as those of white students in 8th grade. Significant differences also persist in the rates at which different groups of students complete high school and in their postsecondary education experiences.

- In the 18- to 24-year-old group, about 90 percent of whites and 94 percent of Asians have either completed high school or earned a GED. Among African Americans, the rate drops to 81 percent; among Latinos, 63 percent.
- Approximately 76 percent of white graduates and 86 percent of Asian graduates go directly to college, compared to 71 percent of African American and 71 percent of Latino graduates.
- Young African Americans are only about half as likely as white students to earn a bachelor's degree by age 29; young Latinos are only one-third as likely as whites to earn a college degree (see fig. 1).

What's Going On?

Over the past five years, staff members at the Education Trust have shared these and related data on the achievement gap with hundreds of audiences all over the United States. During that time, we've learned a lot about what people think is going on.

When we speak with adults, no matter where we are in the country, they make the same comments. "They're too poor." "Their parents don't care." "They come to school without an adequate breakfast." "They don't have enough

Figure 1

Highest Educational Attainment for Every 100 Kindergartners

(Ages 15 to 29)	African Americans	Asians	Latinos	Whites
Graduate from high school	88	90	63	88
Complete at least some college	50	74	33	59
Obtain at least a bachelor's degree	16	51	10	28

Source: U.S. Census Bureau. (1998). Educational Attainment Detailed Tables, October CPS.

books in the home." "Indeed, there aren't enough parents in the home." Their reasons, in other words, are always about the children and their families.

Young people, however, have different answers. They talk about teachers who often do not know the subjects that they are teaching. They talk about counselors who consistently underestimate their potential and place them in lower-level courses. They talk about principals who dismiss their concerns. And they talk about a curriculum and a set of expectations that feel so miserably low-level that they literally bore the students right out the school door.

When we ask, "What about the things that the adults are always talking about—neighborhood violence, single-parent homes, and so on?"—the young people's responses are fascinating. "Sure, those things matter," they say. "But what hurts us more is that you teach us less."

The truth is that the data bear out what the young people are saying. It's not that issues like poverty and parental education don't matter. Clearly they do. But we take the students who have less to begin with and then systematically give them less in school. In fact, we give these students less of everything that we believe makes a difference. We do this in hundreds of different ways.

Let me be clear. It would help if changes were made outside of schools, too: if parents spent more time with their children, if poverty didn't crush so many spirits, and if the broader culture didn't bombard young people with so many destructive messages. But because both research and experience show that what schools do matters greatly, I'll concentrate on what works in education.

Lesson 1: Standards Are Key

Historically, we have not agreed on what U.S. students should learn at each grade level—or on what kind of work is good enough. These decisions have been left to individual schools and teachers. The result is a system that, by and large, doesn't ask much of most of its students. And we don't have to go far to find that out: Ask the nearest teenager. In survey after survey, young people tell us that they are not challenged in school.

The situation is worse in high-poverty and high-minority schools. For the past six years, our staff at the Education Trust has worked with teachers who are trying to improve the achievement levels of their students. But while we've been observing these high-poverty classrooms, we've also looked carefully at what happens there—what kinds of assignments teachers give, for example—compared to what happens in other classrooms.

We have come away stunned. Stunned, first, by how little is expected of students in high-poverty schools—how few assignments they get in a given school week or month. Stunned, second, by the low level of the few assignments that they do get. In high-poverty urban middle schools, for example, we see a lot of coloring assignments, rather than writing or mathematics assignments. Even at the high school level, we found coloring assignments. "Read *To Kill a Mockingbird,*" says the 11th grade English teacher, "and when you're finished, color a poster about it." Indeed, national data make it clear that we expect so little of students in high-poverty schools that we give them *As* for work that would earn a *C* or *D* anywhere else.

Clear and public standards for what students should learn at benchmark grade levels are a crucial part of solving the problem. They are a guide—for teachers, administrators, parents, and students themselves—to what knowledge and skills students must master.

Kentucky was the first state to embrace standards-based reform. Ten years ago, the Kentucky legislature put out an ambitious set of learning goals and had the audacity to declare that all of its children—even the poorest— would meet those goals. Leaders in Kentucky are the first to acknowledge that they are not there yet. But their progress is clear and compelling. And poor children are, in fact, learning in all subjects. For example, in reading, 7 of the 20 top-performing elementary schools are high-poverty; in math, 8 of the top 20 are high-poverty; in writing, 13 of the top 20 are high-poverty.

Lesson 2: All Students Must Have a Challenging Curriculum

Standards won't make much of a difference, though, if they are not accompanied by a rigorous curriculum that is aligned with those standards. Yet in too many schools, some students are taught a high-level curriculum, whereas other students continue to be taught a low-level curriculum that is aligned with jobs that no longer exist.

Current patterns are clearest in high schools, where students who take more-rigorous coursework learn more and perform better on tests. Indeed, the more-rigorous courses they take, the better they do.

- In mathematics, students who complete the full college preparatory sequence perform much higher on the National Assessment of Educational Progress (NAEP) than those who complete only one or two courses.
- The reverse is true of watered-down, traditional "vocational" courses. The more vocational education courses students take, the lower their performance on the NAEP.

- Although some of these differences are clearly attributable to the fact that higher-scoring students are often assigned to tougher classes, careful research shows the positive impact of more-rigorous coursework even on formerly low-achieving students.

Since 1983, we've made progress in increasing the number of students who take a rigorous, college-preparatory curriculum. But the pace is not fast enough.

- Almost three-quarters of high school graduates go on to higher education, but only about half of them complete even a mid-level college-preparatory curriculum (four years of English and three years each of math, science, and social studies). If we also include two years of a foreign language and a semester of computer science, the numbers drop to about 12 percent. The numbers are worse for African Americans, Latinos, and low-income students.

These patterns are disturbing because the quality and intensity of high school coursework are the most important determinants of success in college—more important than class rank or scores on college admissions tests (Adelman, 1998). Curriculum rigor is also important for work-bound students (Bottoms, 1998).

A few years ago, the chancellor of the New York City schools required all 9th graders to take the Regents math and science exams. Though many people were worried that failure rates would be astronomical, in one year the number of Latinos in New York City who passed the Regents science exam tripled, and the number of African Americans who passed doubled. Other groups also had gains in science and mathematics. Did they *all* pass? No, they didn't. But as a principal friend of mine used to say, "At least they failed something worthwhile." And remember, these youngsters previously would never even have been given a chance to learn higher-order content.

Lesson 3: Students Need Extra Help

Ample evidence shows that almost all students can achieve at high levels if they are taught at high levels. But equally clear is that some students require more time and more instruction. It won't do, in other words, just to throw students into a high-level course if they can't even read the textbook.

One of the most frequent questions we are asked by stressed-out middle and high school teachers is "How am I supposed to get my students ready to pass the (fill-in-the-blank) grade test when they enter with 3rd grade reading skills and I have only my 35-minute period each day?"

The answer, of course, is "You can't." Especially when students are behind in foundational skills like reading and mathematics, we need to double or even triple the amount and quality of instruction that they get.

Around the United States, states and communities are wrestling with how best to provide those extras. Kentucky gives high-poverty schools extra funds every year to extend instruction in whatever way works best for their community: before school, after school, weekends, or summers. Maryland provides a wide range of assistance to students who are not on track to pass its new high school graduation test. And San Diego created more time, mostly within the regular school day, by doubling—even tripling—the amount of instructional time devoted to literacy and mathematics for low-performing students and by training *all* of its teachers.

Lesson 4: Teachers Matter a Lot

If students are going to be held to high standards, they need teachers who know the subjects and know how to teach the subjects. Yet large numbers of students, especially those who are poor or are members of minority groups, are taught by teachers who do not have strong backgrounds in the subjects they teach.

- In every subject area, students in high-poverty schools are more likely than other students to be taught by teachers without even a minor in the subjects they teach.
- The differences are often greater in predominantly minority high schools. In math and science, for example, only about half the teachers in schools with 90 percent or greater minority enrollments meet even their states' minimum requirements to teach those subjects—far fewer than in predominantly white schools.
- The patterns are similar regardless of the measure of teacher qualifications— experience, certification, academic preparation, or performance on licensure tests. We take the students who most depend on their teachers for subject-matter learning and assign them teachers with the weakest academic foundations.

A decade ago, we might have said that we didn't know how much this mattered. We believed that what students learned was largely a factor of their family income or parental education, not of what schools did. But recent research has turned these assumptions upside down. What schools do matters enormously. And what matters most is good teaching.

- Results from a recent Boston study of the effects teachers have on learning are fairly typical (Boston Public Schools, 1998). In just one academic year, the top third of teachers produced as much as six times the learning growth as the bottom third of teachers. In fact, 10th graders taught by the least effective teachers made nearly no gains in reading and even lost ground in math.
- Groundbreaking research in Tennessee and Texas shows that these effects are cumulative and hold up regardless of race, class, or prior achievement levels. Some of the classrooms showing the greatest gains are filled with low-income students, some with well-to-do students. And the same is true with the small-gain classrooms. It's not the kids after all: Something very different is going on with the teaching (Sanders & Rivers, 1996).

Findings like these make us wonder what would happen if, instead of getting far fewer than their fair share of good teachers, underachieving students actually got more. In a study of Texas school districts, Harvard economist Ronald Ferguson (1998) found a handful of districts that reversed the normal pattern: Districts with initially high-performing (presumably relatively affluent) 1st graders hired from the bottom of the teacher pool, and districts with initially low-performing (presumably low-income) 1st graders hired from the upper tiers of the teacher pool. By the time their students reached high school, these districts swapped places in student achievement.

El Paso, Texas, is a community that has taken such research seriously. Eight years ago, despite the extraordinarily high poverty of their city, local education leaders set some very high standards for what their students should know and be able to do. Unlike other communities, though, they didn't stop there. At the University of Texas, El Paso, the faculty revamped how it prepared teachers. New elementary teachers, for example, take more than twice as much math and science as their predecessors. More to the point, though, the teachers of these courses are math and science professors who themselves participated in the standard-setting process and who know, at a much deeper level, what kinds of mathematical understanding the teachers need.

The community also organized a structure—the El Paso Collaborative—to provide support to existing teachers and to help them teach to the new standards. The collaborative sponsored intensive summer workshops, monthly meetings for teachers within content areas, and work sessions in schools to analyze student assignments against the standards. The three school districts also released 60 teachers to coach their peers.

The results are clear: no more low performing schools and increased achievement for *all groups of students,* with bigger increases among the groups that have historically been behind.

An Academic Core

El Paso and the other successful communities and states have a lot to teach us about how to raise overall achievement and close gaps. Each community, of course, does things a little bit differently. What we learn is the value of a relentless focus on the academic core. Clear and high standards. Assessments aligned with those standards. Accountability systems that demand results for all kinds of students. Intensive efforts to assist teachers in improving their practice. And extra instruction for students who need it.

Note

1. For state and national data on student achievement, visit the Education Trust Web site . . . and click the data icon.

References

Adelman, C. (1998). *Answers in the toolbox.* Washington, DC: U.S. Department of Education.

Boston Public Schools. (1998, March 9). High school restructuring. Boston: Author.

Bottoms, G. (1998). *High schools that work.* Atlanta, GA: Southern Regional Education Board.

Ferguson, R. (1998). Can schools narrow the black-white test score gap? In C. Jencks & M. Phillips (Eds.), *The black-white test score gap* (pp. 318–374). Washington, DC: The Brookings Institute.

National Center for Education Statistics. (2001). *NAEP summary data tables* [Online]. Washington, DC: U.S. Department of Education. . . .

Sanders, W., & Rivers, J. (1996). *Cumulative and residual effects of teachers on future student academic achievement.* Knoxville, TN: University of Tennessee Value-Added Research and Assessment Center.

Richard Rothstein

 **NO**

Class and the Classroom: Even the Best Schools Can't Close the Race Achievement Gap

The achievement gap between poor and middle-class black and white children is widely recognized as our most important educational challenge. But we prevent ourselves from solving it because of a commonplace belief that poverty and race can't "cause" low achievement and that therefore schools must be failing to teach disadvantaged children adequately. After all, we see many highly successful students from lower-class backgrounds. Their success seems to prove that social class cannot be what impedes most disadvantaged students.

Yet the success of some lower-class students proves nothing about the power of schools to close the achievement gap. In every social group, there are low achievers and high achievers alike. On average, the achievement of low-income students is below the average achievement of middle-class students, but there are always some middle-class students who achieve below typical low-income levels. Similarly, some low-income students achieve above typical middle-class levels. Demography is not destiny, but students' family characteristics are a powerful influence on their relative average achievement.

Widely repeated accounts of schools that somehow elicit consistently high achievement from lower-class children almost always turn out, upon examination, to be flawed. In some cases, these "schools that beat the odds" are highly selective, enrolling only the most able or most motivated lower-class children. In other cases, they are not truly lower-class schools—for example, a school enrolling children who qualify for subsidized lunches because their parents are graduate students living on low stipends. In other cases, such schools define high achievement at such a low level that all students can reach it, despite big gaps that remain at more meaningful levels.

It seems plausible that if *some* children can defy the demographic odds, *all* children can, but that belief reflects a reasoning whose naiveté we easily recognize in other policy areas. In human affairs where multiple causation is typical, causes are not disproved by exceptions. Tobacco firms once claimed that smoking does not cause cancer because some people smoke without getting cancer. We now consider such reasoning specious. We do not suggest that alcoholism

From *American School Board Journal*, October 2004, pp. 17–21. Copyright © 2004 by National School Boards Association. All rights reserved. Reprinted with permission.

does not cause child or spousal abuse because not all alcoholics are abusers. We understand that because no single cause is rigidly deterministic, some people can smoke or drink to excess without harm. But we also understand that, on average, these behaviors are dangerous. Yet despite such understanding, quite sophisticated people often proclaim that the success of some poor children proves that social disadvantage does not cause low achievement.

Partly, our confusion stems from failing to examine the concrete ways that social class actually affects learning. Describing these may help to make their influence more obvious—and may make it more obvious why the achievement gap can be substantially narrowed only when school improvement is combined with social and economic reform.

The Reading Gap

Consider how parents of different social classes tend to raise children. Young children of educated parents are read to more consistently and are encouraged to read more to themselves when they are older. Most children whose parents have college degrees are read to daily before they begin kindergarten, but few children whose parents have only a high school diploma or less benefit from daily reading. And, white children are more likely than black children to be read to in their prekindergarten years.

A 5-year-old who enters school recognizing some words and who has turned the pages of many stories will be easier to teach than one who has rarely held a book. The second child can be taught, but with equally high expectations and effective teaching, the first will be more likely to pass an age-appropriate reading test than the second. So the achievement gap begins.

If a society with such differences wants all children, irrespective of social class, to have the same chance to achieve academic goals, it should find ways to help lower-class children enter school having the same familiarity with books as middle-class children have. This requires rethinking the institutional settings in which we provide early childhood care, beginning in infancy.

Some people acknowledge the impact of such differences but find it hard to accept that good schools should have so difficult a time overcoming them. This would be easier to understand if Americans had a broader international perspective on education. Class backgrounds influence *relative* achievement everywhere. The inability of schools to overcome the disadvantage of less-literate homes is not a peculiar American failure but a universal reality. The number of books in students' homes, for example, consistently predicts their test scores in almost every country. Turkish immigrant students suffer from an achievement gap in Germany, as do Algerians in France, as do Caribbean, African, Pakistani, and Bangladeshi pupils in Great Britain, and as do Okinawans and low-caste Buraku in Japan.

An international reading survey of 15-year-olds, conducted in 2000, found a strong relationship in almost every nation between parental occupation and student literacy. The gap between the literacy of children of the highest-status workers (such as doctors, professors, and lawyers) and the lowest-status workers (such as waiters and waitresses, taxi drivers, and mechanics) was even greater in Germany and the United Kingdom than it was in the United States.

After reviewing these results, a U.S. Department of Education summary concluded that "most participating countries do not differ significantly from the United States in terms of the strength of the relationship between socioeconomic status and literacy in any subject." Remarkably, the department published this conclusion at the same time that it was guiding a bill through Congress—the No Child Left Behind Act—that demanded every school in the nation abolish social class differences in achievement within 12 years.

Urging less-educated parents to read to children can't fully compensate for differences in school readiness. Children who see parents read to solve their own problems or for entertainment are more likely to want to read themselves. Parents who bring reading material home from work demonstrate by example to children that reading is not a segmented burden but a seamless activity that bridges work and leisure. Parents who read to children but don't read for themselves send a different message.

How parents read to children is as important as whether they do, and an extensive literature confirms that more educated parents read aloud differently. When working-class parents read aloud, they are more likely to tell children to pay attention without interruptions or to sound out words or name letters. When they ask children about a story, the questions are more likely to be factual, asking for names of objects or memory of events.

Parents who are more literate are more likely to ask questions that are creative, interpretive, or connective, such as, "What do you think will happen next?" "Does that remind you of what we did yesterday?" Middle-class parents are more likely to read aloud to have fun, to start conversations, or as an entree to the world outside. Their children learn that reading is enjoyable and are more motivated to read in school.

The Conversation Gap

There are stark class differences not only in how parents read but in how they converse. Explaining events in the broader world to children at the dinner table, for example, may have as much of an influence on test scores as early reading itself. Through such conversations, children develop vocabularies and become familiar with contexts for reading in school. Educated parents are more likely to engage in such talk and to begin it with infants and toddlers, conducting pretend conversations long before infants can understand the language.

Typically, middle-class parents ask infants about their needs, then provide answers for the children. ("Are you ready for a nap now? Yes, you are, aren't you?") Instructions are more likely to be given indirectly: "You don't want to make so much noise, do you?" This kind of instruction is really an invitation for a child to work through the reasoning behind an order and to internalize it. Middle-class parents implicitly begin academic instruction for infants with such indirect guidance.

Yet such instruction is quite different from what policy-makers nowadays consider "academic" for young children: explicit training in letter and number recognition, letter-sound correspondence, and so on. Such drill in basic skills can be helpful but is unlikely to close the social class gap in learning.

Soon after middle-class children become verbal, their parents typically draw them into adult conversations so the children can practice expressing their own opinions. Being included in adult conversations this early develops a sense of entitlement in children; they feel comfortable addressing adults as equals and without deference. Children who ask for reasons, rather than accepting assertions on adult authority, develop intellectual skills upon which later academic success in school will rely. Certainly, some lower-class children have such skills and some middle-class children lack them. But, on average, a sense of entitlement is based on one's social class.

Parents whose professional occupations entail authority and responsibility typically believe more strongly that they can affect their environments and solve problems. At work, they explore alternatives and negotiate compromises. They naturally express these personality traits at home when they design activities in which children figure out solutions for themselves. Even the youngest middle-class children practice traits that make academic success more likely when they negotiate what to wear or to eat. When middle-class parents give orders, the parents are more likely to explain why the rules are reasonable.

But parents whose jobs entail following orders or doing routine tasks show less sense of efficacy. They are less likely to encourage their children to negotiate over clothing or food and more likely to instruct them by giving directions without extended discussion. Following orders, after all, is how they themselves behave at work. Their children are also more likely to be fatalistic about obstacles they face, in and out of school.

Middle-class children's self-assurance is enhanced in after-school activities that sometimes require large fees for enrollment and almost always require parents to have enough free time and resources to provide transportation. Organized sports, music, drama, and dance programs build self-confidence and discipline in middle-class children. Lower-class parents find the fees for such activities more daunting, and transportation may also be more of a problem. Organized athletic and artistic activities may not be available in their neighborhoods, so lower-class children's sports are more informal and less confidence-building, with less opportunity to learn teamwork and self-discipline. For children with greater self-confidence, unfamiliar school challenges can be exciting. These children, who are more likely to be from middle-class homes, are more likely to succeed than those who are less self-confident.

Homework exacerbates academic differences between these two groups of children because middle-class parents are more likely to help with homework. Yet homework would increase the achievement gap even if all parents were able to assist. Parents from different social classes supervise homework differently. Consistent with overall patterns of language use, middle-class parents—especially those whose own occupational habits require problem solving—are more likely to assist by posing questions that break large problems down into smaller ones and that help children figure out correct answers. Lower-class parents are more likely to guide children with direct instructions. Children from both classes may go to school with completed homework, but middle-class children are more likely to gain in intellectual power from the exercise than lower-class children.

Twenty years ago, Betty Hart and Todd Risley, two researchers from the University of Kansas, visited families from different social classes to monitor the conversations between parents and toddlers. Hart and Risley found that, on average, professional parents spoke more than 2,000 words per hour to their children, working-class parents spoke about 1,300, and welfare mothers spoke about 600. So by age 3, the children of professionals had vocabularies that were nearly 50 percent greater than those of working-class children and twice as large as those of welfare children.

Deficits like these cannot be made up by schools alone, no matter how high the teachers' expectations. For all children to achieve the same goals, the less advantaged would have to enter school with verbal fluency that is similar to the fluency of middle-class children.

The Kansas researchers also tracked how often parents verbally encouraged children's behavior and how often they reprimanded their children. Toddlers of professionals got an average of six encouragements per reprimand. Working-class children had two. For welfare children, the ratio was reversed—an average of one encouragement for two reprimands. Children whose initiative was encouraged from a very early age are more likely, on average, to take responsibility for their own learning.

The Role Model Gap

Social class differences in role modeling also make an achievement gap almost inevitable. Not surprisingly, middle-class professional parents tend to associate with, and be friends with, similarly educated professionals. Working-class parents have fewer professional friends. If parents and their friends perform jobs requiring little academic skill, their children's images of their own futures are influenced. On average, these children must struggle harder to motivate themselves to achieve than children who assume, on the basis of their parents' social circle, that the only roles are doctor, lawyer, teacher, social worker, manager, administrator, or businessperson.

Even disadvantaged children usually say they plan to attend college. College has become such a broad rhetorical goal that black eighth-graders tell surveyors they expect to earn college degrees as often as white eighth-graders do. But despite these intentions, fewer black than white eighth-graders actually graduate from high school four years later; fewer enroll in college the following year; and fewer still persist to get bachelor's degrees.

This discrepancy is not due simply to the cost of college. A bigger reason is that while disadvantaged students *say* they plan to go to college, they don't feel as much parental, community, or peer pressure to take the courses or to get the grades they need to become more attractive to college admission offices. Lower-class parents say they expect children to get good grades, but they are less likely to enforce these expectations, for example with rewards or punishments. Teachers and counselors can stress doing well in school to lower-class children, but such lessons compete with children's own self-images, formed early in life and reinforced daily at home.

As John Ogbu and others have noted, a culture of underachievement may help explain why even middle-class black children often don't do as well in school as white children from seemingly similar socioeconomic backgrounds. On average, middle-class black students don't study as hard as white middle-class students and blacks are more disruptive in class than whites from similar income strata.

This culture of underachievement is easier to understand than to cure. Throughout American history, many black students who excelled in school were not rewarded for that effort in the labor market. Many black college graduates could find work only as servants or Pullman car porters or, in white-collar fields, as assistants to less-qualified whites. Many Americans believe that these practices have disappeared and that blacks and whites with similar test scores now have similar earnings and occupational status. But labor market discrimination continues to be a significant obstacle—especially for black males with high school educations.

Evidence for this comes from employment discrimination cases, such as the prominent 1996 case in which Texaco settled for a payment of $176 million to black employees after taped conversations of executives revealed pervasive racist attitudes, presumably not restricted to executives of this corporation alone. Other evidence comes from studies that find black workers with darker complexions have less success in the labor market than those with identical education, age, and criminal records but lighter complexions.

Still more evidence comes from studies in which blacks and whites with similar qualifications are sent to apply for job vacancies; the whites are typically more successful than the blacks. In one recent study where young, well-groomed, and articulate black and white college graduates, posing as high school graduates with identical qualifications, submitted applications for entry-level jobs, the applications of whites with criminal records got positive responses more often than the applications of blacks with no criminal records.

So the expectation of black students that their academic efforts will be less rewarded than the efforts of their white peers is rational for the majority of black students who do not expect to complete college. Some will reduce their academic efforts as a result. We can say that they should not do so and, instead, should redouble their efforts in response to the greater obstacles they face. But as long as racial discrimination persists, the average achievement of black students will be lower than the average achievement of whites, simply because many blacks (especially males) who see that academic effort has less of a payoff will respond rationally by reducing their effort.

The Health and Housing Gaps

Despite these big race and social class differences in child rearing, role modeling, labor market experiences, and cultural characteristics, the lower achievement of lower-class students is not caused by these differences alone. Just as important are differences in the actual social and economic conditions of children.

Overall, lower-income children are in poorer health. They have poorer vision, partly because of prenatal conditions and partly because, even as toddlers, they watch too much television, so their eyes are poorly trained. Trying to read, their eyes may wander or have difficulty tracking print or focusing. A good part of the over-identification of learning disabilities for lower-class children may well be attributable to undiagnosed vision problems that could be easily treated by optometrists and for which special education placement then should be unnecessary.

Lower-class children have poorer oral hygiene, more lead poisoning, more asthma, poorer nutrition, less-adequate pediatric care, more exposure to smoke, and a host of other health problems. Because of less-adequate dental care, for example, they are more likely to have toothaches and resulting discomfort that affects concentration.

Because low-income children live in communities where landlords use high-sulfur home heating oil and where diesel trucks frequently pass en route to industrial and commercial sites, they are more likely to suffer from asthma, leading to more absences from school and, when they do attend, drowsiness from lying awake at night, wheezing. Recent surveys in Chicago and in New York City's Harlem community found one of every four children suffering from asthma, a rate six times as great as that for all children.

In addition, there are fewer primary-care physicians in low-income communities, where the physician-to-population ratio is less than a third the rate in middle-class communities. For that reason, disadvantaged children—even those with health insurance—are more likely to miss school for relatively minor problems, such as common ear infections, for which middle-class children are treated promptly.

Each of these well-documented social class differences in health is likely to have a palpable effect on academic achievement; combined, their influence is probably huge.

The growing unaffordability of adequate housing for low-income families also affects achievement. Children whose families have difficulty finding stable housing are more likely to be mobile, and student mobility is an important cause of failing student performance. A 1994 government report found that 30 percent of the poorest children had attended at least three different schools by third grade, while only 10 percent of middle-class children had done so. Black children were more than twice as likely as white children to change schools this often. It is hard to imagine how teachers, no matter how well trained, can be as effective for children who move in and out of their classrooms as they can be for those who attend regularly.

Differences in wealth are also likely to be important determinants of achievement, but these are usually overlooked because most analysts focus only on annual family income to indicate disadvantage. This makes it hard to understand why black students, on average, score lower than whites whose family incomes are the same. It is easier to understand this pattern when we recognize that children can have similar family incomes but be of different economic classes. In any given year, black families with low income are likely to have been poor for longer than white families with similar income in that year.

White families are also likely to own far more assets that support their children's achievement than are black families at the same income level, partly because black middle-class parents are more likely to be the first generation in their families to have middle-class status. Although the median black family income is about two-thirds the median income of white families, the assets of black families are still only 12 percent those of whites. Among other things, this difference means that, among white and black families with the same middle-class incomes, the whites are more likely to have savings for college. This makes white children's college aspirations more practical, and therefore more commonplace.

Narrowing the Gaps

If we properly identify the actual social class characteristics that produce differences in average achievement, we should be able to design policies that narrow the achievement gap. Certainly, improvement of instructional practices is among these, but a focus on school reform alone is bound to be frustrating and ultimately unsuccessful. To work, school improvement must combine with policies that narrow the social and economic differences between children. Where these differences cannot easily be narrowed, school should be redefined to cover more of the early childhood, after-school, and summer times, when the disparate influences of families and communities are now most powerful.

Because the gap is already huge at age 3, the most important new investment should no doubt be in early childhood programs. Prekindergarten classes for 4-year-olds are needed, but they barely begin to address the problem. The quality of early childhood programs is as important as the existence of such programs themselves. Too many low-income children are parked before television sets in low-quality day-care settings. To narrow the gap, care for infants and toddlers should be provided by adults who can create the kind of intellectual environment that is typically experienced by middle-class infants and toddlers. This requires professional caregivers and low child-adult ratios.

After-school and summer experiences for lower-class children, similar to programs middle-class children take for granted, would also be needed to narrow the gap. This does not mean remedial programs where lower-class children get added drill in math and reading. Certainly, remediation should be part of an adequate after-school and summer program, but only a part. The advantage that middle-class children gain after school and in summer comes from the self-confidence they acquire and the awareness of the world outside that they develop through organized athletics, dance, drama, museum visits, recreational reading, and other activities that develop inquisitiveness, creativity, self-discipline, and organizational skills. After-school and summer programs can be expected to narrow the achievement gap only by attempting to duplicate such experiences.

Provision of health-care services to lower-class children and their families is also required to narrow the achievement gap. Some health services are relatively inexpensive, such as school vision and dental clinics. A full array of health services will cost more, but it cannot be avoided if we truly intend to raise the achievement of lower-class children.

The connection between social and economic disadvantage and an academic achievement gap has long been well known. Most educators, however, have avoided the obvious implication: Improving lower-class children's learning requires ameliorating the social and economic conditions of their lives. School board members—who are often the officials with the closest ties to public opinion—cannot afford to remain silent about the connection between school improvement and social reform. Calling attention to this link is not to make excuses for poor school performance. It is only to be honest about the social support schools require if they are to fulfill the public's expectation that the achievement gap will disappear.

POSTSCRIPT

Will School Improvement Efforts Alone Narrow the Racial/Ethnic Achievement Gap?

Challenge Questions

1. What are some barriers that exist in improving the achievement gap?

2. How can school districts with limited resources improve academic achievement of the neediest students?

3. Getting students to read is a common finding among teachers who are successful in closing the achievement gap. Develop a list of your favorite books for K–2 that you would want children of that age group to read. What memories do you have of these books and why are they your favorites?

Suggested Reading

Bell, L. I. (2002/2003). Strategies that close the gap. *Educational Leadership,* 60(4).

Polite, V. C., & Davis, J. E. (Eds.). (1999). *African American males in school and society: Practices and policies for effective education.* New York: Teachers College Press.

Rothstein R. (2004). *Class and schools: Using social, economic, and educational reform to close the black-white achievement gap.* Washington, DC: Economic Policy Institute.

Summary of the nation. (2001). Washington, D.C.: Education Trust (ED 459–220).

Thernstrom, A., & Thernstrom, S. (2003). *No excuses: Closing the racial gap in learning.* New York: Simon & Schuster.

ISSUE 17

Should Corporal Punishment in Schools Be Outlawed?

YES: Paul Ferraro and Joan Rudel Weinreich, from "Unprotected in the Classroom," *American School Board Journal* (November 2006)

NO: Greg Gelpi, from "Some Small Area School Systems Use the Paddle," *Augusta Chronicle* (October 8, 2006)

ISSUE SUMMARY

YES: Paul Ferraro is an elementary teacher in Connecticut and Joan Rudel Weinreich is an associate professor at Manhattanvillle College in New York. They provide information on the twenty-one states that allow the striking of students in schools, why it's wrong and should be abolished.

NO: Greg Gelpi, a writer for the *Augusta, Georgia Chronicle*, writes about the popular practice of administering corporal punishment to students in the state of Georgia.

$\mathbf{T}$he spanking and paddling debate is thrust into the spotlight every few years or so depending on proposed legislation or out-of-control children. In the wake of the many school shootings, attention is turned once again to the need for more stringent discipline methods, including corporal punishment or spanking, to control wayward youth. Nationwide, twenty-one states allow school administrators to implement corporal punishment as a method of disciplining students caught misbehaving.

The first edition of this book contained the controversial issue on parents spanking their children at home. For this edition, the issue centers on corporal punishment used in schools as a method of discipline. Most often, corporal punishment in the schools refers to paddling students with something other than a human hand, most often a wooden paddle of varying lengths and thickness, often with holes drilled in the wood for greater force.

In some states and school districts there are specific policies on administering corporal punishment. Other states and districts leave the decision up to principal or teacher discretion to determine when a paddling is administered, what tool is used, how many swats will be administered, and the force to be applied. In some schools a paddling occurs with a heavy wooden paddle, with great force, ten times to the bare buttocks of a child. The child is helpless in defending him- or herself.

School administrators are facing frustrations with children not respecting teachers, and the learning environment for the other students is disrupted by unruly students. Teachers are stressed as they work to find acceptable methods of discipline that will allow order to be restored to the learning environment. Corporal punishment is legal in schools in twenty-one states. It is however banned in twenty-nine states and the District of Columbia with twenty-three of those states enacting bans from 1985 to the present. The states that do allow corporal punishment in schools allow local school boards of education to set policy. In states where corporal punishment is allowed, mainly in southern states, an adult witness must be present while the physical punishment is being administered.

In "Unprotected in the Classroom," Paul Ferraro and Joan Rudel Weinreich are opposed to paddling and counter that by spanking, switching, or paddling children the message that violence is acceptable is the lesson learned by students.

Proponents of paddling point to the need for more control and order in our society. Greg Gelpi reports on the frustrations many adults are facing related to discipline and how they are using paddling to control unruly students in schools. Gelpi provides information on the common acceptance of paddling in many of Georgia's public school districts.

POINT

- There are many alternatives to corporal punishment.
- Paddling leaves bruises on the body.

- Poor, minority, and male students are paddled more than other students.

- Corporal punishment leads to more aggressive behavior now and in the future.
- Schools are the only institutions in America where striking another person is allowed.

COUNTERPOINT

- Students need to be taught a lesson for misbehaving at school.
- If administered correctly, paddling can be effective and not leave marks.
- Students who do not receive adequate guidance at home are more prone to misbehave at school.
- There is no strong evidence indicating violent behavior is a result of a child being spanked or paddled.
- Schools have the responsibility to provide for the safety and education of all students and a variety of discipline methods are needed.

YES

**Paul Ferraro and
Joan Rudel Weinreich**

Unprotected in the Classroom

"**I**t's prohibited in prisons, the military, and mental institutions. Schools are the only public institutions in the United States where hitting another person is legally sanctioned," says the Center for Effective Discipline. In fact, along with Australia and Canada, the United States has the dubious distinction of being one of the very few industrialized nations that allow educators to intentionally inflict pain on students as a form of discipline.

"Corporal punishment can occur anywhere and encompass everything from paddling to forced exercise to prohibiting use of the bathroom." According to the U.S. Department of Education's Office for Civil Rights, 301,016 students endured some type of physical punishment in the 2002–03 school year. That is a significant reduction from 20 or even 10 years ago, when more than 1 million schoolchildren faced physical pain at the hands of a faculty member.

The decrease is due largely to legislation in many states outlawing the practice. Currently, 27 states have laws banning corporal punishment, 19 of which were enacted within the past two decades. Two states, Ohio and Utah, also have bans, but the prohibition can be overruled by a school board or a parent.

It might appear as though positive gains have been made in banning corporal punishment. But with nearly half of the country allowing its educators to spank, strap, flog, cane, or otherwise humiliate and degrade schoolchildren, there is little to be upbeat about.

Ignorance about corporal punishment no doubt contributes to its continued existence. That appears to have been the case in 1996, when California legislator Mickey Conroy lobbied to reinstate corporal punishment. "Right now [students] can get away with just about anything without fear of punishment," the Republican was quoted as saying. Conroy's logic seemed to appeal to fellow party members, who pushed his bill from the education committee to the assembly floor. Their support waned, however, after a public hearing at which they saw shocking photos of the battered backsides of students. The bill ultimately died.

Such shock tactics still may be needed to persuade some school officials and state lawmakers that meting out physical punishments on unruly children is not an effective method of discipline. In fact, corporal punishment actually can have long-term negative effects on students and on society as a whole.

From *American School Board Journal*, November 2006, pp. 40–42. Copyright © 2006 by National School Boards Association. Reprinted by permission.

Why It's Wrong

Twenty-three states allow "reasonable corporal punishment" in schools. Unfortunately, "reasonable" is not defined in state law, allowing for interpretation according to the vagaries of the state or school district. In 1988, for example, the 5th U.S. Circuit Court of Appeals ruled in *Cunningham v. Beavers* that corporal punishment could be administered up to the point of "deadly force." The case involved two kindergarten girls in Jacksonville, Texas, who had been paddled with a wooden board; the U.S. Supreme Court declined to hear an appeal. (Incidentally, Texas schools led the nation in the number of paddling incidents in the 2002–03 school year, according to the Office for Civil Rights.)

Proponents of corporal punishment argue that it helps establish a scale of disciplinary actions. Corporal punishment, they reason, could be used for an offense too severe for detention, but not severe enough to warrant an expulsion. Yet with so many other methods available to address behavior (including reward systems, short-term suspension, and parental intervention), corporal punishment amounts to an admission of failure on the part of the teacher.

Corporal punishment is degrading. Nothing but humiliation and shame can come from forcing a child to bend over and receive a paddling—especially when it takes place in front of other students. Instead of focusing on the misbehavior, the teacher who paddles a student is not only causing immediate physical pain and suffering, but also may be breaking down the child's psychological defenses, leading to withdrawal, depression, and anxiety or to anger and rebellion.

Research has shown corporal punishment perpetuates a cycle of child abuse. Children who are paddled learn that abuse is justified if an adult deems it's necessary. They learn to solve their problems or express their anger and frustration through violence. When children see adults inflicting pain on other children, they learn to do the same to their smaller and weaker peers.

Worse, children can learn and ultimately mirror sexual deviancy as a result of corporal punishment. The practice of paddling has disturbing sexual undercurrents. Sadomasochistic tendencies or pure sexual excitement may lead a person to choose this method of punishment for certain students. The deviancy can become explicit when children sense the sexual pleasure the beater derives from the act.

Another argument for maintaining corporal punishment is that it creates continuity between home and school. Many parents use spanking to discipline their children. Laws that prohibit corporal punishment in school, proponents of the practice say, send mixed messages to children and diminish the value of the punishments they receive at home. While it's true that schools are being asked to take on more and more responsibilities traditionally left to the home, this is an area where educators should not be expected to tread.

The Unintended Outcomes

Some tout corporal punishment as an immediate and nonburdensome form of discipline that punishes only the guilty. Yet studies have shown that corporal punishment has ramifications extending beyond the school building.

The correlation between corporal punishment and larger societal problems seems clear. A 2002 study by Maryland-based anti-spanking advocate John Guthrow suggests that corporal punishment is a contributing factor in many of society's ills. (Guthrow's study also took a number of other factors into account, including state and local education spending, high school completion rate, percentage of births to unwed mothers, and poverty rate. . . .

Guthrow found, for instance, that corporal punishment is legal in eight of the 10 states with the highest murder rates. Louisiana, which has the highest murder rate in the country, is ranked sixth in the nation in percentage of students struck by educators. Of the states with the lowest murder rates in the nation, educators paddle children in only one. That state, Idaho, has the third lowest murder rate in the country and ranks 18th by percentage of students hit.

Of the states with the 10 highest graduation rates, educators use corporal punishment in only one. Nonpaddling states like Minnesota have relatively better test scores, lower dropout rates, lower poverty rates, and better health care than paddling states like Louisiana.

In short, states that permit the use of corporal punishment in public schools have more negative sociological outcomes than states that have prohibited this violence on schoolchildren.

Evidence also supports the argument that corporal punishment promotes violence and discrimination and creates a hostile school environment. Children find it more difficult to perform and succeed under such pressures. Feelings of anger, resentment, and fear are bottled up and not addressed, which takes a toll on student performance. And as Guthrow surmised in his study, "Once educational achievement suffers, other aspects of society suffer proportionately."

Not the Right Lesson

As with any controversial issue, each side can point to studies and statistics about corporal punishment. But putting all scientific data and findings aside, the primary concern of all educators should be the child's well-being, and that well-being is in jeopardy whenever an adult is allowed to physically harm a child.

On a practical level as well, corporal punishment is not effective. Children who are subjected to corporal punishment are likely to respond with negative behavior. Common sense, compounded by numerous convincing studies, dictates that violence does, in fact, breed violence. Most adults understand that communication is the best vehicle for resolving issues. In times of international conflict, precedent suggests that those involved join to discuss possible remedies. War is never the first suggestion, but rather a last resort. We should model that approach when we discipline children at home or at school.

When big sister Sara grabs little Tommy's toy, Tommy is never taught to hurt Sara and then retrieve the object of contention. Instead, responsible parents teach their children that words are always more effective. Likewise, teachers should nurture, encourage, and protect the children in their care. Violence against children can only poison the student-teacher relationship.

Greg Gelpi  **NO**

Some Small Area School Systems Use the Paddle

When it comes to keeping children in line, many smaller school systems, including Burke County, turn to the paddle.

Although it cut back drastically, Burke County still ranked among the leaders in the state last school year for dishing out corporal punishment. It did so more than 600 times to punish pupils who misbehaved, according to Georgia Department of Education data. The county is also the 10th worst in the state for the rate of discipline problems.

Seventeen of the top 25 school systems issuing corporal punishment were systems of fewer than 5,000 pupils. According to state records, 113 school systems administered corporal punishment last year, with Laurens County, a system of about 6,300 pupils, reporting the most incidents with 3,077.

The number of school systems paddling their pupils was down from 118 a year earlier.

"Principals I've talked to would say it's effective," said James Hyder, an attorney for the Burke County Board of Education, adding that the paddling itself might not be as bad as the experience of getting paddled.

But others said the verdict is still out on the punishment's effectiveness.

Dr. Sabina Widner, of the Augusta State University Department of Psychology, said corporal punishment in and of itself isn't harmful to children, but it's important to balance it with heavy doses of positive reinforcement.

"If you're relying on punishment alone to have a well-behaved child, you're likely not going to be effective," she said.

Dr. Linda Mitchell, of ASU's College of Education, said research on the issue is all across the board. Her thoughts are that it could be effective in a "limited basis" in elementary school, although she has "serious reservations" about its effectiveness in middle schools.

Mr. Hyder said the Burke County school board has a policy in line with state law that establishes guidelines for when and how corporal punishment may be administered.

For instance, the punishment shouldn't be "excessive or unduly severe," the policy states. Rules also dictate that corporal punishment can't be used as the "first line" of punishment unless pupils have been forewarned that specific behavior would result in corporal punishment or the behavior was so "antisocial or disruptive in nature as to shock the conscience."

And even when pupils are paddled, it is done by an administrator with a witness present, Mr. Hyder said. Parents can also opt out of the corporal punishment policy.

POSTSCRIPT

Should Corporal Punishment in Schools Be Outlawed?

Challenge Questions

1. Does the violence that is permitted against students in schools transfer over to other facets of our society?

2. Is paddling the correct path to take to help a child develop a sense of what is right and wrong and how to conduct oneself in society?

3. What are some alternatives to corporal punishment available to school administrators and teachers?

4. If you attended school in a state that allowed corporal punishment, what memories do you have of the practice if used in your schools?

5. Are there times when spanking is an acceptable method of discipline, but other times when it should never be used?

Suggested Reading

Alexander, K. K. (2001). Is spanking ever okay? *Parents,* 76(5), 90–98.

Chenoweth, T., & Just, H. (2000). Corporal punishment: Does it hinder the development of children? (ED 444-759).

Flynn, C. P. (1999). Exploring the link between corporal punishment and children's cruelty to animals. *Journal of Marriage and the Family* (61), 971–981.

Lemonick, M. (1997). Spare the rod? Maybe. *Time,* August 25, 150, 65.

Monaghan, P. (1997). Sparing the rod: A crusader against corporal punishment. *Chronicle of Higher Education,* July 3, 4(43), A7.

O'Callaghan, K. (2006). Is it okay to spank? *Parenting,* 20(7), 142–144, 147–148.

Ramsburg, D. (1997). The debate over spanking. ERIC Digest. ERIC Clearinghouse on Elementary and Early Childhood Education. Urbana, IL. (ED 405-139).

Straus, M. A. (1994). *Beating the devil out of them: Corporal punishment in American Families and its effects on children.* New York: Lexington Books. Jossey-Bass, Inc., Publishers.

U.S. Corporal Punishment and Paddling Statistics by State and Race. (2003). http://www.stophitting.com

ISSUE 18

Are Boys in Crisis in Our Schools?

YES: **Peg Tyre,** from "The Trouble with Boys," *Newsweek* (January 30, 2006)

NO: **Sara Mead,** from "The Truth About Boys and Girls," *Education Sector.org* (June 2006)

ISSUE SUMMARY

YES: Peg Tyre, a Pulitzer Prize-winning editor at *Newsweek* covers a number of issues related to the care and education of children. Her focus in this issue is on what many see as a learning gap between boys and girls.

NO: Sara Mead, a senior policy analyst at Education Sector, says there is ample evidence that boys are not doing worse and that girls have narrowed the achievement gaps that have existed for years.

Eight-year-old James sat up on his knees, perched both elbows on his desk, and placed his bottom on the back of his chair: He was ready to tackle the spelling test. His frustrated teacher asked James politely to sit on his bottom on the chair and then continued with the test. Two minutes later, James was back to his original position. What's a teacher to do? Are our classrooms failing to meet the needs of boys to move, touch, and explore during the learning process? How can the majority of female elementary teachers better meet the needs of the male students in their classes?

In the late 1980s and early 1990s news stories about the failure of girls to excel in math and science pushed educators and researchers to find ways to better meet the needs of girls. There was intense focus on math and science exploration programs for girls and money was spent on summer camps, clubs, and other ways of enticing girls to explore fields traditionally viewed as male-dominated professions. As girls improved their performance in math and science, the gap narrowed and focus turned to the reading and verbal abilities of young boys. Are boys falling behind girls or have girls improved their performance to be even with boys?

Boys are more likely than girls to indicate they are bored in school, and are much more likely to have behavior problems, be referred for special education, be diagnosed with Attention Deficit Hyperactivity Disorder (ADHD), be retained a grade, and drop out. The predominately female elementary teaching population is becoming more in-tuned with the physical needs of boys, but there is not a uniform way of helping young boys adapt to a learning setting that values quiet attentive behavior over an active questioning style. Children are often rewarded for sitting quietly and not yelling out responses. Female teachers tend to value skills such as organization, verbalization, and cooperation, all traits generally found in young girls. Skills traditionally dominate in young boys; competitiveness, quickness, and physical agility are behaviors that can be challenging when practiced in a classroom with twenty-six other bodies. Teachers who value a variety of behaviors and provide ample opportunities for children to interact with others and use skills that are their strengths as well as practice other skills will provide the most learner-friendly environments. Addressing the needs of boys will make a classroom more developmentally appropriate for all students. Some of the unique physical traits for both girls and boys can be accommodated in a classroom with careful consideration by the teacher. Students who are allowed to choose when they want to tackle the activities that require the most concentration can do so, based on their ability to focus throughout the day. The same holds true for students who need to be more physical. Students can be provided manipulatives that will allow them to be physical and still engage in the learning experiences.

Educators, parents, and others who suggest a boy crisis point to college attendance—one of the most striking differences between the sexes. Today colleges are facing a very unique problem with the number of girls on college campuses outnumbering boys by a significant number. The number of males is at an all time low with 44 percent of college students male and 56 percent female. Some suggest the numbers will grow even further apart if boys continue to be miseducated in prekindergarten through the twelfth grade.

Peg Tyre, in "The Trouble with Boys," provides statistics on the differences between boys and girls in elementary, middle, and high school and beyond. Sara Mead, in "The Truth About Boys and Girls," strongly contends there is not a boy crisis and boys are achieving at a high rate. She is worried the hysteria surrounding the purported boy crisis will cause an even greater gap between the sexes in learning situations.

POINT

- There is a crisis in our schools related to the performance of boys.
- Boys are falling behind girls in academic performance.
- There is a preponderance of female teachers in elementary schools.
- Teachers value traits found in girls over those in boys.
- Boys like learning in settings with competition and hands-on experiences.

COUNTERPOINT

- Boys are not doing worse; girls have simply caught up to the boys.
- Girls can be ahead of boys and a crisis does not exist.
- Female teachers can be understanding to the needs of boys.
- There is a perception that classrooms are more girl friendly, but not strong evidence to suggest that is true.
- Teachers need to meet the needs of all learners.

YES

Peg Tyre

The Trouble with Boys

Spend a few minutes on the phone with Danny Frankhuizen and you come away thinking, "What a *nice* boy." He's thoughtful, articulate, bright. He has a good relationship with his mom, goes to church every Sunday, loves the rock band Phish and spends hours each day practicing his guitar. But once he's inside his large public Salt Lake City high school, everything seems to go wrong. He's 16, but he can't stay organized. He finishes his homework and then can't find it in his backpack. He loses focus in class, and his teachers, with 40 kids to wrangle, aren't much help. "If I miss a concept, they tell me, 'Figure it out yourself'," says Danny. Last year Danny's grades dropped from B's to D's and F's. The sophomore, who once dreamed of Stanford, is pulling his grades up but worries that "I won't even get accepted at community college."

His mother, Susie Malcom, a math teacher who is divorced, says it's been wrenching to watch Danny stumble. "I tell myself he's going to make something good out of himself," she says. "But it's hard to see doors close and opportunities fall away."

What's wrong with Danny? By almost every benchmark, boys across the nation and in every demographic group are falling behind. In elementary school, boys are two times more likely than girls to be diagnosed with learning disabilities and twice as likely to be placed in special-education classes. High-school boys are losing ground to girls on standardized writing tests. The number of boys who said they didn't like school rose 71 percent between 1980 and 2001, according to a University of Michigan study. Nowhere is the shift more evident than on college campuses. Thirty years ago men represented 58 percent of the undergraduate student body. Now they're a minority at 44 percent. This widening achievement gap, says Margaret Spellings, U.S. Secretary of Education, "has profound implications for the economy, society, families and democracy."

With millions of parents wringing their hands, educators are searching for new tools to help tackle the problem of boys. Books including Michael Thompson's best seller "Raising Cain" (recently made into a PBS documentary) and Harvard psychologist William Pollack's definitive work "Real Boys" have become must-reads in the teachers' lounge. The Gurian Institute, founded in 1997 by family therapist Michael Gurian to help the people on the front lines help boys, has enrolled 15,000 teachers in its seminars. Even the Gates Foundation, which in the last five years has given away nearly a billion

Figure 1

Elementary School

Boys start off with lower literacy skills than girls, and are less often encouraged to read, which only widens the gap.

■ Girls ages 3 to 5 are **5%** more likely than boys to be read to at home at least three times a week.

■ Girls are **10%** more likely than boys to recognize words by sight by the spring of first grade.

■ Boys ages 5 to 12 are **60%** more likely than girls to have repeated at least one grade.

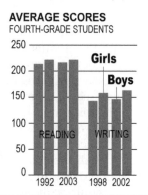

AVERAGE SCORES
FOURTH-GRADE STUDENTS

■ Girls' reading scores improve **6%** more than boys' between kindergarten and third grade.

■ First- to fifth-grade boys are **47%** more likely than girls to have disabilities such as emotional disturbances, learning problems or speech impediments.

■ Fourth-grade girls score **3%** higher on standardized reading tests than boys.

■ Fourth-grade girls score **12%** higher on writing tests than boys.

Sources: U.S. Department of Education, Centers for Disease Control

dollars to innovative high schools, is making boys a big priority. "Helping underperforming boys," says Jim Shelton, the foundation's education director, "has become part of our core mission."

The problem won't be solved overnight. In the last two decades, the education system has become obsessed with a quantifiable and narrowly defined kind of academic success, these experts say, and that myopic view is harming boys. Boys are biologically, developmentally and psychologically different from girls—and teachers need to learn how to bring out the best in every one. "Very well-meaning people," says Dr. Bruce Perry, a Houston neurologist who advocates for troubled kids, "have created a biologically disrespectful model of education."

Thirty years ago it was girls, not boys, who were lagging. The 1972 federal law Title IX forced schools to provide equal opportunities for girls in the classroom and on the playing field. Over the next two decades, billions of dollars were funneled into finding new ways to help girls achieve. In 1992, the American Association of University Women issued a report claiming that the work of Title IX was not done—girls still fell behind in math and science; by the mid-1990s, girls had reduced the gap in math and more girls than boys were taking high-school-level biology and chemistry.

Some scholars, notably Christina Hoff Sommers, a fellow at the American Enterprise Institute, charge that misguided feminism is what's been hurting boys. In the 1990s, she says, girls were making strong, steady progress toward parity in schools, but feminist educators portrayed them as disadvantaged and lavished them with support and attention. Boys, meanwhile, whose rates of achievement had begun to falter, were ignored and their problems allowed to fester.

◦✎⊙✎◦

Boys have always been boys, but the expectations for how they're supposed to act and learn in school have changed. In the last 10 years, thanks in part to activist parents concerned about their children's success, school performance has been measured in two simple ways: how many students are enrolled in accelerated courses and whether test scores stay high. Standardized assessments have become commonplace for kids as young as 6. Curricula have become more rigid. Instead of allowing teachers to instruct kids in the manner and pace that suit each class, some states now tell teachers what, when and how to teach. At the same time, student-teacher ratios have risen, physical education and sports programs have been cut and recess is a distant memory. These new pressures are undermining the strengths and underscoring the limitations of what psychologists call the "boy brain"—the kinetic, disorganized, maddening and sometimes brilliant behaviors that scientists now believe are not learned but hard-wired.

When Cris Messler of Mountainside, N.J., brought her 3-year-old son Sam to a pediatrician to get him checked for ADHD, she was acknowledging the desperation parents can feel. He's a high-energy kid, and Messler found herself hoping for a positive diagnosis. "If I could get a diagnosis from the doctor, I could get him on medicine," she says. The doctor said Sam is a normal boy. School has been tough, though. Sam's reading teacher said he was hopeless. His first-grade teacher complains he's antsy, and Sam, now 7, has been referring to himself as "stupid." Messler's glad her son doesn't need medication, but what, she wonders, can she do now to help her boy in school?

◦✎⊙✎◦

For many boys, the trouble starts as young as 5, when they bring to kindergarten a set of physical and mental abilities very different from girls'. As almost any parent knows, most 5-year-old girls are more fluent than boys and can sight-read more words. Boys tend to have better hand-eye coordination, but their fine motor skills are less developed, making it a struggle for some to control a pencil or a paintbrush. Boys are more impulsive than girls; even if they can sit still, many prefer not to—at least not for long.

Thirty years ago feminists argued that classic "boy" behaviors were a result of socialization, but thes days scientists believe they are an expression of male brain chemistry. Sometime in the first trimester, a boy fetus begins producing male sex hormones that bathe his brain in testosterone for the rest of his gestation. "That exposure wires the male brain differently," says Arthur Arnold, professor of physiological science at UCLA. How? Scientists aren't exactly sure. New studies show that prenatal exposure to male sex hormones directly affects the way children play. Girls whose mothers have high levels of testosterone during pregnancy are more likely to prefer playing with trucks to playing with dolls. There are also clues that hormones influence the way we learn all through life. In a Dutch study published in 1994, doctors found that when males were given female hormones, their spatial skills dropped but their verbal skills improved.

Figure 2

Middle School

Coming of age in a culture that discourages bookishness, boys are more likely to fall victim to drugs and violence.

■ Eighth-grade girls score an average of **11 points** higher than eighth-grade boys on standardized reading tests.

■ Eighth-grade girls score **21 points** higher than boys on standardized writing tests.

■ Between 1993 and 2003, the number of ninth-grade

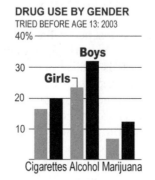

DRUG USE BY GENDER
TRIED BEFORE AGE 13: 2003

boys who skipped school at least once a month because they didn't feel safe increased **22%**.

■ Boys between the ages of 5 and 14 are **200%** more likely to commit suicide than girls.

■ Ninth-grade boys are **78%** more likely than girls to get injured in a fight at least once a year.

■ Between the ages of 5 and 14, boys are **36%** more likely to die than their female counterparts.

In elementary-school classrooms—where teachers increasingly put an emphasis on language and a premium on sitting quietly and speaking in turn—the mismatch between boys and school can become painfully obvious. "Girl behavior becomes the gold standard," says "Raising Cain" coauthor Thompson. "Boys are treated like defective girls."

Two years ago Kelley King, principal of Douglass Elementary School in Boulder, Colo., looked at the gap between boys and girls and decided to take action. Boys were lagging 10 points behind girls in reading and 14 points in writing. Many more boys—than girls were being labeled as learning disabled, too. So King asked her teachers to buy copies of Gurian's book "The Minds of Boys," on boy-friendly classrooms, and in the fall of 2004 she launched a bold experiment. Whenever possible, teachers replaced lecture time with fast-moving lessons that all kids could enjoy. Three weeks ago, instead of discussing the book "The View From Saturday," teacher Pam Unrau divided her third graders into small groups, and one student in each group pretended to be a character from the book. Classes are noisier, Unrau says, but the boys are closing the gap. Last spring, Douglass girls scored an average of 106 on state writing tests, while boys got a respectable 101.

Primatologists have long observed that juvenile male chimps battle each other not just for food and females, but to establish and maintain their place in the hierarchy of the tribe. Primates face off against each other rather than appear weak. That same evolutionary imperative, psychologists say, can make it hard for boys to thrive in middle school—and difficult for boys who are failing to accept the help they need. The transition to middle school is rarely easy, but like the juvenile primates they are, middle-school boys will do almost anything to avoid admitting that they're overwhelmed. "Boys measure everything they do or say

Figure 3

High School and Beyond

Many boys continue to fall behind girls in reading and writing proficiency, and fewer are going to college.

■ Boys are **33%** more likely than girls to drop out of high school.

■ Twelfth-grade girls score **16 points** higher than boys on standardized reading tests.

■ High-school boys are **30%** more likely to use cocaine than high-school girls.

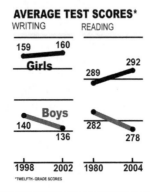

AVERAGE TEST SCORES*

WRITING   READING

159   160
Girls
                    292
              289

Boys
140   282
      136   278

1998   2002 1980   2004
*TWELFTH-GRADE SCORES

■ Twelfth-grade girls score **24 points** higher than boys on standardized writing tests.

■ High-school girls are **36%** more likely to take Advanced Placement or honors biology than high-school boys.

■ **22%** more high-school girls are planning to go to college than boys.

■ The percentage of male undergraduates dropped **24%** from 1970 to 2000.

by a single yardstick: does this make me look weak?" says Thompson. "And if it does, he isn't going to do it." That's part of the reason that videogames have such a powerful hold on boys: the action is constant, they can calibrate just how hard the challenges will be and, when they lose, the defeat is private.

When Brian Johns hit seventh grade, he never admitted how vulnerable it made him feel. "I got behind and never caught up," says Brian, now 17 and a senior at Grand River Academy, an Ohio boarding school. When his parents tried to help, he rebuffed them. When his mother, Anita, tried to help him organize his assignment book, he grew evasive about when his homework was due. Anita didn't know where to turn. Brian's school had a program for gifted kids, and support for ones with special needs. But what, Anita asked his teachers, do they do about kids like her son who are in the middle and struggling? Those kids, one of Brian's teachers told Anita, "are the ones who fall through the cracks."

It's easy for middle-school boys to feel outgunned. Girls reach sexual maturity two years ahead of boys, but other, less visible differences put boys at a disadvantage, too. The prefrontal cortex is a knobby region of the brain directly behind the forehead that scientists believe helps humans organize complex thoughts, control their impulses and understand the consequences of their own behavior. In the last five years, Dr. Jay Giedd, an expert in brain development at the National Institutes of Health, has used brain scans to show that in girls, it reaches its maximum thickness by the age of 11 and, for the next decade or more, continues to mature. In boys, this process is delayed by 18 months.

Middle-school boys may use their brains less efficiently, too. Using a type of MRI that traces activity in the brain, Deborah Yurgelun-Todd, director of the cognitive neuroimaging laboratory at McLean Hospital in Belmont, Mass., tested the activity patterns in the prefrontal cortex of children between the ages of 11 and 18. When shown pictures of fearful faces, adolescent girls registered activity on the right side of the prefrontal cortex, similar to an adult. Adolescent boys used both sides—a less mature pattern of brain activity. Teenage girls can process information faster, too. In a study about to be published in the journal Intelligence, researchers at Vanderbilt University administered timed tests—picking similar objects and matching groups of numbers—to 8,000 boys and girls between the ages of 5 and 18. In kindergarten, boys and girls processed information at about the same speeds. In early adolescence, girls finished faster and got more right. By 18, boys and girls were processing with the same speed and accuracy.

Scientists caution that brain research doesn't tell the whole story: temperament, family background and environment play big roles, too. Some boys are every bit as organized and assertive as the highest-achieving girls. All kids can be scarred by violence, alcohol or drugs in the family. But if your brain hasn't reached maturity yet, says Yurgelun-Todd, "it's not going to be able to do its job optimally."

⋘⊙⋙

Across the nation, educators are reviving an old idea: separate the girls from the boys—and at Roncalli Middle School, in Pueblo, Colo., administrators say, it's helping kids of both genders. This past fall, with the blessing of parents, school guidance counselor Mike Horton assigned a random group of 50 sixth graders to single-sex classes in core subjects. These days, when sixth-grade science teacher Pat Farrell assigns an earth-science lab on measuring crystals, the girls collect their materials—a Bunsen burner, a beaker of phenyl salicylate and a spoon. Then they read the directions and follow the sequence from beginning to end. The first things boys do is ask, "Can we eat this?" They're less organized, Farrell notes, but sometimes, "they're willing to go beyond what the lab asks them to do." With this in mind, he hands out written instructions to both classes but now goes over them step by step for the boys. Although it's too soon to declare victory, there are some positive signs: the shyest boys are participating more. This fall, the all-girl class did best in math, English and science, followed by the all-boy class and then coed classes.

One of the most reliable predictors of whether a boy will succeed or fail in high school rests on a single question: does he have a man in his life to look up to? Too often, the answer is no. High rates of divorce and single motherhood have created a generation of fatherless boys. In every kind of neighborhood, rich or poor, an increasing number of boys—now a startling 40 percent—are being raised without their biological dads.

Psychologists say that grandfathers and uncles can help, but emphasize that an adolescent boy without a father figure is like an explorer without a map. And that is especially true for poor boys and boys who are struggling in school. Older males, says Gurian, model self-restraint and solid work habits for younger ones. And whether they're breathing down their necks about grades or admonishing them to show up for school on time, "an older man reminds a boy in a million different ways that school is crucial to their mission in life."

In the past, boys had many opportunities to learn from older men. They might have been paired with a tutor, apprenticed to a master or put to work in the family store. High schools offered boys a rich array of roles in which to exercise leadership skills—class officer, yearbook editor or a place on the debate team. These days, with the exception of sports, more girls than boys are involved in those activities.

In neighborhoods where fathers are most scarce, the high-school dropout rates are shocking: more than half of African-American boys who start high school don't finish. David Banks, principal of the Eagle Academy for Young Men, one of four all-boy public high schools in the New York City system, wants each of his 180 students not only to graduate from high school but to enroll in college. And he's leaving nothing to chance. Almost every Eagle Academy boy has a male mentor—a lawyer, a police officer or an entrepreneur from the school's South Bronx neighborhood. The impact of the mentoring program, says Banks, has been "beyond profound." Tenth grader Rafael Mendez is unequivocal: his mentor "is the best thing that ever happened to me." Before Rafael came to Eagle Academy, he dreamed about playing pro baseball, but his mentor, Bronx Assistant District Attorney Rafael Curbelo, has shown him another way to succeed: Mendez is thinking about attending college in order to study forensic science.

Colleges would welcome more applications from young men like Rafael Mendez. At many state universities the gender balance is already tilting 60–40 toward women. Primary and secondary schools are going to have to make some major changes, says Ange Peterson, president-elect of the American Association of Collegiate Registrars and Admissions Officers, to restore the gender balance. "There's a whole group of men we're losing in education completely," says Peterson.

For Nikolas Arnold, 15, a sophomore at a public high school in Santa Monica, Calif., college is a distant dream. Nikolas is smart: he's got an encyclopedic knowledge of weaponry and war. When he was in first grade, his principal told his mother he was too immature and needed ADHD drugs. His mother balked. "Too immature?" says Diane Arnold, a widow. "He was six and a half!" He's always been an advanced reader, but his grades are erratic. Last semester, when his English teacher assigned two girls' favorites—"Memoirs of a Geisha" and "The Secret Life of Bees" Nikolas got a D. But lately, he has a math teacher he likes and is getting excited about numbers. He's reserved in class sometimes. But now that he's more engaged, his grades are improving slightly and his mother, who's pushing college, is hopeful he will begin to hit his stride. Girls get A's and B's on their report cards, she tells him, but that doesn't mean boys can't do it, too.

Sara Mead  **NO**

The Truth about Boys and Girls

If you've been paying attention to the education news lately, you know that American boys are in crisis. After decades spent worrying about how schools "shortchange girls," the eyes of the nation's education commentariat are now fixed on how they shortchange boys. In 2006 alone, a *Newsweek* cover story, a major *New Republic* article, a long article in *Esquire,* a "Today" show segment, and numerous op-eds have informed the public that boys are falling behind girls in elementary and secondary school and are increasingly outnumbered on college campuses. A young man in Massachusetts filed a civil rights complaint with the U.S. Department of Education, arguing that his high school's homework and community service requirements discriminate against boys. A growth industry of experts is advising educators and policymakers how to make schools more "boy friendly" in an effort to reverse this slide.

It's a compelling story that seizes public attention with its "man bites dog" characteristics. It touches on Americans' deepest insecurities, ambivalences, and fears about changing gender roles and the "battle of the sexes." It troubles not only parents of boys, who fear their sons are falling behind, but also parents of girls, who fear boys' academic deficits will undermine their daughters' chances of finding suitable mates.

But the truth is far different from what these accounts suggest. The real story is not bad news about boys doing worse; it's good news about girls doing better.

In fact, with a few exceptions, American boys are scoring higher and achieving more than they ever have before. But girls have just improved their performance on some measures even faster. As a result, girls have narrowed or even closed some academic gaps that previously favored boys, while other long-standing gaps that favored girls have widened, leading to the belief that boys are falling behind.

There's no doubt that some groups of boys—particularly Hispanic and black boys and boys from low-income homes—are in real trouble. But the predominant issues for them are race and class, not gender. Closing racial and economic gaps would help poor and minority boys more than closing gender gaps, and focusing on gender gaps may distract attention from the bigger problems facing these youngsters.

The hysteria about boys is partly a matter of perspective. While most of society has finally embraced the idea of equality for women, the idea that women might actually surpass men in some areas (even as they remain behind in others) seems hard for many people to swallow. Thus, boys are routinely characterized as "falling behind" even as they improve in absolute terms.

In addition, a dizzying array of so-called experts have seized on the boy crisis as a way to draw attention to their pet educational, cultural, or ideological issues. Some say that contemporary classrooms are too structured, suppressing boys' energetic natures and tendency to physical expression; others contend that boys need more structure and discipline in school. Some blame "misguided feminism" for boys' difficulties, while others argue that "myths" of masculinity have a crippling impact on boys. Many of these theories have superficially plausible rationales that make them appealing to some parents, educators, and policymakers. But the evidence suggests that many of these ideas come up short.

Unfortunately, the current boy crisis hype and the debate around it are based more on hopes and fears than on evidence. This debate benefits neither boys nor girls, while distracting attention from more serious educational problems—such as large racial and economic achievement gaps—and practical ways to help both boys and girls succeed in school.

A New Crisis?

"The Boy Crisis. At every level of education, they're falling behind. What to do?"

—*Newsweek* cover headline, Jan. 30, 2006

Newsweek is not the only media outlet publishing stories that suggest boys' academic accomplishments and life opportunities are declining. But it's not true. Neither the facts reported in these articles nor data from other sources support the notion that boys' academic performance is falling. In fact, overall academic achievement and attainment for boys is higher than it has ever been.

Long-Term Trends

Looking at student achievement and how it has changed over time can be complicated. Most test scores have little meaning themselves; what matters is what scores tell us about how a group of students is doing relative to something else: an established definition of what students need to know, how this group of students performed in the past, or how other groups of students are performing. Further, most of the tests used to assess student achievement are relatively new, and others have changed over time, leaving relatively few constant measures.

The National Assessment of Educational Progress (NAEP), commonly known as "The Nation's Report Card," is a widely respected test conducted by the U.S. Department of Education using a large, representative national sample of American students. NAEP is the only way to measure national trends in boys' and girls' academic achievements over long periods of time. There are two NAEP tests. The "main NAEP" has tracked U.S. students' performance in reading, math, and other academic subjects since the early 1990s. It tests students in grades four, eight, and 12. The "long-term trend NAEP" has tracked student performance since the early 1970s. It tests students at ages 9, 13, and 17.

Reading

The most recent main NAEP assessment in reading, administered in 2005, does not support the notion that boys' academic achievement is falling. In fact, fourth-grade boys did better than they had done in both the previous NAEP reading assessment, administered in 2003, and the earliest comparable assessment, administered in 1992. Scores for both fourth- and eighth-grade boys have gone up and down over the past decade, but results suggest that the reading skills of fourth- and eighth-grade boys have improved since 1992.

The picture is less clear for older boys. The 2003 and 2005 NAEP assessments included only fourth- and eighth-graders, so the most recent main NAEP data for 12th-graders dates back to 2002. On that assessment, 12th-grade boys did worse than they had in both the previous assessment, administered in 1998, and the first comparable assessment, administered in 1992. At the 12th-grade level, boys' achievement in reading does appear to have fallen during the 1990s and early 2000s.

Even if younger boys have improved their achievement over the past decade, however, this could represent a decline if boys' achievement had risen rapidly in previous decades. Some commentators have asserted that the boy crisis has its roots in the mid- or early-1980s. But long-term NAEP data simply does not support these claims. In fact, 9-year-old boys did better on the most recent long-term reading NAEP, in 2004, than they have at any time since the test was first administered in 1971. Nine-year-old boys' performance rose in the 1970s, declined in the 1980s, and has been rising since the early 1990s.

Like the main NAEP, the results for older boys on the long-term NAEP are more mixed. Thirteen-year-old boys have improved their performance slightly compared with 1971, but for the most part their performance over the past 30 years has been flat. Seventeen-year-old boys are doing about the same as they did in the early 1970s, but their performance has been declining since the late 1980s.

The main NAEP also shows that white boys score significantly better than black and Hispanic boys in reading at all grade levels. These differences far outweigh all changes in the overall performance of boys over time. For example, the difference between white and black boys on the fourth-grade NAEP in reading in 2005 was 10 times as great as the improvement for all boys on the same test since 1992.

And while academic performance for minority boys is often shockingly low, it's not getting worse. The average fourth-grade NAEP reading scores of black boys improved more from 1995 to 2005 than those of white and Hispanic boys or girls of any race.

Math

The picture for boys in math is less complicated. Boys of all ages and races are scoring as high—or higher—in math than ever before. From 1990 through 2005, boys in grades four and eight improved their performance steadily on the main NAEP, and they scored significantly better on the 2005 NAEP than in any previous year. Twelfth graders have not taken the main NAEP in math since 2000. That year, 12th-grade boys did better than they had in 1990 and 1992, but worse than they had in 1996.

Both 9- and 13-year-old boys improved gradually on the long-term NAEP since the 1980s (9-year-old boys' math performance did not improve in the 1970s). Seventeen-year-old boys' performance declined through the 1970s, rose in the 1980s, and remained relatively steady during the late 1990s and early 2000s. As in reading, white boys score much better on the main NAEP in math than do black and Hispanic boys, but all three groups of boys are improving their math performance in the elementary and middle school grades.

Other Subjects

In addition to the main and long-term NAEP assessments in reading and math, the NAEP also administers assessments in civics, geography, science, U.S. history, and writing. The civics assessment has not been administered since 1998, but the geography and U.S. history assessments were both administered in 1994 and 2001; the writing assessment in 1998 and 2002; and the science assessment in 1996, 2000, and 2005.

In geography, there was no significant change in boys' achievement at any grade level from 1994 to 2001. In U.S. history, fourth- and eighth-grade boys improved their achievement, but there was no significant change for 12th-grade boys. In writing, both fourth- and eighth-grade boys improved their achievement from 1998 to 2002, but 12th-grade boys' achievement declined. In science, fourth-grade boys' achievement in 2005 improved over their performance in both 1996 and 2000, eighth-grade boys showed no significant change in achievement, and 12th-grade boys' achievement declined since 1996.

Overall Long-Term Trends

A consistent trend emerges across these subjects: There have been no dramatic changes in the performance of boys in recent years, no evidence to indicate a boy crisis. Elementary-school-age boys are improving their performance; middle school boys are either improving their performance or showing little change, depending on the subject; and high school boys' achievement is declining in most subjects (although it may be improving in math). These trends seem to be consistent across all racial subgroups of boys, despite the fact that white boys perform much better on these tests than do black and Hispanic boys. Evidence of a decline in the performance of older boys is undoubtedly troubling. But the question to address is whether this is a problem for older boys or for older students generally. That can be best answered by looking at the flip side of the gender equation: achievement for girls.

The Difference Between Boys and Girls

To the extent that tales of declining boy performance are grounded in real data, they're usually framed as a decline relative to girls. That's because, as described above, boy performance is generally staying the same or increasing in absolute terms.

But even relative to girls, the NAEP data for boys paints a complex picture. On the one hand, girls outperform boys in reading at all three grade levels assessed on the main NAEP. Gaps between girls and boys are smaller in fourth grade and get larger in eighth and 12th grades. Girls also outperform boys in writing at all grade levels.

In math, boys outperform girls at all grade levels, but only by a very small amount. Boys also outperform girls—again, very slightly—in science and by a slightly larger margin in geography. There are no significant gaps between male and female achievement on the NAEP in U.S. history. In general, girls outperform boys in reading and writing by greater margins than boys outperform girls in math, science, and geography.

But this is nothing new. Girls have scored better than boys in reading for as long as the long-term NAEP has been administered. And younger boys are actually catching up: The gap between boys and girls at age 9 has narrowed significantly since 1971—from 13 points to five points—even as both genders have significantly improved. Boy-girl gaps at age 13 haven't changed much since 1971—and neither has boys' or girls' achievement.

At age 17, gaps between boys and girls in reading are also not that much different from what they were in 1971, but they are significantly bigger than they were in the late 1980s, before achievement for both genders—and particularly boys—began to decline.

The picture in math is even murkier. On the first long-term NAEP assessment in 1973, 9- and 13-year-old girls actually scored better than boys in math, and they continued to do so throughout the 1970s. But as 9- and 13-year-olds of both genders improved their achievement in math during the 1980s and 1990s, boys *pulled ahead* of girls, opening up a small gender gap in math achievement that now favors boys. It's telling that even though younger boys are now doing better than girls on the long-term NAEP in math, when they once lagged behind, no one is talking about the emergence of a new "girl crisis" in elementary- and middle-school math.

Seventeen-year-old boys have always scored better than girls on the long-term NAEP in math, but boys' scores declined slightly more than girls' scores in the 1970s, and girls' scores have risen slightly more than those of boys since. As a result, older boys' advantage over girls in math has narrowed.

Overall, there has been no radical or recent decline in boys' performance relative to girls. Nor is there a clear overall trend—boys score higher in some areas, girls in others.

The fact that achievement for older students is stagnant or declining for both boys and girls, to about the same degree, points to another important element of the boy crisis. The problem is most likely not that high schools need to be fixed to meet the needs of boys, but rather that they need to be fixed to meet the needs of *all* students, male and female. The need to accurately parse the influence of gender and other student categories is also acutely apparent when we examine the issues of race and income.

We Should Be Worried About Some Subgroups of Boys

There are groups of boys for whom "crisis" is not too strong a term. When racial and economic gaps combine with gender achievement gaps in reading, the result is disturbingly low achievement for poor, black, and Hispanic boys.

But the gaps between students of different races and classes are much larger than those for students of different genders—anywhere from two to five times as big, depending on the grade. The only exception is among 12th-grade boys, where the achievement gap between white girls and white boys in reading is the same size as the gap between white and black boys in reading and is larger than the gap between white and Hispanic boys. Overall, though, poor, black, and Hispanic boys would benefit far more from closing racial and economic achievement gaps than they would from closing gender gaps. While the gender gap picture is mixed, the racial gap picture is, unfortunately, clear across a wide range of academic subjects.

In addition to disadvantaged and minority boys, there are also reasons to be concerned about the substantial percentage of boys who have been diagnosed with disabilities. Boys make up two-thirds of students in special education—including 80 percent of those diagnosed with emotional disturbances or autism—and boys are two and a half times as likely as girls to be diagnosed with attention deficit hyperactivity disorder (ADHD). The number of boys diagnosed with disabilities or ADHD has exploded in the past 30 years, presenting a challenge for schools and causing concern for parents. But the reasons for this growth are complicated, a mix of educational, social, and biological factors. Evidence suggests that school and family factors—such as poor reading instruction, increased awareness of and testing for disabilities, or over-diagnosis—may play a role in the increased rates of boys diagnosed with learning disabilities or emotional disturbance. But boys also have a higher incidence of organic disabilities, such as autism and orthopedic impairments, for which scientists don't currently have a completely satisfactory explanation. Further, while girls are less likely than boys to be diagnosed with most disabilities, the number of girls with disabilities has also grown rapidly in recent decades, meaning that this is not just a boy issue. . . .

The Source of the Boy Crisis: A Knowledge Deficit and a Surplus of Opportunism

It's clear that some gender differences in education are real, and there are some groups of disadvantaged boys in desperate need of help. But it's also clear that boys' overall educational achievement and attainment are not in decline—in fact, they have never been better. What accounts for the recent hysteria?

It's partly an issue of simple novelty. The contours of disadvantage in education and society at large have been clear for a long time—low-income, minority, and female people consistently fall short of their affluent, white, and male peers. The idea that historically privileged boys could be at risk, that boys could be shortchanged, has simply proved too deliciously counterintuitive and "newsworthy" for newspaper and magazine editors to resist.

The so-called boy crisis also feeds on a lack of solid information. Although there are a host of statistics about how boys and girls perform in school, we actually know very little about why these differences exist or how important they are. There are many things—including biological, developmental, cultural, and educational factors—that affect how boys and girls do in school. But untangling these different influences is incredibly difficult. Research on the causes of gender differences is hobbled by the twin demons of educational research: lack of data and the difficulty of drawing causal connections among multiple, complex influences. Nor do we know what these differences mean for boys' and girls' future economic and other opportunities.

Yet this hasn't stopped a plethora of so-called experts—from pediatricians and philosophers to researchers and op-ed columnists—from weighing in with their views on the causes and likely effects of educational gender gaps. In fact, the lack of solid research evidence confirming or debunking any particular hypothesis has created fertile ground for all sorts of people to seize on the boy crisis to draw attention to their pet educational, cultural or ideological issues.

The problem, we are told, is that the structured traditional classroom doesn't accommodate boys' energetic nature and need for free motion—or it's that today's schools don't provide enough structure or discipline. It's that feminists have demonized typical boy behavior and focused educational resources on girls—or it's the "box" boys are placed in by our patriarchal society. It's that our schools' focus on collaborative learning fails to stimulate boys' natural competitiveness—or it's that the competitive pressures of standardized testing are pushing out the kind of relevant, hands-on work on which boys thrive.

The boy crisis offers a perfect opportunity for those seeking an excuse to advance ideological and educational agendas. Americans' continued ambivalence about evolving gender roles guarantees that stories of "boys in crisis" will capture public attention. The research base is internally contradictory, making it easy to find superficial support for a wide variety of explanations but difficult for the media and the public to evaluate the quality of evidence cited. Yet there is not sufficient evidence—or the right kind of evidence—available to draw firm conclusions. As a result, there is a sort of free market for theories about why boys are underperforming girls in school, with parents, educators, media, and the public choosing to give credence to the explanations that are the best marketed and that most appeal to their pre-existing preferences.

Unfortunately, this dynamic is not conducive to a thoughtful public debate about how boys and girls are doing in school or how to improve their performance.

Hard-Wired Inequality?

One branch of the debate over gender and education has focused on various theories of divergence between male and female brains. Men and women are "wired differently," people say, leading to all kinds of alleged problems and disparities that must be addressed. There's undoubtedly some truth here. The difficulty is separating fact from supposition.

The quest to identify and explain differences between men's and women's mental abilities is as old as psychology itself. Although the earliest work in this genre began with the assumption that women were intellectually inferior to men, and sought both to prove and explain why this was the case, more recent and scientifically valid research also finds differences in men's and women's cognitive abilities, as well as in the physiology of their brains.

It's important to note that research does not find that one gender is smarter than the other—on average, men and women score the same on tests of general intelligence. But there are differences between men's and women's performance in different types of abilities measured by intelligence tests. In general, women have higher scores than men on most tests of verbal abilities (verbal analogies being an exception), while men have higher scores on tests of what psychologists call "visual-spatial" abilities—the ability to think in terms of nonverbal, symbolic information, measured through such tasks as the ability to place a horizontal line in a tilted frame or to identify what the image of an irregular object would look like if the object were rotated. Quantitative or mathematical abilities are more even, with men performing better on some types of problems—including probability, statistics, measurement and geometry—while women perform better on others, such as computation, and both genders perform equally well on still others.

Much of this research is based on studies with adults—particularly college students—but we know that gender differences in cognitive abilities vary with development. Differences in verbal abilities are among the first to appear; vocabulary differences, for example, are seen before children are even 2 years old, and by the time they enter kindergarten, girls are more likely than boys to know their letters and be able to associate letters with sounds. Male advantages in visual-spatial abilities emerge later in childhood and adolescence.

The research identifying these differences in male and female cognitive abilities does not explain their cause, however. There may be innate, biologically based differences in men and women. But gender differences may also be the result of culture and socialization that emphasize different skills for men and women and provide both genders different opportunities to develop their abilities.

Researchers have investigated a variety of potential biological causes for these differences. There is evidence that sex hormones in the womb, which drive the development of the fetus's sex organs, also have an impact on the brain. Children who were exposed to abnormal levels of these hormones, for example, may develop cognitive abilities more like those of the opposite sex. Increased hormone levels at puberty may again affect cognitive development. And performance on some types of cognitive tests tends to vary with male and female hormonal cycles.

In addition, new technologies that allow researchers to look more closely into the brain and observe its activities have shown that there are differences between the sexes in the size of various brain structures and in the parts of the brain men and women use when performing different tasks.

But while this information is intriguing, it must be interpreted with a great deal of caution. Although our knowledge of the brain and its development has expanded dramatically in recent years, it remains rudimentary. In the future, much of our current thinking about the brain will most likely seem as unsophisticated as the work of the late 19th and early 20th century research-ers who sought to prove female intellectual inferiority by comparing the size of men's and women's skulls.

In particular, it is notoriously difficult to draw causal links between observations about brain structure or activity and human behavior, a point that scientists reporting the findings of brain research often take great pains to emphasize. Just as correlation does not always signify causation in social science research, correlations between differences in brain structure and observed differ-ences in male and female behavior do not necessarily mean that the former leads to the latter.

But these caveats have not prevented many individuals from confidently citing brain research to advance their preferred explanation of gender gaps in academic achievement.

Proponents of different educational philosophies and approaches cherry-pick findings that seem to support their visions of public education. And a growing boys industry purports to help teachers use brain research on gender differences to improve boys' academic achievement. But many of these indi-viduals and organizations are just seizing on the newest crisis—boys' achievement—to make money and promote old agendas. Scientific-sounding brain research has lent an aura of authority to people who see anxiety about boys as an opportunity for personal gain. Many have also added refashioned elements of sociology to their boys-in-crisis rhetoric.

Dubious Theories and Old Agendas

"Girl behavior becomes the gold standard. Boys are treated like defective girls."

—Psychologist Michael Thompson, as quoted in *Newsweek*

Thompson is just one of many commentators who argue that today's schools disadvantage boys by expecting behavior—doing homework, sitting still, working collaboratively, expressing thoughts and feelings verbally and in writing—that comes more naturally to girls. These commentators argue that schools are designed around instructional models that work well with girls' innate abilities and learning styles but do not provide enough support to boys or engage their interests and strengths. While female skills like organization, empathy, coopera-tiveness, and verbal agility are highly valued in schools, male strengths like physical vigor and competitiveness are overlooked and may even be treated as problems rather than assets, the argument goes.

Building from this analysis, a wealth of books, articles, and training pro-grams endeavor to teach educators how to make schools more "boy friendly." Many of these suggestions—such as allowing boys to choose reading selections that appeal to their interests—are reasonable enough.

But many other recommendations are based on an inappropriate appli-cation of brain research on sex differences. Many of these authors draw causal connections between brain research findings and stereotypical male or female personality traits without any evidence that such causality exists, as the sidebar demonstrates. These analyses also tend to ignore the wide variation among individuals of the same sex. Many girls have trouble completing their homework and sitting still, too, and some boys do not.

Members of the growing "boys industry" of researchers, advocates, and pop psychologists include family therapist Michael Gurian, author of *The Minds of Boys, Boys and Girls Learn Differently!,* and numerous other books about education and gender; Harvard psychologist William Pollack, director of the Center for Research on Boys at McLean Hospital and author of *Real Boys;* and Michael Thompson, clinical psychologist and the author of *Raising Cain.* All of these authors are frequently cited in media coverage of the boy crisis. A quick search on Amazon.com also turns up Jeffrey Wilhelm's *Reading Don't Fix No Chevys,* Thomas Newkirk's *Misreading Masculinity: Boys, Literacy and Popular Culture,* Christina Hoff Sommers' *The War On Boys,* Leonard Sax's *Why Gender Matters,* and *Hear Our Cry: Boys in Crisis,* by Paul D. Slocumb. A review of these books shows that the boys industry is hardly monolithic. Its practitioners seem to hold a plethora of perspectives and philosophies about both gender and education, and their recommendations often contradict one another.

Some focus on boys' emotions and sense of self-worth, while others are more concerned with implementing pedagogical practices—ranging from direct instruction to project-based learning—that they believe will better suit boys' learning style. Still others focus on structural solutions, such as smaller class sizes or single-sex learning environments. But all are finding an audience among parents, educators, and policymakers concerned about boys.

It would be unfair to imply that these authors write about boys for purely self-serving motives—most of these men and women seem to be sincerely concerned about the welfare of our nation's boys. But the work in this field leaves one skeptical of the quality of research, information, and analysis that are shaping educators' and parents' beliefs and practices as they educate boys and girls. Perhaps most tellingly, ideas about how to make schools more "boy friendly" align suspiciously well with educational and ideological beliefs the individuals promoting them had long before boys were making national headlines. And some of these prescriptions are diametrically opposed to one another.

A number of conservative authors, think tanks, and journals have published articles arguing that progressive educational pedagogy and misguided feminism are hurting boys. According to these critics, misguided feminists have lavished resources on female students at the expense of males and demonized typical boy behaviors such as rowdy play. At the same time, progressive educational pedagogy is harming boys by replacing strict discipline with permissiveness, teacher-led direct instruction with student-led collaborative learning, and academic content with a focus on developing students' self-esteem. The boy crisis offers an attractive way for conservative pundits to get in some knocks against feminism and progressive education and also provides another argument for educational policies—such as stricter discipline, more traditional curriculum, increased testing and competition, and single-sex schooling—that conservatives have long supported.

Progressive education thinkers, on the other hand, tend to see boys' achievement problems as evidence that schools have not gone far *enough* in adopting progressive tenets and are still forcing all children into a teacher-led pedagogical box that is particularly ill-suited to boys' interests and learning styles. Similarly, the responses progressive education writers recommend—more project-based and hands-on learning, incorporating kinetic and other learning styles into lessons, making learning "relevant," and allowing children more self-direction and free movement—simply sound like traditional progressive pedagogy.

More recently, critics of the standards movement and its flagship federal legislation, the No Child Left Behind Act (NCLB), have argued that the movement and NCLB are to blame for boys' problems. According to *Newsweek*, "In the last two decades, the education system has become obsessed with a quantifiable and narrowly defined kind of academic success, and that myopic view, these experts say, is harming boys." This is unlikely, because high-school-age boys, who seem to be having the most problems, are affected far less by NCLB than elementary-school-age boys, who seem to be improving the most.

Further, many of the arguments NCLB critics make about how it hurts boys—by causing schools to narrow their curriculum or eliminate recess—are not borne out by the evidence. A recent report from the Washington, D.C.-based Center for Educational Policy showed that most schools are not eliminating social studies, science, and arts in response to NCLB. And, a report from the U.S. Department of Education found that over 87 percent of elementary schools offer recess and most do so daily. More important, such critics offer no compelling case for why standards and testing, if harmful, would have more of a negative impact on boys than on girls.

In other words, few of these commentators have anything new to say—the boy crisis has just given them a new opportunity to promote their old messages. . . .

POSTSCRIPT

Are Boys in Crisis in Our Schools?

Challenge Questions

1. What are some common classroom expectations that may be particularly challenging to young boys?
2. What evidence exists that supports a boy crisis?
3. What can be done to better support the unique skills and needs of both sexes?
4. Are the differences between the sexes real or manipulated by the data?

Suggested Reading

Gurian, M. (2006). Learning and gender. *American School Board Journal*, 193(10), 19–22.

Gurian, M., & Stevens, K. (2005). *The minds of boys: Saving our sons from falling behind in school and life.* San Francisco: Jossey-Bass.

King, K., & Gurian, M. (2006). Teaching to the minds of boys. *Educational Leadership*, 64(1), 56–61.

Perkins-Gough, D. (2006). Do we really have a "boy crisis"? *Educational Leadership*, 64(1), 94–94.

Sax, L. (2005). *Why gender matters.* New York: Doubleday.

Contributors to This Volume

EDITOR

KAREN MENKE PACIOREK is a professor of early childhood education at Eastern Michigan University in Ypsilanti, Michigan. For over twenty years she has served as the editor for *Annual Editions: Early Childhood Education*. In addition she edited with Joyce Huth Munro *Sources: Notable Selections in Early Childhood Education*. She has served as president of the Northville Michigan Board of Education, the Michigan Association for the Education of Young Children, and chair of the Michigan Early Childhood Education Consortium. She has a B.S. from the University of Pittsburgh, an M.A. from George Washington University, and a Ph.D. from Peabody College of Vanderbilt University, all in early childhood education. She presents at local, state, and national conferences on curriculum planning, guiding behavior, preparing the learning environment, and working with families. Dr. Paciorek serves on many committees addressing the needs of young children in her community and state and is on the board of directors for Wolverine Human Services and The Karla Fund supporting reading to young children. She is the recipient of the Eastern Michigan University Ronald W. Collins Distinguished Faculty Award for Service.

AUTHORS

KELLY KING ALEXANDER is a contributing editor for *Parents* magazine and writes on a variety of issues that affect children and their families. She writes for numerous other national magazines as well. She lives with her husband and three children in Prairieville, Louisiana, where there is still plenty of playtime.

SUSAN BLACK is a contributing editor for the *American School Board Journal*.

BRENDA J. BOYD is an assistant professor in the Department of Human Development at Washington State University in Pullman, Washington. She teaches in the areas of child development, early education, and parent-child relationships. Her research interests include the play of young children and the professional development of child-care providers.

REGINA G. CHATEL is a professor of education at St. Joseph College in West Hartford, Connecticut.

STEPHANIE CLOTHIER is the chair of the Child Care and Early Education Project for the National Conference of State Legislatures located in Washington, D.C.

SHEREE CRUTE is a freelance health and medical writer and editor based in Brooklyn, New York. Her clients include: The Mayo Clinic, *Health Magazine*, and Consumer Reports on Health. She has a degree in journalism and an M.A. in international politics from New York University and is currently studying public health at the Johns Hopkins Bloomberg School of Public Health in Baltimore.

VERA ESTOK teaches in the Springfield, Ohio, public schools. She has taught both transitional first-grade and kindergarten classrooms for a number of years.

PAUL FERRARO is an elementary teacher at the Bi-Cultural Day School in Stamford, Colorado.

MATTHEW GANDAL works as the executive vice president of Achieve, Inc., which is based in Washington, D.C. This organization was created by governors and corporate leaders to assist states in improving schools and academic performance of students.

GREG GELPI is a staff writer for the *Augusta, Georgia Chronicle*.

BARBARA S. HARRIS serves as associate headmaster at Presbyterian Day School in Memphis, Tennessee.

KATI HAYCOCK is the executive director of Education Trust, an organization dedicated to promoting high academic achievement of all students at all levels from kindergarten through the university level.

MARY M. HITZ is a retired primary teacher and is currently working on her doctorate at Oklahoma State University in Tulsa. For eight years she looped with coauthor Mary Catherine Somers.

TOM JAMBOR is an associate professor of early childhood development at the University of Alabama at Birmingham. He is an international playground designer and the author of many articles and books on children's play and the design of safe and appropriate play spaces.

CHRISTEE L. JENLINK is an associate professor of education with a focus on school administration in the College of Education at Northeastern State University in Broken Arrow, Oklahoma. She spent time as an administrator in buildings where looping was successfully implemented.

OLAF JORGENSON serves as headmaster of the Hawaii Preparatory Academy in Walmea, Hawaii. He writes on school reform and educational leadership.

NANCIE L. KATZ is a freelance writer for the *Christian Science Monitor*.

ALFIE KOHN has authored eleven books, most recently *The Homework Myth: Why Our Kids Get Too Much of a Bad Thing* (DaCapo Press, 2006). He is an outspoken critic of America's keen interest on testing and grades. He speaks nationally on a number of critical issues facing the education profession and parents.

LAWRENCE KUTNER is a clinical psychologist and professor at Harvard University Medical School, where he is codirector of the Harvard Center for Mental Health and Media. He is a contributing editor of *Parenting*, *Family Life*, and *Baby Talk*. Kutner is the author of five books including *Your School-age Child* (Morrow/Avon, 1997) and *Toddlers and Preschoolers* (Morrow/Avon 1995). He speaks nationally on a number of topics related to families and childrearing.

ELIZABETH LARKIN is an associate professor at the University of South Florida at Sarasota/Manatee, Sarasota, Florida.

DIANE E. LEVIN is the author of eight books on the effects of violence and the media on the behavior of young children. She is a professor in the Department of Early Childhood Education at Wheelock College in Boston, Massachusetts. Dr. Levin is the cofounder of Teachers Resisting Unhealthy Children's Entertainment (TRUCE).

MICHAEL I. LOEWY is a professor in the Department of Counseling and School Psychology at San Diego State University, San Diego, California. He serves on the Scientific Advisory Board of the National Association to Advance Fat Acceptance.

HERMINE H. MARSHALL is a professor emerita from San Francisco State University San Francisco, California. She is the author of *Redefining Student Learning* (Greenwood Publishing Group Inc. 1992).

LAURA McGIFFERT is director of the Mathematics Achievement Partnership for Achieve, Inc. Achieve was created by governors and corporate leaders to assist states in improving schools and academic performance of students.

SARA MEAD is a senior policy analyst at Education Sector, an independent education think tank, which is nonprofit and nonpartisan and based in Washington D.C.

EDWARD MILLER is a founding partner and senior researcher at the Alliance for Childhood, which promotes policies and practices that support the healthy development of young children.

DARCY ANN OLSEN was a director of Education and Child Policy at the Washington, D.C.-based Cato Institute at the time of writing this article. The Cato Institute promotes public policy based on individual liberty, limited government, free markets, and peaceful international relations. Her focus has been on parental responsibility in raising children.

JOELLEN PERRY is a writer for *U.S. News and World Report.*

JULIE POPPE follows policy related to preschool education for the National Conference of State Legislatures (NCSL). The NCSL is a bipartisan organization, which serves legislators and staffs of the nation's fifty states, commonwealths, and territories.

KATHY PREUESSE teaches at the Child and Family Study Center at the University of Wisconsin-Stout in Menomonie, Wisconsin.

CHRISTINE ROSSELL is a professor of political science at Boston University in Massachusetts. She holds the Maxwell Chair in U.S. Citizenship and is the author of five books. She has been involved in more than fifty school desegregation and/or bilingual education cases. Dr. Rossell has designed and conducted public interest surveys on a variety of issues.

RICHARD ROTHSTEIN is a research associate of the Economic Policy Institute and a visiting lecturer at Teachers College, Columbia University. He served as the national education columnist for *The New York Times* from 1999-2002. He is currently a senior correspondent for *The American Prospect.* Richard Rothstein is the author of *The Way We Were? Myths and Realities of America's Student Achievement, All Else Equal: Are Public and Private Schools Different?* and *Where's the Money Going? Changes in the Level and Composition of Education Spending* in addition to *Class and Schools: Using Social, Economic, and Educational Reform to Close the Black-White Achievement Gap* from which this selection is taken.

STEPHEN RUSHTON is an associate professor of childhood education at the University of South Florida Sarasota/Manatee in Sarasota, Florida. He is a former teacher at a variety of levels from preschool through the eighth grade.

PAUL V. SEQUEIRA is superintendent of schools in New Britain Connecticut and former associate professor of education at Western Connecticut State University in Danbury, Connecticut.

MARY CATHERINE SOMERS has looped for eighteen of her twenty-nine years teaching elementary school for the Tulsa, Oklahoma Public Schools. Eight of those years were with coauthor Mary M. Hitz. She currently teaches first grade for English language learners.

MARY H. SULLIVAN is an assistant professor in the Department of Education at Western Connecticut State University in Danbury, Connecticut.

PEG TYRE joined the staff of *Newsweek* as a general editor in 2001. She covers criminal justice, media, and social trends. Prior to joining *Newsweek*, she worked for the New York *Newsday* where she won a Pulitzer Prize in 1991. She was also an on-air contributor for CNN's The NcNeil-Lehrer News Hour from 1995–1998.

ALLAN S. VANN is principal of James H. Boyd Intermediate School in Huntington, New York.

JOAN RUDEL WEINREICH has been an associate professor of education at Manhattanville College in Purchase, New York, since 1986. She currently is an associate dean of undergraduate admissions and advising for the school of education.

KENNETH A. WESSON serves as the executive assistant to the chancellor of San Jose/Evergreen Community College in San Jose, California. He consults with educational institutions and organizations whose mission is the education of children from preschool through college. He speaks internationally on the neuroscience of learning.

JUDY WILLIS is a board certified neurologist. Dr. Willis spent over twenty years as a clinical researcher prior to entering the teaching profession. She has authored *Research-Based Strategies to Ignite Student Learning: Insights from a Neurologist/Classroom Teacher* (ASCD 2006). She currently teaches math at a middle school in Santa Barbara, California.

JILL WU is a graduate student in applied linguistics at the University of Colorado at Denver.